Bar Exam PT Success

Strategies & Practice

Third Edition

Sara J. Berman
Professor of Lawyering Skills and Director of the Academic Success Program
University of Southern California Gould School of Law

WEST ACADEMIC

860 Blue Gentian Road, Suite 350
Eagan, MN 55121
1-877-888-1330

Published in the United States of America

ISBN: 979-8-89545-610-1

To UCLA Law Professor Emeritus Paul Bergman—the greatest and funniest law professor ever—and an amazing co-author, friend, and role model. And, to Michigan State Dean Emerita Joan Howarth—legal education visionary and leader, mentor and friend extraordinaire, and tireless advocate for bettering our world.

ACKNOWLEDGMENTS

Deep gratitude to the National Conference of Bar Examiners and the State Bars of California and Nevada for permission to use past exams as part of this book. It is my hope that these brilliant examples of meaningful testing will help law students nationwide in their training to become licensed attorneys, leaders, and professionals.

I would never have started this book had it not been for my extraordinary UCLA Law School professors, particularly Paul Bergman and Carrie Menkel-Meadow. My passion for PTs started in law school and flourished as I taught thousands of students with PTs in law schools and bar review. And, I could never have completed this book without the help of many people including Bryan Kay, Donna Golmer, and others at the ABA who published the first edition and to everyone at West Academic who has collaborated in publishing this new version including but not limited to Pamela Siege Chandler, Louis Higgins, John Moen, Megan Putler, Megan Hoffman, Michele Bassett, and Megan Grove. Thanks too to Sam Farkas, Mike Power, and Marta Young at Barbri for their support, friendship and inspiration.

Many other colleagues and friends reinforced my belief in the performance test as the best form of bar exam testing including but not limited to the members of the *Collaboratory On Legal Education and Licensing for Practice.*

ABOUT THE AUTHOR

Sara Berman is a Professor of Lawyering Skills and the Director of the Academic Success Program at the USC Gould School of Law. Berman previously served as a director at the AccessLex Institute's Center for Legal Education Excellence in Washington, D.C. and has taught in law schools in New York, Florida, and California, and at the nation's first fully online law school. Berman's publications focus on student success, bar exams, professional licensing, distance learning and self-represented litigants and include the books published by West Academic listed below as well as *The Criminal Law Handbook: Know Your Rights Survive the System* and *Represent Yourself in Court: How to Prepare and Try a Winning Case*, both co-authored with Paul Bergman and published by Nolo.com.

WEST PUBLICATIONS BY SARA J. BERMAN

1L Success: Becoming a Lawyer, a Professional Identity Formation Workbook

- Sara J. Berman
- 1st edition, ©2024
- (2d ed forthcoming, 2026)

California Baby Bar Success: A Comprehensive Guide

- Sara J. Berman
- 1st edition, ©2023
- 2d edition, ©2026

2L Success: Lawyering Skills Training & Professional Identity Formation for Upper Division Law Students

- Sara J. Berman
- 1st edition, ©2025

Bar Exam Success: A Comprehensive Guide

- Sara J. Berman
- 2d edition, ©2023
- (3d ed. forthcoming, 2026)

Bar Exam Prep for the Next Generation: Building a Solid Foundation Before Bar Review Begins

- Steven I. Friedland & Sara J. Berman
- 1st edition, ©2026

Office Hours on Academic Success (Audio)

- Sara J. Berman
- Set 1 ©2022
- Set 2 ©2023

Office Hours on Bar Exam Success (Audio)

- Sara J. Berman
- ©2023

Step-by-Step Guide to Torts

- Sara J. Berman & Steven J. Bracci
- 1st edition, ©2022
- (2d ed. forthcoming, 2026)

Step-by-Step Guide to Contracts

- Sara J. Berman & Steven J. Bracci
- 1st edition, ©2022
- (2d ed. forthcoming, 2026)

Step-by-Step Guide to Criminal Law

- Sara J. Berman & Steven J. Bracci
- 1st edition, ©2022
- (2d ed. forthcoming, 2026)

TABLE OF CONTENTS

BAR EXAM PT SUCCESS

Strategies & Practice

Third Edition

CHAPTER 1

INTRODUCTION: GETTING THE MOST OUT OF THIS BOOK

This book is for law students; it is designed to help with practical skills training for the PT portion of the bar exam—skills that will also serve well during law school and in law practice after graduation.

Performance *tests* and performance *tasks* (collectively referred to throughout this book as "PTs") differ in timing, but almost every jurisdiction now uses some variation of this testing format on their bar exams. **After reading this book you will see that PT preparation provides a down payment for success on the bar exam, and, I hope, that PTs *are* the best part of the bar exam!** For now, trust me and read on!

Bar Exam PT Success can be used as part of law school courses, bar review, or independent study to bolster training opportunities for bar success while helping you to develop your identity as lawyers.

Appendix F includes a comprehensive debrief of ten PTs, all housed on West Academic's eProducts site, at https://eproducts.westacademic.com ("eProducts"), accessible to readers of this book. In completing these practice exams on eProducts, you will have the opportunity to "represent" many different and varied "clients." As examples:

- You will help a teenage boy who was injured from wires that fell on him while he was swimming in a local river. (Was he swimming when he should have been in school? You may need to find out!)
- You will represent a local school board trying desperately to keep its high school free of profanity, plays with sexualized content, and scandalous news reporting in the school paper. (Whatever your own free-speech views are, this exam will test your

ability to think in terms of what your client wants and needs.)

- You will act as a prosecutor in two cases, one involving a possible criminal trespass and the other a murder case in which the defendant seeks to suppress evidence alleging that the police violated his *Miranda* rights. And,
- You will counsel a local politician who has gotten into hot water from a string of potential ethical violations.

Reading this book and completing the PTs on eProducts and studying the debriefing content in Appendix F can serve as the basis for a guided or self-study supplemental PT review course.

Some of you will read this book just before your bar exam; others may read the book as early as 1L. The earlier one learns about PTs the better. My initial exposure to a PT was in my first year of law school. I am convinced that completing some PTs *during law school* made bar review after graduation much easier. Early PT exposure provided a distinct advantage in passing the bar exam first time around. I want you to have that advantage too!

PTs bring the law to life. In many doctrinal courses where I taught using a typical casebook, I liked to think my students were engaged. But, when I began introducing PTs to complement casebook readings, my students suddenly showed a profoundly different level of engagement. They sat up. They were excited to see how theories and rules we had discussed in the abstract applied to "their clients." And they had fun. (Fun? In law school? Yes!)

Reading this book and completing the sample exams in the appendices and on eProducts, you will see yourself not just as a student but as a (future) practicing attorney. PTs assist skills training and help you develop your own professional identity in myriad ways. With PT practice, you:

- Gain critical exposure to practical lawyering skills that will help you to pass the bar and transition effectively to the practice of law;

- See law school come alive, especially if your studies have felt so far like you are "just" reading and briefing old cases; and
- Develop practical writing experience by drafting a host of documents (some of which you might be able to adapt and use as writing samples for job interviews), including:
  - Legal memos
  - Briefs to the court
  - Discovery and fact-gathering plans
  - A cross-examination plan to question (and discredit) a key witness at trial

Once you are comfortable with PTs, you too may find (at least *this part* of the bar exam)—dare I say—enjoyable! You may find like many students in a recent study who were interviewed about their bar exam experience that the PT is often the most useful part of bar preparation, the part that aligns in some important ways with new lawyer practice.

Note: I am not knocking casebooks. Cases are as real as it gets; this stuff actually happened, to real people! I tell my students that if you like reality TV you will love cases; they are "reality reading." But PTs are interactive; they are a bit like theater where you not only read, but also role-play, acting the part of the lawyer. Trust me, you can have fun with PT practice!

A. WHO IS THIS BOOK FOR?

Guidance on PT success is primarily for law students and graduates preparing to pass the bar exam, but others may also benefit from reading this book. For example,

- **Law professors:** You may want to introduce PTs into your skills or doctrinal courses. Law professors using this book, please also consult the article from the Journal of the Legal Profession, *Integrating Performance Tests into Doctrinal Courses, Skills Courses, and Institutional Benchmark Testing: A Simple Way to Enhance Student Engagement While Furthering Assessment, Bar Passage, and Other*

ABA Accreditation Objectives at https://papers.ssrn.com/sol3/papers.cfm?abstract_id=3206929.

- **Attorneys:** You may use some of the exams in this book as part of an interview process to select competent new associates. Seeing how the applicants respond to PT prompts may well give some sense of how they would perform in practice.
- **College students in mock trial, prelaw programs, or undergraduate law majors:** You will find the book helpful to train your analytical, persuasive, and writing skills.
- **Readers thinking about applying to law school:** You may find valuable information and help in deciding whether law is the path for you. I hope it is! We want more great minds and great human beings in the legal profession.

B. THIS BOOK'S APPROACH

I am writing directly to you, readers, just as I would speak with you in my office hours—intentionally setting formalities aside with the hope that I can motivate you to really get *into* these exams and enjoy them.

If you have read other books in my West Academic law school success series (perhaps *1L Success*, *2L Success*, or *Bar Exam Success*), you know that my philosophy is one of empowerment. Unlike many who describe the bar exam as "torture," I believe that law school and studying for the bar exam can be a positive and empowering experiences, if you approach them that way. I want you to both succeed *and* to find meaning and fulfillment in the process—this is a wish fully backed by science. Recent learning science studies show and great connection between cognition and emotion, and social science research indicates that finding meaning and purpose in our lives is one of the great keys to happiness.

Doing the work that is necessary to become test-ready involves mental strength-training and physical stamina building; the process will leave you feeling like you can conquer anything. You can be poised to pass your bar exam just as an

Olympic high diver stands ready to plunge gracefully into the pool below.

Take a moment now. Get quiet and into a comfortable position. Close your eyes. Picture yourself as that diver, on the high board, your confidence stemming from years of training and a fundamental belief in yourself. By the time you take your bar exam, you too will have had years of training. Picture yourself plunging straight into the water, strong and sure of yourself. That will be you when you dive into the exam questions on your bar exam!

Notice that nowhere do I say that confidence will appear "just because." Notice that I do *not* say, "Hope for the best and you will *automatically* do well." *Not at all!*

I am all about the hard work, extensive training, and many, many practice tests. What I am saying is that when you pass, all that effort pays off with a lifelong positive ripple effect. You will embody your own "can-do" potential. You will know that you can do virtually anything you set your mind and efforts to.

Throughout this book, as we drill down into the PT portion of the bar exam, we will focus on the positives. We will acknowledge what is tough about this exam, and help you do the "heavy lifting" necessary to become test-ready—but we will do all that with lightness and positivity.

You can think of me as your "trainer" at "the legal gym." Practice tests are workouts, and I will encourage you every step of the way. So? Are you ready to master the PT portion of your bar exam? Let's go!

C. START BAR PREP DURING LAW SCHOOL, IF POSSIBLE

Law students often assume that the bar exam is something far off in the future, a test to be studied for after law school. In years past, many successful law students did not think about the bar exam until after graduation; at that time, they hibernated and did nothing but study for two months, then took and passed the exam.

Those days are history! Today's law students have more pressure, more riding on outcomes, and much more student loan debt than prior generations. Today's law students must start early, during law school, and do everything to ensure success. You cannot risk having to retake the exam.

On a personal note, I was lucky enough to have law professors, experts in clinical legal education, who had the foresight to incorporate PTs in our 1L Legal Writing and Contracts classes. To this day, I am certain that my early exposure to the PT was instrumental in my success on the bar exam. I watched colleagues from other law schools in bar review who were terror-struck when they saw their first PTs in late June.

PTs are not hard when you train and are prepared for them. But trust me, it is much better to get familiar with PTs early on rather than seeing your first PT in bar review just before your bar exam.

DO EVERYTHING YOU CAN TO PASS YOUR FIRST BAR EXAM

The bar exam is not "just another test." Yes, many very successful people have had to repeat the bar exam. But failing the exam now, especially with the cost of legal education and student loans coming due shortly after graduation, can have long-lasting financial and psychological repercussions. Of course, not everyone will pass, but what I am stressing is the importance of taking proactive steps, *beginning during law school, if possible,* to prepare to pass the bar exam first time around. Commit to success! If you sit for the exam having done everything possible to prepare and for some reason do not pass, it will be easier to accept those results, refocus, and pass the next time. If you don't prepare sufficiently and don't pass, that may be harder to accept and recover from. So, let's plan on, and work on (!), first-time bar passage.

1. Getting a Head Start

How do you get that head start? What can you do during school? A lot! Most importantly, get into the habit of effectively completing practice tests. That is what this book is all about:

slow and steady practice PT training so that you can "win" the bar exam "race."

The bar exam is in some ways very similar to a marathon—and I refer to this part of studying as "training" for a reason. The bar exam is too comprehensive an exam to leave to the last minute. You cannot cram for the bar exam. Starting early is a must, and continuing in high gear in the months before the exam is a must. Don't give bar preparation short shrift. When in doubt, train.

Certain parts of most bar exams are closed book; they depend on your having learned and memorized relevant rules of law. Even on parts of the NextGen bar exam where you will only be required to have foundational knowledge of certain subjects, (rather than super detailed knowledge), you may benefit from having a much more thorough understanding of every testable rule than you would think. Why? Let's say, for example, that a criminal law multiple choice question includes a portion of a statute; while you would not have to *memorize* that rule, it may be hard to quickly read, understand, and apply the statute to the stated facts without a very thorough general understanding of criminal law.

The PT, however, the part of the bar exam this book focuses on, *is* open book. The law needed to answer the question is provided in a library and the PT is a skills-based and not a memory-based exam. Because PTs do not require memory or knowledge of specific doctrine, you can master this portion of the bar exam early on, while in law school. That way, during intensive bar preparation after graduation, you can focus more fully on those portions of the exam that require memory and detailed and foundational law knowledge.

There's no way around it; memory fades. Even if you knew every rule that had to be memorized by the March prior to a July bar exam, you would likely forget some by exam time. But skills do not fade. Just as most people don't forget how to ride a bike; you do not forget how to complete PTs. Skills become a part of you; training with practice PTs builds "muscle memory."

What else can you do to get a head start? Well, to effectively *memorize* rules for instant recall on other parts of your bar exam, it is helpful to have already *learned* concepts and be fluent with all the main rules and principles. So, foundational learning in all tested subjects is something to focus on prior to intensive bar review. Study rules you did not understand well in bar classes you took and learn rules in bar-tested subjects you never learned—either because you didn't take the class, the professor didn't cover those rules, or you did not understand them when first exposed to them. Studying for the bar gives you another opportunity to learn everything well.

So, along with early work on PTs (that you will learn about in this book), there is also other early work to do with substantive law learning and in familiarizing yourself with (and taking practice tests in) other testing formats.

How early can you start PTs? If you are in law school, you can start taking practice PTs. By the end of your first year of law school, you should have sufficient skills to be able to complete PT exams. Your finished product may not yet be passing quality, but maintain a practice schedule all through law school, taking a few PTs each semester, and you will build the muscle you need for success on the actual exam.

Gaining exposure to and practicing PTs during law school frees up time during bar review. Why do I stress the need to "free up" time during the months prior to the bar exam? Because as much as you may think you are busy now, during bar review you will likely feel far more time-crunched than ever before—and PT practice takes time. You will have to work to carve out time now, but during bar review, time will be even more scarce; other testing formats will be competing for any available practice test time you do have. So, give yourself the PT advantage; get started on PT work now!

EARLY PREPARATION STEPS FOR BAR SUCCESS

- Read *Bar Exam Success: A Comprehensive Guide*, a West Academic book I wrote detailing general bar exam and bar preparation success strategies and confidence-building tools. The book will help you work through any possible doubts, scheduling issues (including how to get all your studying done), and securing necessary support and buy-in from family and friends so that you approach the exam from a position of strength.

- Familiarize yourself with information about the exam you will take from the website in the jurisdiction where you will sit and the NCBE. With bar exams changing, it is particularly important to get current information from the bar examiners themselves and a reliable bar review course when you are ready for that. *Do not rely on gossip.*
- Get fluent in all the subjects tested on your bar exam. Fill in any knowledge gaps. If there are bar-tested courses you did not take or understand during law school, study them on your own at least briefly before you graduate.
- Make sure that "bar review" is really a *review* and not *bar learning*. It can cause tremendous (wholly avoidable) anxiety to see subjects for the first time in bar review, especially heavily tested subjects, that you either did not take or did not understand well during law school. If you plan not to take certain bar tested subjects during law school, read a reliable quality supplement before bar review begins.
- Complete whatever character and fitness requirements there are in your jurisdiction, including taking and passing the Multistate Professional Responsibility Examination (MPRE).
- Complete any other requirements that may exist in the jurisdiction you seek to be licensed in. (For example, NY has skills and pro bono requirements.)
- Plan ahead, so that you will have at least two months free for nothing but bar study before your bar exam.

Taking practice tests is a bit like going to the law gym, for a legal workout. Once you have committed to passing the bar exam, and once you believe *beyond a reasonable doubt* that *you will pass*, the most important step is to train by regularly completing the types of questions that will be on your bar exam.

In the next chapters, you will learn what PTs are and how to complete them most effectively. The Appendices of this book includes practice PTs of varying lengths. You can access additional exams on eProducts, websites for the jurisdictions where you will sit for the exam, and the NCBE's website. You can also talk with your law school's academic support faculty and law librarians for help in finding practice exams.

CHAPTER 2

PTs: THE BEST PART OF YOUR BAR EXAM

PTs are gifts. When you are skilled and practiced, PTs are straightforward and more "fair" than parts of the exam. PTs are also more useful because they allow you to engage in realistic lawyering simulations; with PTs, you are preparing for actual legal work *while* studying for the bar exam.

In some ways, PTs are like puzzles. I predict that after reading this book and completing 8–10 practice tests, you will find PTs "fun," and you will concur that they are the best part of your exam. If you are a puzzle or word game person, you will really like them!

PT training also helps sharpen your writing, analytical, time-management, and problem-solving skills, many of which are directly transferable to other bar testing formats, and to law practice. Completing the work in this book may also help prepare you for your first law jobs, be they internships during school or new attorney work after graduation. You may be able to use the work you complete on practice PTs as a writing sample.

So, again, why are PTs the best parts of bar exams?

- They are open book and do not put crazy pressure on your memory.
- They are realistic (at least more so than multiple choice questions).
- They mirror the type of work one might do as a beginning lawyer.
- They allow you to think and write somewhat creatively.

Some readers may not welcome this last point. (You know who you are, multiple choice fans!) You don't want options or "creativity" on exams. You want bright lines and blackletter law. Rest assured, once you understand what the bar examiners are up to, you will quickly see that many PTs, at their core, require a type of logical writing style similar to that used for law essays. Even on PTs, effective answers employ some form of IRAC: Issue, Rule, Analysis/Argument/Application (or *proof* as I like to call the "A" portion of IRAC), Conclusion.

You will likely find that you can produce passing PT answers without having to think too far outside the box. But, for those of you who happily receive the news about being *allowed* to think and write creatively (and often being rewarded handsomely for doing so), trust me when I say that you will particularly like the PT portion of the bar exam.

If you yearn to see yourself dealing with real people who have real problems, considering all of the wants and needs of your clients, you will also like PTs. If you are eager to investigate and develop potentially useful facts and not simply analyze whether "frozen" fact patterns include evidence of each element of memorized rules and theories, you may love the PT.

One of my mentors used to describe facts before or during trial as "hot facts," suggesting that they were still malleable, but noting that facts become "frozen" on appeal. Similarly, on other testing formats, such as multiple-choice questions, facts are frozen. You cannot question them or ignore them. In contrast, on PTs, there may be both cold and hot facts. Also, as you will soon learn, PTs typically include some irrelevant and some duplicative facts that you must learn to sift through and separate out. (This is very different from essays where other than the rare red herring, every fact is relevant.)

PTs may end up being your favorite part of the bar exam, or you may remain a multiple choice fan. Nevertheless, every reader can grow to appreciate the PT form of testing if you:

1. Train the underlying skills required to effectively complete PTs
2. Complete many practice PTs under timed conditions
3. Study quality sample answers, working steadily to improve your efficiency and work product

Notice I say that you can "grow to" appreciate PTs. Why? They are open book, but they are not easy! PTs require you to sort through a large amount of material; to absorb, understand, and organize facts and law; and to package your thinking into a well-written, logical, and thoughtful answer in a relatively short amount of time.

Completing PTs within the time limits feels like running a race. Expect your first PTs to be overwhelming. Some of my best students have literally cried the first time they tackled a PT. By exam time, however, my students come to welcome this piece of their bar exam with open arms. One former student referred to the PT with the memorable phrase, a "points volcano," because of the potential grading cushion this open-book exam provides, especially given the possibility of that unpredictable moment on memory-dependent parts of the exam when you know but forget and can't recall a particular rule.

The first PT you complete will seem tough, but they get easier with practice—much easier. If you complete the PTs in the Appendices and on eProducts, you will gain confidence in your fundamental lawyering skills. With continued training, you will get to a place where you know that you can produce a passing answer to any PT the examiners throw at you on your bar exam. (Isn't that the kind of confidence you want!)

A. SUSTAINED AND STRATEGIC TRAINING IS THE KEY TO PT SUCCESS

As noted earlier, I believe in success, but I am also all about hard work. I want you to win, and I want to help you climb the success ladder. I have designed this book precisely with that goal in mind, and with the soundest strategy possible to help you achieve your goals. One key element of this strategy is stamina building.

The first part of this stamina training is to start early, as already discussed, while you are in law school, and not wait until bar review to begin PT training. The second part is to practice with longer and more difficult exams than you will have to complete on your bar exam. Think of it this way: If you want to easily and effortlessly run five laps around the track, start with one lap, build to two, and eventually practice on a regular basis running ten laps each day. If you are used to running ten laps, five will seem easy. My nephew ran track for years. When his varsity team prepared to compete in 3-mile events, his coach made them regularly train with 10 to 15-mile practice runs, sometimes at high altitudes, to make the practice even more difficult than the main event. That is the type of success training I want for you!

PTs in different jurisdictions have different time limits. NextGen PTs are 60-minute exams, MPTs and California PTs are 90-minute exams, Nevada PTs are two-hours each, and old California PTs were three-hours each. Though the timing differs, PTs all involve similar skills and approaches. When you are close to your exam, train with the type of exams that will be on your bar. But when you start early training during law school, it can be very effective and "build PT muscle" to train with PTs of varying lengths. For these reasons, you'll find PTs of differing lengths in the Appendices and on eProducts.

If you start early enough, training with 3-hour PTs can be particularly helpful; they build stamina, focus, and skills. Longer exams include more law and facts to read, sort through, analyze, organize, and write about. And, after completing a few longer PT, shorter PTs seem easy! (It's all relative!) There are also ways to complete parts of PTs in order to get the benefit of training without taking as much time in one sitting; these are detailed in Appendix F.

A LITTLE PRACTICE IS MUCH BETTER THAN NONE AT ALL!

Full-out stamina training is, no doubt, a great way to succeed. But I also know and respect that you are all busy. Therefore, some of the longer practice PTs debriefed in Appendix F) include, "Time Crunch Shortcuts." These describe how to do productive work without completing the entire practice test. Consider a fitness metaphor. If you are looking to get fit, it may well be ideal to commit serious and lengthy blocks of time each day to working out. Still, even a 10-minute jog around the block, on a day when you don't have time for more, is much better than nothing. Similarly, time-saving tips facilitate gaining early exposure to PTs, no matter how busy you are.

> You can also mix and match practice sessions. For some, you can do a "full workout" and complete the entire exam; for others, you can take the shortcut, and come back to that PT (or other full-length PTs) when you have more time.

A last word, for now, on stamina training: Whatever you are working on, be it reading cases to prepare for class, getting a head start for bar success, writing a paper for a seminar, or clerking at a law firm, it can be helpful to practice concentrating for longer stretches of time, without breaks. We live in a fast-paced, multi-tasking society. Most of us break our own concentration stopping every few minutes to check our phones, send messages, watch videos, eat or drink, or engage in any number of other distractions. But bar exam success requires intensity; and you will give yourself a great advantage by bolstering your sustained concentration skills.

The bar exam I took was a three-day exam, with six three-hour blocks of testing. I forced myself, for all of June and July before my exam, to sit and focus each day for *four-hour* blocks of time, without breaks. My reasoning was that if I got used to concentrating for four-hour stretches, three hours of doing so in bar sessions would be easier. That may seem excessive, but it worked well for me and has worked well for the thousands of students I have helped pass bar exams nationwide.

B. THE REST OF THIS BOOK

The next parts of this book serve as a primer on how to take PTs. I describe the skills that PTs test, and walk you step-by-step through a logical approach to successfully tackling any PT question you might encounter. Then, you will train with practice exams in the appendices and eProducts. For some PTs, you will find "spin-off" exercises, suggestions for additional assignments to complete based on the practice PTs to provide more exposure to potential testable tasks. (Appendix F includes a comprehensive debrief of ten PTs, all housed on eProducts. Completing these PTs and studying the debriefing content in Appendix F provides an excellent guided or self-study supplemental PT review course.)

Caveat: Do **not** study PTs to help you master specific rules of law. Reviewing rules in PT Libraries may help bolster your general knowledge of a subject and sharpen your legal analysis skills within the context of that doctrinal area. However, you must *not* expect to use practice PTs to learn particular rules for your bar exam. Why? First, bar examiners may use fictitious law for PT exam purposes, *other than in Nevada where PTs use real law*. (Most PTs contain explicitly warnings that law may be changed for exam purposes.) Second, the PT rules may come from a different jurisdiction and thus not be applicable on your bar exam essays. Third, the law in a PT may be outdated, especially if you are using older PTs to practice with.

So, remember, practice PTs provide excellent *skills training* within the context of subjects you need to learn, and they help you gain general fluency in areas of law that will in turn help when you master the rules tested in your jurisdiction—but do not rely on the accuracy of the law in PT Libraries.

C. KEY TAKEAWAYS

- Practice PTs are one of the best investments of time and energy you can make to set you up for bar success.
- PTs are hard but fair. They are open-book exams, testing skills not memory.
- Stamina training is key. Work harder in practice test sessions so you are ready for the bar exam "marathon" when actual exam time comes.
- PTs can be fun. They provide realistic lawyering scenarios where you jump into role-plays and can show graders that you know how to read cases and statutes, *and* how to help clients. They are opportunities for you to lawyer!

CHAPTER 3

PT STRATEGIES: HOW TO PASS PTS

This chapter explains what a PT is and how to successfully complete this type of exam. If you are already familiar with PTs, this chapter may provide new ways of thinking about your approach. If you have never worked on a PT, this chapter will provide the foundation you will need before testing yourself with practice exam work.

Whether initially familiar with the PT or not, you may find it helpful to return to this chapter as you complete your practice tests. Why? With each re-read, you will gain new strategic insights and confirm your mastery of those skills required to produce passing answers to any new exam you encounter.

A. OVERVIEW

PTs are based on simulated case files. Unlike real-world lawyering, where you must often complete extensive legal research, PTs come in neat packages with (almost) all the facts and law you need to draft the required tasks. (I say "almost" because some PTs involve discovery or fact-gathering tasks, and some PTs require knowledge of ethical rules).

PTs typically provide:

1. ***Instructions:*** General instructions (i.e. how long you have to complete the exam) and detailed directions on how to complete your particular assignment or task. Typical PT tasks include memoranda of law or briefs to the court in support of or opposing motions. Other tasks may include documents such as declarations, statements of facts, closing arguments, opinion letters, letters to clients, discovery plans, or settlement offers.

   Note: PT tasks are judged by the examiners to be work that a beginning lawyer could perform. Do not be concerned if you are not yet familiar with all of these documents. Read on![1]

2. ***Facts:*** Usually in the form of original source documents such as transcripts of interviews, police reports, letters, and contract excerpts, rather than the preset hypothetical fact patterns that are typical of law school essays.
3. ***Law:*** Most often in a "Library" that includes cases and/or statutes. You will read, brief, and analyze these legal authorities, and use them to draft your assigned task(s). The PT is thus an open-book test; virtually all the law you need to know is in your PT Library. Compare with a closed book (essay or multiple-choice) question where you must find the relevant rules in your own memory.

Your first and most important job in successfully completing a PT is to pull together these instructions, facts, and law, as if they were puzzle pieces; organize them logically; and then use them to produce whatever document(s) you are directed to write. At first, PTs seem like a mish-mash of unrelated pages. The more PTs you practice taking, the more you will come to trust that all the materials "fit" together, somewhat like a puzzle. There is a framework and at least one logical organizational structure.

You typically find an organizing structure in either the Instructions or the Library, or a combination of both. This makes sense because facts are not relevant in a vacuum; rather, facts are relevant as they prove or disprove elements of rules of law.

To help visualize the organization of a typical PT, think of the underlying client matter in a PT as a "tree." The "trunk" is a legal theory, cause of action, or crime. The "branches" are elements or factors. The "leaves" on each branch are facts

---

[1] An easy and fun way to get a quick overview of civil litigation and the criminal justice system is by reading two books I co-author: *Represent Yourself in Court: How to Prepare and Try a Winning Case,* and *The Criminal Law Handbook: Know Your Rights, Survive the System.* Both are written for non-lawyers and thus are light reads for law students and tremendously helpful for understanding civil litigation from pretrial discovery to appeal and the criminal justice system from arrest to appeal. Many students have reported that they found these books invaluable in preparing for PT success. It may be especially important to read a resource such as these books if you did not take a trial advocacy course or clinical course in law school.

relevant to proving that particular element or factor. A PT answer may have one or several legal "trees" or organizing principles. (More on organizing PTs later in the book.)

1. Your Role as Lawyer on PTs

In a typical PT, you are acting as a junior associate in a private law firm. Some PTs set you in a government law office as a prosecutor or public defender. You may also role-play as counsel for a nonprofit organization, as a mediator, or as a clerk to a judge or legislator.

> Reflection: Different Tones for Different Tasks
>
> How might your tone and ethical obligations differ if you are an attorney for a private client versus if you are a prosecutor?
>
> ____
>
> ____
>
> ____
>
> How might your tone differ if you are a junior associate in a private law firm versus if you are a law clerk to a judge?
>
> ____
>
> ____
>
> ____

On any given PT, your client may be an individual(s), a business, or another entity. You learn whom you represent on a PT in the Instructions. Just as in practice, you will be expected to be attentive to your client's wants and needs. On a PT, that means taking note every time a File document mentions your client's objectives and concerns. You must be aware of, and sometimes predict, obstacles that may hinder your client's ability to achieve desired outcomes.

PT Instructions will direct you to perform tasks such as analyzing issues, advising and counseling clients or colleagues, or persuading a judge or jurors to decide a matter in your client's favor. You may be called upon to investigate facts or negotiate with opposing counsel. You may have to draft or edit documents.

I often think that if bar examiners had limitless funding, they would call applicants in to appear in person and observe them actually interviewing people posing as clients, reporting to actors posing as colleagues, or arguing in a mock court setting. Instead, they use the PT as a "paper interview." Examiners determine how you handle yourself as a lawyer by reading the documents you draft.

You must be aware at all times of your own professional responsibilities. PTs were designed in part as a vehicle to test ethical rules. Graders may look at your PT responses to assess whether you are ready to be responsible for real clients.

Caveat: Professional responsibility (PR), is the only aspect of PTs that is not necessarily "open book." You will not be expected to cite statutes by number, but you will be expected to know basics about your professional responsibilities. PR is a required course in all law schools. More on PR later in this book.

B. A DETAILED LOOK AT THE PT

PTs were piloted in CA in 1980 and by the NCBE in 1993. Until 2017, the California Bar Exam included two 3-hour PTs; the California Bar now includes one 90-minute exam. The MPT was 90-minutes, Nevada has two-hour PTs, and the NextGen PT will be 60 minutes. (See samples of all of these different exams in the appendices to this book.)

Regardless of differences in length, most PT require examinees to be proficient in a number of lawyering skills. Principal among these are:

- Legal analysis and reasoning
- Factual analysis
- Awareness of professional responsibility: recognizing and resolving ethical dilemmas
- Problem solving
- Communication, including critical reading and effective writing
- Organization and management of a legal task, including time management

- Legal research. (Some NextGen PTs will also test basic foundational legal research skills. An example of this type of PT is at https://www.ncbex.org/exams/nextgen/sample-questions/performance-task/sample-research-pt)

We will discuss these skills as you work through the book and you will train them as you complete practice exams.

C. PT APPROACH: HOW TO FINISH A PT

The following presents an efficient and effective PT approach. Note that because each person thinks differently, and each PT is unique, all times are approximate. And because total completion time varies in different jurisdictions, the time allocation in the approach below is noted in percentages rather than minutes.

The system involves these six steps, easy to remember with the acronym SS-BROW: Study, Skim, Brief, Re-Read, Outline, and Write.

- **S**tudy the Instructions and Task Memo (5%)
- **S**kim the File (5%)
- **B**rief the Library Authorities (20%)
- **R**e-Read Instructions, File, and Library as needed (15%)
- **O**utline (5%)
- **W**rite (50%)

You've got this! SS-BROW. Simple.

The examiners typically recommend that you spend half the time reading and outlining, leaving half to produce your answer. Some people are slower readers and need more time to fully understand the File and Library before they are able to write a passing answer. Others are slower typists; they read quickly but take more time to set out a legible and well-organized answer.

True story: one former student who was following the recommended timing was failing all her practice tests. At my suggestion, she tried incrementally increasing the time she spent reading, thinking, and outlining until she got comfortable using nearly two-thirds of the total time on those parts. (She was a fast enough typist that she was able to complete the exams in the remaining one-third of the allotted time.) She ended up producing much better quality answers and getting much higher scores, and of course, passed her first bar exam.

Most people do well with the recommended 50%–50% split, but, bottom line: these times are guidelines; experiment with timing as you practice and adjust the suggested times based on your own strengths and weaknesses.

The approach expanded just a bit is as follows.

1. **S**tudy General Instructions and the Task Memo General Instructions provide broad guidelines for taking the exam; the Task Memo describes your client's situation, tells you who you are in the exam role-play, and tells you which document(s) you must draft in your answer. The Task Memo is the most important document in the PT. (Some analogize it to "the call of the question" in a law essay.) You may find information in the Task Memo or separate formatting information that tells you how to set up your answer. If there is nothing specific on format, just choose a logical organization. (Much more on how to organize commonly tested tasks appears later in this chapter.)

2. **S**kim the File, to get a sense of your client's situation. Then re-read the Task Memo to focus your Library reading on what is critical to your task(s).

3. **B**rief the Library authorities—typically cases and statutes, but sometimes PT Libraries include other authorities.

4. **R**e-read the Task Memo to remind yourself of exactly what you are to draft. Re-read the File; it should be much easier to spot relevant facts now that you know the law. Think about how the Instructions, Library, and File logically fit together. Re-read the File, Library, and Task Memo again, as necessary.

5. **O**utline your task(s). Logical organization is key to passing.

6. **W**rite your answer. Re-read the Task Memo any time you pause in your writing to make sure you are following directions and answering the question(s) asked.

(7. Optional but often helpful: proofread your answer using any time remaining.)

1. PTs as Training for the Time Pressures of Law Practice

Remember, time flies when you are writing PTs. There is a lot of material to sort through, synthesize, and write about intelligently. So, it is critical to master an efficient approach to the material and to complete many practice tests under timed conditions.

Note again, because times vary, the system above is described in percentage of total time allocated rather than minutes. Thinking in percentages of the time allocated also may be helpful for students with accommodations, who have longer than the standard time to complete these exams.

Some critics believe that the artificial time constraints of PTs make them unfair and unrealistic. They contend that there is too much emphasis on finishing within the allotted time rather than on producing quality work product. It is true that law practice may not obligate attorneys to achieve the rapid turnaround of work product that is required for the PT. However, it is also true that as an attorney in today's fast-paced society, you will likely have to act and react very quickly on many occasions. Clients frequently want instantaneous answers to legal questions. Texting and other direct messaging have become a routine part of law practice. Gone are the days when lawyers could leisurely ponder questions before giving advice. Training under PT time constraints therefore may be a useful learning tool for practice as well as the bar exam.

CHAPTER 4

THE PT APPROACH IN DETAIL

Let's take a closer look at the success steps. (As you review these steps, you can look at samples of PT components in practice exams in this book's appendices.)

You must complete a very specific task(s) in a very limited amount of time, so it is critical to have a picture of what the examiners want before you start writing. Additionally, the examiners expect you to deliver a concise, responsive, well-written, and well-organized answer. For these reasons, the most important parts of every PT are the Instructions.

A. INSTRUCTIONS

PT instructions may take the following forms: General Instructions, a Task Memo, and sometimes formatting instructions.

1. General Instructions

General Instructions are largely boilerplate, meaning the same or similar in every exam. They describe the PT, tell you how long you have to complete the exam, note what fictional jurisdiction you are "lawyering" in, and provide a few other important details. The trend has been to keep these Instructions boilerplate. Jurisdictions and the NCBE post copies of these instructions on their websites, so you can review them ahead of time.

Despite this trend and the fact that you will have studied boilerplate instructions before the exam itself, it may be advisable still to at least quickly skim the General Instructions to confirm certain information. First, look to the General Instructions to confirm what jurisdiction the problem is set in; this is essential to knowing which Library authorities will be binding. Second, General Instructions tell you how many sets of materials you have to work with. Almost always, that is a File and Library. But it is worth confirming that your closed universe consists only of a File and Library because on rare past occasions applicants were given a third set of materials (such as a set of draft trusts) which some Applicants who had not read the Instructions mistook for scratch paper. Also a few past PTs had no Library; the law was provided in something other than a Library, such as in jury instructions located in the File. Third, on many PTs, you only draft one document in your answer. But, if you are assigned multiple tasks, the Instructions or Task Memo usually indicate how much each task is worth; this information is critical to how you apportion your writing time. So, again, just give any General Instructions a cursory skim before moving on to the Task Memo.

2. Task Memo

The Task Memo is the most important part of the Instructions and arguably the most important part of the entire PT. The Task Memo is to the PT what "interrogatories" (or "calls of the question") are to law school essay exams.

The Task Memo is written to you ("Bar Applicant") from the person giving the assignment. Often, that is a senior partner in the fictitious law firm where you work in this PT role-play. For that reason, many people call the Task Memo the "Senior Partner Memo." I refer to this document more neutrally as the "Task Memo" because your assignment may come from someone other than a senior partner. You may not even work in a private firm. You may work in a government office or a nonprofit organization, or you may clerk for a judge.

So, in addition to telling you what your assignment is, the Task Memo also tells you who you are. Knowing your role can be critical to drafting an appropriately worded answer. (In a rare past PT, bar applicants were to play the role of a more experienced lawyer writing to a beginning lawyer. The appropriate tone on that PT was heavily influenced by the fact that applicants were supposed to have had more experience than the person to whom they were writing.)

Bottom line: The Task Memo is your key to success on the PT! It must be your bible, your guide, and your constant companion. Refer back to the Task Memo frequently. Glance at it again after you read the File, after you study the Library, and again periodically as you organize and draft your answer. The further you get into a PT, the more helpful hints you will notice in the Task Memo.

3. Format Pages (Only in Some PTs)

Some PTs include additional instructions that provide a "format" for (and sometimes a sample of) the document you are to draft. A format page may follow the Task Memo, but, more commonly, formatting instructions are part of (embedded within) the Task Memo itself.

If the examiners give you any specific formatting instructions, be happy! That is a gift. If they don't, worry not—just read on; every PT has some logical organizing principle.

Formats may be drafted as internal office memoranda that start with language such as, "Our firm follows the practice of drafting [the particular document type] as follows. . . ." You will see sample format pages in some of the practice tests in eProducts.

If a PT exam provides guidance on how to set up your answer, follow that guidance. **Do not disregard formatting instructions.** The examiners will not give you "extra credit" or think you are creative for setting a document up your own way if they give you formatting instructions. Among other key parts of what bar exams test is your ability to follow directions. People frequently fail PTs because they fail to do as instructed. I have counseled many attorneys who were licensed in one jurisdiction, took the bar in another, and failed because they formatted PT documents as they had in practice and not as directed on the exam.

LAW PRACTICE NOTE

As a practicing lawyer, you often do not need to start from scratch when drafting a motion or other document. Formats (taken from old "form books" or AI, or similar documents drafted by other lawyers in your law firm), can also be invaluable starting places in law practice. In many law firms it is common practice for new lawyers to ask more senior lawyers for similar documents from previous cases to use as samples for guidance when beginning new projects. But be sure to carefully study, edit, and proofread whatever you adapt; do not *assume* that other people's work or AI is correct.

What if a PT does not provide a specific format? When there is no suggested or required format, the key is to know what type of document you are writing, for whom, and why, and then simply choose a *logical and responsive way* to organize and present the information requested. If there is no distinct format guide, there will most likely be organizational clues in either the Instructions or the Library. (More on this later.)

B. FILE

Next, after carefully reviewing all instructional documents, skim the rest of the documents in the File. Note: You will re-read the File later, but the first pass through should be a quick read or skim.

Why a quick read or skim? Because reading every word of each File document now, before you have read the Library, wastes time.

Let me explain why it makes so much sense to skim, rather than read the File carefully, on your first pass through the File. The File will include a great deal of information that you will not need to draft your answer. One major skill tested by a PT is your ability to sort relevant from irrelevant facts. If you read the File carefully, without having any context for the facts, you will likely get mired in irrelevant detours. Only *after* you have studied the Library and are familiar with governing law, will you readily see what is and what is not relevant in the File. Once you know the law, you will be able to identify important facts much more quickly.

You may be asking yourself, "Then why not read the Library first?" Great question! The answer is a bit complicated, but the bottom line is this: Again, you may also waste precious time *wandering* in the Library if you do not first have at least a sense of your client's situation before reading cases and statutes.

So which to read first, File or Library, poses a "chicken and egg" challenge: You really cannot sort relevant from irrelevant information in the File until you know the law. But you also cannot effectively determine how the legal authorities *apply to your client* until you know at least a little about your client's case. For these reasons, the best method is to *skim* the File to get a sense of your client's factual circumstances, then study the Library to see which law applies, then go back and re-read the File. During that re-read, you will readily (and much more quickly) be able to identify relevant facts and start plugging those facts into the legal framework (your outline).

Think of it this way: PTs require you to be on a precision mission rather than a fishing expedition. What does that mean? When you read and brief cases in law school, you are reading every word of each case with an eye toward anticipating any possible question the professor might ask, about any part of the court's decision. If you proceed straight to the Library in a PT without knowing your client's circumstances, you head off on a similar sort of "fishing expedition," finding the cases interesting perhaps, but not knowing what you are looking for in them or how they relate to your case or task.

Instead, you want to read PT Libraries like a lawyer, not a law student. Go into the Library not on the student's fishing expedition, but rather on a lawyer's precision mission. Reading the Library while armed with a sense of what has happened to your client and what your client wants, you will be able to immediately assess whether case law favors your client or not. You will be able to see where a case is factually analogous to or distinguishable from your client's case. Perhaps most importantly, you will understand how to *use* the authorities in your PT answer.

Skimming the File first may also provide hints about how much time to spend on each Library case. Why? If the law supports your client's position, you may be able to quickly get in and out with a holding to cite in your answer. However, if the court has ruled in a manner that would hurt your client, you will likely need to read more closely to see if you can factually distinguish the case from your client's situation.

I hope that you are starting to see now why the read/skim method makes sense. The strategy will come together as you complete practice tests.

In the meantime, you may still be wondering how thorough your initial "skim" should be. How much should someone know after studying the Instructions and skimming the File? This varies from exam to exam, but typically after first skimming the File, you will have a sense of the following:

- Who you work for (private law firm, government, or other entity)
- Who you represent, and some of the basic facts about your client's current situation and problem (What are your client's goals, and what or who is preventing your client from getting what he/she/it wants?)
- What the basic dispute is, if this is a litigation-based problem; or what document is to be drafted or edited to achieve which goals, if a transactional problem
- Where you are located (what fictional state and, if applicable, what fictional federal circuit)
- How many documents the File contains and what sort of information is in the File (e.g., hearing transcript, report, interview or deposition of a witness or party, a map, a photo, a contract, a newspaper article, etc.)
- What type of document(s) you are to draft; if more than one, how much each is worth; and some basic information on format for each task you are to complete

From your skim, you may have learned more than the preceding points suggest, but as you begin reading the Library, you should at least have a basic sense of your client's situation and your assigned task(s).

In the Library, note what types of authorities have been provided: cases, statutes, jury instructions, excerpts from a treatise, or some other source of law. As you study the Library, extract the relevant rules and principles from those authorities (paying attention to the precedential weight of those authorities).

Notice how surgical that sounds: "extract relevant rules." Very different from leisurely reading where you might peruse every fascinating aspect of a case!

Now, once you know what basic rules of law govern your case, you will go back to the File and see how the PT puzzle pieces fit together. After re-reading the File, you can begin your outline and soon start drafting your answer.

Be patient. You may need to re-read parts of the Library and File several times, and re-read the Task Memo, in order to effectively create a working outline. Keep reading, keep reasoning, and trust that the examiners have crafted a doable exam. Believe that each PT is a legal puzzle that fits together, and just keep looking to see how it does.

PT PARTICIPANTS AS CAST OF CHARACTERS IN PLAY

As part of your initial skim, start a "cast of characters" list on your scratch paper or in the table of contents. Sketch the players in the PT as one would the actors in a program for a play, so you have a quick reference guide if you forget someone's role. For example:

Carl Corporate: my client, the defendant in present action

Ms. Bigg: senior partner I work for

Mr. Big-Headed: opposing counsel who represents the plaintiff

Wendy Whistleblower: the plaintiff, fired from her job at my client's company

C. LIBRARY

After skimming the File, check back in quickly with the Task Memo to focus your thinking on your precise mission before you head in to the Library to read the legal authorities. The PT is an open-book test. Unlike in the *Mission Impossible* movies where the directions self-destruct, your Task Memo is always available.

Bar examiners consistently state that one of the most common reasons people fail the PT is not following directions. So, consult the Task Memo frequently as you think, outline, and write your answer.

Once inside your PT Library, if one is provided, start with a quick review of the Library's table of contents to see what sorts of authorities are included. Note that some PTs include one table of contents page for both the File and Library while others include separate tables of contents for the File and the Library. You will see these in the practice tests in eProducts.

As you read, you can take notes directly into the first draft of your answer (noting where the source document you are referring to can be found, for example "F2" for File page 2 or L2 for Library page 2). Be sure on your actual bar exam to delete any notes that are not part of your final answer before uploading the file.

Work on shorthand systems. For example, when briefing cases in the PT Library, you can either type case holdings in your own words on scratch paper or jot down the page numbers corresponding to where you "book-briefed" Library authorities at the top of your answer file. Using annotation software, you can also underline or highlight the holding of a case on a Library page where it appears so you can return to it when you are writing your answer.

1. Briefing the Library Authorities

If your Library includes a case or cases, determine before you read them whether they are binding or persuasive. Then, begin reading each case, paying attention to the dates each case was decided. Summarize each case using the "surgical briefing" system discussed later in this section to get into and out of each with just the information you need to use on your exam. You can always go back and re-read cases if you need more detail, but you do not want to waste time with too slow a Library read; that is time you cannot get back.

I always read the PT Library cases in the order they appear, but some people find it helpful to read them in reverse-chronological order from most recent to oldest. Sometimes a later case will refer to an earlier case, and some PTs include cases that have been overruled by later cases. In one instance, a theory stated in an earlier case had not yet been adopted in the jurisdiction but was embraced by a later case in the same jurisdiction.

In your answer, you will want to cite all the main cases—meaning those listed in the table of contents. You may, but do not have to, cite all of the cases within cases. Recognize that when cases cite other cases, the cited cases may be helpful. If so, reference them in your answer as follows: "*Jones* as cited in *Cray*." (*Cray* was the main case, and *Jones* was a case cited in *Cray*.) Again, you should strive at a minimum to use all the main Library cases.

As you read each case, look for key facts, law, and reasoning, and incorporate them into your answer along with rules and, where appropriate, policy considerations and/or the court's rationale.

As you read each main case, determine three Ws: **W**ho, **W**hat, and **W**here:

- **Who** is suing whom, and which party is in the position analogous to your client? (You must know which party in a case is in a similar position to your client to determine if the court's ruling helps or hurts your client. If the case hurts your client, look further into the facts to try to distinguish the case from your client's situation.)
- **What** did the court rule, and why did it so rule? (To help you keep your case briefing short and surgical, you can combine the holding and rationale.)
- **Where** does the rule from this case fit in your answer? As soon as you know how the rule applies to your client's situation, you can put a reference to the case in your outline. (You may have to come back to this question of where to mention the case in your answer after you have read all the law, re-read the facts, and are putting together your final outline.)

Pay attention to the relative weights of the authorities. If a case that is unfavorable for your client is merely persuasive, it is easy to note in your answer that the decision need not be followed. Do not expect that, though. Often, bar examiners make things more difficult and the best authority may be merely persuasive and those authorities that tend to lean against your client's position may be binding.

When you are faced with a binding decision that is bad for your client, you must usually distinguish the facts of that case from the facts of your client's case. The graders want to see that you can do this! (In rare instances, you may have a good faith argument that the law is outdated and should be overturned, despite its being binding.)

Be sure to read every PT Library case as if it were new to you. Even if a case seems familiar, read it carefully. Do not assume that you know its key facts or holding. In almost every jurisdiction, examiners explicitly state that they may change or edit cases for exam purposes. (Nevada uses actual Nevada cases.)

If the Library provides selected statutes and/or statutes from a subject not on your bar exam, read those too as if they were new to you. Read carefully. Pull the rules out of the statutes; they will likely be key building blocks in your answer. Just as you brief cases and extract the holdings, underline the elements of such statutes and make sure you understand what they require or prohibit. Using annotation software, circle, bold, or underline all the "and" and "or" words so you know whether components of each statute are conjunctive or disjunctive.

If, however, instead of selected statutes, a PT Library provides a block of rules or a series of statutes from a code that you are already charged with knowing for the bar exam, such as the Federal Rules of Civil Procedure, you may want to skim rather than read each statute. Look at the provision headings and know that the precise rules are there for your reference if you need them. Some people call this sort of Library a "reference Library." The statutes are there to consult whenever you need to look up the details of a particular section, just as you would search online or in a code book in practice.

Remember that cases do not form a "reference" Library. In other words, you should always read Library cases as if they were new, even if they seem familiar, because the examiners may edit them for the exam, changing facts and/or the holding.

D. RE-READ, THINK AND START OUTLINING

After reading the Library and extracting rules from cases and/or statutes, consult the Task Memo again. Ask yourself: (1) What document(s) must I draft? and (2) How does the law in the Library fit together?

Look for an organizing principle. There must be a logical organization. There may be more than one, but there is at least one sensible structure in every PT. The examiners create PTs as solvable puzzles.

The Library may contain different theories to support a single cause of action or defense theory. It may include different elements of a single claim, or several possible legal claims. The authorities may include one main rule and exceptions to that rule. There may be a guiding theory or principle with multiple factors or a multipart test.

Whatever the Library includes, the disparate threads of law will fall into an order; you just have to find it. So, after you have looked through all the authorities, stop and take a moment to think about how the cases, statutes, and/or other Library rules fit together. I tell my students at this point to, figuratively, "Put your feet up on the desk, *pretend* that you have all the time in the world, and just think—read and think, really hard."

Re-read the Task Memo. Think back to what you are being asked to draft and determine how the authorities help you draft it. If you are drafting a discovery plan, for example, does the Library include statutes about different discovery devices? If you are drafting a memo, does the Library include cases that all relate to one cause of action, but perhaps address several different elements? Try to see how the authorities can help you form a legal structure into which you will weave the facts when you ultimately write your answer.

If, after thinking for a few minutes, you do not see a pattern or structure emerging, keep moving forward with the process and trust that an organization will come into focus. If you see only a partial pattern—for example, you see how some but not all the cases fit together—start your outline using the pieces you have, and build on them as you proceed.

For your outline, your goal is not to craft a very detailed outline but rather a basic roadmap, preferably including points that you will use as headings and subheadings in your main answers. (The grader will only review your final answer, not your scratch paper.) You will see sample outlines in later chapters.

TREES AND HIGHWAYS: METAPHORS FOR OUTLINING PTs

You can think of your outline as one or more trees with particular branches. The tree trunk(s) are causes of action or defense claims; the elements or factors of those theories are branches. (A torts tree might have a trunk called "negligence" with four branches: duty, breach, causation, and damages. The "causation" branch might itself have two limbs: actual cause and proximate cause.) The "leaves" that cover those branches will be facts from the File. (The kinds of "leaves" that might appear on a "damages" branch could include hospital bills or photos of your client's injuries following an accident.) Your Library may include one tree with a bunch of branches, or several trees.

If you prefer a more urban metaphor, think of your headings and outline as a highway map. There are typically between one and five main legal "highways" in a PT Library. (To finish in the allotted time, and write in an organized way, you need to find them so that you don't get lost on the "side streets.") The main highways will form the main headings or major components of your outline.

Each highway may have main roads or side streets that branch out from that highway. The "cars" that drive on those highways are File facts.

> After you practice with all the PTs in this book, you will get comfortable with finding the "trees" or "highways"—that is, with identifying the organizing principles in each PT.

E. REVIEW THE FILE

Now, go back and re-read the File. You will be surprised at how relevant facts just pop out at you. Before reading the Library, the File seemed filled with random details. Now, as one of my former students put it, your search through the File feels like an Easter egg hunt: you are just pulling out pieces of chocolate!

F. PUT IT ALL TOGETHER AND REFINE YOUR OUTLINE

Re-read the Task and Format Memos. Make certain you understand the exact document or documents you are to produce, for whom you are writing, and why.

What is your goal, who is your immediate audience, and who is your ultimate audience? For example, you might have to draft a brief in support of a motion along with several declarations for your senior partner to file with the court. (The senior partner is your immediate audience; your ultimate audience is the court.) Or, you might have to draft a letter for your boss to send to your client. (Your boss is the immediate audience; the ultimate audience is your client.)

Always remember that the *truly* ultimate audience is your bar grader. The burden is on you to produce a well-organized, responsive answer. Make it easy on that grader to want to pass you. Do not give the grader reasons to want to fail you, such as not following directions or writing in a disorganized manner.

Think first, and then think some more. Think hard. Then, outline your answer before you start writing. Your outline need not be detailed, but it should include all your main headings. It should also note where the main cases and/or other legal rules fit in.

Get organized before you write. (This is especially true of those who hand write on the bar exam.) The clearer you are about what you are to produce, the clearer your answer will be.

Organized, thoughtful writing is what creates passing PT answers.

As you think and outline, refer back to the File, the Library, and any notes you have taken in the margins and/or on scratch paper. Remember that your grader will not consider your notes. You only get credit for your final answers that appear in your final submission, either in an uploaded file or a handwritten bluebook. So, take selective notes, and organize them in a way that you will be able to read and use quickly and easily.

This takes a lot of practice. It is easy to take too many notes. Always remember, though: The PT is an open-book test, so you can go back into any document in the File or Library to pick up details or specific language.

G. YOUR ANSWER

Beware! Graders generally spend very little time grading answers, so write just what the instructions direct and in the order requested. As you write, refer back to the Task Memo and any format guidance to make sure your answer is complete and responsive.

WHAT IF I DON'T KNOW WHETHER TO INCLUDE A POINT OR NOT?

My general rule is that so long as you finish, it is better to err on the side of including something that may not be relevant than to miss something that is relevant and critical. So, if you think of a point that you are not certain should be included and can quickly write it, go ahead, as long as you have a logical tie-in to your answer. If it is a longer point, note it on your scratch paper and decide whether or not to include it after you have written everything you know is critical.

Given that graders are pressed for time, make it easy for them to see your points. Write short sentences and use frequent paragraph breaks. Make your organization explicit, with clearly marked headings and subheadings to indicate main topics and subtopics within a document. You do not have to do this with a fancy numbering system. You can use any logical system that visually sets out your organization. For example, some students left-align all main headings, indent all subheadings once, and indent all sub-subheadings twice.

Type clearly. Try your best to spell key legal terms and names of the parties in your PT correctly. Graders understand and will forgive some typos, but because lawyers are detail oriented, you want to try to keep your presentation as neat as possible. Remember my earlier analogy of the PT to a paper interview: just as you would wear a clean suit to meet with your prospective employer, so too must you present well-organized, neatly drafted documents on your PT.

HANDWRITING

For the rare candidate who handwrites, write legibly. If the graders cannot easily read your answers, they likely will not try too hard to decipher what you have written. Handwriters mostly feel disadvantaged because they cannot "cut and paste." If you are handwriting and think of something that relates back to a section of your answer that you have completed, go back and simply insert a number and write the new thought as a corresponding footnote if you left room at the bottom of the page, or as an endnote if you only have room at the end of the document. That way you can get full credit for "afterthoughts" by indicating the logical place where they belong.

H. YOUR TONE

Whatever your role, part of the test is to see that you approach the task from the perspective of a professional dealing with your client, not as a law student. In other words, when writing a letter to a lay client, you will be judged on your ability to use plain English and define all legal jargon. When preparing a document for court submission, you will be expected to adopt a more formal tone, and use language and legal authorities in a lawyer-like manner.

You will typically adopt a more neutral, balanced, and analytical approach when writing in-house documents (those where you are writing to someone in your own law office or perhaps an investigator or other professional your firm hired).

You will employ a more persuasive tone when you are writing to the court, opposing counsel, or someone who is not "on your side."

A general rule is to avoid slang and to spell out abbreviations the first time you use them. You may use lists in certain documents, such as in-house fact-gathering assignments, but on most PTs you will want to write in complete sentences and complete paragraphs. You will learn much more about appropriate style by completing all the practice exams in this book.

Note: Do not write your name or other self-identifying information in your answer. Grading is anonymous and you will be identified only by the number you are given. Further, avoid humor and politics; the bar grader may not share your views and may take offense to something you write.

I. HOW TO COMPLETE PTs UNDER TIMED CONDITIONS

Now that we have a basic approach, let's look at what is perhaps the most challenging aspect of the PT: how to finish within the time constraints.

After your first practice PT, you may find yourself saying, "I could do this if I had a full day! No problem." Do not be discouraged if you exceed the time limit on your first few practice PTs. (That is a big part of why you are practicing!)

You may have had several weeks to complete a similar type of assignment in a first-year "Legal Research and Writing" course. You must train to complete PTs in a timely fashion. It is not easy!

There are two ways to master PT timing. One, always attempt to complete all practice tests under simulated test conditions. Your first practice PT will likely not be passing quality, but you will improve the quality of your answers with each practice exam. With this strategy, you force yourself to produce better and better quality, within a consistent time frame. Two, complete your first practice PT taking as much time as you need to produce a passing quality answer. Then, with each subsequent practice test, shave off time. You may far exceed the time limits on your first practice PT, but the next one will go faster, and so on. After a number of practice exams, you will get your timing under control.

If you opt for the second strategy, keep close tabs on how far over the time limit you went with each practice exam. If, after completing a half dozen, you exceed the limit by just a few minutes, keep practicing and do not worry. You will have what I call the "adrenaline advantage" on the actual exam. However, if you are consistently taking well more than the allotted time:

1. Keep working to improve your efficiency.
2. Pay attention to time-saving tips and strategies throughout this book.
3. Use the red-line approach.

The red-line approach works like this: Write until the time limit is reached, then note where you are, then finish. Insert a thick red highlighted TIME in the spot where you hit the time limit. See how many paragraphs or pages fall below the red. With each subsequent practice test, try to move that red line closer to the end of your answer. Visualizing how much over time you are often helps you internalize how much faster you must work to complete the exam in time.

Another great thing to do to speed up your timing is to study or even re-type sample answers. Often you will see that something you spent a long time writing was stated much more succinctly—yet still effectively—in a sample answer. Comparing your own work to passing answers will help you see how to improve both your timing and your content.

CHOPPED!

I liken the PT to the TV cooking show *Chopped*, where chefs compete to prepare a three-course meal with each dish featuring all the foods in a particular basket of ingredients. The time limits are strictly enforced. On the TV show when the time limit has passed to prepare a particular dish the host says, "Stop cooking. Put your knives down. Step away from your dishes," just as bar exam proctors will call out, "Time" and say, "Stop typing." On the PT, your "basket of ingredients" includes the Instructions, File, and Library. Just as the

Chopped judges expect contestants to produce a tasty, well-prepared, and beautifully presented meal in a very short amount of time, bar graders expect test-takers to craft well-reasoned, carefully drafted documents that are responsive to the instructions. Chef contestants sweat to finish; so, too, do bar applicants race against the clock. But, just as nearly all the contestants on TV complete each course using all the required ingredients, so too will you. With enough practice, you will become not only proficient but also comfortable completing these PT tasks within the required time frames. *Caveat:* On the very odd chance you run out of time on the actual bar exam, *never* indicate in your answer that you ran out of time. When you see that you have only a few moments to finish, conclude the paragraph you are writing. Skip a line, write the heading, "Conclusion," and finish off as best you can.

J. SELECTED TIME-SAVING TIPS

First, figure out where in the process you get delayed: reading, outlining, or writing?

If you are reading too slowly:

- Resist the temptation to force yourself to "just read faster." It is counterintuitive, but sometimes taking more time to read will actually help you answer faster because you understand more clearly what you intend to write about when you put fingers to keyboard. Consider giving yourself more than the suggested reading time, if you can still manage to complete your writing in less than the suggested time. (It is typically recommended that applicants spend half the exam reading and outlining and half writing. Some people just do not have a thorough enough handle on the problem halfway in, but, by taking a small amount of extra time to read and think, they are better positioned to knock out a good answer in the remaining time. This strategy may work well if you are a slow reader and a fast typist.)
- Read more generally, in and out of law school. The more you read, the faster you will become at reading. Read a news website or blog every day. Try

to summarize in a single sentence the main thesis of at least one article or posting each day. (This is yet another reason to start bar preparation while in law school rather than waiting until intensive bar review.)

If note-taking and outlining bog you down:

- Use skeletal outlines. Your outline should read like a summary of contents rather than a full table of contents; include just headings and subheadings, not every detail.
- Your grader will only read your answer. So, practice writing bare "roadmap" style notes and outlines. What you want in your outline are the main points that will become the headings and subheadings in your answer. Only write a more detailed outline if you can effectively turn your outline into the first draft of your answer.
- You will not get credit for even the most brilliant thoughts unless they are transferred to your official exam answer. Practice with annotation software and try underlining or highlighting key points you want to quote in the File or Library, and use shorthand notes in your answer document to find whether those are.
- Remember that, generally, bar graders do not want to see long passages quoted from the File or Library. (Short quotes are fine, but for longer points, it is better to summarize facts or law in your own words.)

If writing itself takes too much time:

- **Follow directions.** *For example, if they tell you not to draft a Statement of Facts, do* ***not*** *include one.* Give the examiners what they want, and only what they want. Bar examiners design these problems to make them writable within the given time frame; if you do "extra" work, you will likely not finish. (Also, such extra work will not impress the graders. Instead, you will look like someone who does not follow directions.)

- Use short cites. They tell you that you may do this. You will not appear more knowledgeable by taking extra time to include formal citations.
- Finish, and then go back and polish any rough sections. Do not try to write perfectly. To complete the exam in time, you may have to submit what you view as a draft rather than a finished product. That may be fine.
- Remember, bar exams are pass-fail tests. While in law school you worked continuously to get "A"s; here you are striving to do your best, but with an ultimate goal of simply passing—and remember, your quality will improve with continued practice.

Time-saving tips are great . . . in theory. I recognize, though, that sharing these suggestions is a bit like telling you how to run faster in a race. I can explain the theory forever: The real trick is to train. The more "fit" you are, the faster you will run. So, let's get running!

Next we will look at the fundamental skills you need to pass the PT, and then you will go on to practice with actual exams located in eProducts. I am confident that once you see what the examiners really want, you will be reassured that these really are all skills you have learned in law school (and in life!).

CHAPTER 5

FUNDAMENTAL LAWYERING SKILLS TESTED ON PTS

The four core competencies or skills tested on the PT are factual analysis, legal analysis, awareness of professional responsibility, and problem solving. Some newer PTs also include legal research skills. The next sections detail these various lawyering skills and how you will use them on PTs.

These are not the only skills that will be tested on the NextGen bar. The NCBE divides NextGen skills into four groups of skills. The NCBE's website details what is meant by each in their Bar Exam Content Scope outline and lists the following descriptions for each skills group.

- *The purpose of Foundational Skills Group A is to assess the extent to which an examinee can apply fundamental legal principles and legal reasoning to analyze given fact patterns.*
- *The purpose of Foundational Skills Group B is to assess the extent to which an examinee can identify lawyering strategies within the lawyer-client relationship, based on the relevant rules and standards and consistent with a client's objectives, interests, and constraints. Note: Issues related to the rules of professional responsibility listed below frequently arise in the context of Group B Foundational Skills (Client Counseling and Advising, Negotiation and Dispute Resolution, and Client Relationship and Management). Knowledge of the following American Bar Association Model Rules of Professional Conduct (MRPC) will not be assessed in stand-alone questions but may be assessed in the context of assessment of Group B*

Foundational Skills. [Rule sections that will be tested are listed in the scope outline.]

- *The purpose of Foundational Skills Group C is to test the extent to which an examinee can identify and implement legal research strategies, including preliminary issue-spotting, working with provided resources, developing and refining a theory of the case, and reaching closure on research questions.*
- *The purpose of Foundational Skills Group D is to test the extent to which an examinee can complete a legal writing or drafting task based on the relevant rules and standards and consistent with a client's objectives, interests, and constraints.*

Below are descriptions of the core PT competencies. As you practice with PTs in the appendices and eProducts, and take practice exams posted by your jurisdiction and/or the NCBE, you will have the opportunity to train all of these skills.

A. FACTUAL ANALYSIS

You can think of PT factual analysis as a two-part process:

1. Separating relevant from irrelevant facts
2. Tying relevant facts to applicable rules of law

Compare this for a moment to essay exams. Because most facts on essay questions are relevant, the first part of the process (separating relevant from irrelevant facts) may sound unusual. The second part, however, should sound familiar; it mirrors the "A" ("Analysis," or some say "Application") in the logical writing system abbreviated as IRAC which stands for Issue, Rule, Analysis or Application, Conclusion. The factual analysis competency, in the words of bar examiners, is: "Given knowledge of legal rules and preliminary identification of legal issues, the ability to identify areas of factual inquiry, assess facts and marshal facts in support of legal arguments."[1]

---

[1] Quoted from Section II.B. of a pamphlet published by the State Bar of California called *Information Regarding PTs*. This pamphlet notes that: "The description of competencies is based in large part on the work of H. Russel Cort and Jack L. Sammons, described in "The Search for 'Good Lawyering': A Concept and Model of Lawyering Competencies," 29 Cleveland State Law Review 397."

In plain English, your tasks in performing factual or fact analysis are to consider, given the legal rules: (1) What facts do you have, and are those facts credible? (2) What further facts do you need? (3) How do these facts relate to and prove or disprove each element of each cause of action, or each factor or element of each legal theory?

Factual analysis in PTs fundamentally differs from work with facts on law essays or multiple choice questions (MCQs). On PTs, relevant facts generally come from (and may be buried in between irrelevant facts in) original source documents. You will hunt for relevant facts within File documents such as letters, depositions or court transcripts, interview excerpts, articles, medical reports, photos, arrest records, notes, minutes, or statements.

Contrast that with law school essays or MCQ, where facts come from artificially constructed hypothetical fact patterns that you must take as true. Professors sometimes say, "Do not fight the facts." Whoever drafted the exam put each fact in the fact pattern for a reason. Though some law school exams include "red herrings" (or distracter facts) on essays, most bar testing formats other than PTs do not require you to cull out irrelevant facts or assess the credibility of facts. However, those are critical components of the factual analysis skill tested by the PT.

PTs also contain much more information than you will actually need to complete your assigned task(s). Many facts are duplicative or irrelevant to your task.

B. PT FACTS VERSUS ESSAY FACTS

Again, some law professors love "red herrings," or facts meant to distract you, but typical essays contain mostly relevant facts. In contrast, one of the key PT skills is your ability to sort relevant from irrelevant facts. Expect to have to weed out a great deal of information in the File in order to finish in time. Knowing how facts are used in different forms of testing helps you develop appropriate test-taking strategies.

On essay questions, you have probably gotten used to reading the fact pattern and ask yourself why each fact was included and what rule it triggers. (On closed book essays, you have no "Library" and rules must be memorized.) For example, in a criminal law essay, seeing facts such as a "broken" window or "dim lighting" might trigger you to ask yourself if burglary is a discussable issue. *Burglary* at common law was the breaking and entering of the dwelling house of another in the nighttime with intent to commit a felony therein. You would then compare the facts to each element of that rule and analyze whether there is sufficient proof of each element to conclude that the crime has been committed.

It is likely that some elements will be clear and others ambiguous. For instance, the facts may clearly state that the defendant broke and entered the requisite structure at the requisite time, but it may be unclear what her intent was upon entry. There may be facts from which an inference of felonious intent could be drawn, and other facts that refute that inference. In that instance, you may have to analyze the issues from both sides and conclude by showing why the facts logically point toward one or the other party prevailing.

Note: On many law essays, it will be fine to conclude that one or the other party will "likely" prevail (so long as that conclusion logically flows from your thorough and complete analysis). But some professors (and some bar examiners in jurisdictions still using this format) expect a definitive conclusion. Read the call of the question very carefully to get insight into what is expected on a particular question, and study any information you can on new and existing bar exam testing formats to determine the expectations of your bar examiners. Also, heed the advice of your academic support and bar support faculty. (And, of course, in law school essays, ask your professor for guidance and review any past exams your professor has released.)

Notice, even where facts "cut both ways" on an essay question, you do not question the *reliability* of those facts. Back to the preceding burglary example: You would never ask, "Well, what if the window wasn't really broken?" You would not fight the facts and say, "I bet the lighting wasn't really all that dim." No! If essay facts tell you the lighting was dim or the window was broken, those are the facts your professor is requiring you to use. Period. The facts on essays, as in appellate course cases, are frozen. The grader wants to see how you analyze the particular facts given.

In PTs, we know that all the facts will *not* be relevant to our task. (The examiners tell us this!) Hence, there is no way you want to waste time combing through all the facts to see which legal issues the facts trigger, as you would when approaching an essay question. Reverse the thinking process on PTs: Learn the law to see which facts are relevant. Study the Library to determine which legal rules you are working with. Then sift through the facts to pick up the "wheat" (facts that are relevant to elements of those Library rules) and leave aside the "chaff" (irrelevant facts).

File documents in PTs may also include contradictory facts or unreliable facts, leading you to question their credibility. (For example, in a statutory rape-related PT where the age of the victim is critical, you might not take the victim's word about how old she was but suggest your law firm obtain her birth certificate to prove her age.) Keep in mind as you read PTs whether any biases or holes make facts unreliable. As noted earlier, this is the exact opposite of the wholesale acceptance of the fact pattern "as is" that you must do on bar essays.

Also, on some PTs, you may need to think "outside the (factual) box." In other words, part of your PT task may be to discuss what *additional* pieces of evidence are needed and how they might be gathered, such as in a discovery-related assignment. Again, this is a very different way of thinking about facts than what you do on bar essays—but this sort of factual investigation and analysis are precisely what many lawyers do.

C. LEGAL ANALYSIS

Legal analysis skills on PTs include "[t]he ability to analyze and evaluate legal authority, identify legal issues, and generate, assess, and justify the relative merits of alternate or competing legal positions."[2] This skill requires that you read and extract rules from cases and statutes, sift holdings from dicta, and determine the precedential weight of various authorities. You

[2] State Bar of California, *Information Regarding PTs.*

then apply these rules to the factual context in which the client is situated.

Some authorities (sources of law) are binding or mandatory; a court *must* follow them. Others are permissive; if a court finds them persuasive, it *may,* but does not have to, follow them. In order to anticipate how a court will rule or argue how it should rule in your client's matter, you must know these distinctions.

LEGAL AUTHORITIES

Primary authorities (which may be either persuasive or mandatory) that you may see in your PT Library include:

- Legislative authorities, such as constitutions, statutes, court rules, charters, or ordinances
- Judicial authorities, including cases and some court rules
- Administrative authorities, including decisions and regulations

PTs are typically set in a fictional state sometimes called Franklin, Columbia, or Olympia, or in a fictional federal circuit often at the district court or trial court level. The Instructions provide the name of the fictional state or fictional federal circuit so you can determine which authorities are binding in that jurisdiction. In general, primary legislative authorities are mandatory if enacted by the legislature in the jurisdiction. Primary judicial authorities in state courts are generally mandatory if they are decided by the court itself or a higher court in the same jurisdiction (or the Supreme Court if a federal issue) and are still good law, meaning the law has not been overruled. In federal courts, primary judicial authorities are binding if decided by the same court, the relevant federal circuit court, or the Supreme Court, and are still good law.

As distinguished from primary authorities, secondary authorities are never mandatory; however, they can often be quite persuasive. Secondary authorities you might see in a PT Library include dictionaries, treatises, encyclopedias, legal periodicals, *A.L.R.* annotations, law review articles, restatements, and legislative history.

1. Cases

Cases are enforceable decisions made by judges that explain, based on a particular set of facts, what result or outcome applies to the litigating parties and why. *Case holdings* are rulings the court makes that are necessary to the decision's outcome. There may be other legal rules stated in court decisions that are parenthetical and not essential to the particular outcome at hand; these are called *dicta.* (One of my favorite professors in law school, my Nolo.com co-author Paul Bergman, refers to dicta as "Oh, by the way, comments.") You can reference rules from dicta if they are helpful in your PT answer, but do not cite them as holdings. Note: if you want or need additional help with reading and briefing cases, another of Professor Bergman's books may be helpful: *Cracking the Case Method* (West Academic).

Using legal precedent involves referring to past cases to see if a court has already decided the same or an analogous issue to predict how a court would rule in the given new situation. In our judicial system, the core premise is that like situations should be treated alike. As an advocate and as a bar applicant on the PT, you will often be trying to show either that the facts are alike enough for the previous rule to apply, or that they are different enough that a different rule should apply.

In the real world you have many cases to consider, especially because new decisions are handed down regularly. Lawyers must conduct extensive searches to be sure that they have looked into every relevant case. However, PT Libraries typically only include a few cases, making it easy to compare and contrast the facts of the Library cases to your client's situation.

Do not be surprised if the bar examiners give you binding authority (controlling decisions that must be followed) that is bad for or unfavorable to your client, and persuasive nonbinding authority that is good for your client. If you are writing to a court, your job will then be to distinguish the cases and show why they are so factually different that the court you are addressing should not follow this binding rule.

However, remember that on a PT you are not always writing to a court. Often you will be writing a memo or other internal document to someone on your side (your senior partner, your investigator, or your client). Therefore, you may be tasked with exposing the weaknesses as well as the strengths of your client's case, perhaps counseling your client to settle rather than litigate given the facts and unfavorable law. However you handle bad law, on the bar exam and in practice, *do so ethically*. Do not lie, and do not misrepresent what a case (or a statute) says. If binding law does not favor your client's position, deal with that as a zealous, responsible, honest advocate would: argue why it should not apply in this circumstance, make a good faith argument that the law should be overruled or changed if applicable, or (as noted earlier), counsel the client against taking a particular position. Bar graders do, should, and will continue to fail applicants who advocate unethical positions on bar exam answers.

2. Statutes

Statutes, like cases, are primary authority; statutes are created by legislatures, whereas cases are decisions written by judges. Generally, statutes provide rules to govern future matters, and are meant to apply to a category of persons (or entities), whereas cases resolve past disputes between specific parties.

As discussed earlier, statutes may be included in PT Libraries in blocks of code sections that you are familiar with, for your reference. For example, there may be a number of sections excerpted from the Federal Rules of Civil Procedure or the Federal Rules of Evidence. Or, a Library may include one or more selected statutes, such as a section of an environmental regulation, from an area you are not charged with knowing for another part of your bar exam. When given blocks of statutes you are familiar with, they are typically in the Library for your reference. You may skim them and then re-read whichever passages you need to consult. However, when given selected statutes, read every word of each law and assume that it is purposeful. There is no dicta in statutes.

You must read statutory language carefully, section by section, in order. The first sections often define terms used in the body of the law. As you read statutory language, circle every "and" and "or" to know whether provisions are conjunctive or disjunctive.

Also consider legislative intent and public policy, if relevant. Who did the legislature want the statute to affect, and why? Do these rules apply to your client? Would application of the rule to your client have the effect the legislature intended? Would such application be fair and logical?

Concluding our walk through PT Libraries, remember that on PTs, you will *use* cases and statutes differently from the way in which you used them in most law school classes. You will read and analyze cases and/or statutes from the Library, not with general curiosity or to avoid embarrassment should the professor call on you, but with the explicit purpose of learning how the law has treated people whose problems were similar to those of your client, and predicting how a court (or opposing counsel for settlement purposes) will likely treat your client's matter.

Get into the Library, pull out rules from the authorities, and you will start seeing how the facts plug into (and prove or disprove) the relevant rules of law. Do not feel that you must master the Library authorities on your first read. You can go back to the Library any time you want and as many times as you need.

D. MARSHALLING OR ORGANIZING FACTS INTO LEGAL STRUCTURES

We looked at factual analysis and we looked at legal analysis. How do these two skills fit together? On PTs, typically they mesh when you "marshal" or organize facts into legal structures. *Legal structures* include legal theories, causes of action, defenses, and other ways of organizing facts into legally significant frameworks. To *marshal evidence* means to group facts or evidence together so as to help prove or disprove a particular legal element, factual proposition, or factor.

VISUALIZING A LEGAL STRUCTURE

Tree trunk = cause of action, crime, defense, or other legal liability theory

Branches = elements or factors

Leaves = facts

One of the most important skills you are demonstrating on a PT is your ability to show how facts relate to each component of the applicable law. Let's illustrate with a simple contract case. A new client tells you he agreed to loan his business partner $50,000 but the partner never repaid him. The client wants your advice. Even without looking at a Library, you know that for your client to bring a lawsuit to recover the money, you must establish that there was a valid contract that was performed and breached.

You are a lawyer (well, almost!), so you naturally think "formation, performance, breach, and damages." But what *facts* would a jury of lay people have to find in order for those legal elements to be proven?

1. To prove *formation*, jurors would have to find that Client agreed to lend Partner money, and that Partner agreed to pay Client back. (In other words, jurors as factfinders do not "find formation." Rather, they find that certain facts have been established which counsel will argue prove that a valid contract was formed.)

2. To prove *performance*, jurors would have to be satisfied that the evidence shows Client actually lent the money in question.

3. To prove *breach*, jurors must find that Partner failed to repay Client.

4. To prove *damages*, the jury would have to determine that Client is out of pocket $50,000 (perhaps plus interest).

How does this example relate to PTs? Typically, on PTs, you extract applicable rules from the Library authorities and break them down into component or element parts. Then, you search the File to find particular facts in your client's situation that "match up" to (prove or disprove) each part of each rule. Often, to prove to a bar grader that you have a command of the case, your analysis or argument, just like the preceding contracts example, must be simple and straightforward enough that a juror or client could follow your reasoning.

You may also be asked on a PT to gather additional facts. If so, you will want to show how that new potential evidence relates to the elements of the applicable rule(s). For example, earlier we said that "formation" would be established by showing that your client agreed to lend his partner money and the partner agreed to pay your client back.

What evidence would prove this? (1) Testimony that a witness saw or heard the deal being made; (2) Client's or Partner's calendar noting the date an agreement was made; or (3) a written contract, agreement, or IOU that documents the loan in writing. What evidence might you look for to prove that your client actually lent the money? (1) A withdrawal in Client's bank account at the time of the loan; (2) a deposit in Partner's account at the time of the loan; and/or (3) evidence that Partner needed the money at the time of the loan.

You might go through the same sort of reasoning to decide what evidence you would use to prove the remaining elements of the cause of action and to anticipate potential defenses. For example, anticipating that Partner might allege that the contract offer was invalid and thus the contract was never validly formed, you might determine if both parties were sober when the deal was allegedly made. You might find out where they were when the deal was struck (a bar, an office?). What other evidence can you think of that might help, or hurt, your client's case?

We take the time here to make our reasoning explicit because in PT fact-gathering documents, you may be asked to state the evidence you intend to discover, the element it helps prove, and why. You may also be asked to engage in this sort of marshalling of evidence to assess potential facts you want to develop and/or determine the relevance of facts you already have in the File. You will see examples of fact-gathering and marshalling assignments in some of the practice PTs in the Appendices and eProducts.

E. AWARENESS OF PROFESSIONAL RESPONSIBILITY

In the context of PTs, professional responsibility (PR) awareness is described as "[t]he ability to recognize ethical considerations in a factual situation, analyze and evaluate their implications for present and future actions, and behave in a manner facilitates the timely assertion of the client's rights."[3]

All PTs involve legal analysis and factual analysis. Not all PTs have ethics or PR issues, but PTs may be used to examine your knowledge of ethical rules as well as your sensitivity to general client concerns and your sense of good lawyering practices. In other words, you should note and comment appropriately if you see any ethical rule violations in a PT File. Also, you should be aware of, and urge where appropriate, clear and timely communication with clients and other best practices.

I have repeatedly said throughout this book that PTs are open-book tests, meaning that all the law you need is in the Library. Here's where I have to backtrack: *Nearly* all the law you need is in the Library. You are expected to come to the PT as an ethical lawyer who is already aware of his or her professional responsibilities. So, keep your PR antennae up. If, as you read the File, you notice that someone (perhaps even someone in your own office) has committed an ethical violation:

1. Identify the concern; that is, describe the problem and whom it affects.
2. State the rules. (You need not reference a code section number or case name unless those rules are in the Library, but simply state that ethics rules

[3] State Bar of California, *Information Regarding PTs*. Note that another version of the same pamphlet modified the last part, adding "and behave in a manner that is consistent with law and ethics while facilitating the timely assertion of the client's rights."

bar the behavior, and/or professional responsibilities require certain action.)

3. Suggest ways you and/or your firm might resolve the issues.

Sometimes the entire PT is about an ethics matter, and the Library will contain PR authorities. Other times, an unethical or unprofessional action will be suggested somewhere in the File and you will have to call someone or some action out and propose ways to correct the problem.

Ethical issues in PTs may include: (1) a client pursuing an unlawful or unethical objective, such as defrauding a creditor, and trying to get an attorney to go along with this; (2) an attorney breaching client confidentiality; (3) attorneys who are in actual or potential conflicts of interest in representing clients; (4) problems with attorney fees, such as the client's fees being paid by a third party (testing your knowledge of your duties to your client); and (5) obligations of candor and duties to reveal certain information. (Appendix F includes a debrief of an excellent practice PR-based PT that poses a myriad of ethical issues. The exam is located in eProducts.)

In PTs, ethical concerns can often be resolved by obtaining client consent. You can show the grader that you understand there is a problem, and recommend a cure, yet continue to finish the assigned tasks. Even if in real life you might consider withdrawing from a case, do not do that on the bar exam and "write yourself out of the question." Bring the problem to the attention of the person for whom you are writing your assignment (usually a senior partner or head lawyer in your office), and then move on.

If your ultimate audience is the court or opposing counsel, and you have spotted an ethical issue that you want to flag for your boss only, before the document is filed or sent out, write your concern in a short introductory paragraph. Put your note in brackets, addressed only to your senior partner, before writing the rest of your assigned task.

PR REFLECTION

In the following spaces, list at least five things a lawyer may generally not do, and then think of five more actions specifically prohibited during trial. This exercise will help sharpen your PR antennae and spot ethical issues that arise on PTs.

Questions

1. Generally, a lawyer may not:

____

____

____

____

____

____

2. Specifically during trial, a lawyer may not:

____

____

____

____

____

____

Answers

These answers are drawn from PR issues that have arisen in past PTs.

1. Generally, a lawyer:
    - May not counsel or assist in fraudulent or criminal conduct
    - May not use false evidence
    - May not reveal client confidences
    - May not assist a client in committing perjury

- May not force a client to make decisions regarding defenses, settlements, or pleas
- May not litigate in bad faith
- May not talk directly to the represented opposing party

2. Specifically during trial, a lawyer:
   - May not assert personal knowledge of contested facts
   - May not assert personal opinions regarding credibility of witnesses, justness of a cause, guilt or innocence of an accused
   - May not abuse the court process
   - May not violate court orders
   - May not secure the absence or noncooperation of a witness
   - May not pay a witness (except for travel, meals, lodging, loss of time, or expert fees)
   - May not suppress or tamper with evidence
   - May not falsify evidence or assist in perjury

If you spotted at least five for each of these, great! You are likely to see these if they arise on a PT. If not, review these examples and be aware of the types of ethical issues that may be "planted" in a PT on your bar exam.

In addition to concerns that are clear violations of ethical rules, someone in a PT File may suggest actions that are just not good practice, such as deliberately stalling in returning someone's call or replying to an email. Call such actions out the same way you would a PR rule violation. Explain why the behavior is not professional and suggest the best way to proceed. Again, you can sometimes write such a comment in brackets in a note to the person to whom your PT assignment is addressed, either at the beginning or the end of your task.

F. PROBLEM SOLVING

All PTs require competency in the legal analysis and factual analysis skills described earlier. Not all PTs involve PR, as just discussed, or the problem-solving skill discussed here. Nevertheless, perhaps because many complaints are lodged against the practicing bar due to failure to adequately listen to (and hear) client concerns, or perhaps because it is just good practice, listening to clients and helping them accomplish their objectives are themes that have been stressed on some past PTs.

Problem solving on PTs involves "[t]he ability to identify and diagnose problems in terms of client objectives and to suggest measures to achieve those client objectives."[4] On past exams, problem-solving skills have been tested in many different tasks, including in-house memoranda, client letters, and memos to investigators. Applicants have had to identify client concerns and think about ways to meet client objectives in various contexts, such as client counseling and interviewing, negotiation, settlement, mediation and other ADR, as well as in drafting or revising contracts and estate planning documents such as wills and trust instruments.

It may be helpful to think about problem-solving tasks by breaking the definition into two parts:

1. Figure out what the client's problem is (*identify and diagnose problems in terms of client objectives*), and
2. Solve the problem (*suggest measures to achieve those client objectives*).

To competently perform the first part of problem-solving tasks (the identification and diagnosis of problems), you must find those facts from the File that tell you what your client needs and wants. You may see details about the client's concerns, values, and/or priorities in the Task Memo, in letters to or from the client, in transcripts of interviews with the client, or in other client-related documents. Pay attention to these details. At the

---

[4] *See* State Bar of California, *Information Regarding PTs*. Another version of the same pamphlet identified the skill as "[t]he ability to identify and diagnose issues in terms of client goals and to develop lawful suggestions for how best to achieve the client's objectives" (State Bar of California, *Information Regarding PTs.*) See descriptive list of MPT-specific Problem Solving Skills at http://www.ncbex.org/exams/mpt/preparing.

same time, as you read the Task Memo and File, keep the following big-picture questions in mind:

1. Who is my client?
2. Who is suing or plans to sue whom over what, if the problem involves litigation? With whom is my client dealing, and about what specific concerns, if the PT involves a transactional matter?
3. What can I suggest to help my client achieve his/her/its objectives?

Note: It will ultimately be up to the client to decide what choices to make, so better PT answers often include *more than one way* for the client to achieve his/her/its objectives and discuss the pros and cons of each alternative. You may also be called upon to suggest which action is preferable and why.

In some PTs, the types of solutions will be fairly generic. For example, you might suggest that the client settle, sue, or mediate. In other PTs, the solutions are more case-specific. For instance, the client may not be able to have certain goods shipped and delivered on time, so may negotiate a reduced future shipment price to compensate for losses due to delays.

Recall our hypothetical about a client who lent money to his business partner and wants the money back. How might that client accomplish this goal? Of course, the client could bring a lawsuit alleging breach of contract. But he could also ask for the money back, if he has not yet done so. He could write a formal letter of demand (copying you as his lawyer on the letter), or have you write a demand letter. He could propose a payment plan or settle for a smaller sum in cash. Think of and write in the following spaces just a few pros and cons of each of these solutions:

Lawsuit Pros:

____

____

____

Lawsuit Cons:

____

____

____

Mediation Pros:

____

____

____

Mediation Cons:

____

____

____

Arbitration Pros:

____

____

____

Arbitration Cons:

____

____

____

After trying to think of pros and cons on your own, read these suggestions.

Lawsuit Pros:

- If the case is strong, your client may win and be paid back in full.
- It is possible that just filing a complaint will show that your client means business and encourage the business partner to pay up.
- Your client may also feel a sense that justice has been served by bringing the matter to court.

Lawsuit Cons:

- Costs. Attorney fees and costs could easily eat up much of the $50,000 even if the client wins.
- The possibility of losing. No case is a "slam dunk."
- Time. Win or lose, litigation takes a long time.
- Last but not least, being in an adversarial situation with a business partner will likely destroy the relationship.

Mediation: Your client and his business partner could go together to a neutral third party to resolve their dispute.

Mediation Pros:

- May result in an amicable solution that will help if the two want to remain business partners.
- May be quicker and less costly than litigation.

Mediation Cons:

- May require both sides compromising, with no clear "winner" or "loser."

Arbitration: Your client and his partner could select someone to arbitrate their dispute (similar to litigation but less formal).

Arbitration Pros:

- May be quicker, less formal, and less costly than litigation.

Arbitration Cons:

- May still not be easy for parties to work together after going through this adversarial process.

In writing the pros and cons of those dispute resolution scenarios, did any other solutions come to mind? How about:

- *Using a guarantor or providing security:* Perhaps your client's partner could find someone else to guarantee the obligation. Or, maybe the partner could provide your client with some collateral or security for the $50,000.

- *Performing services in lieu of payment:* Maybe the partner could do something for your client in exchange for the money.
- *Force or fear:* Your client could send a thug to rough up his friend and coerce the money out of him. **No way!** I just wrote this to see if you were still awake and reading carefully. No matter what you see on the latest TV law dramas, *do not suggest anything unethical or illegal.* If you do, you may well fail. Likewise, *do not even joke about anything unethical or illegal;* bar graders may not share your sense of humor or realize that you were joking.

You can see that even in a very simple breach of contract scenario there may be many solutions. On PTs, because time is so severely limited, usually thinking of even two alternatives to help the client achieve the client's objectives is enough to answer the question adequately.

Problem solving, though not tested on every PT, is one of the most creative and fun skills tested on these exams. The more you practice, the easier it will become.

G. LEGAL RESEARCH

Some newer performance tasks are also asking students to demonstrate proficiency in certain basic legal research skills. The NCBE notes that the as "foundational skills" the NextGen exam will *"test the extent to which an examinee can identify and implement legal research strategies, including preliminary issue-spotting, working with provided resources, developing and refining a theory of the case, and reaching closure on research questions."*

As of this writing, one sample "research" PT has been published. You can find it here: https://www.ncbex.org/exams/nextgen/sample-questions/performance-task/sample-research-pt. As you read through it, you will see that it largely requires that applicants understand which authorities are controlling and that they have the ability to synthesize cases and/or statutes to solve a problem.

If you are taking a NextGen bar exam, practice these kinds of PTs and other PTs as well.

CHAPTER 6

PT TASKS: WHAT YOU MAY BE REQUIRED TO DRAFT

Now that you have a sense of the basic skills in which you must demonstrate competency for PT success, let's look at frequently tested tasks. On your PT, you will be asked to complete one or more documents that a beginning lawyer might draft in practice. You will likely have specific instructions and may even have a "Format" Memo to guide you. Nonetheless, the more familiar you are with frequently tested tasks, the more prepared and confident you will be.

Here, we look briefly at some of the tasks tested on past PTs. You may want to skip this part of the chapter now and come back to it after having completed a few practice PTs, or you may read it now and then again after you complete some exams.

HAVE NOT TAKEN CLINICAL CLASSES?

For those who have taken trial advocacy or other clinical classes, some of this information will be familiar. If you have not taken such courses and/or want additional background in litigation-related documents, the following may be helpful resources: *Represent Yourself in Court: How to Prepare & Try a Winning Case* (Bergman and Berman, Nolo.com) and *The Criminal Law Handbook: Know Your Rights, Survive the System* (Bergman and Berman, Nolo.com).

A. TEST YOUR KNOWLEDGE OF COMMON PT TASKS

In the following spaces, without looking anything up, write what you know about each document type: its purpose, rules limiting its usage, its typical content or format, and the context in which such a task would be drafted.

NEGOTIATION LETTER:

MEMORANDUM OF POINTS AND AUTHORITIES:

POSITION PAPER:

APPELLATE BRIEF:

DEMAND LETTER:

MEMORANDUM OF LAW:

DISCOVERY PLAN:

CLOSING ARGUMENT:

____

____

____

TRIAL BRIEF:

____

____

____

INTERROGATORIES:

____

____

____

DECLARATION:

____

____

____

AFFIDAVIT:

____

____

____

CONTRACT:

____

____

____

WILL:

____

____

____

TRUST:

STATUTE:

The next subsections contain brief descriptions of selected documents you may be asked to draft, and some strategies for effectively completing these tasks on PTs. On most PTs, you are asked to draft all or part of one or two documents.

1. Legal Memo

This may be called a memorandum of law, memo or memorandum, or analytical memorandum. Memos frequently appear as tasks on PTs. Most students have drafted legal memos in law school legal research courses, so you may have a reasonable comfort level with this task. Nonetheless, be sure to study the PT instructions carefully. A PT memo may require fewer formalities than your legal writing professor required and you would waste time providing anything that was not requested.

You may be asked to draft only a memo, or a memo along with another task or tasks. Depending on the law in the Library, your memo may center on exploring how solid a case your client will have asserting a particular cause of action, legal theory, or potential defense. You may be asked to explore a conflict of laws. You may assess whether and under what theories certain evidence may be admitted. There are infinite legal issues that could form the basis of this type of assignment, but they will all have their foundation in the Library. Study the Task Memo and the Library to determine exactly what the issues are and how to outline your assignment.

A typical legal memo on a PT is written to someone in your office, usually the senior partner or another colleague. You will adopt a balanced tone, explaining the law and, if appropriate and relevant to the task, the strengths and weaknesses of your client's position.

Caveat: Just because a task is called a "memorandum" may not mean it is the classic legal memo you are familiar with. Be certain to ascertain for whom and for what purpose this piece of writing is intended. If it is not an in-house strategizing document, but rather a document you are to file with the court, then it is likely to be a persuasive presentation in disguise. For example, in certain jurisdictions, a persuasive "brief" is called a "memorandum of points and authorities."

You may also be asked specifically to evaluate the likely success of a particular course of action and/or propose alternative solutions for handling your client's problems. *Read the directions carefully.* If you are asked to analyze and then make a recommendation, but all you provide is a neutral discussion, no matter how thorough that discussion/analysis is, you will likely not do well because you failed to follow directions.

a. Format

If the examiners give you a specific format, *follow it*. If they do not provide a format, include an introduction with a simple header as outlined in this subsection, a body that provides an analysis of issues (separated into sections, by issue, if you are addressing more than one question), and a conclusion (short, no more than one paragraph).

Start your memo as indicated in the following, then move into the body of your analysis:

To:

From: [your name on the bar exam is "Bar Applicant" or "Applicant"]

Re:

Date:

Please find the memo you requested regarding [state the general issue, for example, admissibility of evidence] below. If after reviewing it you have additional questions, please let me know and I will be happy to research those.

Unless the instructions tell you otherwise, you need not spend time on "questions presented," "short answers," or other formal parts of a memo that you may have been taught to draft in legal writing courses. In fact, many passing answers on PT memos omit the statement of facts altogether unless it is specifically requested.

If you are asked to write a statement of facts, select only those facts that are relevant to the issues you will analyze. You may want to write the body of your analysis first and then quickly draft the statement of facts, because by that time you will know exactly which facts you used. (If you are typing, it is easy to place the statement of facts above the analysis. If you are writing by hand, you can leave space to insert the statement of facts.)

Be alert for directions that instruct you to omit a statement of facts and proceed directly to your analysis. Follow those directions. You will not "wow" the grader with a superb statement of facts if the directions told you not to include one; in fact, the opposite is likely.

If the directions are silent as to format, and you are not specifically asked to draft a statement of facts, you may typically omit that section and jump straight into the body of the memo (your analysis). But, when you are not told to omit a statement of facts, drafting a short factual summary may help if you are not ready to begin drafting the body of your analysis; starting with a brief statement of facts may unblock your writing and get your creative juices flowing. Again, though, if not specifically requested, do not spend any length of time on this section of the memo; get immediately to what is directly instructed. And, if directed to omit this, leave it out.

Because a legal memo is typically an in-house document, you will want to expose facts that support your client's positions as well as facts that do not. This is very different from the "Statement of Facts" portion of a persuasive brief where your goal is to select those facts that, though stated accurately, paint a picture that helps persuade the reader of the strength of your client's position.

In an in-house legal memo on a PT, you may well end up concluding that your client's position is not supportable, that you do not expect to win on a particular argument, and that therefore you recommend settling or even withdrawing a complaint if necessary.

Caveat: As always, abide by applicable rules of professional responsibility and ethics. In other words, on PTs (and in law practice), *do not* counsel or suggest pursuing a claim that is not well grounded in law and fact.

Following the header and the statement of facts (if requested), organize your analysis around each main legal theory, or each element of each cause of action or defense. To make it easy for your grader to see your main points, give each subsection an appropriate heading.

Headings in legal memos can typically be short, descriptive phrases, similar to headings in typical law essay exams. Their purpose is not to summarize your analysis but to provide a roadmap to the organization of your memo.

Be sure to conclude, briefly, to show the grader that you completed your task.

2. Persuasive Brief

In this type of task, you are typically writing a legal argument to a judge in order to persuade that judge to make a particular decision or ruling. Related tasks may be a brief in support of a motion, a memorandum of points and authorities, a trial brief, and/or appellate brief.

The PT may be set in state or federal court, or some other quasi-judicial body such as an administrative agency. You may be asked to draft a brief covering any area of substantive or procedural law.

You want to use respectful, formal language when addressing a court, just as one would in practice. For example, write out terms in full that you might abbreviate in an informal, in-house memorandum. You may use bullet points where appropriate; for example, in listing reasons for supporting a position that you intend to develop in a later part of your brief. However, do not write in outline style. Rather, write in basic prose, with complete sentences and paragraphs. (By contrast, using more of an outline style might be the perfect format for an in-house investigation or discovery plan task.)

You will not be expected to prepare tables or indices. However, you may be asked to start with a statement of jurisdictional basis. (Unless you are specifically asked to draft this section, leave it out.) If you are asked to draft this section and, for example, your case is set in federal court, you will need to briefly state how your client has satisfied the jurisdictional requirements of either diversity or subject matter jurisdiction. (You would know these basic rules about jurisdiction by the time you get to the bar exam, and the facts would tell you enough about your case to know whether the parties are diverse or suing about a federal question.)

The next part of a persuasive brief-type task is typically a statement of facts. As noted earlier with respect to legal memos, if instructed to omit this section, leave it out. (You will take precious time away from your argument and be graded against others who followed the directions and jumped right into their argument.)

If instructed to draft a statement of facts as part of a persuasive assignment, draft this by summarizing any facts that are relevant to and support your client's legal arguments. Do not distort or fabricate facts. Do be selective, in both the facts you choose and the order in which you present them, to maximize the persuasiveness for your client's position. Look for either explicit directions or descriptive clues about the appropriate length of the statement of facts. Usually, it will be relatively short compared to the argument portion of a brief, but it could be a featured part of the PT assignment. As noted earlier with respect to fact statements in legal memos, it can be helpful in persuasive briefs as well to come back and draft the fact statement last, after completing the body of your assignment.

Next in a brief or persuasive memo is the body of your argument. The most important part of this section on a PT is often your persuasive headings.

Past PT instructions have described headings in persuasive briefs as "carefully crafted subject headings that illustrate the arguments they cover. The argument heading should succinctly summarize the reasons the tribunal should take the position you are advocating. A heading should be a specific application of a rule of law to the facts of the case and not a bare legal or factual conclusion or a statement of an abstract principle." *(NOTE: All credit to the California bar for this guideline and the following examples.)*

EXAMPLES FROM PAST PTs ILLUSTRATING PROPER AND IMPROPER PERSUASIVE HEADINGS

Improper: Defendant had sufficient minimum contacts to establish personal jurisdiction.

Proper: A radio station located in the State of Franklin that broadcasts into the State of Columbia, receives revenue from advertisers located in the State of Columbia, and holds its annual meeting in the State of Columbia, has sufficient minimum contacts to allow Columbia courts to assert personal jurisdiction.

Improper: The evidence is sufficient to convict the defendant.

Proper: Evidence of entry through an open window is sufficient to satisfy the "breaking" element of burglary.

Improper: The plaintiff is not entitled to back pay.

Proper: Because Plaintiff refused to accept Defendant's offer to place her on administrative leave, she is not entitled to back pay.

Improper: The prisoner's rights were violated.

Proper: Requiring the petitioner to take psychotropic medication in the absence of a hearing establishing violent behavior constitutes cruel and unusual punishment under the Eighth Amendment.

Improper: The underlying facts establish Plaintiff's claim of right.

> *Proper:* By placing a chain across the driveway, by refusing access to others, and by posting a "No Trespassing" sign, Plaintiff has established a claim of right.

Under each heading, write the rest of your argument, interweaving facts and law. **Do not list and summarize cases!** Argue why the law and facts together prove that your client should prevail on each particular issue in question.

At the end of your argument section, be sure to include a short conclusion so that the court is reminded of the relief you are seeking and to show the grader that you finished the assignment.

3. Declaration/Affidavit

In a declaration (also called an *affidavit*), you are presenting facts in the name of a witness (called the declarant or affiant, respectively), facts which that person could testify to if he or she were called to the witness stand in court. In other words, you are writing facts that are personally known to the witness and are truthful and relevant. Declarations often provide the supporting documentation that go along with persuasive briefs. Though they are recitations of facts, they are persuasive in nature in that you are selecting those facts that are necessary to and helpful to support your client's legal position.

a. Format

You will typically be given a format to use, but for PT purposes, a declaration may be presented quite simply, as the following examples indicate.

I, [insert name of Declarant], declare as follows:

1.

2.

3.

Signed, Declarant

I, Sara Berman, declare as follows:

1. I have taught as a law professor for more than 20 years.

2. I currently serve as a faculty member and the director of the academic success program at the USC Gould School of Law.

3. I attended the UCLA School of Law where I studied with professors, experts in clinical legal education, who helped in the creation of the first PTs.

4. Since law school, I have been interested in and passionate about PTs.

5. I wrote this book to help law students learn from PTs and do well on that portion of the bar exam.

I declare that the information above is true and correct to the best of my knowledge,

Sara Berman

Note that the first numbered paragraph often contains background information on the declarant and may include the person's connection to the case (for example, whether that person is a party or a witness). The remaining numbered paragraphs each recite important facts that are relevant, truthful, and within the declarant's personal knowledge. (Think: what did the declarant personally observe by sight, hearing, smell, or touch and how are those points helpful to proving something relevant to the case?)

Look for examples within the File itself. On a practice PT that I recently administered to my students, they had to draft declarations for the plaintiff and several witnesses. Some students panicked because they had never drafted a declaration. Others remained calm; they noticed that the File included the defendant's declaration, so they studied that declaration as a sample, and used it along with the formatting instructions to get a handle on how to draft the assigned documents.

4. Closing Argument

This type of assignment is usually a closing argument in court to a jury or judge, but you might be asked to draft a concluding statement in an administrative or other sort of hearing.

For this task, you are expected to write out what you would say at the close of a trial to convince the trier of fact (typically the judge or jurors) to decide in your client's favor, given the evidence presented and the relevant legal rules. You use helpful evidence supporting your client and refute harmful evidence presented by your adversary. You may reference the credibility (or lack thereof) of particular witnesses. And, you attempt to convince the judge or jurors that your client has met its burden of proof and/or that the opposing side has failed to meet its burden of proof. If you are to write a closing argument to a jury, remember that your audience is composed of lay people. Avoid jargon and define any legal terms you use. For example, when discussing the burden of proof, explain carefully terms such as "preponderance of the evidence" or "beyond a reasonable doubt." Use examples. Refer to the ultimate facts that must be proven, perhaps quoting briefly from the jury instructions that the jurors will themselves have to follow, rather than citing cases or statutes.

When drafting a closing argument to the court in a "bench trial" (or trial without a jury) you may (possibly extensively) cite cases and/or statutes in addition to proving how the facts satisfy the elements of those applicable legal rules. When writing to the court, feel free to use legal terms.

You can be less formal when writing to jurors than when you address a judge. However, in a closing argument to a judge or jury, be sure to write in as organized as possible a fashion so that the factfinder (and the bar grader!) can easily follow your points. Even though in a real-life oral argument you would be talking, and one does not generally speak aloud with headings, you still want headings, perhaps in brackets, for the grader to easily identify your main points and follow your organization.

Your organization will most often be an element-by-element approach under each respective crime, cause of action, and/or defense theory. If the PT Library or File (as part of the trial transcript) includes jury instructions, let these be your guide as to which legal elements must be proven. If not, find the elements that must be proven from other Library authorities. Then, using facts that were established as evidence in trial, lay out explicitly for the jurors those inferences you want them to draw from the evidence.

Be sure to anticipate and rebut arguments the other side would make. Even if in the real world you may have a chance to speak again (what is known as "rebuttal"), you will likely only be drafting one document on the PT.

WHAT ARE ULTIMATE FACTS?

In the instructions, you may be prompted to marshal or organize the evidence around what may be referred to as the "ultimate facts." These are plain factual statements of each legal element. For example, in a negligence action where the elements are duty, breach, causation, and damages, "the fact that the plaintiff suffered medical injuries for which she had to pay doctors $100,000" is an ultimate fact; it is the factual restating of the legal element of "damages."

5. Opening Statement

An opening statement is a sort of roadmap or preview that you are giving to jurors at the beginning of a trial to let them know what evidence you intend to present. You can only discuss evidence that you believe, in good faith, will be presented at trial. In other words, you may not discuss evidence that you believe will be found inadmissible. Format: The Task Memo and/or Format Memos will likely give you a sense of how you are to set up the opening statement, but often you will begin by introducing yourself, and then proceed, witness by witness, to discuss the evidence. An example of the type of language that may be used follows:

> *Ladies and Gentlemen, my name is Applicant. I represent __________, the plaintiff in this case, and will be talking to you today about some of the evidence you are going to hear in the coming days. First, you will hear from Mr. _______. Mr. ___ will testify about ______. Next, you will hear from Ms. ___, who will tell you about ___. Last, you will see documentation of ______________* [and you may discuss any exhibits or documentary evidence that will be presented at trial].

In a closing argument you may ask jurors to draw inferences from facts; in an opening statement you may not. You therefore have much more of an opportunity to show your ability to reason in a closing argument assignment. Closing arguments have been tested regularly on past PTs. You may not see an opening statement task on a PT, but if you do, you now know the basics of what it is.[1]

6. Jury Instructions

It is unlikely, but possible, that you could be asked to draft jury instructions. You could also be given proposed jury instructions and asked to edit them to ensure that they comply with relevant, binding case law.

In such a document, you are to present the law or ultimate facts that jurors must find in order to decide the case. Often these instructions are presented in paragraphs or bulleted lists, each paragraph or bullet point discussing one legal element or ultimate fact.

According to the Format Memo in one PT that asked applicants to draft jury instructions: *The objective [of jury instructions] is to fairly state the law while emphasizing factors that support a favorable result for our client.*[2] That same PT gave examples of jury instructions for cases in tort involving issues of negligent infliction of emotional distress, two of which were as follows:

> *If you find that Harry Jones, as an adjacent landowner to the Chesterfield airport, suffered emotional distress as a result of the noise from aircraft landing, taking off and in-flight, you may award damages to the plaintiff.*
>
> *If you find that the employee of the defendant, Speedy Process Service, made an invalid service of the writ on Mary Williams and thereafter knowingly filed a false affidavit of valid service, you may award damages to the plaintiff for negligent infliction of emotional distress.*

---

[1] If you seek more detailed explanations of how to draft closing arguments, opening statements, and other litigation-related items, see Sara J. Berman & Paul Bergman, *Represent Yourself in Court: How to Prepare & Try a Winning Case* (Nolo.com).

[2] California PT, February 1996.

7. Witness Cross- or Direct Examination

Direct examination is the process in which counsel elicits (in question-and-answer form) relevant admissible evidence from counsel's own witnesses. Usually this helps establish facts that support one's case. In *cross-examination*, counsel questions the opposing party's witnesses, with the goal of getting those witnesses to make statements about or admit to facts that support the other side's version of events, or in order to cast doubt on someone's credibility (often the credibility of the witness testifying).

Similar to closing argument, in this sort of task you draft your written answer exactly as the words will be spoken in court. Again, though, do include headings and subheadings to provide a roadmap for graders, even if you would not say aloud in court what is in the headings.

You may be asked to draft an examination (cross or direct) that you or another lawyer in your law firm would conduct. Alternatively, you could be asked to draft questions you think opposing counsel is likely to ask your witnesses and plan for how to respond. In either case, the Instructions will typically give you a precise format to use, one that helps you lay out both the questions and the anticipated responses.

For each witness, you may be asked to list the subject that the questions address, and then write out the questions and anticipated answers in full. After that, you may be asked to note any evidentiary objections that you or opposing counsel might make, give responses to those objections, and finish with the judge's likely ruling as to whether each objection will be sustained or overruled and accordingly whether or not the witness will have to answer each question.

As you can see, the examiners' asking you to draft a cross-examination or direct examination is a backdoor way of also testing you on evidence. Because relevance is one of the most fundamental concepts in evidence, it may be helpful to keep in mind (and, where appropriate, to write out explicitly) why a question is relevant. For instance, assume that you are counsel for the plaintiff in a personal injury action based on alleged domestic violence. You are questioning the witness, a police officer, whose version of events contradicts that of your client. If, in questioning the officer, you were to elicit the fact that the officer was once employed as a personal security guard for the defendant, this would be highly relevant in impeaching the witness's credibility.

I always think students are going to be put off by the rigidity of cross-examination tasks, but inevitably students enjoy drafting them. One of the sample PTs in eProducts, debriefed in this book's appendix, is based on evidence and one of the tasks is to draft a cross-examination plan. Practice with that assignment and get comfortable in case this type of task appears on your bar exam.

8. Discovery/Investigation Plan

Applicants have been tested on both informal fact investigation and "discovery" or formal fact-gathering. In either context, first set out each of the elements to be proven. Then, under each element, list the evidence you wish to locate and why. (State succinctly why the evidence is relevant or what it would help to establish or what it might refute. For example, if an element of particular claim is that the plaintiff must be under age 18, you might suggest obtaining the plaintiff's birth certificate to verify her age.)

Next, list the possible sources you would look to, or tools you might use, to obtain each particular item of evidence. Note that the instructions may ask you to point out any evidentiary concerns with regard to getting a statement or physical evidence admitted into evidence. For instance, you may get credit for noting, in conjunction with the listing of a certain letter that you wish to obtain, that the letter must be authenticated before it will be received into evidence by the court.

For formal discovery, recall that:

- You may depose parties and/or nonparty witnesses. Depositions involve questioning, under oath, with a court reporter making a transcript. You are typically seeking information from the deponent that is within the deponent's personal knowledge about what happened, when, why, and how. You may also ask the deponent about documentary or physical evidence.

- You may only send *interrogatories* to parties. These are written questions asking about facts within the party's knowledge (what happened, when, why, and how), and/or about documentary or physical evidence to which the party may have access. Note that it is generally much less expensive to send interrogatories than to take depositions, because you do not need to hire a court reporter.
- You might send *requests for admission*. These are written questions that ask a party to admit or deny certain facts.
- You might send written requests for a party to *produce documents*. Remember, this discovery tool can only be used for parties, but you can subpoena documents you want from nonparties.

As for informal fact-gathering on PTs, consider everything from talking to anyone who may have relevant information to reviewing public records, social media, or documents obtained via the Freedom of Information Act. However, *do not* suggest talking directly with someone who is represented by counsel; this violates ethical rules. You may suggest examining scientific data (with or without the assistance of an expert), taking pictures or measurements, or doing other sorts of physical testing.

Caveat: Only suggest lawful and ethical ways of obtaining evidence. **Do not** look to the lawyers in most movies or shows for ideas on how to gather evidence.

9. Letter to Client

In order to write an effective client letter for a PT, determine before you begin the exact purpose of the letter. Know why whoever is assigning this task wants you to write to the client.

It may be that your goal is to render some legal opinion to the client. For example, you might need to tell the client how likely the client is to succeed with a particular course of action. If so, you might organize the letter by possible courses of action and then discuss the pros and cons of each. To do this, you must be keenly aware of your client's needs and desires. If you think of different ways to help the client achieve their goals, explain the benefits and risks of any proposed course of action in simple, plain English. Take into account the psychological and financial implications, in addition to the legal aspects, of anything you propose. (Review the problem-solving skills discussed earlier; be alert to any language in the File about what the client wants or needs.) If your client expressly or impliedly suggested some course of action that is illegal or unethical, you must counsel the client as to why that action may not be pursued.

You may be writing to update your client on what has happened in his or her case. If so, you might summarize events to date chronologically, or from most important to least important.

You may be helping to prepare the client for an upcoming court hearing, deposition, or interview. If this is your assignment, you should describe the purpose of the proceeding and tell your client what he or she must do to get ready. Your client will almost always be a nonlawyer or lay person, so this task typically tests your ability to use simple language. Remember to define all legal jargon/terms in plain English.

10. Client or Witness Interview

You may be asked to write out a plan for interviewing your own client or another person who was involved in, observed, or knew about your client and/or the client's story. (On one past PT, applicants were asked to critique an interview plan that a more junior member of their law firm had drafted.)

If you are asked to write or critique an interview plan, you will likely be given a format or guidelines to follow. If you are not given more specific guidance, consider the goals of an interview and set up your answer in a way that logically meets those goals. Generally, in the first part of an interview plan, you want to include language that puts the client or witness at ease as much as possible. For example, tell the person how long the meeting is likely to be and the topics you expect to cover.

If you are meeting for the first time with your own client, this initial interview should also include discussions of fee arrangements. Tell the client how much and on what basis (hourly, contingency, or other) your firm charges.

Next, it may be helpful to try to establish a chronology of events: what happened, what was observed, and when. After that, you may probe one or more areas of questioning further to develop a particular legal or factual theory that is helpful to your client and/or to find out more about something that may be potentially damaging to your client.

Lastly, before the client or witness leaves, it may be important to conclude by confirming any particularly important information that came out during the interview and to thank the person. You may also need to have the person sign something or take documents to review, sign, and return later. You may want to conclude by arranging to meet again and/or to have the person follow-up by sending you physical or documentary evidence that the person has in his or her possession.

11. Client Counseling

Lawyers counsel clients in both litigation and nonlitigation contexts. In each, the lawyer tries to help the client make an informed decision about a particular problem, issue, choice, or path. In a PT, you could be asked to counsel your client by writing a letter to the client, writing an internal memo about counseling the client, or in the context of writing some plan for meeting with the client. Follow whatever specific format or guidelines you are given about how to set up the document. If you are not provided a detailed format, write in an organized, logical manner, keeping in mind the following basics for client counseling.

Start by identifying the client's problems and clarifying the client's goals. (You may do this with the client, or by reading information from the File, such as the transcript of a previous interview with the client or a letter from the client.)

Next, in light of the client's goals, articulate alternative courses of action or competing solutions to the client's problems. Identify the legal consequences of each of these alternatives. You will also want to consider, and likely write about, any important nonlegal consequences to the client, such as the possible effects of these alternatives on the client's business and social life.

Last, you will want to give the client any guidance you can to help the client choose among the various solutions, making certain that you abide by relevant rules of professional responsibility, and, if necessary, request relevant additional information from the client.

12. Negotiation or Settlement

A negotiation or settlement task usually asks you to develop a compromise or settlement offer that helps resolve a number of different areas of conflict that exist between your client and an adversary.

If a format is provided, follow it. If a format is not given, remember that the basics of this type of task involve setting out the factual context for the settlement, what both parties agree to, and what the parties disagree about. Follow that with a specific proposal. Your tone will differ radically depending on whether you are writing an internal (in-house) memo about what to possibly propose by way of settlement or whether you are writing a letter to opposing counsel urging the opposing party to agree to your proposal.

Keep in mind some generally positive aspects to settling a case:

- Cost savings (as compared with litigation)
- Increased privacy (court documents are public records, unless sealed, but you may agree to keep settlement-related documents private)
- Speed (a settlement can resolve matters quickly; litigation is typically a very lengthy process)

Before you can negotiate a successful deal, you must first learn your client's goals and needs. This involves the same first steps as counseling. Then, you will move on and try to persuade the other side either to accept your client's terms or to come to some agreement that is acceptable to all parties.

In practice, you often learn about clients by talking with them. Your client is your first and frequently most helpful source of information. You may also need to talk with others and/or review documents. PT Files may contain notes from meetings with your client, documents the client produced, or notes the client wrote. But you may well need more information than what is given in the File. If that is so, your task may include detailing such potential additional evidence (and possibly thoughts on how to obtain the information) in a memo to the senior partner or an investigator your firm has hired, or in a letter to your client.

Generally, when you negotiate on behalf of a client in the kinds of cases that typically arise on PTs, your primary job as counsel is to present the client's claims, concerns, and proposals to the other side, and try to get the other side to accept your client's terms. Concessions may need to be made on both sides. Remember, your client must consent to any final agreement or bargain reached in the negotiation process.

As with interviewing and counseling, lawyers negotiate for their clients in both litigation and nonlitigation contexts. When a dispute is resolved in the litigation context, the standard legal remedies for a prevailing party come in the form of money damages. In negotiating solutions to clients' problems (both in litigation settlements and in alternate forms of dispute resolution), you may be able to fashion agreements that involve non-monetary terms or deals, either in addition to or instead of money damages. Often such terms will suit your client's needs better than money damages.

A classic example, using a defamation lawsuit, is where the client really wants an apology more than money. Imagine a situation in which your wealthy client was slandered in some tabloid press. (If you are thinking that, technically, this is libel because it is in writing, I am proud of you!) Given your client's finances, negotiating with the newspaper's counsel for a public apology and retraction of its statements, perhaps in a full-page *New York Times* advertisement, might be a perfectly acceptable solution to both parties. Your client's reputation could be restored, at least in the eyes of those who read the *New York Times;* the tabloid, although it may have paid a lot for the ad, probably paid less than it would have paid in legal fees and costs (and possibly a hefty judgment) had the case gone to trial.

In a sales context, suppose that your client is involved in a contract dispute with a regular supplier about the purchase of certain goods. As part of negotiating about damages for goods already shipped, consider shaping an agreement by bargaining about other terms in future deals, such as delivery time, place, or quantity; timing of payment; exchange for related products or services; or anything else your client might want.

Bottom line: Think creatively to find mutually agreeable solutions that meet the financial as well as the legal, practical, and psychological needs of all the parties.

In addition to knowing what *your* client wants, you should know how a court would likely decide the dispute; that is, what are the legal rights and remedies of each party. Even if you fashion a creative agreement, such as those described earlier, knowing the law is vital. It may give you leverage in the negotiation process. If your research shows that your client is not entitled to any legal relief, make sure that you do not file a complaint; if one has already been filed, make sure you withdraw it; as you know, filing a frivolous lawsuit is sanctionable conduct.

You should also consider the amount of time and money it will take for the dispute to be resolved, and how important time, money, and other considerations are to the respective parties. Try to learn as much as you can about the opposing party's wants and needs; this will help you know what to press for and what to concede. (Again, how to you "learn" this in a PT? By carefully reading the Task Memo and File.)

As to tactics and strategies, when you finally sit down to negotiate with the other side after counseling your own client and conducting any necessary legal research (again, on your PT, that means after reading and analyzing the File, Library, and any other documents), you can take several approaches. One is to start with an assertive, but realistic, position and make only a few concessions. When you concede on a small point, you may lose little and in turn get the other side to give in on some terms that really matter most to your client. Another strategy is to start with an aggressive stance, expecting to give in on many terms. A third strategy is to ask for something reasonable that you know the other side will accept, then forcefully state that yours is a "take it or leave it" offer from the outset and you will not bend. (For this last approach, on a PT it could be helpful to clearly state why the offer is reasonable and why they should accept it as is.)

What is essential on this type of a PT task is not to adopt one or another strategy, but to make explicit the reasoning for whatever strategy you choose. Bar graders want to see that you can think like a lawyer, not necessarily that you have "the right answer," especially in negotiation situations where there often is no right answer.

As you read documents in your PT File, take note of the terms and conditions that your client seems adamant about and those about which your client seems open to compromise. Show the grader how your thoughts, critiques, and proposals attempt to meet and fulfill your client's needs and goals. It is vital to demonstrate to the bar grader your ability to act in a *zealous yet ethical manner* on behalf of your clients.

13. Other Transactional Tasks

Although the litigation context is a more common setting for PTs, there have been tests involving or set in other areas. Also, given ongoing trends away from costly, time-consuming litigation and toward both alternative methods of dispute resolution and preventive law (education and planning to stop legal problems from ever arising in the first place), it is quite likely that PTs of the future will be set more frequently in these areas and contexts.

You may be asked to draft documents that cover a broad range of planning, counseling, or deal making, in either a business or a personal context. Business clients may seek advice concerning proposed agreements with other persons or entities, compliance with government regulations, or applications to various government agencies and offices for licenses. Individuals may come to you or your firm regarding the purchase and sale of property, premarital agreements, or estate planning.

On past PTs, applicants have been asked to draft estate plans, evaluate business-related proposals, write marital settlement agreements, and more. For many such assignments, you will be given specific instructions in the Task Memo guiding you on how to format your answer. If not, in order to begin such a task, you would use the same sorts of logical reasoning approaches discussed earlier with respect to counseling, interviewing, and negotiation.

In particular, you would start by developing a clear understanding of your client's objectives and concerns. You begin this process by gathering information from the File. Locate any documents from the client or about the client's situation from other sources such as interview transcripts, letters, contracts, property descriptions, and photographs.

Then, identify the legal and nonlegal issues that are actually and/or potentially raised by the proposed transaction(s). Look at the Task Memo, and study the Library for clues as to the main legal problems or issues you are expected to discuss. Information from the File about the client's goals and desires will help steer you toward the nonlegal problems.

The next part of an analysis of a typical transactional PT will likely involve drafting or editing some proposed agreement or statement of your client's position. You may have to present this to other parties (for example, in negotiating with them), or you may be asked simply to counsel your own client about his, her, or its options. Typically, such documents are organized paragraph by paragraph. The practice PT that is set in the constitutional law context, on eProducts, debriefed in the appendix of this book, will give you training with this sort of a task.

14. Analysis/Editing of a Contract, Will, Trust, or Statute

Applicants asked to handle tasks relating to contracts, wills, trusts, or statutes have typically been asked to review a document that someone else drafted, studying it provision by provision to determine whether the agreement is valid, enforceable, and most advantageously worded for your client. From the File, you can determine your client's specific goals, what terms are essential to your client and what terms your client is willing to yield on; you may also get a sense of the strength of your client's bargaining power. The contracts-based PT in the eProducts (debriefed in Appendix F), will provide practice with this sort of a task.

As always, if the examiners give you a format, follow it. If not, you should proceed through the document, paragraph by paragraph, and suggest what language should be deleted, added, and modified; in each instance, say why. You may also edit the document for ambiguities and ensure that it fits the law provided by legal authorities from the Library.

An example I often give students about editing for ambiguity is if a PT asks you to draft or edit a will and your client wants to disinherit his two children, Sam and Dave, and give his entire estate to charity. Let's say the operative provision says, "I leave nothing to my children." What is wrong with that language? It is not against the law or incorrect. However, it is vague. Your client may at some point have a third child whom he adores. For this reason, the provision should be edited to specify the names and identities of the children he wants to disinherit. "I leave nothing to my twin sons born in 1993, Sam and Dave."

15. Alternative Dispute Resolution (ADR)

In a PT, if you were asked to prepare a client for a mediation and/or arbitration, would you be comfortable doing so? What are arbitration and mediation?

Although in practice there are great differences, for purposes of preparing and completing PTs set in these contexts, you may generally think about preparing for mediation as you would for a settlement conference, and for arbitration as you would for trial. Knowing at least a bit about ADR and understanding some of the practical differences between litigation and alternatives, however, may broaden your base of problem-solving skills and help you with a PT task that involves ADR or settlement.

In *arbitration*, the parties agree to let a neutral third party (often someone knowledgeable about the subject matter of the dispute) make a final and binding decision. Arbitration resembles courtroom litigation but is less formal; for example, rules of evidence may not be adhered to as strictly as in a court proceeding.

In *mediation*, parties also go voluntarily before a neutral third party, the mediator. Unlike arbitrators or judges, however, mediators do not impose a binding decision on the parties. Rather, mediators try to facilitate dialogue between the disputing participants and allow them to come to their own mutually agreeable solution, instead of rendering a judgment for one party. A mediator may also help the parties draft a written memorandum of the agreement reached, which usually takes the form of a binding contract. (If you are unfamiliar with mediation, see the "The Mediation Process" below.)

Mediation resembles negotiation; however, rather than simply pushing one or another party to make concessions in order to arrive at an agreement, the goal is to discover the underlying needs of each side and attempt to find a mutually satisfying resolution. The classic mediation example is two people fighting over one orange. Both want the fruit. In litigation, one would prevail and win the entire orange. In a settlement, the orange might be cut in half. But, in a mediation, if it were revealed that one party wanted the orange for its juice and the other for its zest, both parties might be completely satisfied by splitting the fruit such that the juice is squeezed for one and the entire peel goes to the other.

On a PT, you will seek to understand what each party wants and/or needs by carefully reading the Task Memo and File documents and zeroing in on relevant information about both parties' wants and needs.

If your client is open to contemplating ADR, some of the reasons to consider mediation include:

- Less cost to the client.
- Informality: parties are not bound by evidence rules.
- More control: the parties themselves, not a judge, make the ultimate decisions. Thus, there is truly the potential to get to the parties' underlying needs,

as discussed in the preceding example concerning the orange.

- Convenience: parties also may be able to schedule ADR sessions at times that are more convenient to them, rather than simply when the court clerk places the matter on the judge's calendar.
- Privacy: There is greater privacy in mediation, as there are no court-filed documents that become public record.

THE MEDIATION PROCESS

Conceptually, mediation includes three general phases:

Introductory: *During this part of the process, the mediator helps the parties create a safe environment in which to discuss difficult topics. Depending on the parties' experience with mediation, the mediator may provide a process overview: the role of the mediator, what will happen in the various mediation sessions, and confidentiality. During this phase, the parties may agree to ground rules for the conduct of the mediation (e.g., ensuring that only one person speaks at a time) and a general timetable for the process. This phase includes a joint session among the parties, during which opposing sides have an opportunity to state their views and desired outcomes.*

Problem-Solving Stage: *During this stage, the mediator helps the parties together to focus on issues, interests, options for resolution, and criteria for evaluating those options. The parties may also meet separately with the mediator to share confidences and fully consider options in private.*

Closure: *During this phase, the parties decide whether and on what terms to resolve the dispute. The mediator may help them draft a document that reflects any commitments they wish to make. As needed, the agreement then may be passed to others for approval. If the parties do not reach agreement, the mediator makes sure they understand why and what next steps are available to them.*

See U.S. Department of Health and Human Services, https://www.hhs.gov/about/agencies/dab/adr-services/mediation

16. Legislation

Because lawyers also act as legislators, some past PT tasks have included redrafting statutes and advocating amendments to legislation. As with lawyering tasks, if you are asked to draft or revise/edit legislation on a PT, focus on content and follow any form or format-related instructions that are provided.

Your tone should be formal, similar to how you would write to a court. If you are instructed to advocate the endorsement or passage of certain legislation, your tone should be partisan and persuasive. However, if you are instructed to evaluate the pros and cons of certain legislation, adopt an objective, neutral tone. If you are to edit or draft legislation, consider the suggestions made in the preceding sections on transactional matters and document analysis. Often, the best way to approach this type of assignment is to proceed paragraph by paragraph.

17. Unusual or Unfamiliar Tasks

The material in this chapter will help you familiarize yourself with commonly tested documents. Occasionally, though, bar examiners task you with drafting a document that you have never heard of. If this happens on your bar exam, stay calm, read the instructions carefully (then re-read them) and follow them as closely as possible. It may well be that once you get into the PT, the instructions and assignment will start resembling a task you have seen before, perhaps just called by an unfamiliar name. For example, in California, briefs in support of motions are typically called "Memoranda of Points and Authorities." If you had never heard that term, you could nonetheless clearly see from reading the instructions and putting the task in context that really the examiners are just asking you to draft a "brief."

B. DRAFTING A TASK YOU HAVE NEVER SEEN BEFORE

As noted above, when faced with an unfamiliar task, stay calm and think logically. Begin by studying the instructions. Even before you learn the facts from the File and the law from the Library, you can likely get a pretty good idea of what you need to write by simply thinking things through. Whether your task is determining *how* to draft some document, or strategizing about *when* to do or perform various acts, think and reason through the issues, and you will likely see a way to formulate a responsive answer. For example, let's say you are asked to draft a discovery plan—and that is something you have never done. You don't know what it should look like. How should you proceed? Whatever you do, do not worry. Just stay calm and think. Ask yourself: "What am I being asked to write and why?" Your *thinking* might proceed as follows:

> *I am being asked to draft a discovery plan. I am supposed to be an associate in a law firm. The senior partner said the client is contemplating filing a lawsuit after suffering severe physical injury while trespassing on the defendant's property. I know that discovery is the formal process that allows our client, as a party to a lawsuit, to obtain information, documents, or things that are now in the other side's possession, and which will help us understand the strengths and weaknesses of their case, our case, or both. The partner wants me to plan or strategize about how we are going to get that information—that is, which tools of discovery we will use (depositions, interrogatories, requests for admission, etc.), when we will use them, and why, and what information we are looking for.*

Already, you can begin to see that in asking you to draft a discovery plan, what the examiners are really testing is your ability to analyze the strengths and weaknesses of your client's and the opposing party's cases, and find out more information about them. You can handle that! You can figure out a logical organization if they do not provide a format.

Let's take the example one step further. In considering *when* to use which discovery tools, context and logic will help your analysis. Your *internal thought process* might continue as follows:

> *If we send interrogatories first, we will learn how to proceed with the rest of our discovery; we might find out who has further information and thus learn who to depose and where potential deponents are located. We might learn about documents we will want to review, and more. In addition, interrogatories will be much less*

> *expensive than depositions (as they do not involve court reporters and all that attorney time for preparing and for sitting through the sessions). We should start with less expensive discovery tools and proceed to more costly ones if we need them. We should consult our client before spending more money than we need to.*

You would continue talking yourself through the problem, returning frequently to the instructions, and produce something thoughtful, well-organized, and responsive—exactly what you need to do to pass.

Knowing that it is possible that you will face the task of drafting an unfamiliar document should help you "expect the unexpected." Do not panic. The key to success on the PT is and will always be in reading and carefully following whatever instructions they give you. Look for any clues they do give you about what you are writing, to whom, and why, and pick any logical organization for your responsive writing. Fall back on your general approach, organizing facts around legal principles. Look to the Library for structure and see if you can find a "legal tree and branches" around which to logically organize the "leaves." Think:

- Tree trunk = cause of action, crime, defense, or other legal liability theory
- Branches = elements or factors
- Leaves = facts

Also remember and take comfort in the fact that if the task is unfamiliar to you, it is likely unfamiliar to everyone else around you. Remember too that after completing the practice PTs in the Appendices and on eProducts, you will have been exposed to many of the types of tasks that might appear on your bar exam.

Since you now know a bit about what a PT is and how to complete one, at least in theory, I invite you now to move from theory to practice. Start working through the exams in the Appendices and the eProducts to develop your practical knowledge and hone your PT skills.

By the time you reach the end of the book and have completed a number of practice PTs, I am confident you will agree that the PT is not only wholly doable but it is the best part of the bar exam.

C. KEY TAKEAWAYS

- PTs would be much easier were it not for the time constraints of the exam. Do not get discouraged if you are not completing practice tests in the allotted time; keep up the practice and follow the many time-saving tips detailed in this chapter.
- Master the steps in SS-BROW, a logical approach to handling any PT. (SS-Brow stands for: **S**tudy the Instructions; **S**kim the File; **B**rief the Library Authorities; **R**e-read the Instructions, File, and Library; **O**utline; and **W**rite the tasks as directed.)
- Familiarize yourself with commonly tested tasks such as briefs, memos, letters, fact investigation plans, arguments to the judge or jury, and the other documents discussed in this chapter. Have a strategy for drafting unfamiliar tasks. Bottom line: Be prepared to write any sort of task that might appear on your bar exam.
- PTs test basic lawyering skills including legal analysis, factual analysis, awareness of professional responsibility, problem solving, and legal research. Along with these, PTs test practical skills such as reading comprehension, time management, and clear and effective writing. Train sufficiently so that you are practiced in every testable skill.

CHAPTER 7

SELF-ASSESSMENT AND IMPROVING PT SCORES AND OUTCOMES

Self-assessment is a critical part of training for success on the bar exam. For every practice question you take, set aside time to study sample or model answers and find ways to improve.

As you complete practice PTs, ask yourself the following key questions to self-assess your work. Also, be sure to compare and contrast your answer to reliable sample answers (such as those published by the jurisdictions or the NCBE) to find any ways to improve your own answers.

A. PT SELF-ASSESSMENT CHECKLIST

1. Did I finish the assignment within the allotted time?
2. Did I follow the directions, completing the specific task(s) requested in the Task Memo and only those tasks (being cognizant of the respective weights of different tasks if applicable)?
3. Did I produce a well-written, thoughtful, and organized answer? (Is my answer easy for the grader to read? Did I write in short paragraphs and include headings so that my grader can easily see my organization and main points?)
4. Did I use the authorities (citing to all the main cases and/or key statutes in the Library)?
5. Did I incorporate sufficient facts to support my analysis or argument?
6. Did I employ the proper tone given the audience I am writing to? (If I am writing a letter to a lay client, did I define legal jargon? If writing a brief to

the court, did I write in a persuasive, lawyerly manner?)

After completing some of the practice tests, you may want to return to and re-read earlier sections of this book. Information about PT skills and test-taking strategies will make so much more sense after you did into and finish a number of practice tests.

Keep writing practice PTs until you have it down, until you are consistently producing passing-quality answers under timed conditions. Keep self-assessing and studying sample answers after every practice question you complete. Reverse-engineer: look at those answers and then back at the File and Library to determine how to reference enough of the facts and law to write a complete answer without getting so bogged down that you don't finish.

1. PT "Cheat Sheet"

A favorite law professor of mine advised his students by about two weeks before the exam to boil each subject down to one page, **pretending** that we could bring in one page of notes per subject. (He would ask, "What would you want on your contracts "cheat sheet" if you were hit with a contracts essay?")

You might find such pages invaluable when you want something quick and useful to review before the exam. I loved this advice so much that I not only drafted subject-specific sheets but also a "PT Strategy Sheet."

a. Sample PT Strategy Sheet: Written to You by You

INSTRUCTIONS—Skim general instructions for basic info including anything about task.

TASK MEMO (TM)—Read TM slowly and carefully. This is the most important page of a PT. Look for: 1) Who am I? 2) Who am I writing for? 3) What type of writing is this and what is the goal of the writing task(s)? 4) What exactly am I expected to produce by the end of the exam? 5) Are they giving me any formats or tips on how to organize my answer?

CASE—Big picture. Who is my client and what does my client want? What if anything is preventing my client from getting what my client wants? If the case involves litigation, who is suing whom over what? If transactional, what is my client's main objective(s)?

LAW—1) Try to find the main legal issues and figure out the legal analytical framework—how do the Library rules fit together? 2) Figure out what the legal issues are really about: Is the analysis mainly procedural or substantive or both? Is it expanding or narrowing a legal policy? Is it building a prima facie case or defense theories? Is it distilling a rule from a line of cases, or finding an exception to a general rule? Is it arguing why our case doesn't fit some particular statutory scheme? What is the legal analysis I am to perform? And, again, how do the Library authorities fit together? (Reminder to myself: The law often provides the key logical organizing principle I need to find to write my answer.)

FACTS—On first skim through the File, find out my client's basic story. On second read, after studying the Library, let me think: 1) After knowing what is in the Library and isolating (and if possible breaking down) the main legal rule(s) into element or component parts, let me find some relevant facts that prove or disprove each legal element or component. Remember, there may be irrelevant and duplicative facts. No worries. Just look for some relevant facts on every key component of every main rule. 2) If appropriate, think about how we might gather additional facts that might help my client. Note any inconsistent facts. Note which facts (and which sources of facts) are or are not particularly reliable and why. 3) Again, expect irrelevant and duplicative facts. Don't get bogged down in anything I don't understand the relevance of. I can always come back to it. It's all here right in front of me. Everything I need to answer this question is in my TM, File, and Library.

PROFESSIONAL RESPONSIBILITY—Look for actual or potential conflicts or ethics rule violations; if there are any, think about client consent and other possible ways of resolving such issues.

SOLVE CLIENT'S PROBLEMS—1) Keep my client's objectives in mind. 2) Present alternative strategies; give client at least two choices. 3) Recommend tactics and strategies as well as substantive courses of action.

CONCLUDE!—1) Finish with some obvious concluding line. 2) Ask myself, "Did I perform the task(s) I was asked to in the Instructions and Task Memo? Did I help whomever I'm supposed to help on this project?"

CHAPTER 8

CONCLUSION

The bar review study period you are headed toward does not have to be the torture some describe it as. Bar review can be an empowering experience, an opportunity to review everything you learned in law school, to pull disparate legal threads together, and to get ready to prove to the bar examiners that you are capable of effectively serving clients. Rules and areas of law that may have been murky in school will become crystal clear. And, when you pass, you will feel a sense of achievement and accomplishment that is incomparable. If I haven't yet convinced you and you are still dreading the bar exam, please read my *Bar Exam Success* (free with a West Academic login).

I often say that PTs would be super easy for most law students, if you had several days to complete them. But finishing a thorough answer in the allotted time often proves to be a great challenge. Do not get frustrated. Working thoroughly yet quickly is what clients most often expect in this fast-paced world. And just as answering clients in a timely and accurate manner will become easier as you become more experienced, so too will PTs become easier as you practice them.

By reading this book and completing a good number of the PTs in the book's appendices and on the eProducts site accompanying this book, you will be well on the way to mastering the PT portion of your bar exam. You will also be making serious strides on the path toward establishing a foundation of competency in the kinds of basic lawyering skills needed in law practice and tested on other components of the bar exam.

Role-playing the lawyer in the practice PTs referenced in the Appendices will give you an extensive and diverse "portfolio." After completing the PTs:

- You will have "represented" almost a dozen clients, from an injured teenager to a local school board.

- You will have served as a prosecutor twice: once opposing a motion to suppress evidence based on alleged *Miranda* violations in a murder case, and again in investigating the facts in a heated political case involving alleged assault and trespass in a newsworthy local labor union dispute.
- You will have worked on various aspects of several negligence cases: *Carelton* (where you wrestled with varying duties owed by landowners to trespassers), *Dodson* (which required you to analyze evidentiary and procedural rules in a case stemming from a serious car accident that left your client a paraplegic and put your client in an adversarial position not only against the car manufacturer but also against her own sister), and *Piccolo* (where you helped fight a discovery battle in another car-accident case where a passenger in your client's car was killed).
- You will have dealt with litigation matters, and you also reviewed a contract, analyzed a lease, and scrutinized a proposed communications code as you addressed free speech and other concerns of a school-board client.
- You will have helped a grandmother trying to win visitation rights to see and have a relationship with her granddaughter.
- You will have counseled a colleague about ethical concerns in representing a client who is a local politician.

Your work history in these PT role-plays was varied.

- You worked as an associate in several private firms for private clients and at least one charitable organization.
- You also served as a prosecutor in criminal matters.
- You wrote several legal memos, and you drafted both opening and responsive briefs.
- You analyzed documents.

- You drafted discovery plans and fact-gathering memos for use in pretrial investigation and you drafted a cross-examination plan to question a witness during trial.

Sounds like a lot more than just reading a book, right? You bet!

In addition to helping train your writing and analytical skills, PT answers can sometimes be adapted to serve as writing samples for job interviews. Work with professionals in your law school's career development office and your academic support faculty to help you determine if one of your PT answers might be effectively edited into an appropriate writing sample. If so, this is a nice way to get extra mileage out of work you did while taking practice tests.

With the strategies in earlier chapters and the skills training you will get from taking the practice exams in the Appendices and on eProducts, you will have the tools needed to produce passing-quality answers. Perhaps even more importantly, I hope that after completing these PTs, you see yourself more and more as a beginning attorney, rather than as "just" a law student. You are making your transition from student to professional every day. Your clients will thank you for all that you have put into your studies and training.

With preparation, practice, and a positive mindset, it is my hope that the bar exam will not be a "bar" to your entry into practice but a door of opportunity that leads to a bright future, filled with potential for you to both better your own life and to help make the world a better place.

A. KEY TAKEAWAYS

- PTs are:
  - Open-book and thus fair in that they truly test your skills and not your memory. Once you master the skills, you don't forget them.
  - Realistic. They prepare you for law practice as well as for the bar exam.

  - Fun for many students because they allow for some creative expression, not often as big a part of law essays or multiple-choice questions.

- The best general strategy for completing a PT is to use the SS-BROW approach: **S**tudy, **S**kim, **B**rief, **R**e-Read, **O**utline, and **W**rite.
- To become competent in writing effective PT answers within the allotted time constraints, *practice, practice, practice.*
- Get a head start on PTs:
  - To help make law school come alive,
  - To start seeing yourself as a lawyer, and
  - To give yourself a down payment for success on the bar exam.
- **You've got this! The bar exam is yours to pass. All the best to you on the exam and in practice!**

APPENDIX A

PT-30

Mini-PT 1 The Law Clerk and the Alleged Honor Code Violation: A Mini Performance Test[1]

North & South, LLC., an International Law Firm
45 Main Street
Washington City, Franklin

MEMORANDUM

To: Applicant
From: James North, Senior Partner
Re: Law Clerk
Date: June 4, 2025

I just found out that one of our current law clerks ("Clerk"), a rising 3L student at the Franklin University Law School (FULS) who spent his first summer at the prestigious West & East law firm (W & E), was accused of cheating. The incident stems from Clerk having consulted a 5th year associate, "Alice," who recently lateraled to our law firm from W & E. Clerk disputes the charge of cheating, although he does admit that he spoke with Alice about the assignment.

Given the competitiveness in today's job market, (which I know you are all too familiar with having just graduated from law school and passed the bar), we have already made Clerk an offer of full-time employment for after graduation. This incident is giving me pause, however. If Clerk is found to have violated FULS rules, he may not be the kind of ethical lawyer we pride ourselves on being here at N & S. That said, we all like him a lot or we would not have made him an offer. In addition, Alice is up for partner this year; she is a veritable rock star, so I really hope we don't have to postpone her promotion.

[1] This PT (Task Memo and File) was created by Sara Berman. The scenario and File documents are entirely fictious; the Library contains an excerpt from the publicly available Washburn Law School Honor Code, published at https://www.washburnlaw.edu/admissions/admitted/honor-code.html.

In the File, you will find the email Clerk sent me this morning. In the Library you will find relevant excerpts of the FULS Honor Code. Clerk apparently can present evidence to contest that he violated the FULS Honor Code in the first place. Clerk may also present mitigating factors and defend against aggravating factors when the Honor Committee hears his case to both attempt to refute the charges or to be subject to much more lenient sanctions if he ends up being sanctioned.

I am meeting with Clerk this afternoon. Please draft a memo for me analyzing the charges against him (and if possible to predict, how likely it is that a violation will be found) and analyzing any mitigating and aggravating factors in this case. These are the areas that Clerk has asked for help with, and I want us to help him. After all, he may have been falsely accused. I need your complete, succinct but well-organized memo in 30 minutes. Please also include a short list of additional factual inquiries we might make of Clerk, Alice, or any other evidence we might quickly obtain. You may omit the Statement of Facts, Indices, and Tables, and write only the analysis portion of this memo.

Thank you. The hearing is tomorrow so time is of the essence.

File

Copy of Text of email dated June 4, 2025

Dear Mr. North,

It was great to see you at the dinner last week. Thank you again! I am honored to be working with you and other N & S lawyers on cutting edge environmental cases this summer. I am confident that this is the direction I want my career to head in. I know that our planet can only be saved through the kind of hard work we do at our firm. It is clear that the results of such work will determine whether or not I and my generation will have a safe world to live in.

To advance my goals and perform my work this summer with the most knowledgeable base possible, I enrolled last semester in an environmental law seminar. I was researching my final paper on international global warming legislation and remembered that Alice had a particular interest in that area when we were worked together last summer at W & E. I knew that Alice recently moved from W & E to N & S, so I called Alice for ideas about the paper. I assure you, Alice did not write my paper for me and in no way did I believe that gathering ideas for what to research and write on from a practicing lawyer in the field would be an Honor Code (Code) violation.

Yesterday, I received notice from the Associate Dean of Students saying that it was reported that I cheated on my seminar paper. I was shocked, and frankly, I am panicking a bit. They are threatening to change the A grade I received to an F, and as I read the Code, excerpts of which I am attaching to this email, I could be subject to numerous other sanctions. I felt it important to share this with you right away, so you know that I am not hiding anything. As I said, I believe I am 100% innocent.

I am preparing for a hearing before the Honor Board (Board) tomorrow and wanted to a) let you know that I need the day off to attend the hearing, and b) wanted to respectfully inquire as to whether you or another N & S attorney could help me prepare for the hearing. I feel a bit awkward even asking but I would be grateful beyond words for even some basic advice on how to contest the violation itself and how to appeal to the Board with respect to the aggravating and mitigating factors.

I have attached the relevant part of the Code. Please let me know if you need anything further from me.

Thank you, and most sincerely,

Clerk

Library[2]

[Excerpted language from] **PART I. CONDUCT SUBJECT TO SANCTIONS**

A. * * * The following conduct, if committed by a law student while on University property or while engaged or participating in academic activities or any University sponsored activity, will subject the student to action under this code:

[2] See footnote 1, all credit to the Washburn Law School for these Honor Code excerpts.

1. Academic improprieties. Academic impropriety in all its forms, in course work, on examinations, or in other academically related activities, including but not limited to:

   a. Cheating.

   b. Copying from another student.

   c. Using unauthorized materials.

   d. Collaborating with another person without authorization from the supervising professor.

   * * *

[Excerpted language from] **PART II. SANCTIONS**

A. Mitigating and Aggravating Factors Relevant to the Imposition of Sanctions. This Honor Code does not require the imposition of any particular sanction or range of sanctions for any of the types of misconduct described in Part I. Thus, for any misconduct under this Honor Code, the full range of sanctions described below are available. What sanction or sanctions are appropriate in a particular case will depend on the circumstances of that case. In addition, the following factors may be relevant as mitigating or aggravating factors in determining what sanctions are appropriate.

   1. Conscientious Admissions. A student who voluntarily admits misconduct before gaining any knowledge that someone else may suspect that student of an Honor Code violation, shall be entitled to have this admission considered as a mitigating factor relevant to the determination of appropriate sanctions. A student who has the courage and integrity to come forth with a good-faith admission has reaffirmed a personal commitment to honor. Any student interested in making a conscientious admission should contact the Associate Dean immediately. After discussing the matter with the Associate Dean, the student should prepare a written statement fully acknowledging any and all misconduct. The statement should include a clause attesting to the

fact that the student admitted the acts before being approached by anyone concerning the matter.

2. Other Admissions. Even an admission of wrongdoing made after a student has been accused of misconduct may have some mitigating value. The post-accusation admission shows an acceptance of the wrongful nature of the student's conduct. However, a post-accusation admission is not as strong a mitigating factor as a conscientious admission of wrongdoing because it is not clear that the student would have ever admitted the wrongdoing were it not for the accusation that [h]as been made.

3. Intentional vs. Negligent Conduct. Some conduct described in this Honor Code is only sanctionable if it is done intentionally. Other conduct is sanctionable whether or not done intentionally. However, even in circumstances in which intent is not required, the fact that conduct is intentional is an aggravating factor that may justify the imposition of more serious sanctions. Conversely, the fact that conduct is negligent may be a mitigating factor justifying the imposition of less serious sanctions.

4. Degree of Harm or Seriousness of Offense. The degree of harm to others and the seriousness of the conduct are relevant factors in determining sanctions.

5. Nexus to Professional Standards. The nexus between the student's conduct and the question of character and fitness of the student to practice law is a relevant factor in determining sanctions.

6. Prior Misconduct. Prior convictions under this or other Honor Codes shall be considered aggravating factors in determining sanctions.

7. Discriminatory Motive. If a student, in engaging in conduct found to be in violation of this Honor Code, is also found to have intentionally directed the conduct towards a person or group because of the race, color, religion, age, national origin, ancestry, disability, gender, sexual orientation, marital or parental status of

the targeted person or group, that discriminatory motive is an aggravating factor in determining sanctions.

B. Possible Sanctions. The following sanctions may be imposed for violations of this Honor Code.

1. Expulsion from the Law School;
2. Suspension with the opportunity to apply to the Admissions Committee for readmission after a specified period of time;
3. Suspension for a definite period of time;
4. Partial or total revocation or suspension of scholarship assistance;
5. Probation for a definite period of time under specified terms or conditions with consequences specified for noncompliance;
6. Removal from any student governmental office or position in any Law School sponsored activity or organization or from any other University sponsored position of trust, responsibility or interest;
7. Denial of the privilege of participation in any Law School or University sponsored extracurricular or athletic activity or organization for a definite period of time;
8. Written warning or reprimand;
9. Verbal warning;
10. Prohibiting or restricting access to and/or use of Law School or University facilities or services;
11. Monetary or other restitution;
12. For misconduct related to course work, sanctions may also include:
    a. Change of grade in a course;
    b. Withdrawal of academic credit in a course; or
    c. Receiving no credit for an academic work product, with or without an opportunity to redo the product;

13. For violations of the Residence Hall Behavior Code, sanctions provided therein or by this Code.
14. For violations involving academic improprieties described in the last paragraph of I. A. 1., withdrawal of a previously conferred law degree is an additional possible sanction.

The sanctions of expulsion, suspension and probation are inconsistent and shall not be imposed concurrently. Any suspension will be considered a total suspension from all Law School classes and activities unless it is expressly limited to specified classes or activities. The sanctions of suspension and probation may be subject to conditions.

Mini-PT 1: Sample Answer[3]

Part I: Memorandum

To: James
From: Applicant
Re: Law Clerk
Date: June 4, 2025

Introduction

Clerk, a law clerk in our firm, was just accused of violating Clerk's law school's Honor Code (Code) by consulting with Alice, an attorney who is now with our firm. Below please find the brief memo you requested analyzing Clerk's potential violation of selected Code provisions and assessing how the Honor Board might consider certain aggravating and mitigating factors before imposing sanctions (if any). Note: quoted and italicized language are excerpted directly from Code provisions Clerk provided. Additionally, as you requested, I have provided a short list of additional information we might try to obtain from Clerk, Alice, and others.

---

3 This is a sample student answer, not a faculty-drafted model answer.

Brief Overview of Facts

It is uncontested (Clerk has admitted) that Clerk consulted Alice for ideas for Clerk to write about for a required seminar paper. Clerk said that Alice did not write the paper for him. We do not know if Alice provided any other assistance (for example, we do not know if Alice edited the paper). We also do not know exactly what the professor's instructions were. These are among questions I am sure you will be asking Clerk when you meet with him.

Brief Analysis of Possible Violations

Clerk was accused of violating the Code. The provisions that prohibit the conduct he is alleged to have committed are likely these:

> c. *Using unauthorized materials.*
>
> d. *Collaborating with another person without authorization from the supervising professor.*

First, in order to determine whether Clerk used "unauthorized materials," it must be determined what materials were authorized. Until that is known, it cannot be known if the provision was violated. Note however, if, as Clerk has indicated, all Clerk did was talk with Alice about ideas for a topic or about *where to begin* the research and if all Alice shared were ideas about the area of law, this seems akin to the standard sort of information that a law librarian or even a quick Google search might reveal and likely not the kind of conduct this provision contemplates. (By contrast, such provisions typically prevent the use of answers to tests, teacher's editions, AI, etc.)

The second provision under which Clerk might be found in violation, "Collaborating with another person without authorization from the supervising professor," may pose a greater problem for Clerk. Here, the behavior appears to be a violation if it is not specifically authorized. Another issue however may turn on the meaning of the term, "collaborate." Typically, collaboration means working together. If what Clerk has revealed so far is true, merely consulting about the topic to research would likely not fit the letter of the rule, and certainly not the spirit of a rule prohibiting collaboration. As with the first provision, additional information is required to understand exactly the scope of the interaction between Clerk and Alice, e.g. what action Alice took (if any) beyond simply brainstorming about what to research or write about. And it would also be helpful to know how Clerk's professor and the school has historically defined "collaboration" under the Code.

Brief Analysis of Aggravating and Mitigating Factors

1. Conscientious Admissions

This provision serves to mitigate consequences for a violator who "*voluntarily admits misconduct before gaining any knowledge that someone else may suspect that student of an Honor Code violation.*" It appears from Clerk's email to you that Clerk learned of the issue when the Associate Dean contacted Clerk. Assuming Clerk did not share with anyone else that Clerk had consulted with Alice, it is doubtful Clerk can leverage this factor in his favor. If Clerk told anyone (especially Clerk's professor or even another student) that Clerk consulted Alice with regards to the paper before the Associate Dean contacted Clerk, it might be argued that such an admission is evidence that Clerk did not believe Clerk's actions were in any way wrong. But this factor does not appear to assist Clerk.

2. Other Admissions

If Clerk is prepared to write a complete statement now admitting and explaining the timing and extent of Clerk's contact with Alice, this may lessen any potential sanction. While it is not as powerful as admitting a violation on one's own (before being accused), it is evidence of taking responsibility for one's actions and thus may serve to mitigate any sanctions.

3. Intentional vs. Negligent Conduct

It appears from Clerk's email that Clerk intentionally approached Alice but that Clerk in no way believed that action to be prohibited. Thus, while Clerk intentionally spoke to Alice, Clerk may merely have been negligent in that action as to how it relates to the Code itself. We would need the entire Honor Code (beyond the excerpts provided in the Library) to determine if this is the kind of *"[C]onduct described in this Honor Code [that] is only sanctionable if it is done intentionally."* Regardless, if the Board finds Clerk's conduct here was merely negligent, that "*may be a mitigating factor justifying the imposition of less serious sanctions.*"

4. Degree of Harm or Seriousness of Offense

It is impossible to determine the degree of harm or seriousness of the offense without knowing what exactly Clerk asked of Alice, what sort of help/advice Alice gave, and what the professor's instructions were. Given the egregious nature of many honor code violations (such as plagiarizing the work of another or sharing test answers) however, at least based on Clerk's account, this appears to be fairly minor.

5. Nexus to Professional Standards

This is tricky because, depending on the facts, this could be a direct violation of governing rules or an entirely innocent and perfectly appropriate interview of an original source, an environmental law expert. It is also true that the practice of law often *encourages* collaboration and the exchange of ideas. Professional standards nonetheless require compliance with rules. Thus, in order to determine the potential impact of this factor, we must know more about the professor's rules and Clerk's intent.

6. Prior Misconduct

This cannot be determined from the information in the File. We must determine whether Clerk has ever been accused of or sanctioned for any other Honor Code violations.

7. Discriminatory Motive

This factor does not appear relevant as the alleged conduct was not about a person or group but relating to Clerk's work on Clerk's own paper.

<u>Conclusion to Part I</u>

In conclusion, additional facts are required to determine whether Clerk will likely be found to have violated the Code. If Clerk is found in violation, Clerk may succeed in mitigating any sanctions by leveraging factors 2, 3, and 4: admitting his actions now, pointing out that at most, Clerk was merely negligent in his understanding of the concepts of unauthorized material and/or collaboration, and asking the Board to see the actions as harmless. To that end, hopefully the Board will not sanction Clerk at all, and if they do, that they only give a verbal or at most a written warning or reprimand.

Part II: FURTHER FACTS NEEDED

Below is a list, in no particular order, of information that would be helpful to determine how best to assist Clerk.

- Did Alice provide any other assistance, beyond suggesting topics to research? (We should separately ask this question of Clerk and Alice, if possible.)
- Did Clerk receive any assistance from anyone else (or from AI) on his paper?
- What exactly were the professor's instructions?
- Has Clerk ever been accused of or reprimanded for any Code violations before this?
- What exact Code provision(s) was Clerk accused of having violated?
- Who accused Clerk and is the accuser credible? Have there been other baseless accusations lodged recently?
- Is Clerk prepared to admit his actions and apologize for them?
- Can Clerk request additional time to prepare for the hearing? He was notified yesterday, and the hearing is tomorrow.
- Is Clerk allowed to bring someone to represent him at the Board hearing, or someone to provide moral support?
- What sort of evidence will the Board consider? (Is Clerk allowed to present character witnesses to support him?)

Please let me know if you need anything further before or after you meet with Clerk.

Mini-PT 2[4]

Instructions and File

Memo to Applicant

To: Applicant
From: Ms. X, Sr. Partner at the Law Firm of X, Y & Z
Re: People v. Student A
Date: July 30 ___

Dear Applicant,

As you may know, my niece (referred to in File documents as Student A) is a full-time student at the only law school in our state (the State of Independence), State Law School at Independence University. I am afraid my niece has gotten mixed up with the wrong crowd. Last week, one of my niece's classmates (Classmate C) filed a complaint, and my niece was subsequently accused by the law school's Honor Committee of stealing the notes of a fellow student (Student B) that were allegedly on a small thumb drive in the pocket of Student B's coat. Student B was brought before the Committee and apparently confirmed that his thumb drive had been stolen. We know this because Student B bragged about it, also revealing that the thumb drive had notes and outlines and a very valuable formula Student B planned to sell to a fertilizer manufacturer. Student B had been a chemical engineer prior to law school.

The Honor Committee's rules (which I have yet to get a copy of) prohibit representation at hearings but do allow the accused to submit a letter on the accused's behalf. The rules do not specify who may draft such a letter so we are interpreting this to mean it may be drafted by anyone.

The Committee just let my niece know this morning that whatever she intends to submit must be received by 5pm today. I made a few quick calls and confirmed the statements from a classmate and the Librarian that you will find in the File. The hearing is tomorrow morning. Accordingly, in the next 30 minutes, I would like you to draft, for my review, a letter of no

[4] Consists of Memo to Applicant, Statement from Classmate, Librarian's Statement, and Transcript of Excerpt from Notes of Sr. Partner's Discussion with Student A.

more than one page in length to the Committee, persuading them to drop the charges against my niece.

In the remainder of the File, you will find a report from a classmate and a statement by the librarian on duty at the time of the alleged incident. You will also find notes from my earlier discussion with my niece.

While I am concerned with what the Honor Committee decides, especially if it affects my niece's character and fitness to practice law, I am also concerned that the Committee might forward its case to the local prosecutor's office. For that reason, please also draft a very brief memo to me (again no more than 1 page) outlining potential charges and what more factual or legal research you recommend with respect to either possible criminal charges or Honor Code issues. From my recollection of common law, the following are elements of potentially applicable crimes: 1) Larceny: The taking and carrying away of personal property of another with intent to deprive the owner permanently thereof. 2) Robbery: Larceny committed from the victim's person by force or fear. And, 3) Attempt: An act, done with intent to commit a crime, and tending but failing to effect its commission, is 'an attempt to commit that crime.'

Sincerely,
Sr. Partner

Statement from Classmate

I, Classmate C, do hereby state that on December 1st, during finals week, I saw Student A reach into a coat on a chair in the Library and pull out what looked like a thumb drive. To my knowledge, Student A does not take her own notes or draft her own outlines and frequently asks classmates to see their outlines just before final exams. Student B told me that his notes were stolen and that he thought Student A must have done it because he heard that Student A got As in all her classes last semester.

Librarian's Statement

I have reviewed library logs from December 1. The logs are compiled when students swipe their IDs to enter the library. Student A's name is in that day's logs. Student B's is not. I know both students. I was in the library that day and evening and do not recall seeing either student.

Transcript of Excerpt from Notes of Sr. Partner's Discussion with Student A

Partner: Hi, how are you? How's my niece, the next generation of lawyers in our family?

Student A: Not great. That's why I'm here.

Partner: How can I help?

Student A: Well, one of my weasel classmates reported me—falsely I might add—to the Honor Committee, and I have to appear before them by myself tomorrow morning. I'm scared.

Partner: What happened?

Student A: I have no idea. I hate Student B. "Mr. #1," as he likes to refer to himself, is an arrogant jerk. I would love to see him humiliated as he has humiliated so many of us. I've even thought about various ways to do it. That night, the night I'm alleged to have stolen his notes, I told some friends that it would be funny if someone stole his notes and did better than he did on a final, for a change.

Partner: Did you steal his notes?

Student A: No. He wasn't even in the Library that night.

Partner: What happened after you told your friends it would be funny if someone stole his notes?

Student A: Nothing. One friend, Student F, got really into the idea. She suggested we snoop around his desk at the law review office, see if that is where he keeps his notes and outlines and stuff.

Partner: Did you do that?

Student A: Yeah, I told her that I'd just said it as a joke, but, to humor her and because I needed a study break anyway, we went and looked through his desk. All we saw were prospective articles.

Partner: So, you never took any of his belongings?

Student A: No. We looked around in a few other places we know he hangs out, but nothing. I think Student F was just looking for an excuse not to study. I guess I was too.

Partner: Did you take anything out of a coat in the library that night?

Student A: Yes, I took my own thumb drive out of a coat that I left in the library earlier that day to save a study carrel. Look, this whole thing is a mix-up. Somebody reported me 'cause I'm the only one who ever calls out Student B's bad behavior and the whole class is scared of him.

Mini-PT 2: Self Reflection

1) What was the most challenging part of completing this mini-PT and why?

2) Did you complete your answer in the allotted time? If not, where do you think you might have "wasted" some time—or what might you have done to work more quickly getting through this material?

3) What if anything is similar in the crimes of attempted robbery and attempted larceny?

4) What is different about writing to an Honor Committee than writing to a Court?

5) How did the tone of your letter to the Committee differ from your tone in writing your memo to the Senior Partner?

6) Did it occur to you that the Partner may be biased because the client is his niece? Did you note anything about that in your Memo? Why or why not?

7) Did you believe the niece? Draft a list of questions you would like to ask her if you have a chance to interview

her, and state why you want to ask each question you draft.

Mini-PT 2: Draft Sample Answer[5]

To: Sr. Partner
From: Bar Applicant
Re: DRAFT LETTER AND MEMO

I have gone ahead and prepared the draft letter for your review and the draft memo that you requested. As you will see in the memo, the law provided is not applicable to the internal law school proceedings and additional research is necessary to proceed in an informed way.

DRAFT LETTER TO HONOR COMMITTEE

To the Honor Committee of State Law School at Independence University,

It is unclear why Student A is being called to appear before this Committee. Student A respectfully requests a written statement of any allegations against her and a copy of all relevant rules that the Committee will consider as well as rules of procedure the Committee must follow. Student A also respectfully requests that the hearing be postponed until Student A has had a chance to review those documents, and consult with counsel.

In the event that the Committee decides to move forward on [____ date], less than 24 hours after informing Student A that she must appear for a hearing, the Committee is urged to take into consideration the following:

Student A has apparently been falsely accused of theft of property (namely a thumb drive). The allegations are at best baseless rumors. Neither the classmate who brought the complaint (Student C), nor the alleged victim (Student B) have any firsthand knowledge of whether a theft occurred and, if so, who might have perpetrated it. Further, the Library's own logs indicate that Student B was not even in the library on the night in question so clearly nothing could have been taken from him

5 This is intended as a sample not a model answer.

or from in his clothing. Perhaps Student B misplaced the thumb drive that was claimed to have been stolen.

There is a history of hostile relations between Student B and his classmates, and therefore Student B might have motive to have fabricated this baseless accusation. However, it appears that Student B himself did not even report this alleged theft but another classmate, Student C, did so. What C's motives are at the moment are unclear but what is clear is that Student C was either deliberately fabricating facts or mistaken in believing that Student A took a thumb drive belonging to someone else, someone who was not even in the building at the time in question.

This hearing is a rushed procedure that may have grave consequences if it is allowed to proceed. For the reasons stated above, the Committee is urged to reconsider and drop the proceeding altogether, or at the very least allow Student A the time and information necessary to adequately prepare to contest the baseless accusation that has allegedly been leveled against her.

Sincerely

____

MEMO

To: Sr. Partner
From: Bar Applicant
Re: MEMO
Date:

Assessment of potential charges should Honor Committee share information with local prosecutor

Student A appears to be accused of theft or attempted theft. As you can see from the Draft Letter above, though, what we know so far including with respect to the accusation, is based largely on rumor. Student B allegedly confirmed that his property was missing, but Student A says she did not take Student B's property. Assuming Student A is believed, the only potentially applicable crime for which she could be charged would be attempted larceny. As discussed below, even this is unlikely. To prove attempted larceny, the prosecution would have to show that Student A had the intent to commit larceny and that Student A took actions that caused her to come close to actually taking Student B's property.

From your interview with Student A, it appears that she was more interested in a practical joke, (and possibly even just joking about the idea of playing a prank), than she was in any actual theft. In fact, it appears that she was more interested in procrastination from own studies that in doing anything nefarious or unlawful. If Student A's version of events (what she told you) is not contested (if witnesses do not come forth with a different factual account), there appears to be insufficient evidence to prove that Student had the requisite intent for any crime. Similarly, her actions and circumstances the night in question made her far too remote from being able to effectuate the commission of a larceny. According to her account to you, she never came anywhere near Student B or Student B's property. The only property she took and carried away that resembles what she is allegedly accused of taking on the night in question was her own. For these reasons, based on what we know, it is unlikely that a prosecutor would have sufficient evidence to even press charges let alone convict Student A of larceny or attempted larceny, and certainly not of robbery.

<u>Further research</u>

As to legal research, we will need our state's laws on larceny and attempted larceny. These should be easily locatable in the state penal code. Additionally, with respect to the possible Honor Code violation, we need to know what exactly she is being accused of, and we need a copy of the Student Handbook and any other relevant governing documents, as well as any documents that set forth the procedures the Honor Committee must follow.

As to factual research, we need to substantiate all the rumors—chief among them, we need to find out if Student B really had property that was taken or whether he lost his thumb drive, and any other details about the circumstances surrounding the alleged larceny (or alleged attempted larceny). We need to interview all of Student A's friends and find out if they corroborate, contradict, or add to her story. Note that once we have the Student Handbook and further information from the Honor Code Committee, we may need to conduct additional research to determine if her actions violated some other provision with respect to civility, dealing collaboratively with classmates, etc.

Finally, with all due respect, because she is your niece, even if you are not actually biased there is an appearance of bias, and I would respectfully suggest that you recuse yourself from this matter. Another attorney in our office should interview Student A and confirm her account.

Please let me know if you need anything further at this point on this matter.

APPENDIX B

PT-60 NEXTGEN BAR EXAM PERFORMANCE TASK[1]

About Performance Tasks

Each performance task should take approximately 60 minutes to complete. Performance tasks pose a question or series of questions about a single client matter. The examinee will have two kinds of materials with which to work: a File and a Library. The specific task the examinee must complete will be described in a memorandum in the File. The File may also include interview transcripts, deposition transcripts, or other documents. Both relevant and irrelevant facts will be included, and facts may be ambiguous, incomplete, or even conflicting. Examinees are expected to recognize when facts are inconsistent or missing and to identify sources of additional facts when prompted to do so.

The Library may contain cases, statutes, or other rules, some of which may not be relevant to the assigned lawyering task. The examinee is expected to extract from the Library the legal principles necessary to analyze the problem and perform the task. Performance tasks do not assess memorized substantive law; the Library materials provide the substantive information needed to complete the task.

All performance tasks assess an examinee's skills in legal research and written legal analysis (Groups A, C, and D of the Foundational Skills), but some performance tasks emphasize some skills over others. Performance tasks that focus on legal research skills will consist of a series of multiple-choice and short-answer questions followed by one extended-response question. Performance tasks that focus on written legal-analysis skills will consist of one longer extended-response question.

[1] The material including the practice test in Appendix B is reproduced with permission granted to the author in 2024 from the National Conference of Bar Examiners (NCBE) and is the 2024 copyrighted content of the NCBE.

Performance tasks may assess skills through subject areas that are partially or fully outside of the Foundational Concepts and Principles; however, when such an area is involved, the question will provide the resources the examinee needs to give a complete answer. For example, a performance task may include aspects of state family law when assessing research and writing skills, but the Library will provide all family law rules necessary to give a complete answer.

Below is a sample performance task that is a modified version of the *Butler v. Hill* MPT administered in February 2011.

PERFORMANCE TASK ASSIGNMENT

MEMORANDUM FROM SUPERVISING PARTNER

To:	[You]
From:	[Supervising partner]
Date:	February 22, 2021
Re:	Jennifer Butler v. Robert Hill

We represent Jennifer Butler in a suit against Robert Hill seeking a divorce and property distribution. Jennifer and Robert have two children; temporary custody and child support orders are in place that are not currently at issue. Robert has challenged the validity of the parties' underlying marriage. If there is no valid marriage, Jennifer cannot pursue a claim for divorce or a share of marital property.

I have attached the relevant material from Jennifer's file. I will meet with her later this week in anticipation of trial.

Please draft a short memo that I may use to prepare for my meeting with Jennifer. In the memo, explain whether Jennifer and Robert were legally married under Franklin Family Code § 301 et seq. Do not write a separate statement of facts, but be sure to incorporate the law and the relevant facts and reach a reasoned conclusion.

CLIENT INTERVIEW NOTES MEMORANDUM

To: Jennifer Butler File

From: [Supervising partner]

Re: Client Interview Notes

August 3, 2020

Today I met with client Jennifer Butler regarding a family law matter. Jennifer related her story to me as follows.

In 2013, Jennifer Butler was 17 years old and pregnant with her first child when Robert Hill, the child's father, convinced her to marry him against the wishes of her parents. Robert told her he was single. In fact, unbeknownst to Jennifer at the time, Robert, age 22, was already married and had not yet been legally divorced. Jennifer's parents would not consent to the marriage. Caught in a difficult situation, Jennifer married Robert in a civil ceremony with a forged parental consent form that Robert had signed, and then she moved in with him.

From the date of the marriage ceremony, September 2, 2013, Jennifer and Robert lived together in Franklin. The parties had two children: Christina Hill, born November 14, 2013, and William Hill, born February 22, 2017. Jennifer never changed her surname. Both Jennifer and Robert were employed and contributed financially to the household. Robert consistently earned about twice as much as Jennifer.

In May 2020, Jennifer learned that Robert had been having an affair with a coworker and had lent the woman $10,000. Jennifer immediately decided to end the marriage. She and the children stayed in the home, and Robert moved to his mother's house one week later.

While Robert was moving out, Jennifer found in Robert's dresser drawer a copy of a divorce decree that granted Serena Hill a divorce from Robert. Jennifer had never heard of Serena before and had no knowledge that Robert had been previously married. When Jennifer confronted Robert, he claimed he had not bothered to tell her because he had thought he was divorced from Serena before he married Jennifer and only learned that he wasn't when he was served with the court papers.

EXCERPT OF INTERVIEW TRANSCRIPT

Excerpt of Transcript of Telephone Interview with Louisa Milligan (January 28, 2021)

[Attorney]: Louisa, how well do you know Jennifer?

Milligan: We've been close friends for the past five years. I live just down the block from her. We have kids who are the same ages.

[Attorney]: Do you have reason to believe that Jennifer and Robert are married?

Milligan: Yes, we've been to many social gatherings together, including a celebration of their wedding anniversary.

[Attorney]: When was this?

Milligan: September of 2019. All of their family and friends came. We had a barbecue in their backyard.

[Attorney]: Did they specifically refer to themselves as husband and wife?

Milligan: Yes, always. And, in fact, at the anniversary party, Robert gave a toast saying that marrying Jennifer was the smartest thing he'd ever done.

[Attorney]: Did you ever have any reason to believe that they were not married?

Milligan: No, not until Jennifer called me recently and told me that Robert had apparently been married before and might not have been divorced when they married. She told me that she found a copy of a divorce order in Robert's dresser drawer when they separated last spring. She had not known that Robert was ever married before.

[Attorney]: Louisa, thank you very much for offering to testify to help Jennifer. We will be calling you again before the trial. Please call me if you have any questions or concerns.

CERTIFICATE OF MARRIAGE

Certificate of Marriage
State of Franklin

Ocean City Municipality

License Number 199330

I Hereby Certify that on the **2nd** day of **September 2013**, the following persons were by me united in marriage at the Ocean City Courthouse in accordance with the License of the Clerk of the Court in the jurisdiction shown above.

First Spouse's name: Robert Hill
Age: 22 **Birthplace:** Columbia

Residence: 6226 Berkeley Blvd., Ocean City
Marital Status: Single

Second Spouse's name: Jennifer Butler **Age:** 17
Birthplace: Franklin

Residence: 80 Octavia Street, Ocean City
Marital Status: Single

Relationship to First Spouse if any: None

Consent of Parent of Underage Party (if applicable):
Yes, signed consent form presented at time of application for license.

Monica St. George
Signature of Authorized Officer

District Court Judge
Title and Office

Ocean City Municipal Building
Address of Authorized Officer

August 30, 2013
License Date

JUDGMENT OF DIVORCE

STATE OF COLUMBIA
CIRCUIT COURT FOR BROOKFIELD COUNTY

[caption omitted]

JUDGMENT OF DIVORCE

The Complaint for Divorce was heard before the Magistrate on this 10th day of April, 2018, in the Circuit Court for Brookfield County, Columbia. It is hereby

ORDERED that the Plaintiff, SERENA HILL, is granted a Divorce from the Defendant, ROBERT HILL; and it is further

ORDERED that the Plaintiff is hereby restored to the use of her former name of SERENA JORDAN; and it is further

ORDERED that this judgment of divorce shall become final after 30 days.

Dated: 4/10/2018

Hon. Richard McBain

Hon. Richard McBain
Magistrate Judge

FRANKLIN FAMILY CODE

FRANKLIN FAMILY CODE

§ 301. Marriage of a Minor; Parental Consent; Pregnancy

Marriage of Individual 16 or 17 Years Old

(a) An individual 16 or 17 years old may not marry unless

(1) the individual has the consent of a parent or guardian and the parent or guardian swears that the individual is at least 16 years old; or

(2) if the individual does not have the consent of a parent or guardian, either party to be married gives the clerk a certificate from a licensed physician stating that the physician has examined the woman

to be married and has found that she is pregnant or has given birth to a child.

(b) A marriage by an underage person without valid consent as required by this section, though voidable at the time it is entered into, may be ratified and become completely valid and binding when the underage party reaches the age of consent. Validation of a marriage of an underage person by ratification is established by some unequivocal and voluntary act, statement, or course of conduct after reaching the age of consent. Ratification includes, but is not limited to, continued cohabitation as husband and wife after reaching the age of consent.

* * * *

§ 309. Common Law Marriage—Age Restrictions

(1) A common law marriage entered into on or after January 1, 1990, shall not be recognized as a valid marriage in this state unless, at the time the common law marriage is entered into,

(a) each party is 18 years of age or older, and

(b) the marriage is not prohibited as provided in § 310.

* * * *

§ 310. Prohibited Marriages

(1) The following marriages are prohibited:

(a) A marriage entered into prior to the dissolution of an earlier marriage of one of the parties;

(b) A marriage between an ancestor and a descendant, or between a brother and a sister, whether the relationship is by the half or whole blood;

(c) . . .

(2) Children born of a prohibited marriage are legitimate.

* * * *

Hager v. Hager, Franklin Court of Appeal (2006)

Hager v. Hager
Franklin Court of Appeal (2006)

This is an appeal from a decree of divorce. The trial court ruled that the parties' marriage was valid and granted a judgment of divorce to the Petitioner, Shirley Hager. Respondent Landon Hager has appealed, contending that the trial court erred in upholding the validity of the marriage. We agree and reverse.

In her petition, Shirley Hager alleged that she and Landon participated in a marriage ceremony on July 20, 1988. At that time, however, Landon had not secured a final decree of divorce from his first wife. He subsequently obtained that decree on March 2, 1989. Shirley's petition alleged that she was unaware that Landon was married to another woman at the time of their marriage and that Landon told her he was divorced. The dispositive issue on appeal is whether there was a valid ceremonial marriage.

Shirley argues that the marriage was valid. But a bigamous marriage is void *ab initio*. All marriages that are prohibited by law because one of the parties has a spouse then living are absolutely void. A void marriage is one that has no effect. Notwithstanding Franklin Fam. Code § 301, it cannot be ratified. Indeed, persons who engage in such a marriage may be subject to criminal prosecution.

As a result, the marriage ceremony on July 20, 1988, could confer no legal rights. It was as if no marriage had been performed. The parties' marriage is void and cannot support an action for divorce.

The trial court held that the parties' 1988 marriage was merely voidable and that, since Landon had presented himself as Shirley's husband in all respects, he had ratified the marriage. But, as we have said, the marriage was prohibited, therefore void *ab initio,* and thus not subject to ratification.

We conclude, therefore, that the trial court's ruling that the ceremonial marriage was valid was error and reverse the judgment.

Owen v. Watts, Franklin Court of Appeal (2013)

Owen v. Watts
Franklin Court of Appeal (2013)

Thomas Owen appeals from an order granting summary judgment in favor of Cora Watts, decedent Ruby McCall's surviving sister and personal representative, in her action for possession of McCall's home at 316 Forest Avenue. Owen refused to leave the home after McCall's death, claiming that he was McCall's common law husband and that he was therefore entitled to a possessory dower interest in the property. The trial court held that Owen and McCall had never entered into a common law marriage. The court further held that Owen could not claim an interest in the property. Owen appeals.

The record before the trial court on the motion for summary judgment reveals that Owen moved into McCall's home some time after her husband's death in 1991 but before his own divorce in 1996. Owen testified on deposition that following his divorce, he asked McCall to marry him, but that McCall refused because marriage would jeopardize her continued entitlement to a benefit check she was receiving as a result of her late husband's death. Owen testified that, over the years, he repeatedly asked McCall to marry him but that she refused these requests for the same reason. Owen claimed that McCall finally agreed in 2010 to marry him in 2011 but that she died before the marriage could take place. Cora Watts, McCall's sister, stated in an affidavit that McCall had told her that she had no intention of ever marrying Owen.

Owen represented that he and McCall cohabited and maintained joint bank accounts. He also produced affidavits from two members of the community who regarded him and McCall as husband and wife. Owen offered no evidence, however, that could persuade a rational and impartial trier of fact that, after his divorce, he and McCall had ever manifested an agreement that they were married, as opposed to a belief that they would become married at a later date.

Owen testified that, at the time he moved in with McCall, "she said, 'I want you to come and live with me. I want that we will be as husband and wife.' " He claimed that he "said okay" and moved in with her. He further related that he moved in "because she asked me to come and live with her and make our home together as long as we both shall live, until death do us part."

These words, however, were evidently spoken at a time when Owen was already married and not yet divorced, and therefore could not legally agree to marry McCall. Owen was not divorced until October 22, 1996.

Under Franklin law, a common law marriage requires agreement by parties legally capable of entering into a valid marriage that they have a marriage relationship. Cohabitation continued after the removal of a legal impediment cannot ripen into a common law marriage unless it was pursuant to a mutual consent or agreement to be married made after the removal of the barrier.

Owen and McCall conducted their business affairs as single persons rather than as a married couple. McCall referred to herself as single, or as a widow who had not remarried, in deeds and other documents relating to property transactions, as well as in her tax returns. Similarly, in her will, McCall referred to Owen as a "friend" and left him a bequest in that capacity.

The question before the trial court was whether any impartial trier of fact could reasonably find by a preponderance of the evidence that Owen was McCall's common law husband. We agree with the trial court that no reasonable judge or jury could so find.

Franklin has long recognized common law marriages, the elements of which are a manifestation of mutual agreement, by parties able to enter into a valid marriage, that they are presently married, followed by cohabitation of at least one year, including holding themselves out to the community as being husband and wife. *East v. East* (Fr. Ct. App. 1931).

Since ceremonial marriage is readily available and provides unequivocal proof that the parties are husband and wife, claims of common law marriage should be closely scrutinized, especially where one of the purported spouses is deceased and the survivor is asserting such a claim to promote his financial interest. The burden is on the proponent to prove, by a preponderance of the evidence, all of the essential elements of a common law marriage.

Owen's testimony established at most that he and McCall had, by the end of her life, agreed to be married at an unspecified future time. This is insufficient to establish the existence of a common law marriage under Franklin law.

For the foregoing reasons, the judgment of the trial court is hereby AFFIRMED.

Performance Task Sample Answer Outline

Robert and Jennifer did not have a valid formal marriage.

- Jennifer was 17 years old and had no actual consent from her parents.
- Jennifer was pregnant, but there was no physician-signed document to confirm the pregnancy.
- Robert forged the parental consent form.
- Thus, there was no legal marriage at the time of the ceremony.
- The marriage could not be ratified due to Robert's existing marriage. The marriage could have been ratified once Jennifer turned 18 (due to cohabitation, per Section 301(b)), except that the marriage would be deemed "prohibited" under Section 310(1)(a). Robert was not divorced. Under Hager, it was as if no marriage had been performed, so the marriage could not be ratified.
- The only option to establish a marital relationship is common law marriage.

The facts favor the claim that Robert and Jennifer had a common law marriage.

- **Jennifer and Robert were able to enter into a valid marriage.**

- Jennifer reached the age of 18 before Robert's divorce was final and was then able to enter into a valid marriage.
- Robert's first wife, Serena, obtained a divorce judgment from Robert on April 10, 2018.
- Once Robert divorced, a common law marriage between him and Jennifer became possible.

- **Jennifer and Robert manifested mutual agreement that they were married.**
  - The parties initially expressed their intent to be presently married by participating in the ceremonial marriage.
  - Although the facts present no later restatement of an agreement to be married after the date of Robert's divorce from Serena, the ongoing conduct of the parties as a married couple manifests this intent.
    - The parties shared household expenses and raised children together.
    - Louisa Milligan, a neighbor and friend, said that Robert and Jennifer always referred to themselves as married.
    - This evidence should establish that Robert also had a present intent to be married to Jennifer.
    - At the anniversary party, Robert told everyone that marrying Jennifer was the smartest thing he had ever done.
    - The divorce from Serena had become final in April of 2018, and the anniversary party occurred well thereafter, so this statement was made at a time when a common law marriage was possible.
  - There is no evidence that either party ever changed this intent while they cohabited.

- When Jennifer discovered Robert's affair, she decided to divorce. This demonstrates her agreement and belief that the parties were presently married.
- Robert claims that he thought his first wife had already finalized a divorce before his marriage ceremony with Jennifer.
- After Robert's divorce was final, the parties continued to live together and hold themselves out as husband and wife.
- This is strong evidence demonstrating that both Jennifer and Robert had a present intent to be married at a time when a common law marriage could have been formed.

- **The parties cohabited for at least one year after agreeing to the marriage.**
    - The parties continued to cohabit as husband and wife after Robert's divorce became final on April 10, 2018.
    - This cohabitation continued from the date of their ceremony until their separation in May of 2020.
    - They continued to raise their two children together.
    - They shared household expenses.
- **Jennifer and Robert held themselves out to the community as husband and wife.**
    - Robert and Jennifer both held themselves out to the community as being married.
    - Despite the fact that Jennifer and Robert had different surnames, neighbors believed that they were married.
    - A neighbor stated that she witnessed the parties referring to themselves as husband and wife after the date of Robert's divorce.

- The same neighbor recalled Robert's speech at the anniversary where Robert claimed that marrying Jennifer was the smartest thing he had ever done.
- They continued to raise their two children together.
- They shared household expenses.

APPENDIX C

PT-90

PERFORMANCE TEST AND SELECTED ANSWERS[1]

This publication contains the performance test from the July 2022 California Bar Examination and two selected answers.

The selected answers are not to be considered "model" or perfect answers. The answers were assigned high grades and were written by applicants who passed the examination after the First Read. They are reproduced as submitted by the applicant, except that minor corrections in spelling and punctuation were made for ease in reading. These answers were written by actual applicants under time constraints without access to outside resources. As such, they do not always correctly identify or respond to all issues raised by the question, and they may contain some extraneous or incorrect information. The answers are published here with the consent of the authors.

PERFORMANCE TEST INSTRUCTIONS

1. This performance test is designed to evaluate your ability to handle a select number of legal authorities in the context of a factual problem.
2. The problem is set in the fictional State of Columbia, one of the United States. In Columbia, the intermediate appellate court is the Court of Appeal and the highest court is the Supreme Court.
3. You will have two sets of materials with which to work: a File and a Library.
4. The File consists of source documents containing all the facts of the case. The first document in the File is a memorandum containing the directions for the task you are to complete. The other documents in the File contain information about your case and may include some facts

---

that are not relevant. Facts are sometimes ambiguous, incomplete, or even conflicting. As in practice, a client's or supervising attorney's version of events may be incomplete or unreliable. Applicants are expected to recognize when facts are inconsistent or missing and are expected to identify sources of additional facts.

5. The Library contains the legal authorities needed to complete the task and may also include some authorities that are not relevant to the assigned lawyering task. The cases, statutes, regulations, or rules may be real, modified, or written solely for the purpose of this performance test. If any of them appear familiar to you, do not assume that they are precisely the same as you have read before. Read each thoroughly, as if it were new to you. You should assume that cases were decided in the jurisdictions and on the dates shown. In citing cases from the Library, you may use abbreviations and omit page references. Applicants are expected to extract from the Library the legal principles necessary to analyze the problem and perform the task.

6. In answering this performance test, you should concentrate on the materials in the File and Library. What you have learned in law school and elsewhere provides the general background for analyzing the problem; the File and Library provide the specific materials with which you must work.

7. This performance test is designed to be completed in 90 minutes. Although there are no restrictions or parameters on how you apportion that 90 minutes, you should allow yourself sufficient time to thoroughly review the materials and organize your planned response before you begin writing it. Since the time allotted for this session of the examination includes two (2) essay questions in addition to this performance test, time management is essential.

8. Your performance test answer will be graded on its responsiveness to and compliance with directions regarding the task you are to complete, as well as on its content, thoroughness, and organization.

LAW OFFICES OF CARDINAL AND DEETZ

45 Bennington Circle

Craven, Columbia

TO:	**Applicant**
FROM:	**Carmen Cardinal**
RE:	**Niesi v. Gosling and Hardy**
DATE:	**July 26, 2022**

Grace Gosling is the web host of www.CravenCableConsumers United.com, a consumer website that contains a blog established to provide a platform for dissatisfied cable customers in Craven, Columbia. Gosling has retained our firm for advice concerning a complaint for defamation filed against her and Hank Hardy, a subscriber and poster to her blog, by Jack Niesi. Niesi claims that both Gosling and Hardy are liable as a result of statements Hardy posted about him to Gosling's blog.

I am preparing to meet with Gosling about Niesi's complaint. To help me prepare for the meeting, please draft an objective memorandum that discusses:

1. Whether Niesi would prove that Hardy's statements, as quoted in the complaint, were defamatory if he were to prove the facts alleged.
2. Whether Gosling is immune from liability for Hardy's allegedly defamatory statements.

Do not draft a separate statement of facts, but use the facts in your discussion.

EXCERPTS

www.CravenCableConsumersUnited.com Blog

Welcome to the voice of cable ratepayers in the City of Craven! I inaugurated this blog to highlight the incompetent and overpriced cable "disservice" and mistreatment we consumers receive as a result of the mismanagement and greed of the tone-deaf colossus, Columbia Cable Company. Despite some government regulation, the lack of competition has nevertheless resulted in poor and costly cable service. It is time to educate ourselves about cable services, our rights as consumers, and ways to contain the cost of cable service. I will be posting information on these topics and invite you to participate by posting anything you think will contribute to these goals. My hope is that members of the community will subscribe to this blog and participate constructively in ongoing discussion and action.

Note: To comment, you must be a subscriber. To subscribe, simply log on and, using the pre-populated pull-down menu, insert your first and last names, full physical address and email address, gender, age, and whether you are a Columbia Cable Company customer. There is also a blank box at the end where you can provide any additional information or comments. Each subscriber will have a profile containing all of this information that is accessible to other subscribers. The profiles will allow you to choose which other subscribers to communicate with outside this blog, including to develop ideas and actions against Columbia Cable Company, organize carpools to and from events, and the like.

In Solidarity, Grace Gosling

Oppose Rate Increase!

On June 27, 2022 at 6:00 p.m., the Craven City Council will hear a request from Columbia Cable Company for a 10% increase in cable rates to subsidize its planned re-cabling and the construction of a new store at the Stratford mall! This comes at a time when we are experiencing further deterioration in customer service with even longer waits on the phone and at the stores to talk to a customer service representative, and bait and switch sales tactics! Be sure to show up all together at the meeting in the Council chambers at Craven City Hall to express your opposition to the rate increase request and to demand better service and ethical sales practices. And if you have any other ideas about how to keep cable costs down, please post them below.

In Solidarity, Grace Gosling

Comments:

Grace: Thanks for starting this very necessary dialogue. I'll tell you a big way to keep down cable rates—report cable theft! I live in the Green Hills condominium complex at 451 Green Hills Drive in Craven. Like most of us, I pay a lot for full cable service while one of my neighbors, Jack Niesi, is guilty of cable theft: He uses various unauthorized devices to get free phone, television and internet service to his condo. I'll bet he isn't even a cable subscriber. It's crooks like Jack Niesi who cause cable costs to go up for the rest of us!

Hank Hardy (June 11, 2022)

Hank: That sounds awful! Can you tell us more?? Have you considered reporting Niesi's theft to the Columbia Cable Company's cable theft hotline?!

In Solidarity, Grace Gosling (June 16, 2022)

Grace: This is further to my June 11, 2022 post about Jack Niesi. Since then, I've been watching him closely. And—get this—while his wife is at work, an attractive young woman is at their house most of the day. It looks as though they are watching TV on his stolen cable service. He appears to be a cheating spouse! I put a note on his wife's car windshield telling that nice woman about her husband's infidelity while she is hard at work. What a loser and low life he is!

Hank Hardy (July 1, 2022)

SUPERIOR COURT OF THE STATE OF COLUMBIA
COUNTY OF MOREHEAD

JACK NIESI, Plaintiff, v. GRACE GOSLING and HANK HARDY, Defendants.	CASE NO: 2022–7459 COMPLAINT

1. Plaintiff Jack Niesi is a private individual who at all times mentioned in this complaint was a resident of Morehead County, Columbia.

2. Niesi has worked as an independent television producer for over 20 years and has resided at 451 Green Hills Drive in Craven, Columbia for about 5 years. Niesi has during all this time been faithfully married to his wife, Jill Niesi, and has enjoyed a good reputation, both generally and in his occupation.

3. Defendant Grace Gosling is an individual and is now, and at all times mentioned in this complaint has been, a resident of Morehead County, Columbia. She is the web host of www.CravenCableConsumersUnited.com (3CU.com), which contains a blog. As such, she has unlawfully caused, and is legally responsible for, the injury to Niesi as alleged in this complaint.

4. Defendant Hank Hardy is an individual and is now, and at all times mentioned in this complaint has been, a resident of Morehead County, Columbia. Hardy unlawfully caused, and is legally responsible for, the injury to Niesi as alleged in this complaint.

5. On or about June 11, 2022 and on or about July 1, 2022, Gosling published statements by Hardy on the 3CU.com blog in which Hardy stated:

   a. "I'll tell you a big way to keep down cable rates—report cable theft! I live in the Green Hills condominium complex at 451 Green Hills Drive in Craven. Like most of us, I pay a lot for full cable service while one of my neighbors, Jack Niesi, is guilty of cable theft: He uses various unauthorized devices to get free phone, television and internet service to his condo. I'll bet he isn't even a cable subscriber. It's crooks like Jack Niesi who cause cable costs to go up for the rest of us!"

b. "Since then [i.e., the date of the statement quoted in Paragraph 5.a.], I've been watching him [i.e., Niesi] closely. And—get this—while his wife is at work, an attractive young woman is at their house most of the day. It looks as though they are watching TV on his stolen cable service. He appears to be a cheating spouse! I put a note on his wife's car windshield telling that nice woman about her husband's infidelity while she is hard at work. What a loser and low life he is!"

6. The statements quoted in Paragraph 5 referred to Niesi by name and address and were so understood by those who read them.

7. The statements quoted in Paragraph 5 are false as they pertain to Niesi. Among other things, Niesi has been a Columbia Cable Company customer for over 20 years. In that entire time, he has paid for every type of cable service he has ever received. He works with his technical assistant, Liana Mabry, from his home office. His relationship with Mabry is, and always has been, purely professional.

8. The statements quoted in Paragraph 5 were seen and read by Niesi's neighbors, business associates, and family, including his wife.

9. As a proximate result of the publication of the statements quoted in Paragraph 5, Niesi has suffered injury in the form of loss of his personal and professional reputation and business, shame, and mortification, all to his damage in a total amount to be established by proof at trial.

WHEREFORE, Niesi demands judgment against Gosling and Hardy, and each of them, as follows:

1. For compensatory damages according to proof;
2. For punitive damages;
3. For interest as allowed by law;
4. For costs of suit; and
5. For such other and further relief as this court may deem just and proper.

DATED: July 22, 2022 *Ella Wang*

Ella Wang

Attorney for Jack Niesi

LIBRARY[2]

ANDERSON V. WALSH

Columbia Court of Appeal (2013)

This case arises from an aborted sale of a wig by Wilma Walsh to Ann Anderson. According to Anderson, Walsh represented that the wig was custom made. Anderson, who works for the City of Astoria Building Department, tendered a check from All Coast Building Contractors, a corporation she and her husband own. After realizing the wig was not custom made, Anderson tried to return the wig via FedEx, but Walsh refused the delivery. Anderson stopped payment on the check. Walsh sued Anderson for breach of contract in small claims court. At trial, Anderson introduced a FedEx document confirming that the package containing the wig had been refused by Walsh. Anderson prevailed in the small claims action.

Thereafter, Walsh authored a lengthy statement about the sale on an online consumer blog on RipOffReport.com. Prefaced by the word "Facts" were two allegedly defamatory statements: (1) "Ann Anderson, who works for the Astoria Building Department, wrote an unauthorized check for a wig from her boyfriend's account and at the bottom wrote that it was for a 'prosthetic donation.'" (2) "Ann Anderson brought to court a made-up document from FedEx stating that Walsh had opened the package, saw what was in it, and gave it back to FedEx."

[2] This Library contains two cases.

Thereafter, an anonymous author posted the following to the consumer website Yelp.com: "Thank you Ann Anderson of the Astoria Building Department for hurting the community by giving all the construction business in Astoria to family and friends in exchange for bribes. I hope that an investigation takes place soon and that you end up in prison." Though Walsh denied responsibility for the Yelp.com posting, expert testimony tied the email address used in that posting to her.

Upon reading these statements, Anderson was devastated. She felt compelled to report them to her employer and was thereby humiliated and concerned about losing her job. Shortly thereafter, she sued Walsh for defamation based on false statements imputing dishonesty, fraud, and criminal activity. Walsh asserted the affirmative defense of truth. At trial, Anderson proved that the statements were false and the court entered judgment in her favor. On appeal, Walsh asserts that the statements were opinion rather than fact.

In Columbia, defamation consists of the publication of a false statement to a third party, which proximately results in injury to another. To be false, a statement must be one of fact, and cannot be one solely of opinion. If a statement is reasonably susceptible to an interpretation as either fact or opinion, its proper characterization is determined by asking whether, under the totality of the circumstances, a reasonable trier of fact would conclude that the statement communicates actual fact rather than expresses mere opinion.

Walsh claims that her statements concerning Anderson were not defamatory because they were not factual. Relying on our recent decision in *Insky v. Ilston* (Columbia Court of Appeal, 2011), she argues that, even if they were reasonably susceptible to an interpretation as either fact or opinion, a reasonable trier of fact would conclude that they expressed a mere opinion rather than communicated an actual fact under the totality of the circumstances, including that they appeared on consumer websites, where most readers expect to see opinions rather than facts.

In *Insky*, we stated: "Internet forums promote a looser communication style and an outlet for the user to criticize others. Users are able to engage freely in informal debate and criticism, leading many to substitute gossip for accurate reporting and adopt a provocative tone." There, we held that, under the totality of the circumstances, a reasonable trier of fact would conclude that a statement posted online calling company executives "liars, losers, and crooks" expressed mere opinion rather than communicated actual fact. We explained that, "while unquestionably offensive and demeaning" to the executives, the statement was more emotional catharsis than information.

Here, however, things are different. Walsh's statements on RipOffReport.com, which were labeled "facts," recited alleged facts detailing perjury and fraud by Anderson. Walsh's statement on Yelp.com similarly recited alleged facts detailing Anderson's awarding of city contracts to friends and family in exchange for bribes. We do not believe that these statements were reasonably susceptible to an interpretation as mere opinion. But even if they were, we conclude that, under the totality of the circumstances, a reasonable trier of fact would conclude that they communicated actual fact.

AFFIRMED.

COLUMBIA VALLEY FAIR HOUSING COUNCIL V. ROOMMATE.COM, LLC

Columbia Court of Appeal (2008)

Defendant Roommate.com, LLC (Roommate) operates a website designed to match people renting spare rooms with people looking for a place to live. It features approximately 150,000 active listings and receives a million page views a day. To post or search listings on Roommate's website, Roommate requires subscribers to create profiles. Roommate also requires subscribers to disclose their gender, sexual orientation, presence of children, and to state their roommate preferences under the same three criteria. Lastly, Roommate encourages subscribers to provide "Additional Comments" about themselves and their desired roommate.

The Columbia Valley Fair Housing Council (Council) sued Roommate for violating housing discrimination laws. The trial court held that Roommate is immune from liability under

Section 230 of the General Statutes of Columbia and dismissed the claim. The Council appeals.

The Legislature enacted Section 230 to protect websites from liability for including or failing to remove actionable content in order to preserve the free-flowing nature of internet speech and commerce without unduly prejudicing the enforcement of other important laws. To that end, Section 230 immunizes "interactive computer service providers" from liability arising from content created by third parties. But it does not immunize "information content providers" from liability. Nor does it immunize "interactive computer services providers" from liability to the extent that they act as "information content providers." An "interactive computer service provider" is a person or entity that "enables computer access by multiple users to a computer server." An "information content provider" is a person or entity that "is responsible, in whole or in part, for the creation or development of content." Thus, an "interactive computer service provider" *passively* displays content that may be *actively* created or developed by an "information content provider," whereas an "information content provider" *actively* creates or develops content that may be *passively* displayed by an "interactive computer service provider."

Against this background, we examine whether Roommate is entitled to immunity under Section 230 for the three specific functions the Council alleges violate housing discrimination law.

1. **Roommate's questions to prospective subscribers during the registration process, requiring them to disclose and therefore be subject to discrimination for their gender, family status and sexual orientation**

Because Roommate designed its website registration process around the questionnaire and choice of answers containing discriminatory categories, Roommate is undoubtedly the "information content provider" of the questions and can claim no immunity. Section 230 does not grant immunity for inducing third parties to express illegal preferences.

2. Roommate's development and display of subscribers' discriminatory preferences

If an individual queries for a roommate of a particular gender using a search engine that does not contribute to, but provides only neutral tools to carry out, what may be unlawful searches, the search engine has not engaged in "development" for purposes of Section 230. But by requiring subscribers to provide their preferences using a limited set of pre-populated answers *as a condition of accessing its service*, Roommate is more than a passive displayer of information created by others; it becomes, at least in part, a developer of that information. "Discriminatory" questions solicit, and thereby develop, "discriminatory" answers. Here, Roommate designed its search to limit the listing available to subscribers based on gender, sexual orientation, and presence of children. Roommate both elicits the allegedly illegal content and makes use of it in conducting its business. Roommate's work in developing the discriminatory questions, answers, and search mechanism, and in enforcing a system that subjects subscribers to allegedly discriminatory housing practices, renders it an information content provider and, as such, not eligible for immunity under Section 230.

3. Roommate's display of discriminatory statements in the "Additional Comments" section of subscriber profile pages

Roommate encourages subscribers to personalize their profiles by writing additional comments about themselves and their desired roommate in a blank text box at the end of the registration process, and publishes these comments without revision. It is not responsible, in whole or in part, for the development of this content. This is precisely the kind of situation for which Section 230 was designed to provide immunity.

One final note: We must keep in mind that the Legislature enacted Section 230 to protect websites from liability for including or failing to remove actionable content. Close cases must be resolved in favor of immunity lest websites be forced to face death by ten thousand cuts, fighting off a barrage of claims that they created or developed actionable content. Such an interpretation is consistent with the intent of the Legislature to preserve the free-flowing nature of internet speech and commerce without unduly prejudicing the enforcement of other important laws.

REVERSED in part, AFFIRMED in part, and REMANDED.

PT: SELECTED ANSWER 1

TO: Carmen Cardinal

FROM: Applicant

RE: Niesi v. Gosling and Hardy

Date: July 26, 2022

I. Introduction

You asked me to draft a memorandum analyzing: 1. whether Niesi will be able to prove that Hardy's statements, as quoted in the complaint, were defamatory if he were to prove the facts alleged, and 2. whether Gosling is immune from liability for Hardy's allegedly defamatory statements.

Niesi will likely be able to prove that some of Hardy's statements were defamatory, specifically that Niesi "is guilty of cable theft," and that Niesi "uses various unauthorized devices to get free phone, television and internet service to his condo." The remainder of the statements are unlikely to be categorized as defamatory, either because the statements are mere opinion or because the statements are true. Gosling will likely be able to establish, however, immunity from suit under Section 230 of the General Statutes of Columbia, as the defamatory statement arose out of Gosling's website's user interactive functions, rather than the website's information content provider functions.

II. Niesi Will Likely Be Able to Establish That Some of Hardy's Statements Were Defamatory

Niesi will likely be able to establish that Hardy's statement that "one of my neighbors, Jack Niesi, is guilty of cable theft: he uses various unauthorized devices to get free phone, television and internet service to his condo" is defamatory.

The elements of defamation in Columbia are: 1. publication, 2. of a false statement, 3. to a third party, 4. which proximately results in an injury to another. *Anderson v. Walsh*, (Columbia

Court of Appeal 2013). "To be false, a statement must be one of fact, and cannot be solely of opinion." *Id.*

In *Anderson*, the defendant posted to an online forum that the plaintiff had forged a check in her boyfriend's name and committed perjury in a prior breach of contract action between the defendant and the plaintiff. Essential to the court's analysis was whether the defendant's statements were reasonably susceptible to interpretation as fact or opinion. Where the determination is close, the proper inquiry is whether, under the totality of circumstances, a reasonable trier of fact would conclude that the statement conveys an actual fact rather than the publisher's opinion. The defendant's statements in *Anderson* were couched as facts that the plaintiff had committed several crimes. These sorts of allegations, the court held, were not reasonably susceptible to interpretation as mere opinion.

In online internet forums, general offensive and demeaning words are not sufficient to give rise to a defamation claim. *Insky v. Ilston* (Columbia Court of Appeal, 2011) In *Insky*, the defendant called the defendants "liars, losers, and crooks." The court found that the nature of the internet lends itself to "informal debate and criticism, leading many to substitute gossip for actual reporting and adopt a provocative tone." Whether an online post constitutes such nonactionable insults versus actionable libel centers on a question of whether the statement is "more emotional catharsis than *information*" (emphasis added).

a. Publication

Niesi will easily be able to establish that the statements in question were "published." In *Anderson*, the statements held to be defamatory were published in an online consumer blog, much like the blog in the instant case. Thus, Niesi will be able to show that the statements in question were published.

b. By a Third Party

Niesi will also be able to establish that the statements in question were made by a third party. Each of the allegedly defamatory statements are signed at the end by Hank Hardy, thus establishing that the statements were made by a third party.

c. Damages

Niesi will likely be able to establish that Hardy's statements harmed his reputation. Hardy named Niesi by first and last name and identified Niesi's address. Hardy further alleged that Niesi is a criminal in an online blog. Hardy also alleged that Niesi is an adulterer. His statements were alleged to have been seen by Niesi's neighbors, business associates, and family, including his wife. Niesi properly pleads that as a proximate result of these statements, Niesi suffered injury to his reputation. This element will be subject to proof, but certainly Niesi has sufficiently pled this element of defamation.

d. False Statement

To meet this element, Nisei must prove that Hardy: 1. made a statement of fact, that 2. was false.

1. Statement of Fact

Niesi will likely be able to establish that Hardy's statement that "one of my neighbors, Jack Niesi, is guilty of cable theft: he uses various unauthorized devices to get free phone, television and internet service to his condo," is a statement of fact. Turning once again to Anderson, this statement is similar to the defamatory "facts" published by the defendant. The defendant in *Anderson* posted online that the plaintiff "wrote an unauthorized check" and "brought to court a made-up document." The court points out that both of these statements constitute direct criminal allegations: first of fraud; second of perjury. Statements like these, directly asserting that someone has committed a crime are "not reasonably susceptible to an interpretation as mere opinion." Contrasting Hardy's statements of fact with the mere statements of offensive opinion by the *Insky* defendant (the plaintiffs are "liars, losers, and crooks"), it is clear that where an individual's statement goes beyond mere distasteful insults to assert knowledge of direct criminal misconduct, courts construe such statements as statements of fact. Here, the court is likely to read Hardy's statement as an assertion that Hardy knows that Niesi committed the crime of theft. Thus, the court will hold that this statement is a statement of fact.

Niesi will likely be able to establish that some of Hardy's statements in comment b are statements of fact. Specifically,

Hardy's statement that "while his wife is at work, an attractive young woman is at their house most of the day." Niesi may also be able to establish that "[i]t looks as though they are watching TV on his stolen cable service" is also a statement of fact.

Hardy alleges that he has been watching Niesi and has observed an attractive young woman at his home. This clearly falls under the category as an assertion of fact—Hardy is not saying it is his *opinion* that an attractive woman is at the house, but that he has actually seen an attractive young woman at the house. Further, for the reasons discussed above, Hardy's assertion that the two watch TV on his "stolen cable service" is likely another assertion of fact as Hardy alleges knowledge of Niesi's actual commission of a crime.

The remainder of the potentially defamatory statements are likely to be characterized as opinion and are thus not actionable. Hardy's statement that "I'll bet he isn't even a cable subscriber" is the type of allegation that is clearly by its own words mere speculation ("I'll bet") and even if it were a statement of fact, it is not one that would reasonably give rise to a defamation claim.

The statement "[h]e appears to be a cheating spouse!" is also unlikely to be construed as a factual statement. Though an accusation of adultery is certainly distasteful and offensive, here the accusation is couched as an opinion rather than a statement of fact. Hardy lays out the factual allegation, as discussed above, that an attractive young woman comes to Niesi's home while his wife is away. Hardy then provides his own analysis, that, to Hardy, Niesi appears to be unfaithful. Applying the test in *Anderson*, a reasonable trier of fact would conclude that the statement expressed a mere opinion given the totality of the circumstances, including the previous factual statement and the statement's appearance on the internet.

Thus, Niesi has two statements of fact, of which he will need to prove their falsity.

2. Falsity

In his complaint, Niesi alleges that the statement contained in comment a is false. He alleges that he has been a customer of Columbia Cable Company for 20 years and has paid for every type of cable service he has ever received. If these facts are proved as alleged, Niesi will establish the falsity of the statement of fact in comment a.

Niesi will not be able to establish the falsity of the comment in paragraph b. Niesi admits as such in his complaint: Niesi "works with a technical assistant, Liana Mabry, from his home office." Hardy's statement of fact, that Niesi has a young woman over while his wife is away, is admitted as true. Thus, Niesi will not be able to prove the falsity of comment b. His defamation claim arising from comment b will likely fail.

For the sake of thoroughness, if the court does find that Hardy's accusation of infidelity is factual, then Niesi likely adequately pleads that statement's falsity. Niesi alleges that his relationship with Mabry has always been professional. If proven at trial, such a statement is likely to prove the falsity of the infidelity allegations.

III. Gosling's Immunity Under Section 230

Gosling will likely be able to claim immunity from suit under Section 230 of the General Statutes of Columbia. Under Section 230, "interactive computer service providers" are immune from liability arising from content created by third parties on their websites. "Information content providers" are not immune from liability. An "interactive computer service provider" is a person or entity that "enables computer access by multiple users to a computer server," while an "information content provider" is a person or entity responsible, in whole or in part, for the development of content. In other words, "an 'interactive computer service provider' passively displays content that may be actively created or developed by an 'information content provider.' " *Columbia Valley Fair Housing Counsel v. Roommate.com* (Columbia Court of Appeal, 2008)

As an initial matter, Hardy's statements would be considered statements by a third party under Section 230, as Gosling is the purveyor of the website and Hardy is an unrelated party. Thus, if the comments arise under the site's "interactive computer service provider" functions, Gosling will be entitled to immunity.

In *Columbia*, the defendant website had several functions where the website and its owner solicited information from users, and then *itself* made choices as to what other users would see on the website. The court goes feature-by-feature to determine which features provide the defendant immunity from suit, and which do not. The defendant would collect information from subscribers and then choose which other subscribers that information was conveyed to. Because the defendant took an active role in deciding which information users would see, the court held that, for these functions, the defendant's service was that of an "information content provider," and thus the defendant was not entitled to immunity *on those particular services.*

The court also found that where the defendant gave users a blank text box and published whatever the users typed into it "without revision," it was "not responsible, in whole or in part, for the development of this content." Thus, where an internet service merely displays text entered by a third party without revision as to what people see or who sees it, the service is an "interactive computer services provider" for the purposes of that feature.

Gosling's immunity turns on whether the comments feature to the blog is categorized as an "information content provider" or an "interactive computer service provider." A court would likely find that the comment feature is more like the latter, and thus Gosling is entitled to immunity.

Gosling's website invites users to "participate by posting anything [the user thinks] will contribute" to Gosling's goals in running the website. She does this in the hope "that members of the community will subscribe to the blog and *participate constructively* in ongoing discussion and action." Gosling does not revise comments that are posted on the website, nor does she limit who is permitted to make comments. Though commenters must subscribe to Gosling's website, this does not preclude her immunity. In *Fair Housing Counsel*, the court held that the subscription feature did not give rise to immunity, but that the ability of those subscribers to freely comment without censorship did. It is likely here that the court will find that Gosling's comment section is more like the open comments feature in *Fair Housing Counsel* since Gosling does not edit what her subscribers say in the comments and the comments are entirely provided by third parties.

One area where Gosling may have issue is where she solicits further information from Hardy. In *Fair Housing Counsel*, the court noted that the defendant was "not responsible, in whole or in part, for the development of the content" where it found immunity. In Gosling's comment, she says: "Can you tell us more?? Have you considered reporting Niesi's theft to the Columbia Cable Company's cable theft hotline?!" In commenting as such, the court may find that Gosling did, in fact, solicit the second comment from Hardy, thus weakening her argument for immunity. Further, Hardy addresses his second comment, comment b, to Gosling. Since, as discussed above, Niesi has a weaker argument for defamation in the second comment, it may be that this is not a problem.

It is important to note that the court in *Fair Housing Counsel* urged that "close cases must be resolved in favor of immunity lest websites be forced to face death by a thousand cuts. . . such an interpretation is consistent with the intent of the legislature to preserve the free-flowing nature of internet speech and commerce. . ." To the extent that this is a "close case," it will be important to note that the court found it was the intent of the legislature to err in favor of immunity and to preserve the open forum nature of the internet.

IV. Conclusion

Niesi will likely be able to meet his burden to show that portions of Hardy's statements were defamatory, specifically that Niesi "is guilty of cable theft" and that Niesi "uses various unauthorized devices to get free phone, television and internet service to his condo." The remainder of the statements are unlikely to be categorized as defamatory, either as opinions or statements of fact. Gosling will likely be able to establish immunity arising under Section 230 of the General Statutes of Columbia, as the defamatory statement arose out of Gosling's website's user interactive functions, rather than the website's information content provider functions.

PT: SELECTED ANSWER 2

LAW OFFICES OF CARDINAL AND DEETZ

45 Bennington Circle

Craven, Columbia

TO: Carmen Cardinal

FROM: Applicant

RE: Niesi v. Gosling and Hardy

DATE: July 26, 2022

The following memorandum responds to your memorandum asking whether Jack Niesi's allegations from his complaint, if true, would constitute a claim of defamation against Hank Hardy and whether Grace Gosling would be entitled to immunity from liability for Hardy's allegedly defamatory statements in any event. I first address whether Hardy's statements, as alleged, could be considered defamatory. I then turn to whether Gosling would be entitled to immunity in any event.

For the reasons that follow, I tentatively conclude that Hardy's statements are likely to be considered defamatory under Columbia law because, viewed under the totality of the circumstances, they are statements of fact, not mere opinion. *Anderson v. Walsh* (Colum. Ct. App. 2013). Second, under Columbia General Statutes Section 230, Gosling is likely entitled to at least partial immunity with respect to Hardy's first comments. *See Columbia Valley Fair Housing Council v. Roommate.com LLC (Columbia Ct. App. 2008).* But because Gosling actively sought out further comments from Hardy about Niesi's alleged wrongdoing, her immunity may be limited to Hardy's original comment and not his subsequent comments.

1. Were Hardy's statements defamatory as alleged by Niesi?

Probably yes. Hardy's comments were likely defamatory assertions of fact rather than mere opinion under Columbia law.

The Columbia Court of Appeal in *Anderson v. Walsh* (Colum. Ct. App. 2013) has set forth the applicable standards for determining what statements constitute defamation in the state of Columbia. In Columbia, "defamation consists of the publication of a false statement to a third party, which proximately caused injury to another." *Anderson*. Not all false statements, however, can be considered defamation. Rather, to be a false statement, "a statement must be one of fact and cannot be one solely of opinion." *Anderson*. To determine whether a statement is a statement of fact—which might constitute defamation—or instead a statement of opinion, the courts consider whether a statement "is reasonably susceptible to an interpretation as either fact or opinion" by asking whether "under the totality of the circumstances, a reasonable trier of fact would conclude that the statement communicates an actual fact rather than expresses mere opinion." *Anderson*.

In *Insky v. Ilston* (Colum. Ct. App. 2011), the court of appeals set forth some special considerations that apply to defamation cases involving internet forums. Specifically, *Insky* emphasized that "Internet forums promote a looser communication style and an outlet for the user to criticize others." *Insky*. Because the internet enables users to engage in free informal debate and criticism "leading many to substitute gossip for accurate reporting and adopt a provocative tone," a reasonable trier of fact may be more likely to conclude in cases involving internet defamation that the statements are "mere opinion rather than" assertions of actual fact. *Insky*.

Insky considered posts on an internet forum in which the defendant had called a group of company executives "liars, losers, and crooks." *Insky*. The court in *Insky* held that that kind of language, although "unquestionably offensive and demeaning," was best interpreted as "more emotional catharsis than information," particularly in light of the characteristics of the internet forum on which the comments were made. *Insky*.

Anderson, however, declined to extend the rationale of *Insky* to create a strong presumption that internet defamation is mere opinion as opposed to factual information. There, the court considered a defamation claim brought by a consumer after the proprietor of a store that had attempted to do business with the consumer posted defamatory statements on an online consumer blog about the consumer. *Anderson*. Specifically, the defendant there posted, under the preface word "FACTS," that the consumer had written an "unauthorized check" and had committed fraudulent acts in the course of their contractual relationship. *Anderson*. The retailer also separately commented on a consumer comment website that the buyer was engaging in bribery and hurting the community.

Analyzing these facts in light of *Insky*, the *Anderson* court nevertheless held that, although posted on the internet, the statements were properly considered factual assertions rather than mere opinions. In particular, *Anderson* stressed that the defendant's statements on the consumer website were labeled as "facts," recited alleged facts detailing perjury and fraud by the plaintiff, and therefore were not reasonably susceptible to an interpretation as mere opinion.

Applying both *Insky* and *Anderson* to Hardy's comments, assuming that the allegations in Niesi's complaint are true, a court is likely to conclude that Niesi has stated a valid claim of defamation against Hardy.

To start, Niesi has alleged that he suffered injury to his professional and personal reputation, shame, and mortification. Complaint. He has therefore satisfied the requirement that he show the allegedly defamatory statement proximately result in injury. *Anderson*.

Turning to the substance of the comments, Hardy's comments about Niesi are more similar to the assertions determined to be factual in *Anderson* than the mere opinion considered in *Insky*. Niesi identifies two sets of Hardy's comments as defamatory: First, Niesi points to Hardy's comment from June 11 on Gosling's website accusing Niesi of cable theft. Although, unlike in *Anderson*, Hardy did not expressly characterize these statements as "facts," he used similar language that tends to suggest Hardy intended the statements to be taken as fact, not opinion. For instance, Hardy stated factual information about where he lives in Craven and then asserted, as a definite, actual fact, that his neighbor "Jack Niesi, is guilty of cable theft." Complaint Paragraph 5a. Hardy then went on to assert that Niesi "uses various unauthorized devices to get free phone, television and internet service to his condo." Complaint Paragraph 5a. These sorts of assertions do not present themselves as mere conclusory opinions. Rather, like the statements in *Anderson* that recited alleged fats detailing bribery, perjury, and fraud committed by the plaintiff there, Hardy's statements recite alleged facts detailing specific instances of alleged misconduct by Niesi.

To be sure, as in *Insky*, Hardy's comments also use the kind of "emotional catharsis" language that might be expected on Internet forums, where there is a "looser communication style" and users "substitute gossip for accurate reporting and adopt a provocative tone." *Insky*. For instance, Hardy concludes his first comment by asserting that Jack Niesi is a "crook." Complaint Paragraph 5a. But that statement alone, when viewed in the totality of the circumstances, is not likely to change the conclusion that the other statements were clear assertions of fact and not mere bluster.

Hardy's July 1 comment is likely to be treated the same as his June 11 comment. Again, as with the earlier comment, the overwhelming majority of Hardy's statements appear to make assertions of fact, not just opinion. Again, unlike in *Anderson*, Hardy's comments do not expressly identify themselves as "facts," but the implication of his statements is that he is reciting known facts based on his own investigation, not merely opinions or conjecture. Specifically, Hardy stated that he has been "watching" Niesi "closely," and accused him of engaging in an affair with an "attractive young woman" at his house most of the day while his wife is at work. Complaint Paragraph 5b. Although Hardy stated only that Niesi "appears to be cheating" on his wife, that statement is based on Hardy's first-person reporting of observations of fact, not merely his opinion or conjecture. Complaint Paragraph 5b. Once again, as with the earlier comment, Hardy completed the comment with something more akin to the opinion from *Insky*, stating that Niesi was "a loser and a low life." Complaint Paragraph 5b. But the context of that statement is a paragraph of factual assertions and investigation by Hardy. Again, as in *Anderson*, Hardy's comment detailed specific acts of purported wrongdoing and presented them to the world as fact.

I therefore conclude that a court would likely treat Hardy's comments as defamatory statements of fact, not mere opinion. A reasonable trier of fact, considering the totality of the circumstances, would conclude that the statements are not reasonably susceptible to an interpretation of mere opinion but rather communicated actual fact.

2. Is Gosling immune from liability for Hardy's allegedly defamatory statements under Columbia General Statutes Section 230?

Partially, yes. Gosling is likely entitled to immunity under Section 230 for at least some of Hardy's comments, which he delivered unprompted in response to her open invitation for posts from the community. But insofar as Gosling specifically prompted Hardy to provide further defamatory information, she is likely not entitled to immunity under Section 230.

Applicable Law: Section 230 and *Columbia Valley.*

Whether Gosling is entitled to immunity depends on whether, by running her blog, she was acting as an "interactive computer service provider," or rather as an "information content provider" under Columbia General Statutes Section 230.

In order "to protect websites from liability for including or failing to remove actionable content in order to preserve the free-flowing nature of internet speech and commerce," the state of Columbia enacted Section 230. *Columbia Valley Fair Housing Council v. Roommate.com LLC* (Columbia Ct. App. 2008) (Columbia Valley). Section 230, accordingly, provides immunity for "interactive computer service providers," defined as a person or entity that "enables computer access by multiple users to a computer server." *Columbia Valley* (quoting Section 230). But Section 230 does not immunize an "information content provider" from liability, defined as a person who "is responsible, in whole or in part, for the creation or development of content." *Columbia Valley*. Nor does Section 230 immunize interactive computer service providers from liability to the extent that they act as a content provider. *Columbia Valley*. Accordingly, determining whether Gosling may be immune from liability for Hardy's allegedly defamatory statements depends on whether she was acting as an interactive computer service provider or instead as an information content provider.

The Columbia Court of Appeal in *Columbia Valley* provided a shorthand for determining in what capacity an internet website manager is acting. As a shorthand, Section 230 immunizes conduct if the conduct is limited to *"passively"* displaying content that "may be *actively* created or developed by" a content provider. *Columbia Valley*. In contrast, when a website or entity "*actively* creates or develops content," it is more likely acting as an information content provider and therefore would not be entitled to Section 230 immunity.

Columbia Valley applied these principles in the context of a fair housing lawsuit against a website that matched people renting spare rooms with potential roommates. *Columbia Valley*. Specifically, the court broke down the analysis in three ways. First, to the extent that the website had actually "designed its website registration process around" a questionnaire and choice of answers "containing discriminatory categories," it had acted as an "information content provider" and could not claim immunity. *Columbia Valley*.

Second, the court explained that the website had acted as an information content provider (and was therefore not immune) when it designed its search functions to limit listings available based on gender, sexual orientation, and other prohibited characteristics. *Columbia Valley*. Although merely creating a search engine on its own with "neutral tools" would not be content creation, requiring prohibited pre-populated answers and "developing the discriminatory questions, answers, and search mechanism" was sufficient to go beyond mere hosting of a website and constitute content creation. *Columbia Valley*.

With respect to a third category, the court found the website was entitled to immunity. Specifically, the website also encouraged subscribers to personalize their profiles by writing comments about themselves and then "publish[ed] these comments without revision." *Columbia Valley*. Because the website was "not responsible, in whole or in part, for the development of this content," but merely republished comment after an open-ended prompt to users, it was acting only as an "interactive computer service provider" and therefore was entitled to immunity. *Columbia Valley*.

Gosling's Posts and Hardy's First Comment

Turning to Gosling's blog, it is necessary to compare the characteristics of her blog to the characteristics of the website in *Columbia Valley*. The question is whether Gosling was merely passively hosting Hardy's comments and posting them "without revision" or instead had prompted his creation of the comments by developing questions that were designed to create Hardy's content. *Columbia Valley*.

As a general matter, Gosling identified her blog as being a place where she would "invite" the public "to participate by posting anything you think will contribute" to the goals of improving cable service in the area. Excerpts. Gosling hoped to create "ongoing discussion," but did not claim to have the power to moderate the content of those discussions or pre-approve any particular content. Although Gosling did post to account holders that if they "have any other ideas about how to keep cable costs down, please post them below," that kind of broad, open-ended prompt resembles the kind of open-ended prompt discussed in the third section of *Columbia Valley*. It appears to be the case that Hardy's first defamatory comment was made in response to this open-ended prompt. But because Gosling did not in any way limit Hardy's response to providing only a defamatory answer, her conduct with respect to Hardy's first comment is likely more the passive variety that resembles an interactive computer services provider, not a content creator. She "publish[ed] these comments without revision" and "is not responsible, in whole or in part, for the development" of Hardy's initial comment. *Columbia Valley*.

Niesi might argue that, like the website in *Columbia Valley*, Gosling "elicits the allegedly illegal content" and exercises some control over it by requiring commenters to subscribe. *Columbia Valley*. Niesi would contend that, like the website in *Columbia Valley*, Gosling uses the commenters to conduct her business by requiring them to subscribe and provide information to her about themselves. Although this is a superficial similarity, it is not likely to convert all of Gosling's website into an information content provider. To be sure, Gosling requires commenters to subscribe, but, unlike in *Columbia Valley*, the requirement that commenters subscribe here has nothing to do with Hardy's allegedly defamatory statements. Moreover, unlike in *Columbia Valley* where the website required users to create profiles using certain discriminatory prompts and thereby creating discriminatory answers, Gosling did not restrict users to creating only defamatory speech on their profiles. Rather, she explained that the profiles will allow users to choose how to communicate outside of the blog and develop their own ideas. For this reason, a comparison of Gosling's website to the Roommate.com website in *Columbia Valley* is likely inapposite, at least with respect to Hardy's initial comments.

Gosling's Immunity Regarding Hardy's Second Comment

Niesi may have a stronger argument, however, that Gosling is not entitled to immunity with respect to Hardy's second comment. After Hardy's first comment, Gosling wrote back and asked Hardy if he could "tell us more." Excerpts. Specifically, she further prompted Hardy to provide additional information about Niesi by asking if he had considered reporting Niesi's theft to the cable company. Excerpts. In making this statement, Gosling did not merely permit Hardy to produce content on her hosted site but rather joined in his comment creation by ratifying his characterization of Niesi as a thief. As such, she had essentially engaged in the kind of "development" and active creation of content that is not protected by Section 230.

Furthermore, by prompting Hardy to post additional information—asking if he can "tell us more???"—Gosling again likely acted as an information content provider or at least as a service provider behaving in the capacity of a content provider. In particular, Gosling's conduct in this respect resembles the website in *Columbia Valley* prompting its users to provide discriminatory preferences with a set of pre-populated answers. *Columbia Valley*. To be sure, unlike in *Columbia Valley*, Gosling did not require Hardy to provide more information "as a condition of accessing" her service. *Columbia Valley*. But at the same time, by asking Hardy for more information and implicitly blessing that additional statement Gosling was "more than a passive displayer of information created by others" but rather was "at least in part, a developer of that information." *Columbia Valley*.

Gosling's best chance at avoiding liability with respect to Hardy's later comments is the admonition from *Columbia Valley* to tread lightly when interpreting the scope of Section 230. Specifically, the court emphasized that the legislature enacted Section 230 to protect websites from liability "for including or failing to remove actionable content." *Columbia Valley*. "Close cases," the court held, "must be resolved in favor of immunity lest websites be forced to face death by ten thousand cuts" and to protect the "free-flowing nature of internet speech and commerce." *Columbia Valley*.

Even in light of this language in *Columbia Valley*, however, a court is more likely to find that Gosling's comments prompting Hardy's second post goes beyond the scope of Section 230's immunity provision. Gosling, by prompting Hardy specifically to provide more specific information about Niesi, did more than merely "including or failing to remove actionable content;" she quite clearly assisted in its creation by soliciting it. *Columbia Valley*. Accordingly, notwithstanding *Columbia Valley*'s admonition that Section 230 be interpreted in favor of immunity in close cases, Gosling will likely be unable to seek immunity for this aspect of her conduct.

Conclusion

Because Hardy's comments, although they occasionally contained language similar to that found in *lnsky,* were primarily presented as assertions of fact based on his own investigations, Hardy's comments are likely to be considered defamatory under Columbia law, assuming the complaint to be true. And, although Columbia Section 230 provides immunity to at least some of Gosling's conduct insofar as she merely passively hosted Hardy's comments, Gosling may have lost that immunity when she prompted Hardy to provide more specific details about Niesi's conduct.

APPENDIX D

PT-120

TRANSIT CENTER

FILE

MEMORANDUM

From: City Attorney

To: Applicant

Re: Transit Center Regulations

As you know, The City is dealing with a controversy about whether the Transit Tax should be repealed by a referendum. A group is attempting to gather signatures to get a referendum on the ballot to repeal the transit tax. Mayor Lane called me yesterday about this group's activities at the City Transit Center. The Transit Director told the Mayor that something needs to be done because the people gathering petition signatures at the Transit Center are making upsetting and unfair accusations about the transit department and getting into heated arguments with the staff and patrons about the bus service.

The Mayor wants the petition area shut down and, failing that, wants something done to address the suggestions referenced in the attached memorandum from the Transit Director. I explained to the Mayor that the petition area cannot be shut down because it is required by NRS 293.127565, but that we would develop Regulations to address the Transit Director's concerns as much as possible within the confines of the Nevada and U.S. Constitutions and NRS 293.127565.

---

1 The material including the practice test in Appendix D is reproduced with permission granted to the author in 2025 from the State Bar of Nevada and is the copyrighted content of the State Bar of Nevada.

I am providing you with Draft Regulations that were started several months ago regarding signature-gathering activities at the City Transit Center. This project is now urgent.

Please write a memorandum for me analyzing the legality of the three provisions in Section 2 ("Restrictions") of these Draft Regulations under NRS 293.127565 and the Nevada and U.S. Constitutions.

For each Section 2 provision, using the authority in the Library, analyze the applicable constitutional and statutory law and explain why the provision as written is or is not lawful. You may use abbreviations when citing to cases. Omit page references.

If any provision would not be lawful, please recommend new language for a substitute provision that would address the Transit Director's concerns in a permissible manner. Explain why your new language would be lawful, again using the relevant legal authority from the Library.

MEMORANDUM

From: Transit Director

To: Mayor

Re: Political Activities at Transit Center

A group has been using the designated Signature Gathering Area at the Transit Center in attempt to get signatures for a referendum petition to repeal the transit tax. I have concerns with how this group's activities are causing problems at the Transit Center. I believe we should shut down the Signature Gathering Area because of these issues.

The morale of the Transit Center employees is being hurt by comments made to passengers in the area that the bus system "sucks" and needs to be defunded as reasons for why passengers should sign their petition. Recently this group got into a shouting match with bus drivers who took offense at the complaints about the bus system. The police were called and defused the situation without making any arrests. Why should anyone have to come to work to listen to complaints by people who are trying to cut funding and maybe cost our employees their jobs?

I respectfully request that you consider enacting regulations to bring some control to these activities. I suggest that we (1) get rid of the petition area; and (2) prohibit such demoralizing and disruptive opposition to the transit department.

* * *DRAFT* * *

REGULATIONS FOR CITY TRANSIT CENTER SIGNATURE GATHERING ACTIVITIES

Section 1: <u>Statutory Requirements for Designated Area</u>

(A) The City Transit Center is a public building required by NRS 293.127565 to include a designated area where people seeking signatures for referendum or initiative petitions as defined in NRS 293.127565 may gather signatures on such petitions.

(B) The designated area for gathering signatures for referendum or initiative petitions within the meaning of NRS 293.127565 shall be the left side of the main lobby bounded by the main entrance door (south), windowed wall (west), interior doors (north) and a line from exterior to interior doors halfway between the east and west walls, as indicated by permanent tape on the floor.

Section 2: <u>Restrictions</u>

(A) Notice. Members of the public seeking to gather signatures pursuant to NRS 293.127565 must submit by phone or email to the Transit Director or his or her designee the name and contact information of any person intending to gather signatures at the City Transit Center; the organization of the requestor; the subject of the petition for which signatures will be gathered; and the date on which the activity is to occur. This notification must be given no later than 24 hours before the time such activities are intended to be initiated.

(B) The use of any language that is demeaning, critical, or disrespectful to employees of the City Transit Center is prohibited and will result in removal of the speaker from the City Transit Center.

(C) Signature gathering activity pursuant to NRS 293.127565 will be permitted between noon and 6:00pm daily.

LIBRARY

EXCERPTS FROM NEVADA REVISED STATES

Title 24. Elections

Chapter 293—Elections

Circulation and Sufficiency of Certain Petitions

NRS 293.127565 Use of public buildings to gather signatures on petitions; remedy for violation; regulations.

1. At each building that is open to the general public and occupied by the government of this State or a political subdivision of this State or an agency thereof, other than a building of a public elementary or secondary school, an area must be designated for the use of any person to gather signatures on a petition at any time that the building is open to the public. The area must be reasonable and may be inside or outside of the building. Each public officer or employee in control of the operation of a building governed by this subsection shall:

(a) Designate the area at the building for the gathering of signatures; and

(b) On an annual basis, submit to the Secretary of State and the county clerk for the county in which the building is located a notice of the area at the building designated for the gathering of signatures on a petition. The Secretary of State and the county clerks shall make available to the public a list of the areas at public buildings designated for the gathering of signatures on a petition.

2. Before a person may use an area designated pursuant to subsection 1, the person must notify the public officer or employee in control of the operation of the building governed by subsection 1 of the dates and times that the person intends to use the area to gather signatures on a petition. The public officer or employee may not deny the person the use of the area.

EXCERPTS FROM THE CONSTITUTION OF THE UNITED STATES

First Amendment

Congress shall make no law respecting an establishment of religion, or prohibiting the free exercise thereof; or abridging the freedom of speech, or of the press; or the right of the people peaceably to assemble, and to petition the Government for a redress of grievances.

EXCERPTS FROM THE CONSTITUTION OF THE STATE OF NEVADA

Article 1—Declaration of Rights.

Section 9 Liberty of speech and the press.

Every citizen may freely speak, write and publish his sentiments on all subjects being responsible for the abuse of that right; and no law shall be passed to restrain or abridge the liberty of speech or of the press. In all criminal prosecutions and civil actions for libels, the truth may be given in evidence to the Jury; and if it shall appear to the Jury that the matter charged as libelous is true and was published with good motives and for justifiable ends, the party shall be acquitted or exonerated.

REGIONAL TRANSPORTATION COMMISSION OF WASHOE COUNTY V. NEVADANS FOR SOUND GOVERNMENT

Supreme Court of Nevada (2004)

In this appeal, we examine the constitutional boundaries of the government's right to impose "time, place, and manner" restrictions on the use of its property for petition-circulating activities. The First Amendment to the United States Constitution and Article 1, Section 9 of the Nevada Constitution protect the rights of persons to engage in expressive speech activity. NRS 293.127565 governs the right to use public buildings to collect petition signatures.

Nevadans for Sound Government [NSG] filed a complaint in the district court alleging that various actions taken during the previous months by the Regional Transportation Commission of Washoe County (RTC) had unlawfully restricted its access to RTC properties for signature collecting purposes.

RTC guidelines provide that an RTC request form must be submitted three business days before the date of the intended activity. The request form asks for the name, telephone number, and organization of the requestor. It also asks for the subject of the petition, and for the dates on which the activity is to occur.

Freedom of Speech

The First Amendment to the United States Constitution, as applied to state governments through the Fourteenth Amendment, prohibits a state from "abridging the freedom of speech." Similarly, Article 1, Section 9 of the Nevada Constitution protects the general right of the people to engage in expressive activities in this state. We have held that Article 1, Section 9 affords no greater protection to speech activity than does the First Amendment to the United States Constitution. Therefore, under the Nevada Constitution, the appropriate analysis of appellants' restrictions is identical to that under the First Amendment.

The circulation of ballot petitions constitutes core political speech for which First Amendment protection is at its zenith. Nevertheless, the First Amendment does not grant a circulator the right to access all government property without regard to the nature of the property or to the disruption that might be caused.

Time, place, and manner restrictions under the First Amendment

When analyzing the constitutionality of restrictions placed on protected speech activities that take place on government property, the United States Supreme Court has differentiated between public and nonpublic forums. Public forums encompass places which by long tradition or government fiat have been devoted to assembly and debate, such as streets and parks. Public forums may also be created by government designation. However, when the government designates a forum as public, it must intend to open the forum for use by all or part of the public for discourse. Mere permission to freely go onto government land is not enough to create a designated public forum. Thus, the government does not create a designated public forum by permitting limited discourse.

All remaining property is nonpublic fora. Within the nonpublic forum description, falls a subset, the limited public forum. A limited public forum is created when a state designates an area for speech activities by certain groups or for certain subjects. In limited public forums, the state must respect the lawful boundaries it has itself set. When nonpublic or limited public forums are involved, government restrictions on time, place, and manner will be upheld if they are viewpoint neutral and related to a legitimate government purpose served by the forum. Moreover, the government's decision to restrict access to a nonpublic forum need only be *reasonable;* it need not be the most reasonable or the only reasonable limitation.

In determining whether a forum is public or nonpublic, courts consider the policy and practice of the government and the nature of the property and its compatibility with expressive activity.

Forum characterization

In contending that the RTC CitiCenter is a limited public forum, RTC asserts that its primary purpose is to allow the transfer of passengers between buses, not to provide a forum for the free exchange of ideas. RTC concedes that, under the statute, it was required to open its facilities to petition circulators for signature-gathering activities. However, according to RTC, neither the statute nor RTC guidelines compel it to grant access for expressive activity to the public at large. Therefore, RTC asserts that with the enactment of NRS 293.127565, the state purposefully created a limited public forum or nonpublic forum at certain public buildings, including the RTC CitiCenter. We agree.

Clearly, the RTC CitiCenter was not designed for and dedicated to the advancement of expressive activities. Although NRS 293.127565 creates an obligation for the CitiCenter to provide areas for signature gathering, the statute applies only to people gathering signatures for petitions; it does not grant rights to the general public to engage in any type of speech activity that would normally be permitted in a traditional public forum. Nor does RTC permit speech activities on its premises other than those mandated by the statute. Further, the CitiCenter is of limited space and its patrons have limited time in which to make connections. If unrestricted expressive activity were allowed, the principal operations of the transportation system could be severely disrupted. Accordingly, we conclude that the RTC CitiCenter is a limited public forum, and RTC policies should be reviewed under the reasonableness standard generally applied to time, place, and manner restrictions of limited public and nonpublic forums.

Restrictions' reasonableness

At issue in this appeal are the RTC policies concerning advance notice, identification of the petition's subject and the petition circulator, and pre-authorization. Neither written policy discriminates amongst signature gatherers based on the content of the petition or the viewpoint of the petition circulator. Therefore, we must decide whether the policies are reasonable in light of the RTC CitiCenter's transportation purposes.

RTC contends that its guidelines were created in order to accommodate petition circulators while also ensuring the safety and security of RTC patrons and preserving efficient operations of its transportation system. In addition, with respect to its designated-area provision, RTC asserts that its CitiCenter is a cramped area in which patrons are often pressed up to the curb edges, and through which patrons have to quickly cross in order to make connections, and notes the potential dangers of permitting groups of signature gatherers or their equipment to become obstacles to unwary or distracted patrons.

We conclude that, under the First Amendment, the regulations are permissible restrictions related to legitimate government safety and functional operating purposes. There is nothing inherently unreasonable in requiring a petition circulator to provide advance notice of his or her intended signature-gathering activities. Advance notice serves a variety of purposes, including enabling building operators to better accommodate multiple signature gatherers and individual petition circulators' particular needs, and to have a chance to make other employees aware of the intended signature-gathering activities so that they will be able to adjust their duties accordingly.

Additionally, the RTC requirements that a signature gatherer provide his or her contact information before being allowed to use RTC property are reasonable. The requested information is reasonably related to RTC aims of accommodating all requestors and unusual circumstances while maintaining safe and efficient operations of their affairs.

As the above discussion demonstrates, none of the RTC time, place, and manner restrictions challenged by NSG discriminates amongst petition circulators based on the content of the petition or the viewpoint of the petition's promoter. Further, all of the restrictions are reasonable and all are related to RTC's goals of promoting safety and efficiency in conducting their legitimate transportation purposes. RTC's time, place, and manner restrictions are constitutionally valid.

GRIFFIN V. BRYANT

United States District Court, D. New Mexico (2014)

In analyzing the constitutionality of restrictions on speech that occurs on public property, the Supreme Court has identified three types of forums: the traditional public forum, the public forum created by government designation, and the nonpublic forum. The Supreme Court has determined that this tripartite framework is necessary, because the First Amendment does not guarantee access to property simply because it is owned or controlled by the government. The Supreme Court has explained that the State, no less than a private owner of property, has power to preserve the property under its control for the use to which it is lawfully dedicated.

Nonpublic forums are sometimes referred to as limited public forums. Governmental restrictions on access to a nonpublic forum are valid so long as the restrictions are reasonable and not an effort to suppress expression merely because public officials oppose the speaker's view.

With respect to activities on government property, the Constitution does not require the Government freely to grant access to all who wish to exercise their right to free speech on every type of Government property without regard to the nature of the property or to the disruption that might be caused by the speaker's activities.

The Supreme Court determined that airport terminals are nonpublic forums, and the government could thus impose reasonable, viewpoint-neutral, speech restrictions. Regarding speech restrictions in a nonpublic forum, the Supreme Court emphasized that the "restriction need only be *reasonable;* it need not be the most reasonable or the only reasonable limitation."

The Defendants contest the proposed finding that a provision, which forbids speakers from making any negative mention of any Village personnel, staff, or of the Governing Body during the public input portion of Governing Body meetings, is an unconstitutional speech restriction. Instead, they contend that it is a content-neutral time, place, or manner restriction designed to prevent disruption during Governing Body meetings.

The Court determines that this provision violates the First Amendment.

First, the Court determines that the public input portion of the Governing Body meetings constitutes a limited public forum, and, thus, any government restriction on speech must only be reasonable in light of the purpose served by the forum and be viewpoint neutral.

A limited public forum is a subset of the nonpublic forum classification. The core pursuit of Governing Body meetings is to make decisions and conduct business on behalf of the municipality. To assist itself in this core pursuit, the Governing Body has chosen to open its meetings to limited public comment so that it can be informed of its constituents' opinions, and, with this information, be better situated to make decisions that are more democratic, and, sometimes, more competent.

On its face, a restriction that "no negative mention will be made of any Village personnel, staff or the Governing Body" is viewpoint-based, because it allows praise or neutral comment, but not criticism or disapproval, about government employees or the Governing Body. The restriction eschews a limitation that could cure its constitutional infirmity: narrowing the phrase "negative mention[s]" to an equivalent phrase that would include only personal attacks and breaches of decorum.

The Court can imagine three potential government interests that the Village could assert to justify this restriction: (i) preventing disruption of the Governing Body meetings; (ii) maintaining decorum and an atmosphere of respect in the meetings; and (iii) preventing criticism and potentially damaging job-related embarrassment to government employees and the Governing Body. The first interest is constitutionally permissible. The third is not. The second might not be.

The serious way in which this restriction is viewpoint-based is, again, that it allows praise but not criticism of the Governing Body and its employees. It goes beyond the prohibition against personal or slanderous attacks upheld in *Scroggins v. City of Topeka, Kan.* and takes one side of the conversation—a conversation of public importance, in which citizens opine on their leaders' performance—off the table, while leaving the other side unimpeded. The suppression of political dissent is the core evil the First Amendment seeks to prevent, and that the viewpoint suppressed by this restriction is all negative feedback to the government—rather than one side of a single, discrete issue—makes things worse, not better, for the rule. This restriction is a viewpoint-based speech restriction.

BREES V. HMS GLOBAL MARITIME, INC.

U.S. District Court, W.D. Washington (2020)

Speech in a non-public forum may be regulated as to time, place, manner, and content so long as the content regulation is viewpoint neutral. Where a non-public forum is at issue, the court must inquire whether the challenged restriction is reasonable in light of the purpose served by the forum, and is viewpoint neutral.

Plaintiff's First Amendment claim is without merit. The Pierce County Ferry System ("PCFS") regulates speech, through its Passenger Code of Conduct ("PCC"), by precluding "foul, abusive, or disruptive language" to "provid[e] a safe and enjoyable experience for all . . . passengers." Approximately 12 times per year, HMS Ferries bars a passenger from boarding due to unruly and disruptive behavior; if a passenger persists in this behavior, they are banned. The ferry holding area is a non-public forum. It is demarcated by physical barriers and signage, and vehicles and pedestrians not boarding the ferry at not permitted in the holding area during ferry operations.

To the extent that Plaintiff was precluded from boarding the ferry because he said to Mr. Caputo, "I'll see you in court, asshole," or used any other foul, abusive, or disruptive language, this behavior was in violation of the PCC. The PCC's regulation of speech does not violate Plaintiff's rights under the First Amendment as it is a reasonable regulation in light of the purpose of the ferry system—safely and efficiently transporting passengers and crew—and is viewpoint neutral.

Memorandum

FROM: Applicant

TO: City Attorney

RE: Transit Center Regulations

The following memo addresses the legal validity of the draft regulations proposed for the City Transit Center (CTC), both under Nevada statutes (specifically, NRS 293.127565), and the Nevada and federal constitutions. As requested in your previous memo, to the extent that the legality of any regulation is questionable, the memo proposes potential revisions.

I. General considerations

A. Interaction between NRS 293.127565 and the Nevada, and federal constitutions.

As a threshold matter, the First Amendment to the United States Constitution prohibits a state from "abridging the freedom of speech." The Nevada Supreme Court has have held that Article 1, Section 9 of the Nevada constitution affords no greater protection to speech activity than does the First Amendment to the United States Constitution. *RTC v. NSG* (Nev. 2004). For the purposes of the constitutional discussion that follows, then, the appropriate analyses under the Nevada and federal constitutions are identical. *See id.*

With regard to NRS 293.127565 (the "limited public forum" or "LPF" statute), subsection (1) only opens up certain publicly held property as limited forums during the hours that property is open to the public—it bears emphasis that the LPF statute does *not* purport to extend the constitutional protections offered pursuant to the state or federal constitutions. *See RTC.* Accordingly, compliance with the subsection (1) of the LPF statute only ensures that the government is opening the particular property statutorily identified as a limited forum. It does not bear on the restrictions on speech that might be put in place there, if that area is statutorily designated to be a limited forum.

Subsection (2) places some limited requirements as to notice required to circulate petitions, but, as will be discussed herein, they fall short of those set in the draft regulations. Note though, that subsection (2) does not prohibit more restrictive requirements on notice.

B. Valid restrictions on speech in limited forums.

The scope of constitutional speech protections are somewhat dependant on whether the law in question occurs in a public forum (which is a location that has been traditionally open to speech), a designated public forum (a location that the government opens up for the purpose of public discorse), or a nonpublic forum (all that remains). *RTC.* A limited public forum of the sort that the LPF statute designates, is a subset of nonpublic fora that the government opens up for limited speech by certain groups or on certain topics.

Accordingly, under the state and federal constitutions and as well as the statutory authority, where a limited public or nonpublic forum is at issue, the government make make reasonable "time, place, and manner" restrictions. However, to be upheld, the provision in question must be "viewpoint neutral and related to a legitimate government purpose served by the forum." *RTC.* The Nevada Supreme Court has already held that the RTC area opened under the LPF statute (the "petition area") as a limited public forum because the statute only allows a certain type of speech (signature gathering). Thus, the legality of each specific draft provisions at issue turns on whether they respectively satisfy the standard stated above.

II. Discussion of specific Section 2 draft provisions.

1. Section 2.A. (the "24-hour notice provision").

Briefly, the 24-hour notice provision requires that an individual seeking to gather signatures submit by phone or email, the name and contact information of signature gatherers, the organization of the requestor, the subject of the petition, and the planned date.

Statutory limitations: There is nothing in the LPF statute that would prohibit the requirement of 24-hour notice of the name and contact information of signature gatherers, the organization of the requestor, the subject of the petition, and the planned date. Indeed, this seems only to add aditional requirements—namely, 24-hour notice—based upon subsection (2), which states that "Before a person may use an area designated pursuant to subsection 1, the person must notify the public officer or employee in control of the operation of the building governed by subsection 1 of the dates and times that the person intends to use the area to gather signatures on a petition." As discussed above, nothing in the LPF statute forbids a more stringent notice requirement.

I would note, however, that subsection (2) makes the addtion that the public officer or employee may not *deny the person the use of the area.*" That is, this is not an application for permission to collect signatures, but pure notice of the intent to collect signatures. I would recommend adding similar language to the proposed regulations to avoid any implication that the RTC or transit director would exercise discriminatory discretion based on content of speech.

Constitutional limitations: The Nevada Supreme Court has upheld similar guidelines from the RTC. *RTC.* The court described the valid guidelines as follows: "an RTC request form must be submitted three business days before the date of the intended activity. The request form asks for the name, telephone number, and organization of the requestor. It also asks for the subject of the petition, and for the dates on which the activity is to occur." Without having the actual wording of these previous guidelines it is difficult to tell how closely they are in line with the proposed draft regulation. Potential similarities and differences are discussed herein.

The Nevada Supreme Court held that the RTC guidelines at issue in *RTC* (the "RTC guidelines") were viewpoint neutral. Specifically, the court noted that the RTC guidelines did not "discriminate[ ] amongst signature gatherers based on the content of the petition or the viewpoint of the petition circulator." I would argue that the draft regulations are likewise without any reference to viewpoint and are likely to be considered viewpoint neutral. I would note, however, that the 24-hour notice provision here only requires advance notice from "members of the public," which would appear to exclude employees of the RTC. This is, arguably a restriction based on content as an RTC employee is far less likely than a member of the general public to, for example, say that the RTC "sucks." To the extent that the 24-hour notice provision can be brought into line in this respect with the former RTC guidelines already upheld by the Nevada Supreme Court, I would recommend that change to ensure the regulation is deemed viewpoint neutral.

To the extent that the regulation is viewpoint neutral, *RTC* essentially controls the question of its constitutionality. All that is required is a reasonable relationship between the RTC's purpose and the regulation at issue. *RTC.* The Nevada Supreme Court has already identified that advance notice requirements such as the one at issue "serve[ ] a variety of purposes, including enabling building operators to better accommodate multiple signature gatherers and individual petition circulators' particular needs, and to have a chance to make other employees aware of the intended signature-gathering activities so that they will be able to adjust their duties accordingly." Moreover, the Nevada SUpreme Court found the RTC guidelines' requirement of contact information from the requestors was "reasonably related to RTC aims of accommodating all requestors and unusual circumstances while maintaining safe and efficient operations of their affairs." *RTC.*

I would note two potential differences. One is that the instant regulation only requires 24 hour notice, while the RTC guidelines upheld in *RTC* required 72 hours. This supports the constitutionality of the regulation as requiring less notice could only make the provision more reasonable. On the other hand, I would note is that 24-hour notice provision here asks for notification via phone or email, while the former RTC guidelines only asked for submission of an RTC request form, apparently without specifying the mode of communication. The addition of the requirement that notice be sent by phone or email, arguably, makes the proposed regulation less reasonable because it could limit access by people who do not have the means to maintain such modes of communication. To the extent that this was a deliberate change, based on some sort of necessity by the RTC—perhaps, again related to the RTC's aims of maintaining efficient operations"—this is unlikely to be constitutionally fatal to the provision as a restriction need not be "the most reasonable or the only reasonable limitation." *RTC*. If, however, there is no reasonable justification for the change, I would recommend removing the specifications by which the request communications must be sent.

Suggested alterations: As a threshold matter note that there appears to be a typographical error in this provision. The subpart title reads "otice," which I believe should read "Notice." Beyond correcting this, I would recommend removing the reference to "members of the public," and not delineate any category of petition circulator that might be subject to more strict regulation than another. I would recommend further, that a brief examination of the reasons for including the "phone or email" requirement be conducted, to ensure that it is included for a legitimate purpose. I would further recommend adding a sentence to the end of 2.A stating that the government officer responsible for receiving the notices may not "deny the person the use of the area," consistent with subsection 2 of the LPF statute.

2. Section 2.B (the "morale" provision).

Section 2.B. prohibits [t]he use of any language that is demeaning, critical, or disrespectful to employees of the City Transit Center in the petition area.

Statutory limitation: Again, there is nothing in NRS 293.127565 that would impact this regulation.

Constitutional limitations: Because this regulation restricts the content of speech ("demeaning, critical, or disrespectful" language), it is not viewpoint neutral but a content-based regulation of speech. *Griffin v. Bryant.* A similar provision, prohibiting "any negative mention of any [local government] personnel, staff, or of the Governing Body" in a limited public forum (there, the "public input portion of the Governing Body meetings") was challenged before the Supreme Court. *Griffin.* The court determined that the restriction was viewpoint-based "[o]n its face" because it allowed speech that was neutral or favorable to the government and prohibited the rest. *Id.*

In *Griffin* the Court identified a potential limitation that would resolve the problem inherent in that particular statute, exchanging the problematic wording with an equivalent phrase that "would include only personal attacks and breaches of decorum." This is consistent with the other case in the library, *Brees*, where a passenger was precluded from boarding a ferry because he called a ferry driver an explative. The regulation at issue in *Brees* was viewpoint neutral because it precluded all "foul, abusive, or disruptive language." I would recommend revising the draft regulations in line with *Griffin* and *Brees.*

Suggested alterations: I would recommend replacing the phrase "demeaning, critical, or disrespectful to employees of the City Transit Center is prohibited" to say "any foul, abusive, or disruptive language, personal or slanderous attacks, and breaches of decorum are prohibited. . .". This largely addresses the Transit Directors concerns regarding the morale of his employees. I recognize it does not prohibit all negative speech regarding the Transit Center employees, and perhaps stops short of what the Transit Director might be requesting. Note though, that the expression of an opinion as to government operations, i.e. "Transit sucks," is the suppression of political dissent which is "the core evil the First Amendment seeks to prevent, and that the viewpoint suppressed by this restriction is all negative feedback to the government—rather than one side of a single, discrete issue—makes things worse, not better, for the rule." *Griffin.*

3. Section 2.C (the "timing" provision).

This provision limits the period of signature to between noon and 6:00 pm daily.

Statutory limitation: This is in violation of NRS 293.127565(1), which requires that the petition area be open "at any time that the building is open to the public."

Constitutional limitation: This is viewpoint neutral, to the extent it applies to all signature gathering, and is only a limitation on the timing for that speech. It is a time-based restriction. Absent the violation of NRS 293.127565(1), this would likely be a restriction reasonably related to the RTC's goals of "promoting safety and efficiency in conducting their legitimate transportation purpose." *Griffin.*

Suggested alterations: I recommend changing "between noon and 6:00 pm daily" to adhere to the language in NRS 293.127565(1), and be replaced by "only when the building is open to the public."

APPENDIX E

PT-180[1]

PERFORMANCE TESTS AND SELECTED ANSWERS JULY 2008 CALIFORNIA BAR EXAMINATION

This publication contains two performance tests from the July 2008 California Bar Examination and two selected answers to each test.

The answers received good grades and were written by applicants who passed the examination. The answers were produced as submitted, except that minor corrections in spelling and punctuation were made for ease in reading. The answers are reproduced here with the consent of their authors.

INSTRUCTIONS

1. You will have three hours to complete this session of the examination. This performance test is designed to evaluate your ability to handle a select number of legal authorities in the context of a factual problem involving a client.
2. The problem is set in the fictional State of Columbia, one of the United States.
3. You will have two sets of materials with which to work: a File and a Library.
4. The File contains factual materials about your case. The first document is a memorandum containing the instructions for the tasks you are to complete.
5. The Library contains the legal authorities needed to complete the tasks. The case reports may be real, modified, or written solely for the purpose of this performance test. If the cases appear familiar to you, do not assume that they are precisely the same as you have read before. Read each thoroughly, as if it were new to you. You should assume that cases were decided in the jurisdictions and on the dates

---

1 California PTs from before July 2017 were three-hour exams. The material including the practice test in Appendix E is the copyrighted content of the State Bar of California, publicly available and reproduced here with permission.

shown. In citing cases from the Library, you may use abbreviations and omit page citations.

6. You should concentrate on the materials provided, but you should also bring to bear on the problem your general knowledge of the law. What you have learned in law school and elsewhere provides the general background for analyzing the problem; the File and Library provide the specific materials with which you must work.

7. Although there are no restrictions on how you apportion your time, you should probably allocate at least 90 minutes to reading and organizing before you begin preparing your response.

8. Your response will be graded on its compliance with instructions and on its content, thoroughness, and organization.

HAMLINE & BUTTRAM, LLP

Santa Claritan, Columbia

MEMORANDUM

To:	Applicant
From:	Mary Hamline
Date:	July 29, 2008
Re:	**Chris Pearson v. Savings Galore**

Our client, Chris Pearson ("Pearson"), was held for about an hour by the Savings Galore supermarket because his buddy, with whom he shopped, was suspected of shoplifting and took off when confronted. I've checked out the criminal aspect, and Pearson did not commit any illegal acts.

Please write a memorandum that evaluates his possible civil claim against Savings Galore. Your memorandum should do the following:

1. Explain the elements that must be proven in order for Pearson to succeed on a false imprisonment claim.

2. Apply the facts of Pearson's situation to the elements and assess the likelihood that Pearson would prevail on the merits of the claim.

3. Identify the injuries incurred by Pearson that would be compensable given these facts and assess the likelihood that punitive damages would be awarded given these facts.

4. Identify any defenses the store may raise, and explain and assess the likelihood that the store would prevail on each defense.

TRANSCRIPT OF JULY 24, 2008 INTERVIEW WITH CHRIS PEARSON

Mary Hamline (Q): The tape recorder is running now. As I said, the reason why I like to record initial interviews is that it will give me an accurate record of what you say, and I will be able to listen and use it later on.

Chris Pearson (A): Okay.

Q: I understand that you got into some sort of a dispute with a store, and that you might want to sue them, but that's about it.

A: Well, I live with about 5 other people in a rented house over near the campus.

Q: Okay. Are you a student at the University of Columbia?

A: Yes, I'm a student, a biosciences major. I'm going to finish up pretty soon. I'm 22 years old, single, and pretty much impoverished. Well, one of my roommates and I went to do the weekly food shopping for the whole house.

Q: Went where?

A: Right. We went down to that combined warehouse store and market, you know, that huge thing down on the corner of Euclid and Sligo?

Q: Do you mean Savings Galore?

A: Yes, that's the name of it. We almost always go there to do the shopping unless we can get a car, and then we go somewhere better.

Q: What was your roommate's name, the one who went with you?

A: Do I have to tell you that?

Q: It is always possible that we might need to talk to this person or even get him to testify, depending on what is going on. But for now, just use a first name at least, just so you can tell the story.

A: Okay. My roommate is named Jeff.

Q: Is he a student at the University of Columbia too?

A: No. He finished up about a year ago.

Q: Why don't you just tell me what happened when you and Jeff went shopping?

A: Well, we started to do the shopping, putting some stuff in the cart. We would split up to go get things; we had a list, but then we would come back to the cart and talk and look for other stuff, too. After we had been there for about 20 minutes, I thought I saw

Jeff open up a can of cashews and eat them while we were shopping. But I didn't pay too much attention to it.

Q: How long did it take you to shop?

A: About an hour. There was a long wait at the check-out stand, and we finally got up to the front and paid and headed out of the store. We were both kind of loaded down - I was carrying about 6 bags of groceries, and Jeff had about 4 bags.

Q: How were you carrying so many bags?

A: If you get your hand through the handle of those plastic bags, you can hold a whole bunch - I had three in each hand - well balanced.

Q: I'll have to try that some time. Had you paid for the cashews?

A: At that point, I didn't really notice. I didn't think we had, but there was quite a wait at the check-out stand and I had forgotten about it, to tell you the truth.

Q: How long ago was this?

A: About 2 months ago.

Q: What happened next?

A: We were walking out of the parking area and towards the street back to our house, when a big, strong-looking woman came walking right up to us. She yelled, "Hold it right there!" And I remember thinking "Who is this lady?" She got right next to us and grabbed me and said, "I saw you take those cashews and you didn't pay for them." I said, "I didn't take any cashews." She said, "That's right, you didn't; it was this guy, right here." And she grabbed hold of Jeff's arm. Jeff said something like: "Oh yeah, I forgot to pay for them; here, let me pay for them right now." And the lady said: "No, it was deliberate; I'm going to have to take you in."

Q: Interesting. Did you both go back to the store?

A: No. As soon as that woman said "I'm going to have to take you in" - and you could just tell she was trouble and meant it from the tone in her voice and her look - Jeff dropped his bags of groceries, shook himself off from her hold, and took off around the corner of the store. There is a wetlands area around the back.

Q: But you didn't go with him?

A: No. He split, and I was left holding the bags. I just stood there with my mouth open.

There I was with a couple of hundred dollars worth of groceries, that detective, and no Jeff.

Q: Did she identify herself as a detective?

A: Not until later. She just gave me a glare and said, "You come with me." I said, "I didn't do anything," but she said, "I don't care. You come with me right now. You and your fast friend are in big trouble."

Q: Did you think at all about running yourself?

A: Not really. She looked like a big, strong football player, and I was holding a lot of stuff.

Q: Did she grab you or force you into the store?

A: Not exactly. She picked up the bags Jeff had dropped and got sort of in back and sort of to the side of me and herded me in, kind of like a dog herding sheep.

Q: What would have happened if you had tried to just walk away at that point?

A: I don't know for sure, but it didn't seem like an option to me. She would probably have tackled me.

Q: So did you go on your own?

A: I sure wouldn't say that. I went along, but I didn't see what else I could do.

Q: What happened when you got into the store?

A: We went into an office and she tossed the bags down, and I put the ones I was carrying down, and I said something like "Why don't you leave me alone? I didn't take any cashews and you know it." She took me to another office, way in the back, one with no windows. I had no idea they had rooms like that in those buildings. We sat down in there and she called someone on the phone and after a few minutes two very large men, who looked like they were former boxers, came in. They left me in there for a while with the door locked and I could hear her talking to them right outside the door.

Q: How do you know the door was locked? Did you try to get out?

A: Well, no. It sounded like they locked the door. I wasn't about to try to take off. I was pretty scared, actually. I get anxious sometimes, and I was having some trouble breathing and my heart was pounding, so I just sat there and tried to take some deep breaths. Then all three of them came back in. The woman told me she was the house detective, and the two guys were security staff, and that they just wanted to talk to me.

They said, "Let's see some identification." I told them, "You have no right to do this." But I showed them my student registration card, partly because I figured it was better if they knew who I was and that I was a student at the University, and partly because I didn't really see any choice. I didn't give them my address.

Q: Did you think they were going to rough you up?

A: Actually, no, even though Jeff and I look like young punks and they looked like professional wrestlers. I thought they were going to try to intimidate me somehow, and I didn't think they were going to let me go for maybe a long time, but they didn't say they were going to beat me up, either.

Q: Okay. What did they say to you?

A: They said: "Because you are a college kid, you must be pretty smart. Is your friend a college student too? He was pretty dumb to run." I didn't want to say anything about Jeff, so I tried not to look at them, and that kind of angered them. The lady said: "Your friend isn't much of a friend - he took off and left you to take the rap. We've got you. But if you give us his name and address, we'll let you go." I was pretty scared about that. I was mad at Jeff, because he is always pulling stuff like that.

Q: What do you mean, stuff like that? Has he ever been caught shoplifting before?

A: No. But he is such a clueless idiot. He actually is kind of a slacker. You know, he opens up food in stores, forgets to pay for it, and I think he steals stuff from time to time. But he's never been caught.

Q: What did you do when they asked you for his name?

A: They kept saying, "Give us his name and address and we'll let you go." And I was mad at him, especially for taking off and leaving me with all of this trouble but I wasn't about to give them his name. So I kept saying: "You have no right to keep me here. I have not done anything illegal. Let me go immediately." And they kept saying stuff like: "Hey, figure it out; we don't have to let you go, but we will if you give us his name and address." And I just kept saying the same thing: "You have no right to keep me here. I have not done anything illegal. Let me go immediately." Sort of like a mantra. I just kept repeating that and trying not to make eye contact. I didn't want to antagonize them.

Q: Did you think you were actually right about their having no right to hold you?

A: I didn't think they were going to let me go, but I didn't think they could prove I did anything illegal, because I hadn't. So I didn't know. I was trying not to be anxious.
Q: They must have eventually let you go?
A: Yeah. This went around and around, and they'd come ask, all three, and then they would leave for a while, and then come back and try again, and I'd say the same thing. I never tried to just walk out of there, but I thought if I did they would just grab me and put me back there, or arrest me, so I just waited. After I had been there quite a while, I'm guessing about an hour, I was starting to get worried, because the only person who knew I was there was Jeff, and he obviously wasn't going to get me out, and then they came in with a piece of paper and said, "Here, if you sign this, we'll let you go." I signed it and they let me go. I don't know what happened to the groceries; I didn't even think about them until much later.
Q: What did the piece of paper say?
A: Here. This is the copy of what they gave me. But I didn't read it too closely. I probably would have signed it no matter what it said. At the time, I just wanted to get out of there.
Q: Can I keep this?
A: Sure.
Q: Did they ever find out who Jeff was and have him arrested?
A: No, they never did. He was amazed I didn't tell. He was going around the house looking for anything the police would be interested in when I showed up. He also told me he had stuck a pair of garden gloves in his pants, which was one reason why he had taken off, as it was more than just the cashews.
Q: Am I right that they never physically harmed you, and never did arrest you or even really make a move to arrest you?
A: In thinking back on it, I'm not sure they ever actually touched me other than when the detective first put her hands on me in the parking lot. They never did strike or hit me, or arrest me. So maybe I should just leave it alone.
Q: Well, you can always just leave things where they are. But it sounds like you want to at least consider your options?

A: Yes. I'm kind of mad because of what they did, so I'm interested in knowing, I guess, if I can sue that store. I haven't really been able to sleep at all since then. If I do get to sleep I have nightmares about being locked away in little places. I've been to a psychiatrist quite a few times since this happened, and I don't have any health insurance, and that actually has been expensive. We all lost the money from the food. Who knows what they did with it? Although I guess that was sort of Jeff's fault for just dropping those bags, and mine for not remembering them. But I don't think they should be allowed to get away with that, when I didn't do anything except go shopping with a screw-up. I could have had a panic attack or heart failure in there. I was really scared and I'm not sure they had any right to do that to me. So I guess I think someone should call them on that, and not let them get away with it. And it sure can't be Jeff.

Q: Would it be okay with you if I talked with your psychiatrist briefly about how you are feeling and what treatment is necessary? It would be helpful if your doctor could verify your condition.

A: That's okay.

Q: What is his name, and if you have it, his phone number?

A: His name is Dr. Romeo. I don't have his phone number with me right now, but we could look it up in the phone book. That's what I do when I want to change an appointment.

Q: That's okay; we'll look it up. How do you spell it, like the Shakespeare character?

A: R-o-m-e-o. So do you think I should sue the store? Or is it not worth it?

Q: I'd like to have someone do a little research so we will know for sure what we are dealing with before we give you advice. Why don't you set up a meeting with my secretary and . . .my secretary is the guy sitting over in the other office. There isn't a real hurry on this. Can you come back in a week?

A: Sure.

END OF TRANSCRIPT

SAVINGS GALORE, INC.

SUSPECTED SHOPLIFTER RELEASE FORM

YOU HAVE THE RIGHT TO REMAIN SILENT. RATHER THAN SPEAK WITH US, YOU MAY FIRST CONSULT WITH AN ATTORNEY.

NOTICE: THIS IS A LEGALLY BINDING AGREEMENT. By signing this agreement, you waive your right to bring a court action to recover compensation or obtain remedy against Savings Galore, Inc.

WAIVER/RELEASE/COVENANT NOT TO SUE

In consideration for Savings Galore, Inc. releasing me from their custody, and in consideration for Savings Galore, Inc. not filing criminal charges against me or seeking civil liability against me, I hereby release Savings Galore, Inc., a Columbia corporation, and its officers, agents, and employees from and WAIVE MY SUBSTANTIAL RIGHTS TO ASSERT any cause of action, claims or demands of any nature whatsoever, including but not limited to a claim of false imprisonment, false arrest, intentional infliction of emotional distress, duress, or negligence which I, my heirs, representatives, executors, administrators and assigns may now have, or have in the future against Savings Galore, Inc. on account of the store detaining me on 5/29/08 for purposes of investigation of shoplifting. I further agree that Savings Galore, Inc. had reasonable cause to detain me because they suspected me of shoplifting and that they did not detain me for longer than a reasonable period of time. I understand that the terms of this agreement are legally binding and I certify that I am signing this agreement, after having carefully read it, of my own free will.

Chris Pearson 5/29/08	*John de Majo*
Signature and Date	Witness
Chris Pearson	*Kent Wong*
Printed Name	Witness

HAMLINE & BUTTRAM, LLP

Santa Claritan, Columbia

MEMORANDUM

To:	Chris Pearson Client File
From:	Mary Hamline
Date:	July 24, 2008
Re:	**Phone conversation with Dr. Fred Romeo, a psychiatrist treating Chris Pearson**

On July 24, 2008 I called Dr. Fred Romeo, phone # 555-3882, 550 Bootwide Ave., Santa Claritan, Columbia. Dr. Romeo is a psychiatrist who has been treating our client Chris Pearson. He has been a practicing psychiatrist for over 10 years. I explained that Pearson was our client, and that Pearson had authorized Dr. Romeo to discuss his current condition with me as a privileged communication. Romeo said that Pearson had told him I might call, so he wasn't surprised by it. We then had a conversation concerning whether Pearson had suffered emotional injuries due to the episode at Savings Galore, the nature of the suffering, and whether Romeo would be willing to sign an affidavit and/or testify if Pearson asked him to.

Dr. Romeo said he knows and remembers Pearson quite well, but he also went and retrieved and reviewed his notes. He said that Pearson had been to see him a couple of times before the episode at Savings Galore, so he had a chance to compare, but only a little. Dr. Romeo said he concluded that Pearson was currently suffering from significantly lower than usual energy and low motivation, as well as sleep disorder, loss of concentration, tearfulness, and loss of general interest in previously pleasurable activities. He said these symptoms were all quite consistent with posttraumatic stress disorder, and predicted that they may persist, on and off, for as long as a year, and might return. He also said, however, that he had seen a lot worse cases of posttraumatic stress disorder, although Pearson does seem to be suffering.

I asked him if he was reasonably confident that the posttraumatic stress suffered by Pearson was brought about by the episode at Savings Galore. Dr. Romeo said yes. He said Pearson hadn't mentioned the episode extensively, but that his current condition was connected to a traumatic event. I asked if Pearson's symptoms could be triggered even though there was not any physical injury associated with the event. Dr. Romeo said, "Oh, sure. Posttraumatic stress is often created by a stressful event that turns out not to cause physical injury. It is the fear and lack of control over the situation that create the conditions for posttraumatic stress in a lot of cases."

Dr. Romeo said he has never testified in a court setting, but has had his deposition taken several times. He would be happy to sign an affidavit concerning Pearson's condition, and he would be willing to testify if necessary, although he'd like to avoid it. I thanked him and said that it was probable that we would get back to him on this, although that decision in the end was up to Pearson.

SELECTED PROVISIONS OF THE COLUMBIA PENAL CODE

§ 13–1 Shoplifting; detaining suspect; defense to wrongful detention

A. A person commits shoplifting if, while in an establishment in which merchandise is displayed for sale, such person knowingly obtains such goods of another with the intent to deprive that person of such goods by:

1. Removing any of the goods from the immediate display or from any other place within the establishment without paying the purchase price; or

2. Charging the purchase price of the goods to a fictitious person or any person without that person's authority; or

3. Paying less than the purchase price of the goods by some trick or artifice such as altering, removing, substituting or otherwise disfiguring any label, price tag or marking; or

4. Transferring the goods from one container to another; or

5. Concealment.

B. Any person who knowingly conceals upon himself or another person unpurchased merchandise of any mercantile establishment while within the mercantile establishment shall be presumed to have the necessary culpable mental state pursuant to subsection A of this section.

C. A merchant, or a merchant's agent or employee, with reasonable cause, may detain on the premises in a reasonable manner and for a reasonable time any person suspected of shoplifting as defined in subsection A of this section for questioning or summoning a law enforcement officer.

D. Reasonable cause is a defense to a civil or criminal action against a peace officer, a merchant or an agent or employee of such merchant for false arrest, false or unlawful imprisonment, or wrongful detention.

ALICE JAMES V. SMITTY'S

Columbia Court of Appeal (1998)

Alice James ("James"), her son Steven James ("Steven"), and her friend Nancy Robertson ("Robertson") were shopping at Smitty's, a supermarket chain store. James placed a pair of children's sandals in her shopping cart and covered them with an advertising flier. James later said she: (1) placed the sandals in the cart to quiet Steven, who wanted them; (2) covered them to make Steven forget them, planning to return them; and then (3) forgot them herself. Robertson later said she was only vaguely aware that James had placed the sandals in the cart and was entirely unaware that James had placed the flier over the sandals.

Karen Wilkerson, a Smitty's security officer, observed James's actions on a surveillance monitor and followed James and Robertson to the check-out stand. Though James paid for other items, she did not pay for the sandals, which remained in the bottom of her cart.

James and Robertson left the store. Robertson waited outside the car while James placed the groceries and her purse inside the car and then lifted Steven from the cart. She then picked up the sandals. She later said she had just discovered them and was about to return them to the store. At that moment, Wilkerson approached, identified herself as a Smitty's security officer, pointed to the sandals, and motioned James and Robertson back into the store. James, who is very hard of hearing, originally did not understand what Wilkerson said. She first thought Wilkerson wanted the advertising flier. When Wilkerson pointed at her purse, James thought Wilkerson was trying to rob her. When Wilkerson pulled at her purse and pointed at the sandals, James understood that Wilkerson thought she had stolen the sandals and, accompanied by Robertson and Steven, followed Wilkerson to the security offices inside the store.

Wilkerson directed Robertson to remain in one small office. (There is conflicting evidence concerning whether the door to Robertson's office was locked, but that fact is not relevant to the issues in this appeal.) Wilkerson then escorted James and Steven to a separate office. Wilkerson searched James's purse, photographed her against her will, showed her part of the surveillance video, and presented a form letter demanding payment of a statutory civil penalty plus the sandals' purchase price. James, increasingly distraught, wrote her phone number on the form letter, hoping Wilkerson would call her husband. Wilkerson did not perceive a hearing problem and did not call the number that James had written. James (and Robertson, who claimed she could hear through the wall) claimed that Wilkerson was abusive, yelling and slamming objects. After about 45 minutes in the office, James hyperventilated and lost consciousness. Wilkerson and the night manager called for paramedic assistance. Wilkerson testified that she took Steven from the security office when the paramedics arrived to attend to James and that Robertson and one of the paramedics took Steven to the parking lot to see a fire engine. The paramedics took James to the hospital. Robertson called James's husband, who came to pick up Steven and went to the hospital where the paramedics had taken his wife.

James and Steven sued Smitty's for negligence and false imprisonment. The jury awarded James $8,500 in damages on her false imprisonment claim and awarded Steven $12,500 on his false imprisonment and negligent infliction of emotional distress claims. From judgment on the verdict and the denial of its posttrial motions, Smitty's appeals. These appeals concern the finding of liability and award to Steven.

At the close of Plaintiffs' evidence, Smitty's moved for a directed verdict on Steven's negligent infliction of emotional distress claim, arguing that Plaintiffs neither alleged nor presented evidence of compensable harm. Smitty's claims that the trial court was required to grant their motion for a directed verdict against Steven because there was no evidence offered that Steven suffered physical injury. His damages were transitory nightmares and sleep disturbance, for about two months, which subsided without medical treatment. Under these facts, this motion should have been granted.

In Columbia, a plaintiff may not recover for negligent infliction of emotional distress unless the shock or mental anguish is accompanied by or manifested as a physical injury. Transitory physical phenomena such as nightmares and sleep disturbance are not the type of bodily harm that would sustain a cause of action for emotional distress. In contrast to a negligence claim, however, a false imprisonment claim does not require proof of physical injury to go forward. Steven's false imprisonment claim is therefore not impeded by the absence of physical damages. Consequently, the injuries suffered by Steven are sufficient injuries to justify an award under a false imprisonment claim.

Smitty's, however, alleges errors concerning Steven's false imprisonment claim. It claims that the trial court should have directed a verdict because Smitty's neither accused nor suspected Steven of shoplifting. We disagree.

Smitty's intended to confine James with the necessary consequence of also confining Steven, her four-year-old child. Its liability to Steven under these circumstances is explained in the Restatement (Second) of Torts. According to Restatement § 35, an actor is subject to liability for false imprisonment for the wrongful confinement of another if "he acts intending to confine the other or a third person within boundaries fixed by the actor. . .his act directly or indirectly results in such a confinement of the other, [and] the other is conscious of the confinement or is harmed by it." If a confinement of one party imposes confinement on another party, "the actor is subject to liability to such other as fully as though it were intended so to affect him."

These provisions are dispositive of Smitty's first argument. That Steven was merely an indirect, not the direct, target of confinement does not relieve Smitty's of liability on Steven's false imprisonment claim. Steven is entitled to compensation for loss of time, for physical discomfort or inconvenience, and for any resulting physical illness or injury to health. Since the injury is in large part a mental one, he is entitled to damages for mental suffering, humiliation, and the like. The damages that flow foreseeably from a false confinement of a caretaker flow equally foreseeably to an accompanying small child.

Smitty's also argues that Steven's false imprisonment case should have been dismissed due to the statutorily granted shopkeeper immunity for detaining suspected shoplifters. A merchant may detain a suspected shoplifter without incurring liability if the storekeeper has reasonable cause to believe that the person shoplifted and if the detention is performed in a reasonable manner and for a reasonable length of time. Columbia Penal Code § 13–1 C and D. Reasonable cause for the shopkeeper to detain a suspected shoplifter is not dependent on guilt or innocence of the person detained, or whether a crime was actually committed. If the facts and reasonable inferences therefrom are not subject to material dispute, reasonable cause is a question of law to be determined by the court.

Smitty's argues that it had reasonable cause to detain James, and thus it had reasonable cause to detain Steven as well. While we agree that ordinarily reasonable cause to detain a parent suspected of shoplifting gives the merchant reasonable cause to detain minor children of the suspected parent, given the facts of this case we do not agree that Smitty's had reasonable cause to detain Steven.

We have previously indicated our acceptance of Restatement § 35, which explains the potential linkage of false imprisonment of a suspect and another. Had Smitty's detained James without reasonable cause, it would have detained Steven without reasonable cause as well. But Smitty's had reasonable cause to detain James, because she picked up the sandals, placed them in the cart, covered them with an advertising flier, and left the store without paying for them. This may have been inadvertent; it may have been deliberate; but the appearance was such that it gave Smitty's reasonable cause for suspicion of shoplifting.[2]

But the real question is whether Smitty's needed to detain Steven, a person not suspected of shoplifting, for as long as they did under these circumstances. We conclude that it was not reasonable under the circumstances for Smitty's to detain

---

2 Because no fact-finder could reasonably conclude otherwise, the trial court could have directed a verdict for Smitty's on the issue of reasonable cause to detain James.

Steven for more than the time necessary to make sure Steven would be under proper supervision.

Smitty's had several alternatives available for Steven's supervision other than detaining him. Most notably, Wilkerson could have immediately asked Robertson to care for Steven while James was detained for investigation of shoplifting, yet she made no effort to do so and in fact impermissibly detained Robertson as well as James and Steven. There was no reasonable cause to detain Robertson. Wilkerson had no basis to believe Robertson had shoplifted or assisted in the shoplifting in any way, and Wilkerson testified that she did not consider Robertson to have been involved in any illegal activity. A merchant does not have immunity to detain a companion of a suspected shoplifter unless the store has reasonable cause to believe the companion was involved in the illegal activity. Because Smitty's did not have that reasonable cause, Robertson was a fully viable alternative for the supervision of Steven. If in fact James had not wished Robertson to supervise Steven, Smitty's would have grounds for avoiding liability for false imprisonment of Steven. Smitty's took all of that opportunity away by simply detaining James, Steven, and Robertson. In addition, they could have had Steven come into the store, asked James to call an acceptable supervisor for Steven, and detained Steven only until the acceptable supervisor arrived.

Accordingly, Smitty's was not by statute granted immunity from liability on Steven's suit for false imprisonment.

Affirmed.

GASPARD V. AMERICAN TELCO

Columbia Court of Appeal (2001)

Tracey Gaspard sued her former employer, American Telco, for retaliatory discharge after she filed a workers' compensation claim. The trial court granted summary judgment to her employer on the basis that Gaspard had signed a release of all claims against it. Gaspard appeals, contending that the release was ambiguous and procured by duress, and thus the trial court erred in granting summary judgment. We affirm.

Gaspard worked for American Telco as a district sales manager. While driving to the office after a sales appointment in August

1997, she was involved in a car accident in which she claimed neck and back injuries. She continued to work, although in pain and under the care of a chiropractor, for two months. Then, in October 1997, she was unable to get out of her bathtub without assistance. An MRI revealed two ruptured discs in her back. A doctor advised that she take several weeks off work in order to rest.

Just eleven days later, while at home on medical leave, an American Telco employee who "shared lodgings" with Gaspard came home with bad news. He told Gaspard that she was being fired from her job. He gave her a release, by which she was allowed to resign, receive $4,500, and keep her health insurance for another month in exchange for her waiver of all claims against her employer. If she did not sign the release, she would be terminated without continued benefits or pay. He told Gaspard she had until the next morning to make her decision.

Gaspard signed the release and received the month's insurance and money. Two years later, she brought suit for wrongful termination, alleging the discharge was in retaliation for her having filed a worker's compensation claim. The trial court granted summary judgment to her former employer based on the release, and Gaspard appeals.

To prevail on a motion for summary judgment, a defendant must establish that no material fact issue exists and that it is entitled to judgment as a matter of law. If a defendant moves for summary judgment on the basis of an affirmative defense, it has the burden to prove conclusively all the elements of the affirmative defense as a matter of law. In conducting our review of the summary judgment, we take as true all evidence favorable to the nonmovant, and we make all reasonable inferences in the nonmovant's favor.

In general, a release surrenders legal rights or obligations between the parties to an agreement. A release is a complete bar to any later action based on matters covered by the release. American Telco, who in this case is the party asserting summary judgment on the basis of the release, undertook its burden to prove the elements of its defense as a matter of law by attaching a copy of the release signed by Gaspard to its motion for summary judgment. A signed release contains a strong presumption of enforceability. To presume otherwise would throw into doubt the validity of every settlement and create strong disincentives for parties to settle. Because American Telco has provided presumptive evidence of the release, the burden then shifts to Gaspard to directly attack the release or establish a fact issue in avoidance of it.

Gaspard first attacks the validity of the release by arguing it is ambiguous. The release that Gaspard signed states in pertinent part as follows:

"I hereby release American Telco from any and all claims, charges, liabilities, causes of action, and demands arising from or in connection with my employment with American Telco or the termination thereof, which I ever had, now have or may have from the day of the commencement of my employment to the date of this waiver and release. This waiver and release includes, without limitations, claims and causes of action arising under federal and state fair employment practice laws as well as the common law of torts and contracts, relating in any way to my employment with American Telco, treatment while employed with American Telco and the termination of my employment. I hereby agree not to bring any lawsuit, charge or claim against American Telco in any court or administrative proceeding relating in any way to my employment, my treatment while employed, and the termination of my employment."

This release expressly includes all claims arising from Gaspard's employment or termination from employment with American Telco. Because the release mentions claims arising from termination of employment, we hold that the release unambiguously bars Gaspard's retaliatory discharge claim.

Gaspard also argues that she was under duress when she signed the release. In the early common law, duress *per minas*, i.e., by threats, was available to void a contract where the threat involved imprisonment, mayhem, or loss of life or limb. Through the years, there has been a steady expansion of the duress principle such that direct dire harm is no longer essential, the focus instead being on whether the threat is so overbearing that the victim had no reasonable alternative. If a party's manifestation of assent is induced by an improper threat by the other party that leaves the victim no reasonable alternative, the contract is voidable by the victim.

Thus the modern defense of duress, used to avoid enforcement of an agreement, is met by demonstrating the following elements: (1) The promise must be made in response to a threat. Ordinarily it must be the promisee who created or issued the threat, although in some cases a successful showing of duress was made when the threat did not originate with the party seeking to enforce the promise. (2) The threat needs to be severe enough to reasonably convince the will of the promisor to make the promise. If sufficient alternatives to making the promise were available to the promisor, the threat will not be considered severe and duress will not succeed as a defense. (3) The threat must be improper rather than just hard bargaining.

A difficult issue is determining what type of threat is sufficient to invoke the rule. Courts tend to use as a shorthand summary, words such as "wrongful," "oppressive," or "unconscionable" to describe conduct, but the complexity of the term "threat" is demonstrated in Section 176 of the Restatement (Second) of Contracts, which provides:

> "(1) A threat is improper if:
>
> > (a) what is threatened is a crime or a tort, or the threat itself would be a crime or a tort if it resulted in obtaining property;
> >
> > (b) what is threatened is a criminal prosecution;
> >
> > (c) what is threatened is the use of civil process and the threat is made in bad faith; or
> >
> > (d) the threat is a breach of the duty of good faith and fair dealing under a contract with the recipient.
>
> (2) A threat is improper if the resulting exchange is not on fair terms, and
>
> > (a) the threatened act would harm the recipient and would not significantly benefit the party making the threat;

> (b) the effectiveness of the threat in inducing the manifestation of assent is significantly increased by prior unfair dealing by the party making the threat; or
>
> (c) what is threatened is otherwise a use of power for illegitimate ends."

In this case, Gaspard's argument is that she faced economic duress. She does not claim that she was physically threatened as a reason to have agreed to the release promise. Gaspard claims in her affidavit "I had no money in the bank and I was in financial straits." Economic duress may be claimed, however, only when the party against whom it is claimed was responsible for claimant's financial distress. None of the summary judgment evidence indicates that American Telco was responsible for Gaspard's economic distress. Accordingly, Gaspard has failed to meet her burden of establishing duress.

We find that American Telco established the requisites of release and there is no ambiguity in the language of the agreement. We have also concluded that the release was not obtained by economic duress. Accordingly, we overrule Gaspard's sole issue and affirm the trial court's judgment.

PETERSON V. ZELIE CORP.

Columbia Court of Appeal (1979)

Defendant Zelie Corp. ("Zelie") appeals from a judgment finding it liable for false imprisonment and awarding $10,500 in actual damages and $20,000 in punitive damages to Plaintiff Mary Peterson ("Peterson").

At the time the incidents leading to the false imprisonment suit took place, Plaintiff Peterson was twenty-three years old and pregnant. Plaintiff went to the Zelie store with instructions from her mother to complete the purchase of items which her mother had placed in the store's layaway department. She was driven to the store by a neighbor, Mike Taylor, and was accompanied by her two sons Tom and Jim, ages 1 and 3 years, and by her 14-year-old brother, Bill. The Plaintiff entered the store, went to the layaway department, and handed the clerk the layaway receipt that her mother had given her. According to Plaintiff Peterson, the clerk handed her, in addition to the items listed on the layaway receipt, a box containing a Chipshot hockey set. This item, as boxed, was approximately as large as the counsel's table in the trial court. Plaintiff accepted this item, she argued, because she did not know exactly what was to be picked up from the store.

Plaintiff Peterson paid the balance due on the items listed on the layaway receipt. She then put all the items except the hockey set in a shopping cart along with her two children. At Plaintiff's direction the hockey set was placed in another cart. Plaintiff's brother, Bill, pushed the cart containing the hockey set toward the store's exit, while Plaintiff propelled the cart containing her children and the balance of the items. As they neared the door Plaintiff found a "Paid" sticker on the floor and placed it on the box containing the hockey set. Plaintiff Peterson claimed Bill, her brother, told her that the sticker had fallen off one of the items she had purchased.

A guard at the store's exit checked each item for a paid sticker and allowed Plaintiff Peterson to pass. However, once outside the door Plaintiff was stopped by a security guard, whose suspicion was aroused because he had observed Plaintiff place the paid sticker on the hockey set's box. The guard identified himself and asked Plaintiff whether she had paid for the hockey set. Plaintiff claimed she had paid for the item. The guard then asked Plaintiff and her brother to follow him to a room in the back of the store used by the security staff. Once in this room three security officers questioned Plaintiff, at various times.

Initially, Plaintiff Peterson maintained she had purchased the hockey set. However, when Plaintiff was shown the layaway receipt, which did not list the hockey set, she admitted that the hockey set was not one of the items that her mother had previously placed in the store's layaway department. She subsequently filed a suit for false imprisonment which resulted in the judgment from which defendant Zelie appeals.

Defendant Zelie argues that the facts did not warrant the imposition of punitive damages. Under Columbia law, punitive damages are recoverable for false imprisonment when the plaintiff proves, by clear and convincing evidence, that the defendant has been guilty of oppression, fraud, or malice. "Malice" is defined as conduct which is intended by the defendant to cause injury to the plaintiff or despicable conduct which is carried on by the defendant with a willful and conscious disregard of the rights or safety of others. "Oppression" is despicable conduct that subjects a person to cruel and unjust hardship in conscious disregard of that person's rights. "Fraud" means an intentional misrepresentation, deceit, or concealment of a material fact known to the defendant with the intention on the part of the defendant of thereby depriving a person of property or legal rights or otherwise causing injury.

That the jury found Zelie's detention of Plaintiff Peterson constituted a false imprisonment does not necessarily mean the jury concluded the interview was conducted with the intent to cause harm or was despicable. The only mental state required to be shown to prove false imprisonment is the intent to confine, or to create a similar intrusion. Thus, the intent element of false imprisonment does not entail an intent or motive to cause harm; indeed false imprisonments often appear to arise from initially legitimate motives.

Similarly, even if some force had been used to detain Plaintiff Peterson it would not mean there was sufficient evidence of oppression, fraud, or malice to warrant a trial on the punitive damages issue. In *Beau v. Ketchum* (Columbia Supreme Court, 1953) for example, the plaintiff recovered only nominal damages for being falsely imprisoned, because no actual damages were sustained and there was no evidence of oppression, fraud, or malice. Although the defendants in *Beau* had caused the plaintiff's forcible removal and arrest, the court found that the mere use of force does not constitute evidence of oppression, fraud, or malice where only a reasonable and necessary amount of force was used in the detention.

Under a reading of the facts most generous to Peterson, defendant Zelie cannot be viewed as having been guilty of the oppression, fraud or malice necessary to justify a punitive damage award for the tort of false imprisonment. The facts contain no suggestion of fraud. The facts only mildly hint at malice, and while Zelie did confine Peterson, it was for only a brief period of time sufficient to demonstrate that in fact Peterson had not paid for the hockey game. There are no facts indicating the confinement was intended to cause injury to

Peterson or was undertaken by Zelie with a willful and conscious disregard of the rights and safety of Peterson. Similarly, there is no evidence that Zelie subjected Peterson to a cruel and unjust hardship in conscious disregard of Peterson's rights. Zelie thought Peterson was attempting to steal the hockey game, and in fact Peterson had not paid for the hockey game. We note that since these events occurred, the legislature has enacted a "shopkeeper immunity" statute that provides a shopkeeper with immunity not only from punitive damages but from liability at all when the store detains a customer whom the store has reasonable cause to believe was stealing for a reasonable period of time. Columbia Penal Code § 13–1. This statute cannot be applied retroactively, but does suggest a societal indication that the store's detaining, investigating, and ultimately releasing Peterson under the circumstances cannot be said to be despicable. Accordingly, Peterson did not present clear and convincing evidence of oppression, fraud or malice sufficient to justify a punitive damages award.

Defendant Zelie also argues the trial judge should have granted its motion that judgment for the defendant should be ordered because plaintiff's pleadings and evidence established that plaintiff had released defendant from any liability arising out of plaintiff's detention. Plaintiff Peterson, in response, claims that the release was obtained by duress and it is therefore voidable.

A signed promise by a plaintiff to refrain from suit is entitled to a strong presumption of enforceability. Nevertheless, a plaintiff can avoid summary judgment by demonstrating that there are factual matters to be resolved concerning the existence of the release, the meaning of the release, or the enforceability of the release. For example, if a plaintiff can demonstrate that there are disputed facts concerning whether the release was obtained by overreaching, or was the result of economic duress, or the plaintiff lacked the capacity to enter into the release, the matter cannot be resolved by summary judgment. The parties must go to trial, not on the underlying matter of the lawsuit, but on the issue concerning whether the release is valid and enforceable.

Affirmed in part, reversed in part.

RAFTON V. DORMAN'S DONUT HOUSE, INC.

Columbia Court of Appeal (1985)

Plaintiff Nancy Rafton ("Rafton") appeals from an order of the trial court granting defendant Dorman's Donut House, Inc.'s ("Dorman's") motion for summary judgment. Plaintiff Rafton contends that the trial court erred in entering summary judgment against her because a genuine issue of material fact existed concerning her charge that she was falsely detained and imprisoned. For the reasons that follow, we affirm the trial court's decision.

Plaintiff Rafton's complaint alleged that she was employed as a clerk in defendant's donut shop in Meyers, Columbia, for approximately three years; that defendant Dorman's, through its agents and employees, Mac Betts, William Conn, and Joseph Jackson, accused her of selling donuts without registering sales and thereby pocketing defendant Dorman's monies; and that she was falsely detained and imprisoned against her will in a room located on Dorman's premises, with force, and without probable and reasonable cause, by defendant Dorman's employees.

Defendant Dorman's denied the material allegations of Rafton's complaint and filed an affirmative defense that alleged it was a merchant; that any questioning of Rafton by its employees, Betts, Conn, and Jackson, was performed only after the employees had reasonable grounds to believe that Rafton had committed retail theft while working for defendant Dorman; that any alleged detention for questioning was limited solely to an inquiry as to whether Rafton had failed to account for certain retail sales; and that such inquiry took place in a reasonable manner and for a reasonable length of time. Defendant Dorman's subsequently moved for summary judgment, arguing that the Plaintiff Rafton's false imprisonment complaint that she was held against her will by her employers in a certain room of a Dorman's Donut House was contradicted by her testimony in a discovery deposition. The transcript of the deposition indicated that Plaintiff Rafton testified that she had voluntarily complied with Betts, Conn, and Jackson's request to speak privately with her regarding the matter of shortages in her cash register on April 9, 1981, and that when she no longer wished to continue her conversation with her employers, she got up and went home, electing never to return to her job. Rafton's response to Dorman's motion for summary judgment did not contradict the statements that she had made in her discovery deposition.

The trial court entered summary judgment for defendant Dorman's. Plaintiff Rafton appeals from that order.

Plaintiff Rafton asserts that the trial court erred in granting defendant Dorman's motion for summary judgment as there exists a genuine issue of material fact. She posits that she felt compelled to remain in the baking room, where she had gone after Betts and Conn requested they speak privately with her, so that she could protect her reputation by protesting her innocence to the two men, and that she left the room once she began to shake and feel ill. Additionally, she attributes her "serious emotional upset" to her feelings of intimidation that she contends were caused by: William Conn and Joseph Jackson each sitting directly next to her during questioning, yellow pad and pencil in hand; Mac Betts' repeated statement that his briefcase contained proof of her guilt; and his raised voice.

The common law tort of false imprisonment is defined as an unlawful restraint of an individual's personal liberty or freedom of locomotion. Imprisonment has been defined as any unlawful exercise or show of force by which a person is compelled to remain where he does not wish to remain or to go where he does not wish to go. In order for a false imprisonment to be present, there must be actual or legal intent to restrain. Unlawful restraint may be effected by words alone, by acts alone, or both; actual force is unnecessary to an action in false imprisonment. The Restatement of Torts specifies ways in which an actor may bring about the confinement required as an element of false imprisonment, including (1) actual or apparent physical barriers; (2) overpowering physical force, or by submission to physical force; (3) threats of physical force; (4) other duress; and (5) asserted legal authority. Restatement (Second) of Torts §§ 38–41 (1965). It is essential, however, that the confinement be against the plaintiff's will and, if a person voluntarily consents to the confinement, there can be no false imprisonment. Moral pressure, as where the plaintiff remains with the defendant to clear himself of suspicion of theft, is not enough.

In the case at bar, we are confronted with Plaintiff Rafton's testimony, given under oath, that she voluntarily accompanied Mac Betts and William Conn to the baking room; that she stayed in the room in order to protect her reputation; that she was never threatened with the loss of her job; that she was never in fear of her safety; and that at no time was she prevented from exiting the baking room. Her affidavit, in which she averred that she left the baking room after she began to shake and when she felt that she was becoming ill, does not place into issue material facts which she had previously removed from contention. In her discovery deposition, given under oath, she stated that she "got up and left" when Mac Betts asked her how long the cash register "shorting" had been going on.

In the tort of false imprisonment, it is not enough for Plaintiff Rafton to have felt "compelled" to remain in the baking room in order to protect her reputation, for the evidence must establish a restraint against her will, as where she yields to force, to the threat of force, or the assertion of authority. In the present case, our search of the record reveals no evidence that Plaintiff Rafton yielded to constraint of a threat, express or implied, or to physical force of any kind. Also, absent evidence that Plaintiff Rafton accompanied Betts and Conn against her will, we cannot say that she was imprisoned or unlawfully detained by defendant Dorman's employees.

For the reasons stated above, we conclude that the trial court properly granted defendant Dorman's motion for summary judgment, as there exists no question of material fact in the present case.

Answer 1 to Performance Test A

Memorandum

To: Mary Hamline

From: Applicant

Date: July 29, 2008

Re: Chris Pearson v. Savings Galore

Below is the requested information regarding our client, Chris Pearson's ("Pearson") possible civil claim against Savings Galore supermarket ("the store").

I. Elements of False Imprisonment

Under the Restatement of Torts section 35, an actor is subject to liability for false imprisonment if the actor (1) intends to confine the plaintiff or a third person; (2) within fixed boundaries; (3) there is actual confinement; and (4) the person confined is aware of the confinement or is harmed by it. James v. Smitty's ("James"). Similarly, the common law tort of false imprisonment is defined as an unlawful restraint of an individual's personal liberty or freedom of locomotion. Rafton v. Dorman's Donuts ("Rafton").

A. Intent to Confine

First, Pearson must establish that the detective intended to confine him. In the interview, Pearson indicated that as he exited the store, the detective approached him and yelled, "Hold it right there!" The detective then indicated that she was going to "have to take [Pearson] into [the store]." After Pearson's friend fled, the detective told Pearson to come with her into the store. She then picked up the bags and herded Pearson into the store and into the office. She left Pearson in the [room] with the door closed. These facts indicate that the detective intended to confine Pearson.

B. Confinement to Fixed Boundaries

Second, Pearson must establish that the confinement was to a bounded area. As noted, the detective placed Pearson in a room, in the back of the store, with no windows. She left Pearson in the room and closed the door. While Pearson did not check to see whether the door was locked, he believed he heard the detective lock the door. Further, he was frightened and could hear the detective talking to the other security guards right outside the door. Because he was in a closed room, with no windows, and the store's agents stood directly outside the door, Pearson had no reasonable means of leaving the room. Thus, he was confined to a bounded area.

C. Actual Confinement

To imprison the plaintiff, "there must be an unlawful exercise or show of force by which a person is compelled to remain where he does not wish to remain or go where he does not wish to go." Rafton. However, actual force is unnecessary and the restraint my be by words alone. Rafton. Similarly, under the Restatement (Second) of Torts, a plaintiff can be confined by actual or apparent physical barriers, overpowering physical force, threats of physical force, other duress, or asserted legal authority. Rafton.

Here, Pearson was compelled to follow [the] detective into the room and to remain in the room against his will. Although the detective did not force him into the room, she picked up the grocery bags and herded him into the store. She was a large and strong woman, and Pearson has indicated that he felt he could not have left at that point because the detective likely would have tackled him if he tried. Further, the detective asserted that she had legal authority to detain Pearson as an associate of a known shoplifter. For example, she stated that Pearson was in "big trouble" and ordered him to come with her. Thus, Pearson was compelled against his will to follow the detective into the room.

Once in the room, Pearson was not able to leave. The room had no windows and only one door. The store might argue that there was no actual confinement because the door was not locked. Although, Pearson is not certain whether the door was locked, he believed that he heard them lock the door. Nonetheless, whether the door was locked is not controlling because imprisonment does not require actual force preventing release. Instead, words or threats of force can be enough to establish actual confinement.

Similarly, the store might argue that there was no confinement because Pearson did not believe that the store's agents were going to physically harm him. However, as noted in Rafton, words alone can be sufficient to effectuate an unlawful restraint. So long as the confinement was against the plaintiff's will and a result of threatening words or conduct, there is imprisonment.

Here, although Pearson did not believe the store's agents were going to rough him up, he believed they were going to try to intimidate him somehow and hold him for a long period of time. While in the room, either the detective or other agents accompanied Pearson or they stood directly outside of the door, physically preventing his exit. Further, the agents directly stated that they did not have to let Pearson go, implying that they had legal authority to detain him.

It should be noted that where the plaintiff voluntarily consents to the confinement, there can be no confinement. Moral pressure, such as remaining to clear one's own name, is not sufficient to establish actual confinement. For example, in Rafton, the plaintiff voluntarily accompanied the defendants' agents into a room. She stayed in the room to protect her reputation, was never threatened, and never feared for her safety. Further, she was able to actually leave the room when she decided that she wanted to leave. Under those circumstances the court found that the plaintiff was not restrained against her will merely because she felt compelled to stay to protect her reputation.

On the other hand, here, Pearson did not consent to the confinement. Although the detective did not physically force Pearson into the room, she picked up the grocery bags and herded him into the store. The detective was a large strong woman, and Pearson has indicated that walking away did not seem like an option because the detective likely would have tackled him. He felt as if he had no other options and was compelled to follow Pearson into the store. Once he was in the store, the door remained closed and the store's agents continued to indicate that he was not free to leave by implying that he could only leave if he told them his roommate's name and address.

Thus, given that the store's agents confined Pearson by actual or apparent physical barriers (the closed door, lack of windows, and their physical presence) and asserted a claim of legal authority, Pearson will likely be able to establish that he was actually confined against his will.

D. Awareness of or Harm by Confinement

Finally, here Pearson was both aware of and harmed by the confinement. He was aware of the confinement because the detective closed the door, Pearson believed she locked the door, and the agents stood directly outside of the door, preventing his departure. Further, as noted below in the damages section, the confinement harmed Pearson because he suffered mental distress and financial harm as a result of the confinement.

E. Likelihood of Pearson's Success on a Claim of False Imprisonment

Because the store's agents intended to confine Pearson to a bounded area resulting in his actual confinement and his awareness of and harm by the confinement, Pearson will likely to be able to succeed on the merits of a false imprisonment claim.

II. Compensable Injuries

A claim of false imprisonment does not require proof of a physical injury. As the court noted in James v. Smitty's (James), while negligent infliction of emotional distress requires a physical manifestation of injuries, a claim for false imprisonment does not required such physical injury. It is sufficient for a plaintiff to suffer "transitory physical phenomena" such as nightmares and sleep disturbances. There, the court awarded claimant, a child incidentally confined because of his parent's confinement, compensation for loss of time, for physical discomfort or inconvenience, and for resulting physical illness or injury to health. The court noted that the injury resulting from false imprisonment is largely mental suffering, including humiliation.

Thus, here, if Pearson establishes his claim for false imprisonment, he will be able to recover damages for his mental suffering. Pearson's doctor, Dr. Romeo, has indicated that Pearson suffers from significantly lower than normal energy and motivation levels, a sleep disorder, loss of concentration, tearfulness, and loss of general interest in previously pleasurable activities. Dr. Romeo [is] reasonably confident the injuries are a manifestation of posttraumatic stress disorder caused by the incident at Savings Galore. He is willing to sign an affidavit stating such facts and conclusions and may be willing to testify.

Further, Pearson will be able to recover for any physical and economic suffering, including compensation for loss of time, physical discomfort or inconvenience, and for the groceries lost and retained by the store as a result of the improper detention.

Punitive Damages

Under Columbia law, a plaintiff may recover damages for false imprisonment if the plaintiff establishes, by clear and convincing evidence, that the defendant is guilty of oppression, fraud, or malice. Peterson v. Zelie ("Peterson"). Where the defendant uses reasonable and necessary force to detain the plaintiff, the fact of force is not sufficient to establish oppression, fraud or malice.

For example, in Peterson the court found that the defendant was not liable for punitive damages because they did not act with fraud, malice, or oppression. There, the defendant detained the plaintiff for only a brief period of time sufficient to show that the plaintiff had not paid for the item in question. There was not evidence that the confinement was intended to cause injury to the plaintiff or was undertaken with a willful and conscious disregard of the rights and safety of the plaintiff. Further, there was not evidence of cruel and unusual hardship in conscious disregard of the plaintiff's rights.

Malice

Malice is conduct intended to cause injury to the plaintiff or despicable conduct carried on by the defendant with a willful and conscious disregard for the right or safety of others. Peterson. Here, there does not appear to be conduct rising to the level of willful or conscious disregard for Pearson's rights. The store's agents may have reasonably believed that they had a right to detain Pearson and there is no evidence of an improper motive. The detention was for only one hour and therefore not for an unreasonable period of time. There is no indication that the agents were aware of Pearson's nervousness or tendency to suffer anxiety, and there is no indication that they attempted to exploit this tendency in holding Pearson. As a result, there was no malice subjecting the store to punitive damages.

Oppression

Oppression is despicable conduct that subjects a person to cruel and unjust hardship in conscious disregard of that person's rights. In this case, there is no indication that Pearson suffered cruel and unjust hardship. The detention was only for one hour and, as noted above, the agents did not exploit a known weakness in Pearson or subject him to physical or severe mental abuse.

Fraud

Fraud is an intentional misrepresentation of concealment of a material fact known to the defendant with the intention of the party of the defendant to deprive a person of property or legal rights or otherwise causing injury. There is no indication that the store's agents misrepresented or withheld a material fact in detaining Pearson. They may have believed they had a lawful right to detain Pearson. They may have believed they had a lawful right to detain Pearson. If they knew they did not have a lawful right to detain Pearson, then their misrepresenting this fact or their failure to disclose this fact might rise to the level of fraud. However, further evidence is needed.

Thus, because the store's agents did not act with fraud, malice or oppression, Pearson is unlikely to succeed if he claims punitive damages.

III. The Store's Defenses

The Store will likely argue that they are entitled to the Shopkeeper's privilege in detaining Pearson and that Pearson waived his right to bring a false imprisonment claim against the store by signing the release form.

A. Shopkeeper's Privilege

Columbia Penal Code Section 13–1 provides a defense to a claim of false imprisonment. Subsection C provides that a merchant or a merchant's agent or employee may detain an individual reasonably suspected of shoplifting on the store's premises in a reasonable manner for a reasonable time for questioning. Further, under Subsection D, where the merchant or merchant's agent has reasonable cause to suspect an individual of shoplifting, they have a valid defense to a claim of false arrest, false or unlawful imprisonment, or wrongful detention.

Reasonable Suspicion: The Companion of a Shoplifter

In James, the court discussed the reasonableness of detaining an individual not suspected of shoplifting. There, the defendant detained the person suspected of shoplifting's four year old son. The court held that it was not reasonable for the defendant to detain the son for more than the time necessary to make sure the son would be under proper supervision. Further, in dicta, the court noted that the defendant lacked reasonable cause to detain the individual accompanying the suspected shoplifter because the defendant's agents testified that they did not consider the companion to have been involved in any illegal activity. Thus, it would not have been reasonable for the defendant to detain the companion.

Here, the detective did not suspect that Pearson shoplifted. When she originally stopped Pearson and his roommate, she acknowledged that she did not suspect Pearson of shoplifting. Pearson stated that he did not take the cashews, and the detective stated, "That's right, you didn't." As in James, where the defendant lacked reasonable suspicion to believe the shoplifter's companion was involved in the shoplifting, here, the detective lacked reasonable suspicion to believe that Pearson had shoplifted, and, in fact, admitted that she did not believe that Pearson had shoplifted. Because the store lacked a reasonable suspicion, under the dicta in James, the store cannot invoke the shopkeeper's privilege to justify Pearson's detention.

Reasonable Manner

The store's detective "herded" Pearson into the back office. While the agents did not threaten Pearson with physical force, they did impliedly threaten him with the threat of criminal or civil liability by asserting that they did not have to let him go and that he was not free to leave. However, as noted above, they may have reasonably believed that they were entitled to detain Pearson. Thus, because there was no overt physical force or threats of physical force, a court is likely to find that the manner of detention was reasonable.

Reasonable Time

The store's agents detained Pearson for approximately one hour. This does not appear to be an unreasonable time. However, Pearson can argue that it was an unreasonable time because the detective knew that he did not commit the crime. Nonetheless, as noted above, even if the detective knew he did not commit the crime, the agents may have had a reasonable basis for believing they were entitled to detain Pearson. If the agents had such a reasonable basis, then detaining him for one hour does not appear unreasonable.

Likelihood of Success

Although a court will likely find that the manner and time of detention were reasonable, as noted above, the store cannot invoke the shopkeeper's privilege as a defense to their detention of James because the agents lacked a reasonable suspicion to believe that Pearson shoplifted.

B. Waiver by Release of Liability

"In general, a release surrenders the legal rights or obligations between the parties to an agreement." Gaspard v. American Telco ("Gaspard"). If valid, a release completely bars a later action based on matters covered in the release. A signed release creates a strong presumption of enforceability. Gaspard. Nonetheless, a victim can void a signed release if they establish that the terms of the release are ambiguous or the signing of the release was a result of duress.

Here, Pearson clearly signed the release. Thus, the release is entitled to the presumption of enforceability. However, Pearson may be able to void the release if he establishes that the release was ambiguous or a result of duress.

Ambiguity

In Gaspard, the court held that because the release expressly mentioned the claim that the plaintiff asserted (claims arising from termination of employment), the release was not ambiguous. Similarly, here the release expressly mentioned claims arising from false imprisonment. Thus, under the reasoning of Gaspard, Pearson cannot argue that the release is ambiguous because the release expressly covers his potential claim.

Duress

To establish a claim of duress, Pearson must show that (1) the promise was made in response to a threat; (2) the threat was severe enough to reasonably convince the will of the promisor to make the promise; and (3) the threat was improper rather than just hard bargaining. Gaspard.

The Sufficiency of the Threat

First, Pearson must show that he signed the agreement because of a threat. While there is no clear test for determining what is a sufficient threat to invoke the rule, section 176 of the Restatement (Second) of Contracts indicates that a threat is improper if the threat itself constitutes a crime or a tort, the threat is of criminal prosecution, or the threat is of civil process and is made in bad faith.

Here, it is not entirely clear what the store threatened. The detective told Pearson that if he gave the store his roommate's name and address, the store would let him go. Further, the store directly indicated that they did not have to let Pearson go and told Pearson that if he signed a release, they would let him go.

While the store did not directly threaten criminal prosecution or a civil suit, Pearson could have reasonably believed that, in stating that they had a right to detain him, the store was indicating that they could file criminal charges or bring a civil claim against Pearson. In addition, the continued detention of Pearson might qualify as a tort or a crime in and of itself. As noted above, the store's threats and intimidation led Pearson to reasonably believe that he was not free to leave. This is an element of the false imprisonment claim.

In Gaspard, the plaintiff claimed only economic duress and not a physical threat inducing her to sign the release. Here, on the other hand, Pearson was told that he would not be able to leave if he did not sign the release. This, coupled with the intimidation and Pearson's belief that the door was locked, is a physical threat because it restricted Pearson's movement, making him believe that he had to stay where he was.

Reasonable Inducement to Act

Here, the threat reasonably induced Pearson to sign the waiver because he believed he was not free to leave. Further, Pearson did not believe anyone would come to his assistance. Under the circumstances, a reasonable person would believe they did not have a right to leave and might be held indefinitely. Thus, the threat reasonably induced Pearson to sign the release.

An Improper Threat

Finally, the threat rose above hard bargaining to impropriety. The agents indicated that they had a lawful right to detain Pearson and gave no indication that they would release him. Pearson could have been detained indefinitely, which is a significant violation of his freedom. Thus, the threat rose above hard bargaining.

Conclusion:

Pearson will not be able to rebut the defense of a liability waiver by establishing that the waiver was ambiguous. He may be able to establish that the signing of the release was a result of duress. If he establishes this, then he can void the release and sue under a claim of false imprisonment.

Answer 2 to Performance Test A

Memorandum

To: Mary Hamline

Re: Chris Pearson v. Savings Galore

As requested, here is an evaluation of Mr. Pearson's civil claim for false imprisonment against Savings Galore. The memorandum includes: (I) the elements necessary to succeed on a false imprisonment claim, (2) a factual analysis of the likelihood of Mr. Pearson prevailing on a false imprisonment claim, (3) an analysis of the injuries incurred by Mr. Pearson that may be compensable, (4) the likelihood of punitive damage awards given Mr. Pearson's injuries, and (5) the defenses that Savings Galore may raise and the likelihood o their success.

I. Elements that must be proven for Pearson to succeed on a false imprisonment claim

False imprisonment is defined as the unlawful restraint of an individual's personal liberty or freedom of locomotion (Rafton v. Dorman's Donut House). Under the Restatement (Second) of Torts, an actor is subject to liability for false imprisonment if the actor: (1) acts intending to confine another person within boundaries fixed by actor, (2) the act directly or indirectly results in such a confinement of the other person, and (3) the other person is conscious of confinement or harmed by it.

A. The actor acts intending to confine another person within boundaries fixed by actor.

The actor must actually intend to restrain the victim/plaintiff. The intent may be actual or legal intent. The actual unlawful restraint may be effected via words, acts, or both. Actual force is not necessary for liability in a false imprisonment claim (Rafton).

B. The act directly or indirectly results in such a confinement of the other person.

The act must result in confinement of the victim. Confinement can be brought about in many ways, including (1) actual/apparent physical barriers, (2) overpowering physical force or submission to physical force, (3) threats of physical force, (4) other duress, or (5) asserted legal authority (Restatement Second of Torts). The confinement must actually be, against the plaintiffs will—voluntary consent to a confinement is not against the plaintiff's will. Furthermore, moral pressure to accede to a confinement is not enough (Rafton).

C. The other person is conscious of confinement or harmed by it.

The victim/plaintiff must know of the confinement or be harmed by it.

II. Application of the facts of Pearson's situation to the elements and assessment of the likelihood that Pearson would prevail on a claim.

Mr. Pearson's situation would have to meet all three elements of the false imprisonment tort in order to succeed.

A. Did Savings Galore act intending to confine Mr. Pearson within boundaries fixed by Savings Galore?

Savings Galore (SG) would have to act intending to confine Pearson within fixed boundaries. There are several instances where SG's house detective and security officer's actions could rise to the level of intending to confine Pearson within fixed boundaries.

I. Grabbing Pearson's arm.

The SG detective yelled "Hold it right there!" and grabbed Pearson's arm. Grabbing a person's arm is likely an attempt to prevent them from leaving. Accompanied with her words, it is clear that the detective's actions were meant to prevent Pearson from leaving the area. SG is unlikely to be able to argue against this. However, this confinement only resulted in Pearson's confinement in that spot in the parking lot, and was over once she removed her hold on his arm.

II. Threats to Pearson

Restraint may be affected via words or threats; actual force is unnecessary. Here, the house detective of Savings Galore told Pearson, among other things, "I'm going to have to take you in" and "You come with me right now. You . . .are in big trouble." Here, the implied threat that Pearson would be in legal trouble should be enough to constitute action intending to confine. Even though Pearson protested that he had done nothing wrong, the detective replied that she "didn't care," and repeated that he was to go with her. This threat of legal action is likely enough action to lead a reasonable person to believe he had no other choice.

Pearson may also argue the threat of force, since he said that "she would probably have tackled me," if he tried to run. Though this argument is less plausible considering that the detective made no such move, he may argue that her appearance and large[ness], combined with her earlier hold on his arm and the threats that he was in trouble and should come with her, would constitute a threat of force.

The detective also took hold of his groceries that Pearson's roommate had dropped and "herded" Pearson into the room. Although courts have not addressed the issue of whether taking a person's rightful belongings consists of the necessary action for false imprisonment, it is likely that taking the groceries would suffice. The groceries belonged to Pearson and had been paid for; they were his rightful possessions. The detective deprived Pearson of the groceries and implied that she was taking them with her. Pearson could argue that he should not be forced to give up his rightful possessions and was forced to follow her in order to recover them; this could constitute a wrongful threat sufficient for an action to confine.

III. Placing Mr. Pearson into a windowless room

The detective took Pearson to a windowless office in the back of the store, summoned two large security officers, and closed the door, leaving Pearson inside. Pearson also states that he believed they locked the door, although he is unsure. Courts have not addressed issues of belief of confinement via locks, but looking at the totality of the circumstances—the three people standing outside, the windowless room, and the admonition to Pearson that he was in trouble, confinement in the room should be sufficient to constitute an action intending to confine.

B. Did Savings Galore's actions directly or indirectly result in the confinement of Mr. Pearson?

SG would argue that Pearson's confinement was not the direct result of its employees' actions. They would argue that Pearson came voluntarily, of his own free [will], and that he was free to leave at any time. They would also argue that he came with them due to moral pressure, or an attempt to protect his reputation.

However, Pearson would argue that the confinement was due to either threat of physical force or asserted legal authority. The threat of force argument would be that there were three people, all significantly larger than him, standing outside the door or with him in the room at all times. This would be enough to prevent a reasonable person from leaving, due to the threat of being tackled or overpowered. The threat of asserted legal authority was via the detective's statement that P had to come with her, and that he was in "big trouble," which implied trouble with the law. This threat of legal authority should be considered enough to result in P's confinement.

SG may also argue that Pearson was free to leave at any time. If they did not in fact lock the door or intend to hold him, then P's waiting would simply be of his own volition. They would argue that P did not simply try to walk out of there. This argument is unlikely to succeed, again given the circumstances—there were security guards standing around, and they repeatedly told him that he could leave only after giving up the name and address of his roommate, or additionally after signing the release form. They were aware that P considered himself confined, as he repeatedly requested to be allowed to leave, and did not disabuse him of that notion. Additionally, P feared that if he did try to leave, he would be assaulted by the guards. This is probably a reasonable fear considering the disparities in their sizes and their hostile attitudes towards P. Thus, this argument is unlikely to succeed.

SG may also argue that P stayed due to moral pressure and to clear his reputation. According to Rafton, moral pressure is not enough to constitute confinement. In Rafton, the plaintiff testified that she voluntarily accompanied the defendants into a room and stayed there in order to protect her reputation. Additionally, the plaintiff eventually left the room on her own. Rafton can be distinguished here, as Pearson's interview reveals that his accompaniment was not voluntary—he felt like he had no other choice, as leaving "didn't seem like an option." He makes no mention of staying behind to protect his reputation—he thought he had no other choice, and wished to leave during the confinement. He believed that he was not allowed to leave until they had given him the release to sign. His belief is likely reasonable given the circumstances—3 people in the room with him, constantly telling him that they would only let him go after he gave them his friend's name and address, and stating that "if you sign [the release], we'll let you go."

Therefore, it is likely that SG's actions will be found to have directly resulted in P's confinement.

C. <u>Was Mr. Pearson conscious of his confinement or harmed by his confinement</u>?

Pearson's testimony is clear that he was conscious of his confinement and also harmed by it. Pearson stated that he "was pretty scared," was having trouble breathing, and his heart was pounding. He repeatedly told SG employees that "You have no right to do this to me," and that he wished to be let go immediately, showing that he understood he was being confined and wished to be let go. (The harm resulting from his confinement is addressed below.) He, at the very least, clearly understood that he was confined. This factor is likely met.

For these reasons, Pearson should be able to make out a prima facie case of false imprisonment.

III. Identify the injuries incurred by Pearson that would be compensable given these facts

A claim of false imprisonment does not require proof of physical damages—a plaintiff will be entitled to compensation for loss of time, physical discomfort, inconvenience, resulting physical illness or injury (James v. Smitty's). In Smitty's, a child defendant's injuries consisting of nightmares and sleep disturbances for two months were considered sufficient damages to justify compensation under a FI claim.

A. Sleeplessness and nightmares

Here, P's injuries were very similar to the child in Smitty's. P stated that he cannot sleep, that he has nightmares, and that he has consulted a psychiatrist several times despite not having any health insurance. These damages would probably be recoverable.

B. Posttraumatic stress disorder

Additionally, Dr. Romeo stated that the symptoms P suffers from, including low energy/motivation, sleep disorder, loss of concentration, tearfulness, and loss of general interest in previously pleasurable activities, are consistent with posttraumatic stress disorder. Dr. Romeo stated that such symptoms may persist for as long as a year and P does seem to be suffering, and that posttraumatic stress is often created by a stressful or traumatic event. It is likely that the event in question was P's confinement in the store. Dr. Romeo would be willing to sign an affidavit and testify if necessary. Therefore, it is likely that P will be able to recover for his posttraumatic stress.

P also stated that he "could have" had a panic attack or heart failure, and that he was "really scared." These injuries are sufficiently uncertain that he would probably not be able to recover for them.

C. Monetary damages

As stated above, P consulted a psychiatrist for his problems despite not having health insurance. His consultation with the psychiatrist arose directly due to his imprisonment and thus, he would probably be able to recover for the cost of seeing the psychiatrist.

Additionally, P was not allowed to take his food or groceries that had already been purchased for a couple of hundred dollars. The guards kept the food (and P stated that he "lost the money from all the food. Who knows what they did with it"?) P would probably be able to recover the cost of those groceries.

IV. The likelihood of punitive damages given Pearson's situation

Under Peterson v. Zelie, punitive damages are recoverable for false imprisonment when the plaintiff proves by clear and convincing evidence that D is guilty of oppression, fraud, or malice. Under Beau v. Ketchum, the mere use of force is not evidence of oppression, fraud, malice, if the force is only reasonable and necessary for detention.

Here, in order to recover punitive damages, P will have to show that SG acted with fraud, oppression, or malice.

A. Fraud

Fraud is defined as intentional misrepresentation, deceit, or concealment of material facts known to D with the intention of depriving person of legal rights or otherwise causing injury.

Here, there is unlikely to be a showing of fraud. SG's employees did not act to deceive P or misrepresent/conceal a material fact. Though P may have an argument that they knew he was free to leave and did not have any right to keep him there, the fact that they repeatedly told him that he would be free to leave after he did give up his roommate or signed the release could constitute fraud. This is a rather attenuated argument as they never explicitly said that they had the right to hold him, nor did they lie in refusing to let him go after he had signed the release. It is unlikely that P would be able to show fraud.

B. Oppression

Oppression is defined as despicable conduct that subjects P to cruel and unjust hardship in disregard of that person's rights.

Here, P would argue that holding him while knowing he had done nothing wrong is despicable conduct. Although Zelie stated that exercise of a shopkeeper's privilege in detaining a suspect with reasonable cause was not despicable, here it was clear that the SG employees knew P had done nothing wrong. The detective stated that she "didn't care" that P hadn't done anything. The guards repeatedly stated that he would be let go if he gave up his friend show[ing] that they knew P was not at fault and they thus did not have the right to hold him.

P would argue that his confinement for over an hour in a windowless back office, with several security officers surrounding him, was a cruel and unjust hardship. However, although false imprisonment does disregard a person's rights, it may be difficult to argue that confinement of only an hour consists in "cruel and unjust" hardship. P may also argue that the harassment and coercion he faced during that hour, combined with the confinement, should be enough to constitute oppression. However, this would be a difficult argument. A court is unlikely to find any oppression was present.

C. Malice

Malice is defined as conduct intended by D to cause injury to P, or despicable conduct carried on by D with willful/conscious disregard of rights/safety of others.

P may have the most luck with this prong of the argument. The conduct of the security cops showed that they intended to falsely imprison him (which would qualify as an injury). The despicable conduct analysis would be similar to above, but here the despicable conduct must be accompanied by willful and conscious disregard of P's rights. As analyzed above, the guards clearly knew they did not have the right to hold P and were simply threatening him in order to get information about his roommate—they consciously ignored his right to leave (despite his constant pleading) and continued questioning him. This unfair pressure/coercion may rise to the level of despicable conduct with conscious disregard of P's rights.

In the end, P may be able to obtain punitive damages by showing that SG acted with malice via despicable conduct carried on with willful and conscious disregard of his rights, although this would be a difficult argument.

V. Possible defenses that Savings Galore may raise, and an assessment of the likelihood that store would prevail on each defense.

Savings Galore may raise three possible defenses against a claim of false imprisonment. The defenses are the release he signed, voluntariness, and shopkeeper's privilege.

A. Release

Under Gaspard v. American Telco, a release is a complete bar to recovery and comes with a strong presumption of enforceability. If P signed a release, the burden would be shifted to P to attack the release or establish a fact issue in avoidance of it. Releases can be attacked via ambiguity and duress.

Since P did sign the release, he would have to attack it via one of these methods.

1. Ambiguity

A release may be attacked for being ambiguous. In Gaspard, the court held that a release that stated the signor was releasing D from all claims arising from employment with D was an unambiguous release.

Here, P is unlikely to succeed with this argument. The release clearly and ambiguously states that P released SG from all causes of action, including claims of false imprisonment, on account of his detainment. Although P could argue that he did not read the release, he did sign it and therefore has no defense of ambiguity.

2. Duress

Alternatively, P could attack the validity of the release via duress. Duress traditionally required some sort of harm; modern courts have interpreted it to require an overbearing threat that leaves the victim with no reasonable alternative. (Gaspard). This can be shown by demonstrating three elements: 1. a promise made in response to threat (where the promisee created or issued the threat), 2. that the threat was severe enough to reasonably convince the will of the promisor to make promise, and that there were no sufficient alternatives to making the promise, and 3. the threat was improper, not just hard bargaining.

i. Was the promise made in response to a threat where the promisee created the threat

Here, P would argue that the "threat" was continued imprisonment. SG clearly told him that they would let him go if he signed the release, which he did, so the element of the promise made in response to a threat is met. The threat of imprisonment was also created by SG, since they were the ones who held him in the first place.

ii. Was the threat severe enough to reasonably convince the will of the promisor to make promise to make promise, and were there any sufficient alternatives?

P would argue that the threat was severe enough to make him sign the release. He would argue that he had been there over an hour, had been constantly questioned and harassed, and did not know when he would be let go. P was also extremely anxious and earlier had had trouble breathing. P could argue that the prospect of continued imprisonment was severe enough to convince him to sign the release, and, as he stated, he "would have signed it no matter what it said."

Additionally, no one besides his roommate (who was not going to come to his aid) knew he was there, so he had no alternative since no one else would come looking for him. His only options were to sign the release or wait for SG to release him. It should not be considered an "alternative" to have to rely on the person creating or making the threat and demanding the promise to provide a better option. Therefore, this prong was likely met.

iii Was the threat improper and not just hard bargaining?

Here, the question is whether the threat (of continued imprisonment) was improper or just "hard bargaining." According to the Restatement (2d) of Contracts, a threat is improper if it threatens a crime or tort. Additionally, a threat is improper if the resulting exchange is not on fair terms, and either the threatened act would harm the recipient and would not significantly benefit the threatening party, or what is threatened is a use of power for illegitimate ends.

Here, the threat was the threat of continued false imprisonment, which is an improper tort. While SG might argue that they never actually threatened to hold him further if he did not sign, they did state that they would let P go if he did sign the release. P's options were therefore to continue his imprisonment and hope that they would release him later, or just sign the release. This is not truly a "choice" made by anyone with free will. Given the totality of the circumstances, including his previous confinement for over an hour, P would likely be able to show that this threat was improper.

Additionally, P could argue that the exchange was not on fair terms. Here, his part of the bargain was to sign a release that gave up his legal right to sue for a wrongful tort. SG's side of the bargain was simply to give up someone who had done nothing wrong and they clearly could not gain any information from. SG had no benefit (or right) to continue keeping P confined, since he was refusing to give any information about his roommate. Therefore, giving up this nonexistent right/benefit in exchange for a waiver of a legal right is an unbalanced bargain. Furthermore, this is a use of SG's power for illegitimate ends, as they held him in their custody and threatened to continue the false imprisonment if he did not sign.

In the end, P will probably be able to show that the release is invalid because it was a result of duress (a threat by D that left P with no reasonable alternatives).

B. Voluntariness

SG may also raise a defense of P's voluntary acquiescence to the confinement. Although this is not a defense per se and rather goes to one of the elements of the claim, it may still be a valid argument. SG would argue that P accompanied the guard of his own free will, remained in the room despite it not being locked and being free to leave, or stayed there out of a sense of moral pressure (Rafton).

As addressed above, these arguments are unlikely to succeed given the circumstances of the confinement (threats of legal action, confinement in a small room, 3 guards standing around, harassment, etc.) Please see the above analysis distinguishing Rafton from the instant case.

C. Shopkeeper's Privilege

Lastly, SG may assert the "shopkeeper's privilege" in S.13–1 of the Columbia Penal Code. 13–1 provides that merchant (and its agents/employees) may, with reasonable cause, detain persons suspected of shoplifting in a reasonable manner and for a reasonable time, for questioning or summoning a law enforcement officer. A shoplifter is defined as someone who knowingly obtains the goods of another with the intent to deprive the other of the goods, by removing goods from the establishment without paying, or by concealment. The Code further provides that reasonable cause is a defense to civil action against a merchant (agent/employee) for false imprisonment.

It is difficult for SG to argue that it had reasonable cause to detain P. The detective's statement, upon being told that P had not done anything, was that she "didn't care." The actions of the guards in pressuring P to give up his friend, and their repeated claims that P would be free to go as long as he gave up his friend (who they said was "not much of a friend" since he had abandoned P), all go to show that the guards did not reasonably believe that P was the one who had shoplifted. Rather, they were detaining him because his friend was unavailable.

SG may argue that P knew that his friend had shoplifted, and thus P assisted in the shoplifting. However, James v. Smitty's is directly on point here. In Smitty's, a friend of the Defendant, who was vaguely aware that an item had been placed in the shopping cart and was not paid for, but had not seen the item being hidden, was detained. The court found that the friend was wrongfully detained, since the defendant "had no basis to believe [friend] had shoplifted or assisted. . .in any way." Furthermore, the court held that "A merchant does not have immunity to detain a companion of a suspected shoplifter unless the store has reasonable cause to believe that the companion was involved in the illegal activity."

Here, P was not involved in taking the cashews or consuming them, nor in leaving without paying. He was also not involved in taking or concealing the garden gloves. Although SG may argue that P did believe that his roommate stole things from time to time, in this case the detective clearly did not have reasonable cause to believe that P was involved in the shoplifting, as she stated that she "didn't care" that he had done nothing wrong and continuously pressured him to give up his roommate [or] rather pressure him to admit to being involved in the shoplifting. Therefore, this defense is unlikely to succeed.

PEOPLE v. DUNCAN

INSTRUCTIONS

1. You will have three hours to complete this session of the examination. This performance test is designed to evaluate your ability to handle a select number of legal authorities in the context of a factual problem involving a client.
2. The problem is set in the fictional State of Columbia, one of the United States.
3. You will have two sets of materials with which to work: a File and a Library.
6. The File contains factual materials about your case. The first document is a memorandum containing the instructions for the tasks you are to complete.
7. The Library contains the legal authorities needed to complete the tasks. The case reports may be real, modified, or written solely for the purpose of this performance test. If the cases appear familiar to you, do not assume that they are precisely the same as you have read before. Read each thoroughly, as if it were new to you. You should assume that cases were decided in the jurisdictions and on the dates shown. In citing cases from the Library, you may use abbreviations and omit page citations.

6. You should concentrate on the materials provided, but you should also bring to bear on the problem your general knowledge of the law. What you have learned in law school and elsewhere provides the general background for analyzing the problem; the File and Library provide the specific materials with which you must work.
7. Although there are no restrictions on how you apportion your time, you should probably allocate at least 90 minutes to reading and organizing before you begin preparing your response.
8. Your response will be graded on its compliance with instructions and on its content, thoroughness, and organization.

Warren County Prosecutor Alicia Ouelette,
District Attorney Averil Park, Columbia

MEMORANDUM

To:	Applicant
From:	Laurie Shanks, Deputy District Attorney
Date:	July 31, 2008
Re:	**People v. Duncan**

We have indicted Raymond Duncan for the murder of Jennifer Clark. Mr. Duncan confessed to police detectives during an interview at the Averil Park police station. The interview was tape-recorded. We have, of course, turned the recording and transcript of the interview over to defense counsel. Defense counsel has filed a Notice of Motion to Suppress Evidence, seeking to suppress evidence of all statements made during the interview. We will oppose that motion. The defendant has ten days after filing his notice of motion to suppress to file the actual motion and accompanying Memorandum of Points and Authorities. I, however, want you to start work on our reply immediately. Please prepare a draft of a persuasive Memorandum of Points and Authorities that argues the motion should be denied.

Arguments on motions to suppress require a detailed showing of how the facts in the case relate to specific factors identified by the courts in suppression cases. Therefore, your memorandum should relate specific facts to those specific factors and conclude how your analysis would establish that the evidence should not be suppressed. Where appropriate, explain how the defendant's version of the facts is not credible. Finally, take care to anticipate arguments defense counsel is likely to make and explain why they are not persuasive. Your memorandum should dispense with a statement of facts. I will draft the statement of facts later.

EXCERPTS OF INTERVIEW OF RAYMOND DUNCAN BY DETECTIVES TIMOTHY JAMES AND GREGORY MANDEL

Detective Timothy James ("James"): Mr. Duncan, it is now 12:25 p.m. on January 2, 2008, and you are here in the Averil Park police station with me, Detective Timothy James, and Detective Gregory Mandel. Is that correct?

Raymond Duncan ("Duncan"): Yes.

James: This interview is being tape-recorded. Is that okay with you?

Duncan: Sure.

James: How old are you, Mr. Duncan?

Duncan: 24.

James: Did you know Jennifer Clark?

Duncan: Yes. I met Jennifer in high school, but I didn't see her after she graduated. Last year, Jennifer and I reconnected through mutual friends.

James: Were you good friends?

Duncan: Sure.

James: How good a friend were you? I mean, did you have a key to her apartment?

Duncan: No. I mean we saw each other occasionally. She allowed me to borrow her car three or four times. I don't have a key to either her apartment or her car.

James: When did you last have contact with Jennifer?

Duncan: It was probably between 10:00 p.m. and 11:00 p.m. on Wednesday, December 20. Jennifer picked me up and left me at her apartment. Jennifer said her rent was due and she had to go somewhere and do something.

James: Were you still at her apartment when she returned?

Duncan: She returned about six hours later, around 4:00 a.m. on December 21.

James: What did the two of you do then?

Duncan: We watched television in the living room. I stayed until maybe 9:00 a.m., when she asked if I wanted to go home because someone was coming over.

James: Who was coming over?

Duncan: She didn't say who it was.

James: Did she drive you home?

Duncan: No. I borrowed her car and left. Jennifer told me to call her in a couple of hours.

James: Did she walk you to the door?

Duncan: Yes.

James: Did she lock the door behind you?

Duncan: She always locked the door. It's not the best neighborhood.

James: Did you see her after that?

Duncan: No.

James: What was Jennifer wearing when you left?

Duncan: She was wearing a short-sleeve, white T-shirt, and light-colored shorts.

James: Did you try calling her like she asked you to?

Duncan: Sure. I drove home in Jennifer's car and took a shower. I called Jennifer's cell and home telephones at least twice between 10:30 a.m. and 12:15 p.m., but there was no answer. Around 1:00 p.m. or 2:00 p.m., I drove to a friend's house and tried to reach Jennifer. Later I went to Pat Kinnikin's house and again tried to reach Jennifer but was unsuccessful. So, Pat and I went to a restaurant later that evening.

James: Did you try to contact her again?

Duncan: Between 6:00 p.m. and 7:00 p.m. we left the restaurant to return Jennifer's car, and Pat followed in his car. We drove to Jennifer's apartment and I parked her car. I hid the key inside the car like the other times I borrowed it.

James: You didn't knock on her door?

Duncan: No. She hadn't been answering the telephone. She did that sometimes. I assumed she wanted to be left alone.

James: When did you find out Jennifer was dead?

Duncan: The next day. I saw it on the news.

James: Mr. Duncan, I'm going to ask you some direct questions and I want you to give me direct answers. And, you need to realize what I'm looking for. I need to establish that what other people told me is credible and I'm also looking to see how truthful you are with me in our conversations here, okay?

Duncan: Sure.

James: Why didn't you contact the police after you learned she was dead?

Duncan: Look, I don't have a clean record. Besides, my fingerprints were probably everywhere around her apartment and car and I figured the police would contact me. And see, that's what happened. You came to my apartment, left a message. I called you back and agreed to come down to this interview. I don't have anything to hide, but let's be real, I have a record.

James: Did you stab Jennifer?

Duncan: No.

James: Did you mess with any windows in her apartment?

Duncan: No.

James: Were you on the patio or did you use the sliding glass door during your last visit? Would your fingerprints be out on the patio?

Duncan: I didn't use the patio the last time I was there.

James: Are you sure?

Duncan: Uh, I think I'd know, unless I—unless—unless I just peeked out there. But I wasn't out there for a second or two if I was.

James: That's interesting. I talked to the people who live in the apartment complex, and so you're sure?

Duncan: Well, I could have stepped out on the patio. I may have even stuck my head out and looked. I might have, you know. But, I left out of the front door, and she locked the door behind me, and I went to the car.

James: That's a little more in line with what we're hearing, that you were on that patio. Two people were pretty darn sure you left from the patio.

Duncan: Not true. I left through the front door.

James: Who killed Jennifer?

Duncan: I don't know. I don't have a clue.

Detective Gregory Mandel ("Mandel"): I have to tell you, Mr. Duncan, I still am stuck on why you didn't call the police when you found out what happened.

James: Let's cut to the chase. We've talked to a lot of people and you need to be honest because we need to put this thing to an end. If you'd like to tell us that?

Duncan: What do you want to know?

James: I want to know what happened with Jennifer.

Duncan: I swear I don't know what happened with Jennifer.

James: Raymond, Raymond. We're past that, dude. We're way past that. You know what I mean? Would you like to tell me what happened? I know this is bugging you, man.

Duncan: I don't know what happened.

James: You know what happened to her. We already know what happened.

Duncan: Okay, what happened then?

James: Ray. There's no doubt in my mind that you did this to her. You know what I'm talking about. Don't put yourself in a position anymore where you have to lie. Okay? We just need to put a closure to this thing. You know what I mean. If there's a reason, there's a reason. But you need to let us know what that reason was.

Duncan: I have no reason for it, because I didn't do it.

James: Ray, Ray.

Duncan: Yes.

James: Take a deep breath. Okay. Tell me what happened.

Mandel: You made mention of the. . . .

James: Hold on a second. . . .

Duncan: Do you mind if I have a glass of water?

James: Sure.

Duncan: Thanks.

James: Ray, you've got to help us here. Tell us what happened. I have to say, what you've told us so far just doesn't fit with the evidence. Not just the witnesses, either.

Mandel: Come on, Ray. Jennifer's family needs to know. You've got to realize this is tearing them apart.

James: We've got physical evidence and witness statements. Now's the time to tell your side of the story.

Duncan: I've told you my side of the story. I wasn't there. Jennifer was my friend. I had no reason to kill her, and I didn't kill her.

Mandel: I have to say, Ray, all our information points to you. Your story doesn't quite add up and you need to clear the air because I understand it was probably not planned.

Duncan: I can't explain what happened because I don't know.

James: Well, I'll tell you how you can explain it, Ray, because when she died you were there. And I can establish that based on your own statements about the times you were there, coupled with scientific facts establishing the time and cause of death.

Duncan: I'm telling the truth. I wasn't there. I didn't do it.

James: There's no doubt in my mind, Ray, you did it, and I can prove it. The problem here is that you, for no reason, other than maybe fear, are painting yourself into a corner. You're putting yourself in a position where you're having to justify the time of death.

Duncan: Not true.

James: Here's what I think, Ray. You were angry with Jennifer because she slept with another guy that night.

Duncan: I don't know about what she did with other guys.

James: We have no doubt what happened. Ray, she was killed by somebody in that apartment that knew her. That apartment told us a lot of stuff, Ray. You go to church, Ray?

Duncan: Yes. Sometimes.

James: You know then, you've got to be forthright with this thing.

Duncan: I have been.

James: You didn't approve of Jennifer's lifestyle, did you?

Duncan: I don't judge people.

James: Let's go back to the time line.

* * * * *

James: But you did go out on the patio, didn't you?

Duncan: Okay. I unlocked the living room's sliding glass door and went to the patio. But I went back inside and locked the door.

James: See, Ray, this is what I figure. The killer must have been inside the apartment for a while because you had been there, alone, for nine hours on Wednesday evening until Jennifer returned at 4:00 a.m. on Thursday. Jennifer slept on the couch while you watched television until 9:00 a.m. You went out to the patio to look for her car, returned inside and locked the patio door. You said Jennifer locked the front door when you left. Jennifer was killed when she was asleep on the sofa, so how did the killer get inside the apartment with all the doors locked?

Duncan: That's your problem. Maybe someone could have come over after I left with her car.

James: There's no way anyone came over. Look, Ray, this doesn't appear to be a first-degree murder, but it wasn't a random crime. Looks more like a heat of passion kind of thing. And, I have to tell you, everything points to you, Ray, and you know, again, I'm still sitting right here, trying to appeal to you and your sense of fairness.

Duncan: I didn't do it.

James: I'm going to tip my hand on one thing. Okay? I can put you on that patio. I can put you exiting that way. All right? I need you to give me a justification for going out that way instead of going out the front door. Otherwise, your story doesn't hold water.

Mandel: You need to know, Ray, Jennifer's neighbor was always sitting there watching people come and go. Why did you go out the patio and over that fence on the back porch? Why did you leave that way?

Duncan: Didn't I explain to you that I had entered that way, too?

James: Well, Ray, no you didn't. Explain it to us; put the cards on the table for us, man.

Duncan: I jumped over the balcony and I tapped on the window, and I jumped back over because nobody answered. And that was that morning after I had gone to the car. I went back for something. She didn't answer the door. I didn't have the house key. All I had was the car key. And, I knocked and she didn't answer, and I jumped over the balcony, and then knocked on the glass door, and nobody answered so I jumped back over and I left. I didn't go back into the apartment.

Mandel: Well, the neighbors said something else, so I guess we're still not on the same page. You need some more water?

Duncan: Please.

Mandel: Okay, let me get it for you. . . . Here, now, let's just sit back and relax for a minute and give this some thought.

Duncan: Can I get a cigarette?

Mandel: We can't smoke in the building, but, hey, let's get some coffee and go sit on the rooftop courtyard for that cigarette. Let me go and check it out.

James: Mandel is a good guy, but more direct than I am. We need to solve this thing.

Duncan: I'll tell you, when I offered to come in for questioning, I felt it wouldn't be too bad, but oh boy!

James: Well, it's a far cry from how it was in the 60's and 70's, where they used to have a bunch of guys yelling at you, threatening and deprivation. Things have changed over the years. You know, we're just doing our job and we won't start yelling at you.

Mandel: I'm back; here's the coffee. You know, I've been thinking about your story about jumping over the balcony and tapping on the window. It doesn't make sense, because Jennifer would have been dead already, and the sliding glass door would have been unlocked. A reasonable person would have tried the door when there was no answer. Did you walk into the apartment when Jennifer was already dead?

Duncan: No. You know what's so bad about this? It's that you guys are saying I did it, and it doesn't matter what I say. Did the neighbors see anyone else at the apartment?

Mandel: We showed your picture at the apartment complex and people have already picked you out. But look, I might be able to understand. Maybe you had to defend yourself if Jennifer's methamphetamine use made her paranoid. You know, that crank can make you crazy. What happened? She tweaked and went nuts?

James: And, I have to say, your story that you jumped over the balcony, knocked on the window, and left wasn't entirely true.

Duncan: I just have the strong feeling that. . . . If you guys want it to be me, it's going to be me. I don't know what happened.

Mandel: You might not have meant it to happen; it just might be something ticked you off, something got you upset. But, it happened. I'm aware of that, and the only thing I can say is, man, it's going to torment you, and it's going to bug you, and it's going to cause you untold anguish like it's doing to her family right now. I know it's been bugging you. I could tell when I saw your face when you opened that front door earlier today.

Duncan: I did not do it. Can I have some fresh air, please?

Mandel: Sure. It is now 3:30 p.m. and we are stopping the tape recorder.

* * * * *

Mandel: Okay, it is now 3:50 p.m. We've taken a 20-minute break and in the room are myself, Detective Mandel, Detective James, and Ray Duncan.

James: Need some water?

Duncan: No, I just want to get this over with.

James: I think it's almost over. I want to compliment you on how polite you have been in this interview. If you just opened up, the hard part would be over. We know what happened. Did Jennifer do something to get you upset? Give me something.

Duncan: I didn't do it.

* * * * *

James: Look, Ray, we've been at this for hours. We know you did it. We know it. I told you that scene spoke volumes. And it wasn't the scene of a cold-blooded killer. It wasn't that kind of a crazed scene.

Mandel: We're way beyond you not having anything to do with her death. We can place you at the crime scene at the time that she was killed. We have witness statements placing you there. On top of that, you finally have admitted to jumping over that balcony on that patio.

Duncan: I was at the apartment but she wasn't dead and I didn't stab her. I didn't leave through the sliding glass door. I just jumped over the balcony and tapped the glass.

James: There were only two possibilities: either you killed her or you went back into the apartment and saw her dead.

Duncan: Yes. Okay, but I don't know what happened. I entered her apartment through the sliding glass door and saw her lying on the couch. Jennifer was covered by a blanket, she was lying on her stomach and facing the cushions, her right hand was by her face, and there was a bunch of blood. I didn't see any wounds but the blood was just like soaked into the couch. I didn't touch anything. I left through the patio, closed the sliding glass door, and drove Jennifer's car back to my place.

Mandel: When was this?

Duncan: Between 8:30 a.m. and 9:00 a.m. on Thursday, December 21.

Mandel: Did you really spend Wednesday night at her apartment?

Duncan: I spent the night on Wednesday, and left around 4:00 a.m. on Thursday. I walked out through the front door. I took Jennifer's car, drove to my place, and then went to a friend's house. I returned to Jennifer's apartment between 8:30 a.m. and 9:00 a.m. Jennifer didn't answer and the front door was locked, so I entered through the sliding glass door. I left through the sliding glass door and jumped over the patio balcony. I used Jennifer's car to leave.

Mandel: Did you tell anyone what you saw?

Duncan: No.

James: Why did you call Jennifer's house later that day, even though you knew she was dead?

Duncan: So the police wouldn't suspect me.

Mandel: Why would we suspect you?

Duncan: I was the only one that was there around that time, and I knew that, like I told you before, that I had touched everything.

Mandel: Let's take a break. It's currently 5:15 p.m. and we are turning off the tape recorder.

* * * * *

James: Okay, we are back from our break. It is 5:35 p.m. and Detective Mandel, Raymond Duncan, and I, Detective James, are back in the interview room. Okay, let's finish this up. You killed your friend. Why?

Duncan: Look, I've got a question.

Mandel: Go ahead, ask.

Duncan: I halfway know the answer already. Are you guys going to go ahead and process me, or what are you going to do with me? I appreciate the fact that you guys have been patient with me. What are you guys going to do? I mean, are you guys going to process me, or what? I don't want to go to jail. I didn't stab her. But if you guys are going to process me and say that I did, why don't you just go ahead and do it?

James: What would you like us to book you for?

Duncan: I don't know. 'Cause you guys say I did this murder.

James: Well, I'll tell you what we've done. I think what we've established at this point, Ray, is that you saw your friend in her apartment, stabbed, okay, because you at least established that.

Mandel: You need to get this off your chest. Did you use crank with Jennifer on Wednesday night?

Duncan: We had been smoking crank. Listen, guys, I'm getting scared now.

James: Do you still want to talk to us? To tell us about the crank?

Duncan: Sure, I'll talk. I used a substantial amount of crank with Jennifer that night.

James: What were you thinking, Ray, when you were using the crank?

Duncan: I don't know, man. All of the drugs—I don't know.

James: Was it the crank, Ray? Is that what made you do it?

Duncan: Look, okay, Jennifer was arguing with me when it happened.

James: Were you trying to have sex with her, Ray? Were you trying to rape her?

Duncan: No.

James: But you stabbed her, didn't you Ray?

Duncan: Okay, okay. I don't remember stabbing her, but we argued.

James: Tell us what you remember, Ray.

Duncan: We were near the couch and I stood up. I remember us arguing. I remember standing up, and I remember seeing a knife with blood and then leaving. I left through the sliding glass door to throw off the police. I drove away in Jennifer's car and threw away the knife in a trash can.

James: Where'd you get the knife?

Duncan: I probably got the knife from the kitchen counter.

James: Why 30 times, man? She had to be screaming.

Duncan: No, no. All she did was ask what I was going to do, but she didn't scream.

James: Why 30 times?

Duncan: It was more than once, but not 30 times.

James: I think it's time we read you your rights, Ray. Now, Ray, you have the right to remain silent. Anything you say can and will be used against you in court. You have the right to the presence of a lawyer. If you can't afford a lawyer, one will be provided at no cost. Do you understand these rights, Ray?

Mandel: Ray, you are under arrest for the murder of Jennifer Clark. We may as well turn off the tape recorder. It's 6:03 p.m.

END OF TRANSCRIPT

IN THE SUPERIOR COURT OF THE STATE OF COLUMBIA
IN AND FOR THE COUNTY OF WARREN

People of the State of Columbia	)	
	)	
	)	Criminal Division
v.	)	
	)	2008–2341
	)	
Raymond Duncan	)	
______________________________	)	

NOTICE OF MOTION TO SUPPRESS EVIDENCE

PLEASE TAKE NOTICE that upon the annexed affidavit of Raymond Duncan, defendant, and upon all the previous papers and proceedings in this matter, the undersigned will move this Court at the Courthouse located at 1435 Elm Street, Averil Park, Columbia, on August 7, 2008, at 9:00 a.m. or as soon thereafter as counsel can be heard, for an order:

1. Suppressing evidence of all statements made by defendant to the police during an interview conducted on January 2, 2008, as obtained in violation of *Miranda v. Arizona*; and

2. For such other and further relief as to the Court may deem just and proper.

Dated: July 30, 2008

Mary Lynch

Mary Lynch
Attorney for Defendant

IN THE SUPERIOR COURT OF THE STATE OF COLUMBIA
IN AND FOR THE COUNTY OF WARREN

People of the State of Columbia	)	
	)	
	)	Criminal Division
v.	)	
	)	2008–2341
	)	
Raymond Duncan	)	
	)	

DEFENDANT'S AFFIDAVIT IN SUPPORT OF MOTION TO SUPPRESS EVIDENCE

I, Raymond Duncan, being duly sworn, state:

1. I am the defendant in the above-entitled action.

2. At approximately 12:30 p.m. on January 2, 2008, I was arrested and taken into custody at the Averil Park Police Station by Detectives Timothy James and Gregory Mandel ("James" and "Mandel," respectively).

3. Detectives James and Mandel never attempted to question me at my home.

4. Detectives James and Mandel never told me I could have refused to go to the police station.

5. Once I arrived at the police station, Detective James or Mandel never told me I could leave.

6. I was placed in a small interrogation room that unlocked only from the outside.

7. I spent five hours being questioned by the two detectives.

8. Detective James accompanied me on two cigarette breaks and never left me . . .alone.

9. Detectives James and Mandel repeatedly accused me of killing Jennifer Clark.

10. Detectives James and Mandel communicated their subjective belief that I was the killer and made it objectively reasonable for me to believe I was not going to leave the police station.

11. During the course of this interrogation one or both of the detectives informed me repeatedly that it was to my advantage to cooperate with them.

12. During the course of the interrogation I was told of several items of evidence, including eyewitnesses and forensic evidence, which allegedly constituted evidence against me, and was told by my interrogators that it was useless for me to deny my guilt in the face of such evidence.

13. Finally, after a total of approximately six hours of interrogation I was placed in handcuffs, left alone in the locked interrogation room for approximately one hour and then transported to the city jail.

14. It was after more than five hours of interrogation that I was advised that anything I said might be used in evidence

against me, that I was not required to make a statement, that I had a right to the assistance of counsel, or that if I could not afford counsel, one would be appointed for me without charge.

Raymond Duncan

Raymond Duncan

Subscribed and sworn to before me on July 30, 2008.

Guido Zanani

Notary Public

TRANSCRIPT OF INTERVIEW OF DETECTIVE TIMOTHY JAMES

BY LAURIE SHANKS

Laurie Shanks ("Shanks"): Thank you for coming in, Detective James. As I said on the phone, Ray Duncan's attorney has requested a hearing seeking to exclude the statements her client made to you during your interrogation. We need to prepare for hearing. You're obviously likely to be called, so I wanted to go through your version of the interview. I have reviewed the transcript, but I have a few questions.

Timothy James ("James"): Fine.

Shanks: I'll be tape-recording this so I can refer to it for that preparation. First, how did Duncan come to be at the police station?

James: Well, the fact is he came down on his own.

Shanks: Did he just show up at the station?

James: No. We had been out to his apartment a couple of times and he wasn't there. We called a couple of times and left messages. And, apparently knowing we were looking for him, he called me and left a message saying when he would be home. Detective Mandel and I went out to his apartment and he invited us in. About the time we told him we were investigating Jennifer's death, we got a call from a crime scene and had to leave. He told us he would wait.

Shanks: When was this?

James: About 11:00 a.m., January 2. The call turned out to be nothing, so we went back to the apartment. We got there about 11:30, maybe 11:45.

Shanks: Then what happened?

James: Again, we told him we were investigating Jennifer's death and that he was one of several people we wanted to talk to because her cell phone indicated she had talked to him the day she was murdered. We asked if we could talk to him at his place, but he suggested that it would be better for him if we met him at the police station.

Shanks: Did he indicate why he'd rather be at the police station?

James: Not really. I just assumed he might be concerned about the neighbors, or maybe he didn't want the police there if someone stopped by.

Shanks: So what did you do?

James: He said he didn't have a car and asked if we would give him a lift, so we drove him down to the station.

Shanks: What kind of car were you in?

James: An unmarked sedan.

Shanks: Where did he sit on the ride to the station?

James: The front seat.

Shanks: Was he handcuffed?

James: No.

Shanks: What were you guys wearing?

James: No uniforms. We were both in business suits.

Shanks: Did either of you ever display your guns?

James: No.

Shanks: During the drive to the police station, what did you talk about?

James: Small talk mostly, but I did advise him that he was going to a voluntary interview and he was free to leave at any time.

Shanks: When did you arrive at the station?

James: About noon. I got a phone call just as we arrived at the station, so we had him sit there in the reception area for about half an hour.

Shanks: When you interviewed Duncan, was he a suspect in Jennifer's death?

James: He was a subject, like everyone we had talked to.

Shanks: Did you say suspect or subject?

James: He was a subject. He was not suspected of doing anything wrong. We wanted to determine if he had any helpful information about the case.

Shanks: Why did you and Detective Mandel not advise Duncan of his *Miranda* rights at the beginning of the interview?

James: Like I said, he was not a suspect, he had not been linked to the murder, there were no independent witnesses, and there was no evidence he had been at the scene. The evidence was developed from Duncan himself during the interview.

Shanks: Did it become apparent to you during the interview that he was being caught in inconsistencies in what he was telling you happened on the day Jennifer was killed?

James: As you can see from the transcript, it became evident that there were several inconsistent statements he was making during the interview.

Shanks: At any time did he ask to leave?

James: After he was inside the interview room, he could have told us he was going to leave and walked out of the police department without talking to anyone. The complete interview lasted about five hours, but he never asked to leave.

Shanks: Was the interview room locked?

James: No, the room doesn't lock. We interview all kinds of people in there. There's no real need to lock the room. If a person was in custody, he'd either be in handcuffs, or there are these rings bolted in the floor and we would chain him to the rings.

Shanks: Tell me about the breaks you took.

James: He asked for water and it was provided for him. We took two cigarette breaks during the interview. The first break occurred when Duncan asked for a cigarette and some fresh air. There is no smoking in the police department building, so we decided to take a break outside and we went up on the roof, which is the building's designated smoking area for employees. It's got a gazebo.

Shanks: Did Duncan have any cigarettes?

James: No. We got one from another officer.

Shanks: Did you stay with him during the break?

James: Yes.

Shanks: Why did you stay with him?

James: No real reason other than the fact that I was just out there. I had given him the cigarette and, you know, I knew he didn't know the way to the smoking area. Also, there are some security concerns. You don't want the general public wandering around the station. Doesn't happen often, but you can imagine what would happen if someone under arrest got violent and someone just happened to walk by and got injured.

Shanks: What did you talk about during the break?

James: Nothing much. He asked if he was under arrest and I repeatedly told him that he was not under arrest and that he was free to leave.

Shanks: Did Duncan ever ask to leave?

James: He never asked to leave and he never tried to leave.

Shanks: Was he handcuffed while on the break?

James: He was not handcuffed or restrained in any way on the trip to or from the roof.

Shanks: You took a second cigarette break later. Was he handcuffed then?

James: No.

Shanks: Did you go with him to the roof?

James: Yes.

Shanks: How long was that break?

James: Like the first, maybe 20 minutes—the length of the time it took to walk and get the cigarette and allow him to smoke the cigarette. We didn't rush the breaks.

Shanks: And, at any time during the breaks, did he tell you that he wanted to leave?

James: No.

Shanks: Did he ask if he could leave?

James: He never made that request.

Shanks: What did you say when he finished his cigarette? I mean, did you say, "Are you ready to go back now?" Or do you recall what you would say in that regard?

James: Well, right before we actually walked out of the gazebo we would ask, "Are you ready to go back and talk some more?"

Shanks: And what did he answer you?

James: I don't recall the specific answer, but I know that the response was affirmative.

Shanks: Now, you interviewed other people as part of your investigation. Were they questioned in the same manner as Duncan? Did you confront other individuals with the accusation that you knew they killed the victim?

James: I interviewed three others before I talked to Duncan. I asked each of them whether they killed Jennifer and if they had anything to do with her murder. These three were also subjects rather than suspects.

Shanks: Did any of these other three interviews last five hours?

James: No, but one might have been for three hours. In fact, I think it was Brandy Gentry. I conducted an interview at the police department that lasted several hours. She made obscene remarks during the interview, and I became more aggressive and accused her of killing Jennifer. She was interviewed in the same room, and she got up, said the interview was over, and left the police station.

Shanks: Was Duncan ever left alone at any point in the interview?

James: No.

Shanks: Could someone have entered the police station and walked to the second floor interview room without interference by any officers?

James: Sure, a person could walk into the station and take the elevator to the second floor, and go to the interview room without being stopped. But, witnesses or suspects are usually accompanied by an officer to protect the integrity of the department's internal security.

Shanks: After Duncan was placed in the interview room, if he had decided to leave, could he have said, "Excuse me, gentlemen, I think I'm going to leave now?"

James: Yes.

Shanks: You know that technique you used with Duncan where you and Detective Mandel told him repeatedly that you knew he committed the crime, you had the evidence to prove it, and you just want to know why, and when he denied doing it you repeated the accusations? Did you use that technique with Gentry or any other person?

James: Yes. I specifically asked Gentry if she committed the crime and accused her of lying, but I never told her there was no doubt in my mind that she killed Jennifer.

Shanks: So, to be clear, was Duncan physically restrained in any way prior to his arrest?

James: He was arrested at 6:03 p.m., when the interview concluded, and he was handcuffed and chained to the bolt in the floor. Up to that point he was not restrained.

Shanks: Thank you, Detective. I think that will do for now.

STATE OF OREGON V. MATHIASON

United States Supreme Court (1977)

Carl Mathiason was convicted of first-degree burglary after a bench trial in which his confession was critical to the State's case. At trial he moved to suppress the confession as the fruit of questioning by the police was not preceded by the warnings required in *Miranda v. Arizona* (U.S. S.Ct., 1966). The trial court refused to exclude the confession because it found that Mathiason was not in custody at the time of the confession.

The Oregon Supreme Court reversed the conviction. It found that although Mathiason had not been arrested or otherwise formally detained, the interrogation occurred in a coercive environment of the sort to which *Miranda* was intended to apply. We think that the Oregon court has read *Miranda* too broadly, and we therefore reverse its judgment.

The facts are straightforward. An officer of the Oregon State Police investigated a theft at a residence near Pendleton. The officer asked the lady of the house which had been burglarized if she suspected anyone. She replied that Mathiason was the only one she could think of. Mathiason was a parolee and a "close associate" of her son. The officer tried to contact Mathiason on three or four occasions with no success. Finally, about 25 days after the burglary, the officer left his card at Mathiason's apartment with a note asking him to call because he'd like to discuss something with him. The next afternoon Mathiason did call. The officer asked where it would be convenient to meet. Mathiason had no preference, so the officer asked if Mathiason could meet him at the State Police patrol office in about an hour and a half, about 5:00 p.m. The patrol office was about two blocks from Mathiason's apartment. The building housed several state agencies.

The officer met Mathiason in the hallway, shook hands and took him into an office. Mathiason was told he was not under arrest. The door was closed. The two sat facing each other across a desk. The police radio in another room could be heard. The officer told Mathiason he wanted to talk to him about a burglary and that his truthfulness would possibly be considered by the district attorney or judge. The officer further advised him that the police believed Mathiason was involved in the burglary and (falsely stated that) Mathiason's fingerprints were found at the scene. Mathiason sat for a few minutes and then said he had taken the property. This occurred within five minutes after Mathiason had come to the office. The officer then advised Mathiason of his *Miranda* rights and took a taped confession.

At the end of the taped conversation the officer told Mathiason he was not arresting him at this time; he was released to go about his job and return to his family. The officer said he was referring the case to the district attorney for him to determine whether criminal charges would be brought. It was 5:30 p.m. when Mathiason left the office.

The Oregon Supreme Court reasoned from these facts that the interrogation took place in a "coercive environment." The parties were in the offices of the State Police; they were alone behind closed doors; the officer informed Mathiason he was a suspect in a theft and the authorities had evidence incriminating him in the crime; and Mathiason was a parolee under supervision. We are of the opinion that this evidence is overcome by the evidence that Mathiason came to the office in response to a request and was told he was not under arrest.

Our decision in *Miranda* sets forth rules of police procedure applicable to custodial interrogation. By custodial interrogation, we mean questioning initiated by law enforcement officers after a person has been taken into custody or otherwise deprived of his freedom of action in any significant way. Subsequently we have found the *Miranda* principle applicable to questioning that takes place in a prison setting during a suspect's term of imprisonment on a separate offense, *Mathis v. United States* (U.S. S.Ct., 1968), and to questioning taking place in a suspect's home, after he has been arrested and is no longer free to go where he pleases. *Orozco v. Texas* (U.S. S.Ct., 1969).

In the present case, however, there is no indication that the questioning took place in a context where Mathiason's freedom to depart was restricted in any way. He came voluntarily to the police station, where he was immediately informed that he was not under arrest. At the close of a 1/2-hour interview, Mathiason did in fact leave the police station without hindrance. It is clear from these facts that Mathiason was not in custody or otherwise deprived of his freedom of action in any significant way.

Such a noncustodial situation does not become one where *Miranda* applies simply because a reviewing court concludes that, even in the absence of any formal arrest or restraint on freedom of movement, the questioning occurred in a coercive environment. Any interview of one suspected of a crime by police will have coercive aspects to it, simply by virtue of the fact that the policeman is part of a law enforcement system that may ultimately cause the suspect to be charged with a crime. But the police are not required to administer *Miranda* warnings to everyone whom they question. Nor is the requirement of warnings to be imposed simply because the questioning takes place in the station house, or because the questioned person is one whom the police suspect. *Miranda* warnings are required only where there has been such a restriction on a person's freedom as to render him in custody. It was that sort of coercive environment to which *Miranda* by its terms was made applicable, and to which it is limited.

The officer's false statement about having discovered Mathiason's fingerprints at the scene was found by the Oregon Supreme Court to be another circumstance contributing to the coercive environment that makes the *Miranda* rationale applicable. Whatever relevance this fact may have to other issues in the case, it has nothing to do with whether Mathiason was in custody for purposes of the *Miranda* rule.

The judgment of the Oregon Supreme Court is reversed.

UNITED STATES V. CRAY

United States Court of Appeals, 15th Circuit (2004)

The government appeals from an order of the district court suppressing a written statement that Dr. Michael Cray, a chiropractor, signed at the conclusion of an interview with FBI agents. The district court determined that the statement should be suppressed because it was the product of custodial interrogation that was conducted without informing Cray of his rights under *Miranda v. Arizona* (U.S. S.Ct., 1966). We respectfully disagree, and we reverse.

FBI agents Timothy Bisswurm and Sean Boylan went to Cray's home the morning of February 16, 2001, to interview him regarding a health care fraud investigation. Prior to their arrival, the agents called Cray at 4:30 a.m. to ensure that Cray was home, stating they had the wrong number. At 6:30 a.m., the agents approached the home. When Cray did not answer the door, Agent Boylan called Cray by telephone and told him that he needed to come to the front door. When Cray appeared, Boylan identified himself and Bisswurm as FBI agents and told Cray they would like to speak with him for a few minutes. Boylan further informed Cray that he did not have to speak with the agents.

Cray admitted the agents into his home, and the three men proceeded to the living room to discuss the investigation. Over the course of the ensuing interview, which lasted nearly seven hours, Cray was informed several times that his participation was voluntary, and that he was free to ask the agents to leave his home. About three hours into the interview, Cray told the agents that he was late for work. The agents instructed Cray to call in sick, and directed him not to inform his office about the investigation. Cray complied.

Although the telephone rang several times as the interview progressed, the agents instructed Cray not to answer, and Cray did not do so. When Cray moved about his home on two occasions to go to the bathroom and his bedroom, Boylan accompanied him to check the rooms for telephones. During the interview, Cray was told that if he did not cooperate, the agents would interview his 75-year-old father and others. The agents further told Cray that they would "light up his world," and also suggested that if he did not cooperate, then they could use the power of the FBI to pressure insurance companies to withhold payments to his business.

Cray did not resist the agents' questioning during the interview, and he never asked them to leave. At the conclusion of the meeting, Cray signed a written statement (after making one correction and initialing each page) acknowledging that "no one has threatened, coerced, or promised me anything." The written statement contained admissions that Cray had knowingly caused insurance companies to reimburse at least one hundred false claims, and knowingly paid illegal fees to persons who referred new patients to Cray's chiropractic clinic. There was no threat of arrest during the encounter, and the agents never displayed weapons. Cray was not arrested until weeks later.

Cray was charged in a twenty-seven count indictment with various crimes relating to an alleged health care billing fraud scheme. He brought a motion to suppress his signed statement.

The ultimate question in determining whether a person is in "custody" for purposes of *Miranda* is whether there is a formal arrest or restraint on freedom of movement of the degree associated with a formal arrest. The only relevant inquiry in considering that question is how a reasonable person in Cray's position would have understood his situation. In making that evaluation, we consider the totality of the circumstances that confronted the defendant at the time of questioning.

Courts have identified at least eight factors for consideration in making the custody determination: (1) whether the suspect was informed during the interview that the questioning was voluntary, that he could ask the officers to leave, or that he was not considered under arrest, and whether the person's conduct indicated an awareness of such freedom; (2) whether the suspect possessed unrestrained freedom of movement during questioning; (3) whether the suspect voluntarily acquiesced to official questioning or initiated contact with authorities; (4) whether strong-arm tactics were used, *e.g.*, the police manifested a belief that the person was culpable and they had evidence to prove it, the police were aggressive, confrontational or threatening; (5) whether there was a police-dominated atmosphere, *e.g.*, where the interview took place or how many police officers participated; (6) whether the suspect was placed under arrest at the termination of the questioning; (7) whether the express purpose of the interview was to question the person as a witness or a suspect; and (8) how long the interrogation lasted. *United States v. Jones* (15th Cir. 1995).

The most obvious and effective means of demonstrating that a suspect has not been taken into custody is for the police to inform the suspect that an arrest is not being made and that the suspect may terminate the interview at will. The FBI agents who interviewed Cray testified they informed Cray at least eight times that his participation in the interview was voluntary, and that he was free to ask the agents to leave his home.

We believe that this abundant advice of freedom to terminate the encounter should not be treated merely as one equal factor in a multi-factor balancing test designed to discern whether a reasonable person would have understood himself to be in custody. That a person is told repeatedly that he is free to terminate an interview is powerful evidence that a reasonable person would have understood that he was free to terminate the interview. So powerful, indeed, that no governing precedent of the Supreme Court, or this court, or any case from another court of appeals that can be located, holds that a person was in custody after being clearly advised of his freedom to leave or terminate questioning.

The weighty inference that Cray was not in custody after receiving such advice is strengthened further by the context in which the interview occurred—the living room of Cray's home. When a person is questioned on his own turf, the surroundings are not indicative of the type of inherently coercive setting that normally accompanies a custodial interrogation. Indeed, an interrogation in familiar surroundings such as one's home softens the hard aspects of police interrogation and moderates a suspect's sense of being held in custody. The custodial surroundings are important to consider. The principal psychological factor of concern is isolating the suspect in unfamiliar surroundings for no purpose other than to subjugate the individual to the will of his examiner.

Although these nonexhaustive factors and their attendant balancing test are often cited in our decisions concerning *Miranda*, there is no requirement that they be followed ritualistically in every *Miranda* case. When the factors are invoked, it is important to recall that they are not by any means exclusive, and that "custody" cannot be resolved merely by counting up the number of factors on each side of the balance and rendering a decision accordingly. Exploring the nuances of such vague factors as voluntary acquiescence, strong-arm tactics, and a police-dominated atmosphere in order to place them on one side or the other of a balancing scale may tend one to lose sight of the forest for the trees. The ultimate inquiry must always be whether the defendant was restrained as though he were under formal arrest.

The district court relied heavily on its finding that the FBI agents instructed Cray not to alert others by telephone of the FBI's presence during the interview, and escorted Cray to his bedroom and bathroom to check for telephones before Cray entered the rooms. There are two difficulties with this emphasis on telephones. The first is precedent. In *United States v. Sutera* (15th Cir. 1999), officers conducted a three and one-half hour search of Sutera's apartment, and then interviewed him for one hour. They prevented him from using his phone during the search, and then questioned him in isolation in his apartment.

We rejected Sutera's contention that prohibition on use of the telephone was one of several factors that demonstrated custody.

The second difficulty presumably explains the precedent: That a suspect is discouraged from using a telephone in his home during an interview often is not probative of whether he is free to terminate the interview altogether. In this case, the FBI agents testified that they requested (or, as the district court found, "directed") Cray not to use the telephone to disclose the presence of FBI agents, because such disclosure would interfere with Cray's ability to cooperate with an ongoing investigation. If his cooperation with the FBI were known by alleged coconspirators, then he could not assist the government (and potentially himself) through undercover telephone calls or recorded meetings with other suspects. This likely is a common request (or direction) from investigators who are soliciting cooperation.

We also conclude that Cray's lack of voluntary acquiescence in questioning does not tend to show that he was in custody. The district court thought the mere absence of resistance by Cray, such as his making no attempt to terminate the interview and allowing the interview to proceed to its closing, did not rise to the level of active cooperation that our court has found to constitute voluntary acquiescence as used in our third factor. We conclude that the initiation of questioning by FBI agents in this case is not significant evidence of restraint on Cray's freedom of movement. Against a backdrop of repeated advice that he was free to terminate the interview, Cray's decision not to terminate the interview and to allow the interview to proceed to its closing suggests an exercise of free will, rather than restraint to a degree associated with formal arrest.

Judgment reversed.

PEOPLE V. ADAMS

Columbia Supreme Court (1996)

Defendant Joseph Adams appeals from a judgment entered after a jury convicted him of involuntary manslaughter. Defendant claims his statements to police were involuntary and obtained in violation of the *Miranda* rule. *Miranda v. Arizona* (U.S. S.Ct.,

1966). We agree and conclude that their admission at trial compels reversal.

Officer Cindy Torres testified that she and her partner Officer Mike Sterner learned from Jessie Badillo that defendant was "involved" in a shooting death by a group of "gang bangers" at Washington School on January 27. They went to defendant's residence and asked him and his mother if he would talk to them at the police station about the homicide. They offered to bring him back home. Defendant and his mother agreed that he would go. Defendant's mother also consented to a search of her house for evidence of the homicide and gang involvement.

The officers brought defendant to an interview room at the police station. Although he was not physically restrained, Officer Torres did not recall whether defendant ever left the room. The interview lasted two hours, and, when it was over, the officers drove defendant back home. Officer Torres told defendant he was not in custody. However, she then said they would bring him home when they were finished, explaining that "[i]t really depends on how long you want to take and how quickly you tell us the truth." Torres later testified that what she meant was if defendant told the truth in one hour or two hours, the interview would take that long. She further explained, "There's a possibility that he would never tell us the truth; then we would give him a ride home without him telling us the truth." However, Torres admitted she did not tell this to defendant.

Officer Torres next informed defendant they knew what had happened at Washington School, who had been present, and who had done what. Officer Sterner said they just wanted to know how he got involved. Defendant denied being involved. He said that, after school, he declined an invitation to join a group of people and instead walked home with Richard Badillo. The officers rejected this story, and accused him of fabricating an alibi with Badillo. They told him not to "play games" and confronted him repeatedly with incriminating evidence of his involvement with "gang bangers." They falsely suggested they had his fingerprints from one of the cars.

Defendant continued to deny involvement. The officers became exasperated and annoyed and assailed him for hiding behind lies and not taking responsibility for his conduct. They warned that his lies would not protect him and that while the truth might exculpate him, his lies plus the evidence they had would probably lead to murder charges and his being labeled a liar. Defendant nevertheless refused to admit involvement. The officers pressed on. They said other officers were with his mother, and she would not corroborate his story. They said his story might be an effort to conceal complicity in the murder. They asked him to think about family events (his sister's marriage) and personal opportunities (going to college) that he would miss if sent to prison. They said he owed the victim the real story and invoked his mother's guidance to tell the truth.

After a while, the officers decided to leave defendant alone for a while. Before leaving, they advised him to clear his conscience and not to waste any more of his or their time. When the interview resumed, defendant stuck to his story. The officers again said he was lying and continued to pressure him to tell the truth. They warned that "[l]ying isn't gonna get you anything, nothing good. It'll sink you, but it ain't gonna save you." Torres advised him that "[i]f you tell us a lie and we know it's a lie, then that story is what's gonna get tacked onto you, and I can't protect you from that. Nobody can protect you from that."

After further pressuring, defendant partially abandoned his story. Asked if he intended to kill anyone while driving around, defendant said "No." Sterner expressed disbelief, asserted that was the purpose. "That was stated clear and upfront." Defendant denied he intended to get involved if there was fighting and said he thought the group was out looking for girls. Sterner said others had given this story, but he did not believe it. Defendant then said he just wanted to cruise around with the group but soon realized they were out to "gang bang." He denied seeing a gun but admitted hearing someone mention that somebody else had a gun and that it was "no good."

Defendant then said that after the group left a restaurant, he left them to go with a girl he had seen. Sterner responded, "You know how this is gonna work. You're gonna tell us some girl's name. We're not gonna let you leave here until we go talk to the girl, and she's not gonna be able to confirm the story, Joe." He then pressed defendant to tell him about the incident at

Washington School. At that point, defendant dropped all resistance and explained what happened that day.

In *Miranda v. Arizona* (U.S. S.Ct., 1966), the United States Supreme Court held that a person questioned by the police after being "taken into custody or otherwise deprived of his freedom of action in any significant way" must first "be warned that he has a right to remain silent, that any statement he does make may be used as evidence against him, and that he has a right to the presence of an attorney, either retained or appointed." Statements obtained in violation of this rule cannot be used to establish guilt.

It is settled that the *Miranda* advisements are required only when a person is subjected to custodial interrogation. Custodial means any situation in which a person has been taken into custody or otherwise deprived of his freedom of action in any significant way. Interrogation refers not only to express questioning, but also to any words or actions on the part of the police that the police should know are reasonably likely to elicit an incriminating response from the suspect.

It is beyond reasonable dispute that defendant's interview was reasonably likely to elicit incriminating responses and thus was interrogation within the meaning of the *Miranda* rule. The People do not claim otherwise. The primary issue is whether defendant was taken into custody or otherwise deprived of his freedom of action in any significant way.

To make this determination, a trial court must first establish the circumstances surrounding the interrogation. It must then measure these circumstances against an objective, legal standard: Would a reasonable person in the suspect's position during the interrogation experience a restraint on his or her freedom of movement to the degree normally associated with a formal arrest?

Courts have identified a variety of relevant circumstances to consider in deciding whether an interrogation was in a custodial environment. *United States v. Jones* (15th Cir. 1995). No one factor is dispositive. Rather, we look at the interplay and combined effect of all the circumstances to determine whether on balance they created a coercive atmosphere such that a reasonable person would have experienced a restraint tantamount to an arrest.

Here, defendant agreed to an interview at the station, and Officer Torres initially said defendant was not in custody. However, we find it significant that Torres then explained that the interview would end and they would bring him home after he told them the truth. Given the officers' repeated rejection of defendant's story, a reasonable person eventually would have realized that telling the "truth" meant admitting the officers' information was correct and explaining how and why one was involved and that until this "truth" came out, he or she could not leave. The officers later expressly reinforced this implication by explicitly telling defendant he would not be allowed to leave if they had to go interview an alleged alibi witness.

Next, we note that Officers Torres and Sterner did not tell defendant he was free to terminate the interview and leave if he wished. Furthermore, defendant's conduct here does not indicate he was aware of his personal rights during the interrogation. Indeed, it does not appear that defendant ever left the interview room, and Torres could not recall whether defendant ever did. Nor does it appear defendant had a means of getting home on his own if he had tried to leave before the officers were finished with him.

We observe that the officers did not interview defendant only as a potential witness. The officers unmistakably informed defendant he was a potential suspect and repeatedly told him they had evidence to prove his involvement. The People candidly concede that defendant was made aware "that the police officers fully suspected the worst possible scenario regarding his involvement in the crime."

Concerning the manner of interrogation, this court has consistently held that accusatory questioning is more likely to communicate to a reasonable person in the position of the suspect that he is not free to leave than would general and neutral investigative questions. Thus, on the issue of custody, courts consider highly significant whether the questioning was brief, polite, and courteous, or lengthy, aggressive, confrontational, threatening, and intimidating.

The "tag team" interrogation lasted two hours and was intense, persistent, aggressive, confrontational, accusatory, and, at times, threatening and intimidating. Although the officers' tactics and techniques do not appear unusual or unreasonable, we associate them with the full-blown interrogation of an arrestee, and except for a *Miranda* advisement, we cannot conceive how defendant's interrogation might have differed had he been under arrest.

Given the totality of circumstances, we conclude that at least by the time defendant partially abandoned his story, if not before, the environment during the interrogation had become coercive, and a reasonable person would have understood he or she was required to remain for questioning indefinitely at the sole discretion of the officers and was not free to leave until he or she satisfied the officers' demand for the truth.

Thus, a reasonable person would have felt deprived of liberty in a significant way and that the restraint was tantamount to being under arrest. Here the interview was a typical custodial interrogation, during which the suspect feels completely at the mercy of the police and frequently is prolonged, and in which the suspect is aware that questioning will continue until he provides his interrogators the answers they seek.

The judgment is reversed.

Answer 1 to Performance Test B

Memorandum of Points and Authorities Opposing Defendant's Motion to Suppress Evidence

Defendant Raymond Duncan has moved to suppress all statements he made to the police during an interview conducted on January 2, 2008, as obtained in violation of Miranda v. Arizona. The people oppose this motion and respectfully submit, for those reasons listed below, that defendant's motion should be denied.

A. Defendant's motion to suppress should be denied because he did not confess during a "custodial interrogation," as he was fully informed that he was not under arrest and could terminate the interview at his discretion.

Under Miranda v. Arizona, police are required to give suspects a litany of warnings before engaging in custodial interrogation. The United States Supreme Court has defined custodial interrogation as "questioning initiated by law enforcement officers after a person has been taken into custody or otherwise deprived of his freedom of action in any significant way." Mathiason. In other words, according to the Supreme Court, "Miranda warnings are required to be given only where there has been such a restriction on a person's freedom as to render him in custody." Id (emphasis added).

The Columbia Supreme Court has followed the Supreme Court's lead, and it requires the Miranda warnings to be given only if "a reasonable person in the suspect's position during the interrogation [would] experience a restraint on his or her freedom of movement to the degree normally associated with a formal arrest." Adams. In determining whether an interrogation took place under custodial circumstances, the Columbia Supreme Court has adopted the balancing test used by the 15th Circuit in Jones. Under this test, the factors to be considered in determining whether a custodial interrogation occurred are: 1) whether the suspect was informed during the interview that the questioning was voluntary, that he could ask the officers to leave, or that he was not considered under arrest, and whether the person's conduct indicated an awareness of such freedom; 2) whether the suspect possessed unrestrained freedom of movement during questioning; 3) whether the suspect voluntarily acquiesced to official questioning or initiated contact with authorities; 4) whether strong-arm tactics were used; 5) whether there was a police-dominated atmosphere; 6) whether the suspect was placed under arrest at the termination of the question; 7) whether the express purpose of the interview was to question the person as a witness or a suspect; and, 8) how long the interrogation lasted. Jones.

In this case, the vast majority of the factors to be examined weigh in favor of denying defendant's motion to suppress. Though the defendant's questioning might have been an uncomfortable experience, it never rose to the level of custodial interrogation required by this state, the 15th Circuit, or the Supreme Court.

1. The defendant was repeatedly informed during the interview that his questioning was voluntary, and that he was not under arrest.

This first factor, weighing whether the suspect knew he could terminate the interrogation, has been described by one court as "powerful evidence that a reasonable person would have understood that he was free to terminate the interview." Cray. In fact, neither the Supreme Court, nor any other court of appeals, has ever held "that a person was in custody after being clearly advised of his freedom to leave or terminate questioning."

Here, the defendant was clearly informed that the questioning was voluntary and that he could leave or terminate questioning. First, The defendant voluntarily agreed to come down to the interview, in fact proclaiming "I don't have anything to hide," He was told by Defective James that he was going to a voluntary interview and that he was free to leave at any time. And, as the interview progressed, it was again indicated to the defendant that he was in control of the interrogation—when the defendant asked for a break, he was given one without hesitation. Even towards the end of the interview, and even after the defendant had contradicted himself several times, he was once again asked "Do you still want to talk to us?" Only after he agreed did the interview continue.

At no point during the interview was the defendant restrained from leaving. The defendant has alleged that he was kept in a locked room, but according to Detective James, the room in which the interview took place does not lock. The defendant was not in handcuffs nor was he chained, and Detective James has noted that while he and the defendant were on the police roof smoking, he "repeatedly told him that he was not under arrest and that he was free to leave." The 15th Circuit has noted that the "most obvious and effective means of demonstrating that a suspect has not been taken into custody is for the police to inform the suspect that an arrest is not being made and that the suspect may terminate the interview at will." Detective James did just that, and so the defendant was fully aware that the questioning was voluntary, that he could ask the officers to leave, and that he was not considered under arrest.

The defendant has claimed that the detectives never told him he could leave. He claims they never told him he could have refused to accompany them to the station, and that while on his cigarette breaks Detective James never left him alone.

But the defendant's recollection is directly contradicted by both his own statements on tape—during which he specifically stated "I called you back and agreed to come down to this interview"—and by the accompanying circumstances. Whenever the defendant asked for a break, he was granted one. When he asked to get fresh air, he was allowed to. He never once asked to leave, and was not physically restrained in any way.

Further, the defendant has rendered himself not credible based on inconsistencies with his affidavit. In his affidavit, the defendant declares that at 12:30 p.m. on January 2, he "was arrested and taken into custody." However, the fact that he was taken into the station in the front seat of an unmarked sedan, was not placed in handcuffs until after 6:00 pm, was allowed to leave the building to smoke, all contradict that contention. Even stronger evidence of this false allegation is his statement on tape that, "I called you back and agreed to come down to this interview." Given such direct contradictions between the defendant's statements on tape, and his declarations in his affidavit, the Court should discount as untrustworthy all the defendant's contentions. What is more, the defendant has every incentive to lie concerning the circumstances of his confession, as suppression of the evidence will likely be the only realistic way for him to defeat liability at trial.

In denying that he was free to leave, the defendant compares his circumstances to that of Adams, where the police told the defendant that the length of his interrogation "really depends on how long you want to take and how quickly you tell us the truth." Given this statement, Adams had every reason to believe that he would be detained as long as was necessary for him to confess. But here, on the other hand, there was never any suggestion that the length of the interview would be the defendant's willingness to confess.

While "any interview of one suspected of a crime by police will have coercive aspects to it, simply by virtue of the fact that the policeman is part of a law enforcement system. . . . .police are not required to administer Miranda warnings to everyone whom they question." Mathiason. Here, the defendant's interrogation was no more coercive than what is inherent in any interview where the police are seeking to solve a crime and interview an individual they believe involved. Therefore, this most important factor weighs in favor of not suppressing the defendant's confession.

2. The defendant had unrestrained freedom of movement during questioning, and he used this freedom on several occasions.

Under the second factor, courts examine whether the defendant had complete freedom to move around during the questioning. However, the simple fact that the questioning took place in a police station does not render a defendant in custody. Mathiason.

Here, detectives had in fact given the defendant a choice of where he wanted the interview to occur. The police offered to question him in his home, where he would have a great deal of freedom of movement and could be free from any of the pressures that might be attached to a police station. See Cray. He chose not to accept their offer. And, during the interview at the station, the defendant was granted every request he made—whether for water, a cigarette, or some more fresh air. During these breaks the defendant was allowed to leave the room, and in fact, went outside onto the station's rooftop gazebo. There was never any show of force made to the defendant—the detectives were wearing business suits, he was never handcuffed, and there was never any display of guns. In fact, as Detective James has stated, the defendant was repeatedly told that he was free to leave.

The defendant has argued that because Officer James accompanied him during his breaks, he was not free to leave. However, in Cray, the court rejected precisely this argument. There, the suspect was followed into his bedroom and to the bathroom to ensure that he was not using the phone. However, even such invasive actions by police was not considered sufficient to render his interview custodial.

The defendant has further argued that he was never told that he was free to leave, and that he of course did not possess unrestrained freedom of movement given all the circumstances. However, this argument is contradicted by the fact that Brandy Gentry, another subject interviewed in connection with this crime, was interviewed under quite similar circumstances—she even got aggressive towards the detectives—and was allowed to walk out the exact same room in which the defendant was interviewed.

The defendant also relies on the Columbia Supreme Court's decision in Adams as evidence that he did not possess unrestrained freedom of movement. He compares his interview to the interrogation in Adams, and argues that he was similarly restrained. However, in Adams, the suspect was repeatedly told that he would not be released until he agreed with the accusations the detectives were levying at him. What is more, the defendant in Adams never once left the examination room, supporting his contention that he really was not free to leave. This situation was different—though the detectives refused to believe the defendant's story, they never once told him that his release would be conditional on his accepting responsibility for the crime. And, though the door to the interview room was closed during the interview, the defendant left it on more than one occasion.

This defendant had every opportunity to move about during question[ing], and his own decision not to take advantage of such freedom by leaving the station is no reason to suppress his properly obtained confession. This factor thus supports the confession's admissibility.

3. The defendant and police engaged in a voluntary and informal soliloquy to determine the time and manner of the interview.

In this case, officers initiated contact with the defendant, but did so in such a way that a reasonable person would not have felt that he had to speak with them. All the evidence suggests that the detectives left several messages for the defendant and went to his apartment a couple times, and that the defendant eventually called and left a message saying when he would be home. Though the officers made the first move to speak with the defendant, this informal back and forth presents strong evidence that there was never any coercion in how they approached him.

In fact, the facts of this case are remarkably similar to how contact was initiated in Mathiason. There, police officers initially left a card with the defendant and asked him to call. Here, the officers left word for the defendant, but the defendant called on his own volition—without the officers asking him to. There was no coercion found based on such actions then, and police here did nothing to materially distinguish that case.

What is more, when the officers got to the defendant's house in this case, there was a back and forth where the interview would take place, and all questioning ultimately took place where the defendant specifically asked it to. It was for the defendant's benefit that questioning took place at the police station.

Therefore, even though officers technically spoke to the defendant before he reached out to them, contact was initiated by both sides, and this factor should be of limited use to the Court in determining whether a custodial interrogation took place.

4. Strong-arm tactics were not used during the defendant's interview.

In Cray, the 15th Circuit gave two examples of improper strong-arm tactics that might be used by police. First, the court offered that "police manifested a belief that the person was culpable and they had evidence to prove it." Next, "the police were aggressive, confrontational or threatening."

Here, the police may have manifested a belief that the defendant was culpable, but they only did so once the defendant's statements themselves gave them that reasonable belief. As Detective James has said, the police did not consider the defendant a suspect when they initially sought him for questioning. Rather, it was only once he contradicted himself that their questioning truly manifested a belief that the defendant was culpable. In fact, reviewing the transcript of the defendant's interview, it is clear that the police became more accusatory only once the defendant contradicted himself for the first time—by stating "didn't I explain to you that I had entered that way, too?" about how he had left the apartment—a clear contradiction to what he had said earlier.

The defendant has also alleged that police told him of several items of evidence that constituted evidence against him, and has insinuated that such statements were false. However, the defendant's contentions are irrelevant. As the Supreme Court declared in Mathiason, "[w]hatever relevance this fact may have to other issues in the case, [a false statement by a police officer to a suspect] has nothing to do with whether Mathiason was in custody for purposes of the Miranda rule."

Further, the police were not aggressive, confrontational, or threatening in this case. They were accusatory, to be sure, but the courts have not suggested that mere accusations of guilt, without being coupled by more aggressive or threatening behavior, are sufficient to rise to the level of custodial interrogation. Rather, in Adams, it was repeated accusations of lying, made in an aggressive fashion, coupled with direct threats that he would miss important family events, that led to the defendant's confession. There, true duress and coercion was imposed on the defendant, and he was made to feel as though he had no way out but to confess.

The defendant relies on these facts in Adams to analogize his case. However, in this case, unlike Adams, the detectives asked "direct" questions but were not rude. They expressly told the defendant that they would not yell at him. Moreover, the defendant's own statements suggest that he was not intimidated by the police. At one point he even joked with Detective James: "I'll tell you, when I offered to come in for questioning, I felt it wouldn't be too bad, but oh boy!" Then, towards the end of the interrogation, he even thanked the police for being so patient with him.

Each of these specific instances belies the defendant's argument that police only obtained his confession through the use of strong-arm tactics. This factor further supports the contention that the defendant did not confess during a custodial interrogation.

5. Any police-dominated atmosphere at the station existed only due to the defendant's choice of the interview's location.

The Cray court also offered two examples of when an interview might take place in a police-dominated atmosphere: where the interview took place, and how many police officers participated.

Here, the defendant notes that the interview took place in a police station. However, as described above, the interview took place in the police station only because the defendant chose not to use his house for the interview. The police made every attempt contrary to defendant's contentions, to interview him at his house, and the defendant should not now be entitled to claim a police-dominated atmosphere when it was his choice of atmosphere in the first place.

Further, only two officers participated in this case. There is nothing to suggest that officers were rotated in and out of the interview in order to throw the defendant off, or to confuse or intimidate him.

Therefore, this factor is neutral at best in determining whether the defendant's confession was given in a custodial atmosphere.

6. Though the defendant was placed into custody at the termination of the interview, this factor offers him only minor support for his claims.

The defendant was placed under arrest at the termination of the questioning. However, this was not a situation in which the defendant was initially a suspect and would have been placed under arrest regardless of what he had told the police. Rather, the defendant was not a suspect in this crime until after he contradicted himself on material elements of his story. Therefore, this factor provides only minimal support for the defendant's contention that his confession occurred in a custodial environment.

7. The express purpose of the interview was to question the defendant as a witness, not as a suspect.

Detective James made it quite clear to the defendant that the purpose of the interview was to question him as a witness. The objective circumstances surrounding how the parties began questioning—the informal back and forth as to where the interview would take place—would have been a strong indication to anyone in that circumstance that he was only a witness in the killing. This fact is further confirmed by the circumstances in which the defendant arrived at the police station—in the front seat of an unmarked sedan, with detectives wearing business suits, without any physical restraint of any kind.

Further, Detective James has unequivocally stated that he repeatedly told the defendant that he was free to leave, and that he was not under arrest. In fact, the defendant, in his affidavit does not contest the fact that the purpose of the interview was to question him as a witness. Nowhere in the defendant's affidavit does he dispute the suggestion that he arrived at the police station as a witness to a crime like any other.

8. The interrogation did not last an unreasonable length of time.

The defendant points to Adams and claims the case provides him strong support for his contention that the long duration of the interview—over five hours—supports his contention that this was a custodial interrogation. And, it is true that the confession suppressed in Adams was obtained after only two hours of interrogation. However, the Adams court, after noting that the interrogation lasted two hours, only once made mention of that fact again, and then in the context of noting the threatening, confrontational, and intimidating atmosphere of the interrogation. It simply was not a fact that the court found especially compelling in determining the confession was taken within a custodial interrogation.

Further, in Cray, the court found that an interview of seven hours was not enough to render a noncustodial interrogation custodial. There simply is no set time limit after which any interrogation is inherently custodial. The defendant was interviewed for five hours, but it was during the middle of the day, between lunch and dinner, and not in such a way so as to prevent him from working or engaging in other activity he had already scheduled.

What is more, the defendant himself did not seem to think the interview was unfairly long. Though he insinuates in his affidavit that the police unfairly kept him in captivity for almost six hours for the express purpose of obtaining his confession, this fact is belied by his own statements on tape. Towards the end of the interview—minutes before it ended—the defendant told the detectives "I appreciate the fact that you guys have been patient with me." Such a statement is entirely inconsistent with any suggestion that the interview's length was a major factor in obtaining the confession.

Therefore, though this interview was longer than that in Adams, the difference in length is irrelevant when compared with the vast distinction between the custodial nature of the two interviews.

B. Conclusion

The totality of the circumstances balancing test used by Columbia in determining whether an individual confessed during a custodial interrogation plainly shows that Mr. Duncan did not need to be read his Miranda rights at any point before he confessed. Though balancing is not a strict counting exercise, the factors, viewed as a whole, consistently support the People's contention that the defendant was never restrained as though he were under formal arrest. As in Cray "[a]gainst a backdrop of repeated advice that he was free to terminate the interview," [Mr. Duncan]'s decision not to terminate the interview and to allow the interview to proceed to its closing suggests an exercise of free will, rather than restraint to a degree associated with formal arrest.

Therefore, we respectfully ask this Court to deny defendant's motion to suppress evidence, and to allow his full confession to be admitted into evidence.

Answer 2 to Performance Test B

IN THE SUPERIOR COURT OF THE STATE OF COLUMBIA IN AND FOR THE COUNTY OF WARREN

People of the State of Columbia v. Raymond Duncan

Criminal Division 2008-2341

MEMORANDUM OF POINTS AND AUTHORITIES IN SUPPORT OF OPPOSITION TO MOTION TO SUPPRESS

Raymond Duncan ("Defendant") has been charged with the murder of Jennifer Clark ("victim"). While being questioned by police detectives, Defendant admitted to the killing. He now seeks to suppress his confession as being taken in violation of his right to a Miranda warning. Because Defendant was not subject to a custodial interrogation under the Cray factors, he was not entitled to a Miranda warning. Thus, his confession is admissible.

Applicable Law

The U.S. Supreme Court held in Miranda v. Arizona that police must first warn a person being questioned of his rights in certain circumstances. Oregon v. Mathiason; United States v. Cray; People v. Adams. As noted in Adams, the police must give a Miranda warning only to a person subjected to a custodial interrogation. At issue in the case of Defendant's confession is whether the situation was custodial. "Custodial" includes any situation in which a person has been taken into custody or otherwise deprived of his freedom of action in any significant way. Id. To make this determination, a court must determine whether a reasonable person in the suspect's position during the interrogation would experience a restraint on his or her freedom of movement to the degree normally associated with a formal arrest. Id.

In making this evaluation, courts will consider the totality of the circumstances that confronted the defendant at the time of questioning. Cray; Adams. However, courts have identified eight factors in making the custody determination: 1)whether the suspect was informed during the interview that the questioning was voluntary, that he could ask the officers to leave, or that he was not considered under arrest, and whether that person's conduct indicated an awareness of such freedom; 2) whether the suspect possessed unrestrained freedom of movement during questioning; 3) whether the suspect voluntarily acquiesced to official questioning or initiated contact with authorities; 4) whether strong-arm tactics were used; 5) whether there was a police dominated atmosphere; 6) whether the suspect was placed under arrest at the termination of the questioning; 7) whether the express purpose of the interview was to question the person as a witness or a suspect; and 8) how long the interrogation lasted. United States v. Jones.

While no one factor is dispositive, Adams, courts have found evidence that repeated communications that the person is free to terminate an interview is powerful evidence that a reasonable person would have understood that he was free to terminate the interview. No Supreme Court, Fifteenth Circuit or other appellate precedent holds that a person was in custody after being clearly advised of his freedom to leave or terminate questioning.

Analysis

Applying the United States v. Jones factors, as stated in Cray, establishes that Defendant was not subject to a custodial interrogation when he confessed his murder of the victim.

Suspect Was Informed During the Interview that the Questioning Was Voluntary; Conduct Indicating Awareness of Such Freedom.

As the court of Cray noted, the "most obvious and effective means of demonstrating that a suspect has not been taken into custody is for the police to inform[him] that an arrest is not being made and that the suspect may terminate the interview at will." This exactly describes the facts of this case. While Defendant states that the officers arrested him before the questioning began, he was never placed under arrest according to Detective James. He voluntarily accompanied the detectives to the station, as will be discussed later.

Significantly, Defendant was repeatedly informed over the course of his encounter with the police that he was free to leave any time. He was informed of this on his way to the station house, and repeatedly again on his breaks with Detective James.

While Defendant claims that it became objectively reasonable for him to believe he was not going to leave the police station, this was not the case. Though he stated that he thought he had to tell the officers what they wanted to hear in order for him to be able to leave, the officers never indicated anything like that to the Defendant. In Adams, the interview of a high school boy became custodial because the police conditioned taking him home on his telling the "truth." The court found that a reasonable person eventually would have realized that telling the truth meant admitting the officers' information was correct. However, as, demonstrated by the taped recording of the interview with Defendant, the officers in this case never made such statements. They only encouraged Defendant to confess as an appeal to his sense of fairness, and because otherwise living with the murder would "bug" him.

In addition to the statements of the officers being much different from those in Adams, it must further be considered that the police in that case were questioning a high school age boy who had no way to get home except through the police. In this case, although Defendant got a ride from the police, he is a 24 year old man who would certainly find other ways to get home from the police station. (In any event, he requested the ride to the police station.) They never gave him any indication that he couldn't leave unless he told them what they wanted to hear. Though Defendant stated as much during the interview, the test for a custodial interrogation is whether a reasonable person would feel as though they had been restrained as if formally arrested.

Furthermore, the defendant in Adams was told he would not be allowed to leave if the officers had to leave to interview an alibi witness. The officers in this case made no such statements about the Defendant not being able to leave. In addition, the defendant in Adams was never allowed to leave the room, which was not the case here.

Suspect Possessed Unrestrained Freedom of Movement During Questioning

Defendant was not restrained during his interview with the police. According to Detective James, he was never handcuffed or physically restrained in any other way. While Defendant claims that he was in a locked room, in fact the room he was in was not capable of being locked. He could have left at any time, and, in fact, did leave the room he was in. He twice went on cigarette breaks with Detective James on the roof of the police station. Being able to take cigarette breaks and walk through the police station unrestrained would not indicate to a reasonable person that they were in custody and unable to leave.

While Defendant was always accompanied by an officer while he moved about the police station, this would not necessarily indicate custody to a reasonable person. The defendant in Cray was always accompanied by an officer when he moved about his own home during questioning, and the court there found that there was no custodial interrogation.

Suspect Voluntarily Acquiesced to Official Questioning

Though Defendant claims that he was arrested, and thus did not voluntarily acquiesce to questioning, this is not the case. In fact, the detectives tried several times to contact him but were unable to. Defendant was finally the one who got in touch with the detectives. When the detectives came to his home to talk to him, they were called away and left the Defendant by himself. If the officers were going to arrest him, a reasonable person would not think that they would leave him alone while taking care of other business.

In addition, the method by which the Defendant arrived at the station house should have indicated to him that he was not under arrest. He rode with the officers in an unmarked car, while they weren't wearing uniforms. Most significantly, he did not sit in the back seat. He sat in front. A person under arrest does not usually sit in the front seat of a police car. Furthermore, James informed him on the way to the station house that he was voluntarily coming in for questioning, and was free to leave at any time.

This situation is extremely similar to that in Mathiason. In that case, officers tried to contact the defendant with no success, left a card at his apartment with a note to call them. The defendant did. In that case, the defendant also accompanied the officers to the station house, where he gave a confession. This was not considered to be a custodial interrogation. Though the interview in that case was extremely short, the Mathiason Court did not give that fact much weight. It focused its attention on how his freedom to depart was restricted in any way. Therefore, the length of this interview should not take away from the fact that the Defendant volunteered to answer police questioning, indicating it was not a custodial interrogation.

Strong-Arm Tactics

According to the Jones factors, strong-arm tactics could include that the police manifested a belief that the person was culpable and they had evidence to prove it, as well as aggressive, confrontational and threatening behavior on the part of the police.

In this case, the police did indicate to the Defendant that they thought he had committed the crime. However, they were not being aggressive or threatening about it. Rather, they told the Defendant he should get the murder off his chest so it wouldn't "bug" him. They tried to appeal to his sense of compassion for the victim's family, as well as his sense of religious obligation. The Defendant even specifically discussed police tactics with Detective James, who assured the Defendant that police questioning was very different than in the past, and they would not yell at the Defendant.

This conduct is markedly different from the tactics used in the Adams case, where the police were found to have created a custodial interrogation in part by their use of strong-arm tactics. The tag-team environment contributed to the finding. While there may have been two officers in this case, in Adams, the officers were "intense, persistent, aggressive, confrontational, accusatory, and, at times, threatening and intimidating." As noted above, this description [does] not comport with the officers' actions in this case. Furthermore, and as previously noted, the defendant in Adams was in high school, and would be more likely to be pressured by threatening and aggressive questioning.

A better comparison to this case is with the defendant in Cray, in which two government agents were dealing with an adult man. In Cray, the FBI agents interviewed that defendant for seven hours and threatened to "light up his world," and put financial pressure on him if he did not cooperate. This was not found to create a custodial interrogation. The police behavior in this case fell far short of the conduct of the police in both of those cases, and is thus noncustodial.

As to fabricated evidence, the Supreme Court in Mathiason rejected this as a factor creating a custodial interrogation. In that case, the suspect was confronted with fabricated evidence. While the interrogation was much shorter than the Defendant's in this case, the court explicitly stated that "whatever relevance this fact may have to other issues in the case, it has nothing to do with whether Mathiason was in custody for purposes of the Miranda rule." Therefore, this should not be considered as supporting Defendant's belief that he was in custody.

Notably, the officers in this case subjected others to similar questioning, and those persons knew that they could leave. In fact, those other persons did leave police custody. This indicates that the police tactics would not indicate to a reasonable person that their freedom of movement was restricted to the extent of someone who was under formal arrest.

<u>Police-Dominated Atmosphere</u>

According to the Jones factors, this could include such factors as where the interview took place or how many police officers participated. In this case, although Defendant claims the police did not try to question him at his home, this was not the case. They tried several times to contact him at his home, and when they finally met up with Defendant they gave him the option of staying at home for questioning.

The claim that the police never attempted to interview him at his home is belied by the many times the police tried to contact him there, as well as their offer to question him at his home on the day of confession. While the questioning did take place at the police station rather than at the Defendant's home, this was only the case because Defendant requested it. Finally, as the Supreme Court noted in Mathiason, the police are "not required to give Miranda warnings. . . simply because the questioning takes place in the station house." Just because the Defendant was questioned at the police station does not mean he was under arrest. A reasonable person who requested to be interviewed at the police station would not take that as an indication that they were in custody.

Suspect Placed Under Arrest at Termination of Questioning

The Defendant was placed under arrest at the termination of questioning. However, it was only after he confessed to the murder. This does not indicate anything about the nature of the rest of the interrogation.

<u>Express Purpose of Interview</u>

The Defendant was not a suspect at the time of his interview. They just wanted to see if he had any helpful information about the case. In fact, Defendant knew this when he accompanied the officers to the police station. They informed him that they just wanted to talk to him because he had spoken with the victim on the day she died. This is a rational reason that the police would want to interview someone, and would not indicate to a reasonable person that the police were taking them into custody just based on that fact. This is more in line with the police interviewing the Defendant as a potential witness than as a suspect. They never indicated to the Defendant that they thought he might have committed the murder until well into the interview.

<u>Length of Interview</u>

The length of the interview goes to whether a reasonable person would believe they were in custody. Defendant in this case was interviewed by the police for a little over five hours. However, this is not dispositive of the issue. The defendant in Cray was questioned for seven hours, but was found to have not been subject to a custodial interrogation. And while he was in his own home, he was not allowed to contact anyone and he was always in the presence of the FBI agents. Here, Defendant was being interviewed by police for less time. Significantly, the questioning, though long, was not continuous. The Defendant was allowed to take cigarette breaks, and received water when he asked for it. The detectives gave Defendant the space he needed by telling [him] things like "take a deep breath," and "sit and relax and give it some thought." The interview was not of an intense and continuous nature as in Adams, and thus would not indicate to a reasonable person that they were unable to leave.

Conclusion

As the Cray court noted, there is no requirement that these factors be followed ritualistically in every Miranda case. The issue of custody cannot be resolved merely by counting up the number of factors on each side of the balance and rendering a decision accordingly. Cray. The ultimate inquiry must always be whether the Defendant was restrained as though he were under formal arrest. In this case, the court must be careful not to "lose sight of the forest for the trees," as the Cray court cautioned. Though the other factors also suggest there was no custody, great weight must be given to the fact that Defendant was informed on several occasions that he was free to terminate the questioning and leave at any point. The court must find that the Defendant was not subject to a custodial interrogation.

APPENDIX F

DEBRIEF OF SELECTED PRACTICE PTS AND SAMPLE ANSWERS HOUSED ON EPRODUCTS

Appendix F serves as a companion guide to ten of the PTs posted as practice exams on the book's West Academic eProducts website, at https://eproducts.westacademic.com. These exams are set in the following contexts: 1. Criminal Law, 2. Criminal Procedure, 3. Torts, 4. Contracts, 5. Civil Procedure, 6. Evidence, 7. Constitutional Law, 8 Professional Responsibility, 9. Real Property, and 10. Family Law. Readers should study the sections in this Appendix as you complete the corresponding practice task. You can:

1) Take each practice PT while enrolled in or shortly after you take the corresponding class in school. This will train lawyering skills while you are in the context of a particular legal subject area. Or,

2) Take all ten as supplemental PT training in the order they are described below. This is an excellent opportunity for students who want a longer runway for bar review, to complete these exams independently or in a law school pre-bar skills course. The suggested order for this second approach is:

- You will first take four 3-hour PTs in criminal law, criminal procedure, torts, and contracts.
- Then, you will take a 90-minute PT (in civil procedure).
- Next is the evidence-based PT that was designed to be completed in 3-hours or to break evenly into two 90-minute PTs. You can take it in one 3-hour sitting for endurance and stamina training or as two separate 90-minute PTs.
- Next, you will take another 90-minute PT on constitutional law.

- The last three PTs based respectively in professional responsibility (PR), real property, and family law are also 3-hour PTs, providing still more of the stamina and endurance training that is so essential for bar passage. PR is tested in many ways on most bar exams, so it can only help to give yourself an additional three hours of exposure to PR.

  I chose the practice PT for real property as the ultimate empowerment tool. Along the same lines as running 10 laps to get ready to easily run 5 laps, it is an excellent strategy to at least see the worst-case scenario and know that you will be OK. In real property, for many students the worst case would be an exam on the rule against perpetuities, a most dreaded rule. So what did I choose for you? Of course! A PT that allows you to face the rule against perpetuities for three hours. Tackle this PT, and you will know you can handle anything the examiners throw at you.

  The last PT is based in family law—a topic that will be tested on the NextGen bar exam. It is a 3-hour PT but one that you can easily shave time off of it you cannot afford to dedicate the full three hours. The family law PT is a creative and interesting exam that demands thinking outside the box and also provides excellent reinforcement of element-based analysis skills. The task in this family law PT is an investigation/discovery plan and thus provides exposure to both family law and civil procedure.

The text in this Appendix provides time-saving tips on how to complete a variation on each PT if do not have time to complete the entire exam. Remember, after graduation and during bar review, you will train under timed conditions. Thus, during law school is a great time to train PT muscle and stamina with longer exams, enabling you easily pass this portion of your bar exam. So, although I provide time-crunch tips, please do try to complete as many of the full PTs as possible.

1. CRIMINAL LAW

Bar exams may lump them together but in law school, criminal law and criminal procedure are very different courses. Criminal procedure courses typically focus on studying the Fourth, Fifth, and Sixth Amendments to the Constitution, looking at defendants' rights in cases of arrest and search and seizure of evidence, and considering constitutional rights with respect to defendants' statements. You learn about the history and evolution of the rights, how they have been guaranteed, when and where exceptions have been carved out, and more. You study mostly Supreme Court cases in law school criminal procedure courses.

In criminal law courses, you most often read appellate cases that focus on what is required for proof of certain elements of certain crimes. In typical criminal law courses, you study the elements of crimes, including:

- Homicidal offenses such as murder and manslaughter
- Structure crimes such as burglary and arson
- Theft crimes such as larceny and embezzlement
- Preliminary (or inchoate) crimes such as solicitation, attempt, and conspiracy
- Defense theories, such as self-defense and insanity

For teaching purposes, those cases are heavily edited to drill down into particular aspects of each concept. You may read cases illustrating different tests that have been adopted in different jurisdictions to establish certain legal theories. For instance, you will likely read about a number of tests for the insanity defense. You may also study the differing approaches various jurisdictions have taken to establish that a defendant has engaged in sufficient action (when coupled with the requisite intent) to support a conviction for attempt crimes. Casebooks often include historical perspectives, so you can see how the law has evolved over time in certain areas. You may study decisions that illustrate how courts may create exceptions to rules to mitigate the harshness of certain results, such as restricting criminal liability under the felony murder rule.

In bar exam criminal law essay questions, you are typically given a set of facts from which you have to determine the defendant's guilt with regard to one or more offenses. The interrogatory or query at the end of the fact pattern may ask if a defendant is guilty of particular crimes, or, simply, whether or not any crimes have been committed. To determine this, you will consider both the elements of relevant crimes themselves and relevant defenses. In criminal procedure essays, you are often considering whether the defendant's arrest, statements, or evidence seized from the defendant (or others) may be used against the defendant at trial, or whether such evidence will be suppressed.

The following are some of the many possible scenarios that could be tested on criminal law and procedure PTs:

- You may be asked to role-play as either a government attorney (a prosecutor) or a defense lawyer. As a prosecutor, you may have to determine whether the law and evidence support charging the defendant and/or convicting the defendant of particular crimes. As a defense attorney, you may be asked to prepare the defense case or prepare to plea bargain.
- You may be given statutory law and/or cases that specify what must be proven beyond a reasonable doubt, and you may have to study testimony or documentary evidence to determine the likelihood of conviction.
- You may have to write an investigation plan to determine how evidence may be obtained to prosecute or defend against a conviction.
- You may be asked to draft an argument to a judge to suppress evidence before a trial, or to draft a closing argument to a judge or jury to urge a conviction or argue that the prosecution has not met its burden of proof at the close of a criminal trial.
- You may be asked to draft an appellate brief arguing that a conviction at the trial level should be

overturned, or, if you represent the government, that the conviction should be upheld.

State v. Burke

Take three hours and complete the exam called *State v. Burke*. I strongly recommend that you complete this exam in full under timed conditions. If you do not have time, however, and prefer to take this exam in shorter sittings, read the following Time-Crunch Tips.

TIME-CRUNCH TIPS

You will see that *State v. Burke* involves two drafting tasks, both of which relate to several crimes the defendant may be charged with. To divide the exam into two practice tests, in your first sitting complete the part of Task A that relates to the possible violations of Columbia Criminal Code §§ 18–602(D) and 18–602(F), and also complete the part of Task B that relates to those same charges. In your second sitting, complete the part of Task A that relates to the possible violation of Columbia Criminal Code § 18–745 and the part of Task B that relates to that same charge. The Library divides neatly: the *Wallace* and *Zerbe* cases relate to the § 18–602 charges and the *Polin* and *Lathus* cases relate to the § 18–745 charge. You will need to read the entire File to write about all three charges, but because it will be familiar when you go to complete your second "practice test," you may need to spend about 100 minutes on §§ 18–602(D) and 18–602(F), and only 80 minutes on § 18–745. If you have even less time, just complete the document requested in Task A for the crimes in Columbia Criminal Code §§ 18–602(D) and 18–602(F), referring only to *Wallace* and *Zerbe* (about 60 minutes total), and then complete only Task A for the crime in Columbia Criminal Code § 18–745, referring only to *Polin* and *Lathus* (about 30 minutes).

DEBRIEFING TIPS AND STRATEGIES

Note: Read this section only **after** completing the *State v. Burke* assignments.

Why *State v. Burke* as a practice criminal law exam? I chose *State v. Burke* for a few reasons. The first is that this test provides a superb review of one of the most fundamental underpinnings of criminal law: the requirement of proof beyond a reasonable doubt. Next, the highly structured tasks in *Burke* also remind us that crimes (like torts and many other areas of law) are element based. Typically, each element of each cause of action in a civil case must be proven by a preponderance of the evidence; each element of each crime must be proven beyond a reasonable doubt. Third, the *Burke* exam provides exposure to some crimes that one may not study in criminal law classes: criminal trespass and assault with a deadly weapon. Finally, the exam is set in the early stages of prosecution, while the government is deciding whether there is enough evidence—and if that evidence is credible enough and persuasive enough—to proceed to trial. Therefore, this PT provides a good opportunity for you to look at facts when they are most malleable: before trial, when they are not yet proven "evidence."

Instructions/Assignment

In *Burke*, you play the role of an assistant district attorney; in other words, you are a government prosecutor. The case is realistic, especially compared with typical law school essays and multiple-choice style exams, both because of the uncertainty about the facts and because it brings in political concerns as well as legal concerns. You might think it is not realistic that a new lawyer would be asked to make such an important determination, but a former student of mine, when she was still in law school, was clerking for a district attorney's office when a recession hit; due to budget constraints and attorneys being tied up with other cases, research assignments just like this one regarding *Burke* were regularly given to law clerks.

Doctrinal classes in law school look at whether a party will likely prevail on the merits of a lawsuit, but they generally avoid discussion of why parties bring or fail to bring lawsuits, or resolve actions prior to trial. I raise this topic because a big part of law practice is advising clients on whether to file lawsuits in the first place, how to solve their problems without litigation, and/or whether to settle (civil cases) or plea bargain (in criminal cases) prior to trial. (According to some sources more than 95%

of criminal cases end in plea bargains.) These questions involve assessment far beyond simply whether the elements of each cause of action or crime can be established.

As far as facts go, both in PTs (and in this one in particular) and in the real world, witnesses are not always credible. Certain versions of "the facts" may not always be reliable. This is radically different from law school or bar exam essay questions on which you must accept facts as given. On law essay exams, you are being tested precisely on your ability to apply the facts, as stated, to the law you know. On essays, you must not question whether the facts are believable. In contrast, in this PT and in most day-to-day lawyering, you *must* question facts.

I use a criminal law example to explain why *not* to question facts in essays. In this particular essay, the facts say that the defendant "shot at the victim" from a "very far distance away," in a "dark alley," and "aimed at the victim's toe." Students frequently will argue: "But, Professor, there is no way a person could aim at the toe, especially from that far away in the dark." My reply? "So what?! These are the facts. Use them." I then urge my students to ask why exam drafters might have included the fact that the defendant "aimed at the victim's toe." Readers, you will likely see this! These facts allow the test taker to argue that the defendant did not intend to kill but merely to injure the victim, thus potentially affecting the determination of whether the defendant acted with malice aforethought. (Aiming at the toe negates the intent-to-kill presumption raised by the use of a deadly weapon because, generally, one who intends to kill aims at a vital area, such as the head or chest.) Note that malice might nonetheless be established here, but only through intent to seriously injure or reckless disregard for human life rather than intent to kill (which in turn affects whether the resulting crime might be murder in the first or second degree). Do you see how many discussable issues (and points) stem from the test taker's thorough use of the facts presented? Do you also see that a reader who told himself or herself "No one could possibly aim at the toe in this situation, so I'm going to ignore this silly fact" may well fail the essay!

The point is that, unlike in essays where you must use even implausible facts, in PTs you can and often must question the facts. In *State v. Burke*, there were many potential factual problems. Did you see them? There are witnesses whose vantage points were such that they may not have gotten a good look at what happened between Burke and Passon. Other witnesses had motives to exaggerate (i.e., they were biased). Yes, this skeptical thinking goes beyond the "four corners" of the exam, but it is highly relevant to what is being asked of you on this PT, which is to determine if the prosecution (your office) has sufficient evidence to prove guilt beyond a reasonable doubt of each element of each crime. To respond effectively on this PT, you *had* to question the "facts."

Let's walk through the File and make some observations about what you saw or should have seen as you were reading.

The General Instructions

The first thing that you should have noticed was the percentage split, telling you how much each of the two required tasks was worth. On this exam, the only place to find this information was in these General Instructions; it was not repeated anywhere else in the exam. It would be helpful to transfer such information immediately to either the Task Memo or your scratch paper.

Here, Task A is worth 50% to 60% and Task B is worth 40% to 50%. That is close to equal, with Task A being weighted slightly more heavily than Task B. Your takeaway? You needed to allocate slightly more time to complete Task A than Task B. But, given that Task B was worth up to 50%, you had to give it almost equal attention, and clearly a poor job on Task B could sink your final score. (Many students who failed this exam made the mistake of spending too much time on Task A and running short on Task B.)

TIP: COMPLETE PT TASKS IN ORDER

When a PT includes more than one task, complete them in order. Finishing the first task often helps you complete the second one. Also, if you happen to run short on time as you are finishing the second task (which should *not* happen if you have trained thoroughly and practiced with all the exams in this book), others may also be rushing to finish that second task, so your answer will be comparable in thoroughness. Generally, write the documents out of order only if you freeze or have writer's block against the first task and are able to begin the second task more easily. In that case, do what it takes to get your brain and fingers moving.

In *Burke*, the General Instructions tell you that you are an assistant district attorney. Thus, you know—and should keep in mind as you read through the File and Library—that you have certain additional ethical obligations required of prosecutors.

The Instructions also tell you, and you see this again in the Library, that all four cases are Supreme Court of Columbia cases. The pending matter, the prosecution of Burke, is set in state court in the State of Columbia. What do you know from this? That unless one case overrules another, all of the Library case law is binding.

The Task Memo

The next File document is the Task Memo. (The Task Memo has historically always followed the General Instructions.) The Task Memo explains some of the complicating factors in our case, namely:

- The prior history between defendant and victim
- The victim's and even the police's alleged ties to one of the entities in the case, and the money that is generated from the racetrack
- That this case is what D.A. Boland describes as a political "hot potato." (Note that the politics are underscored in the article at the end of the File. Pay attention when information is repeated by bar examiners, on PTs and essays!)

In the Task Memo, D.A. Boland gives you background on and a nice summary of the case, then requests that you complete two tasks. The first task he calls a "second assessment of the case." That term always throws students. They think, "I have never done this; I have no idea what a 'second assessment' is." Then they panic. But you need not be rattled, and I hope you weren't. Read beyond the name of the task to see what they really want, and you discover that the "second assessment" is simply an internal memorandum with a special name. Specifically, in this "second assessment" memo, you are to:

- Advise the DA whether, based on evidence you currently have in the File, there is sufficient proof of each element of each crime to support a conviction (i.e., whether each element is established beyond a reasonable doubt)
- Consider potential defenses and credibility or proof problems
- Conclude with a recommendation of whether to proceed to trial or not

How should you organize your answer? The instructions make it clear: element-by-element, under each respective count. The fact that these instructions were so specific was a gift.

While reading the instructions, you might have helped yourself by writing exactly what is being asked of you in your notes. Pull components out of the Task Memo and get them either on your scratch paper or typed into your first "draft" of your answer. As you complete your final answer, look back at the Task Memo and be sure you included all parts of what was requested. In other words, confirm the task to be sure that your answer was responsive and complete. For example, did you write about the proof that exists to establish each element beyond a reasonable doubt *and* about defenses and credibility concerns, but forget to conclude with a final recommendation on whether to prosecute? That final recommendation on each count was critical. Failing to make such a recommendation would show the grader that you did not read the directions and possibly make it look like you did not finish analyzing that particular count. (The examiners put a premium on *completing* PT tasks.) Re-reading the Task Memo several times (before, during, and after you draft your final answer) will prevent your uploading an incomplete answer.

In the second document, you are again asked to proceed element by element on each charge, but here you are to determine what *additional evidence* might be gathered. For the second task, you are given a Format Memo on how to set up the assignment, which they call a "Follow-Up Investigation Plan." (Again, the name threw people who did not read carefully and see that everything requested was spelled out explicitly.)

The first page of this office procedure memo tells you what a "Follow-Up Investigation Plan" is; the second page gives an example. The first page says, among other important points: "Each charge is to be stated separately, and the additional evidence related thereto listed under the element . . . to which it applies, with a notation of the possible source from which the evidence may be obtained."

If you are a visual person, you might actually "see" this language in a tiered outline format such as this:

Charge 1

____

Element 1

____

> Additional evidence proving element 1 (and where to find that evidence). Note here that you may have several pieces of evidence that you could investigate or discover that might prove element 1. List everything you can think of and note where and how you might *ethically* find it.

____

____

____

Element 2

____

> Additional evidence proving element 2

____

____

____

Charge 2

____

Element 1

____

Additional evidence proving element 1

____

____

____

Element 2

____

Additional evidence proving element 2

____

____

____

Note: In this PT, you are role-playing a lawyer for the government. Pay close attention to the ethical obligations of prosecutors. Also, no matter who you represent on any PT, *never* suggest an illegal or unethical means for discovering evidence, no matter how much it might help prove your case.

The sample you are given on the next page of the Format Memo illustrates this format: the first count, "robbery," under which elements are listed: (1) the identity of the perpetrator; and (2) the force or fear element. Under each element is a brainstorming list of all the evidence that might prove that element, and, where applicable, how one might obtain such evidence. (For example, under force or fear, it is suggested that there may be a weapon; to get that weapon, we may need a warrant to search the house.)

A key part of PT success is following directions; where they are specific about a format, such as here, you must follow it. Such specificity is a gift. It takes all the guesswork out of how to respond. You just need to follow the sample precisely. You may have to read that sample two or three times to fully understand it and see how to translate the elements of your case into that format, but the organization is given to you.

Remainder of the File

The next document you see, the "Information" or criminal complaint, clearly sets forth the elements of the two charges: criminal trespass and assault with a deadly weapon. Remember, you were told in the Task Memo that these were the two charges, so you should have been expecting to see them in this charging document.

> **TIP: USE FILE DOCUMENTS AS SAMPLES FOR DRAFTING PT TASKS**
>
> When working through practice PT Files, take a step back and look at the various documents in the File for ideas on how you would draft this sort of document if it were your task. Looking at this Information, you can see what goes into a criminal complaint: just a plain and simple statement of the defendant's having committed the elements of each charged offense. (Would you have been comfortable if you had been asked to draft a criminal complaint? I hope that after completing this practice PT, you would!)

Now, the Library will also provide the relevant Criminal Code sections, but this Information tells you which particular sections the defendant is charged under, and you can begin separating them out into elements:

Under § 18–602(D), that the defendant:

(1) entered the property,

(2) with the intent to interfere or obstruct.

OR, under § 18–602(F), that the defendant:

(1) entered the property which was enclosed by a fence, **AND**,

(2) refused **OR** failed to leave when requested to do so.

Notice that in the previous outline I bolded and wrote my "OR" and "AND" in all caps. Whenever I read a statute, I circle or put a box around the words "and" and "or" so that I know if elements or provisions must all be proven (if they are conjunctive), or if only one or the other must be proven (if they are disjunctive). Use this technique when reading statutes on PTs.

In the second charge, the assault, you see two elements: (1) the assault to the victim's person, **AND** (2) with a deadly weapon or instrument **AND/OR** with force likely to produce great bodily injury.

Note: Do not rely on the Information alone to determine the elements. These code sections are in the Library. Read them carefully there as well to see if this Information document has stated the law correctly. (A document drafted by someone in your office may be correct, but it is also possible that the document contains errors and thus should be amended.) Also, as you can tell by the sample with the Robbery charge in the Format Memo, "identity of the perpetrator" must necessarily be established in order to charge that particular person with the crime. So, we also may need to add that, especially if it becomes unclear as we read whether the defendant in question committed the criminal acts in question. (You might make a note to yourself as soon as you think of this to add "identity of the perpetrator" as an element in both the second assessment and follow-up investigation plan.)

The following is my continued debriefing of the File, which I wrote in the first person, telling you what I would say to myself while reading each document. (It often helps to talk to yourself as you read PTs—it keeps you awake and focused!) Print a copy of the File (from the eProducts) and refer to it as you read the following.

> My next File document is the sheriff's arrest report. Before I even start reading this document, I remember that my boss, the DA giving me this assignment, told me that these sheriffs may be biased. I know generally that an arrest report may be impeached. And, I know one of my tasks is to see if there is enough evidence right now, based on what we have, to convict. But I also know my other task is to write a plan about getting additional evidence. So, I skim the police report with those thoughts in mind. The police report, signed by a deputy named Angel Coderra, includes a great deal of information about where the picketers allegedly were and what exactly they were doing, and specifically

where the defendant allegedly was and what he allegedly did or failed to do.

For this first read-through of the File, my plan is to skim each document, just to see what it is, who wrote it, and basically what sort of factual information it contains. I know that I will not yet know what specifically to look for in the File documents until I read the Library. So I know I will return to these File documents once I know the law that governs. (It's an open-book test. The File will be there for me when I need it.) I keep the word "allegedly" in my mind as I'm reading the police report because, as the prosecutor, I have to be certain I can prove the requisite facts in court, establishing each element beyond a reasonable doubt. A police officer may be biased, mistaken, or lying; and, again, here I know from the Task Memo that there are at least suggestions of sheriff bias.

The next document is a statement of the alleged victim, Joe Passon. This is Passon's account of events. Again, only after reading the Library will I know exactly what I am searching for in this document. At that time, I definitely will want to compare what Passon said happened to other witnesses' versions of events.

The next document is a report from the chief county investigator, the same man District Attorney Boland directed to interview witnesses. The investigator indicates that each of the five witnesses' statements is "summarized." In other words, this document is what the investigator says they said, not necessarily in their own words, so we are not certain that these witnesses will testify exactly as these summaries indicate. (We may immediately note in our second task that this is information we will need to confirm.)

Be skeptical. The hint that you should question "facts" in the File was in the Task Memo when you were told to take into account witness credibility. Were you thinking that these summaries may or may not be completely accurate? Were you telling yourself we may need to double-check certain points? If so, great! You should be skeptical and thinking about getting more information, because you know your second task is precisely about conducting further investigation.

The investigator's first witness (Pentivo) clearly was not present at the scene; he was at the north gate of the property and the alleged incidents occurred at the south gate. You may want to draw a diagram of the property where the incident occurred to try to keep straight what allegedly happened where.

The Memo tells you more than once that Pentivo does not have firsthand knowledge of the events but just heard about them from others. What Pentivo does give is background on both Passon (the alleged victim) and Burke (the defendant and alleged perpetrator), and about the "bad blood" (as Boland described it in the Task Memo) or past history between the two.

The investigator's second witness (Joey Culmone) was present at the scene of the alleged incident but does not seem eager to testify about what he knew. (Why might he be reluctant to testify? Think about how that affects our case, if at all.) Culmone's version of events also differs drastically from both the police report and Passon's account. If Culmone were to be believed, this would cast significant doubt on our ability to prove either the trespass or the assault charges beyond a reasonable doubt.

Note: You may not have seen all this until your re-read of the File.

The investigator's next witness (Jack Beta) was allegedly present, but could not see clearly because of the crowds surrounding the car in which Passon claimed to have been assaulted. Jack Beta may therefore easily be impeached, because he did not have a clear line of sight at the time.

The investigator's next witness was Joseph Passon, the alleged victim. Interestingly, the investigator notes that Passon's statement was identical to the statement included earlier in the File (that the deputy attached to the police report), with certain exceptions the investigator enumerates. The investigator's report fleshes out further information about bad blood between Passon and Burke, but also notes these inconsistencies in Passon's statements. These will be critical in efforts that defense counsel might make to discredit the victim.

The investigator's final witness is Junior Harwood, the alleged passenger in Joseph Passon's car at the time of the incident. The investigator notes that Harwood is both a friend and neighbor of Passon's, so there is great room for bias. It also notes that Harwood himself says he did not clearly see what happened or whose stick hit Passon.

The last item in the File is a newspaper editorial. Even newspaper articles written by respected journalists are not fact, but this is especially true here because this is an *editorial* piece. Including this sort of document in the File is a classic PT move; you must be able to see that what is stated in such a document is not fact but someone's opinion. It does, however, provide a great deal of food for thought on bias.

If at all possible, you should try to weave in mention of this editorial somewhere in your memo. This document highlights the political pressure that the DA is under from opposing constituencies to bring or drop the charges against Burke, and you may want to underscore that your office is obligated to follow the law, not public opinion.

Note: Many students avoid referring to this newspaper piece altogether because they do not know what to say about it. Here, because your task is to draft an internal memo to the DA, rather than a document meant for someone outside your office, you can easily weave this in either in an introduction or a conclusion if you do not see another spot for it, to reiterate that despite political pressures the DA should hold firm in prosecuting or not, per your recommendations.

Bottom line: Try to make at least some mention of every document in the File and make every effort to reference all the main cases in the Library. (You do not have to mention every case within the main cases, but try to mention every main case, meaning every case listed in the table of contents.)

Library

The Library (your closed legal universe) includes a few code sections (Columbia Criminal Code) and four cases (Columbia Supreme Court). This case was filed in state court in Columbia, so everything in the Library appears to be binding authority.

NOTE-TAKING TIPS

As suggested earlier, it is helpful to experiment with note-taking systems while completing practice tests. The exam is "open book." You can always and at any time go to the Library and look up any rules or to the File and locate additional details you want to reference. Still, it can be useful to have all the main rules on one page. You can also "book brief" on the actual cases, noting the issue, holding, key facts, rationale, and dicta. Then "key" your book briefing to page numbers that you jot down on one page (that you will delete before uploading) in your answer file. For example, write something like "H at p. 3" next to the printed case name to indicate that you have marked the holding of that case on page 3 of the Library.

The Code Sections

Note that here you are provided only selected relevant statutes, so you must read them carefully. Compare this with a PT Library in which you are given a block of a particular code, with sections numbered sequentially, and where only certain sections apply to your case. Examples of such a "reference Library" are in the PTs in the contracts, evidence, and professional responsibility debriefed in this appendix.

Here, you have the criminal trespass and the assault with a deadly weapon statutes under which Burke was charged, and an exemption for union activity. If that exemption is applicable, it would serve as a defense and would negate Burke's guilt with respect to the criminal trespass. You will need to study each provision; as you read, circle every "and" and "or" and underline elements to learn exactly what is required under each statute.

Cases

Here I highlight just a few points about each case. I have noted the years only because the instructions told us they were all Columbia Supreme Court cases, so you must keep track of whether a case might be older and no longer applicable for some reason. (The *Burke* matter took place in 1987.)

Wallace and *Zerbe* both relate to the criminal trespass, whereas *Lathus* and *Polin* both relate to the assault. The Library will not always divide that neatly, but here it does, and seeing that would be helpful to your organization.

Note: You will not organize your PT answer in a case-by-case fashion. Rather, you will weave important points from the cases, as relevant, into your answer, and organize your answer using an element-by-element approach, under each charge. (An answer organized case-by-case would likely have failed. The instructions told you how to organize your answer, so you had to do what was asked to pass.)

TIP: SAVING TIME WITH CASE CITES

The Instructions tell you that you may abbreviate cases. You score no additional "points" with the grader by providing full cites, and it wastes your time to do so. On PTs, typically you reference civil cases by the plaintiff's or appellant's name. In criminal cases, you reference using the defendant's name because the other party is typically the "state" or the "people" in every case. You can see, in my debriefing of the cases, that I use short cites just as you would have wanted to do in your answer to this PT.

Wallace (1970)

In this case, the court (the Supreme Court of Columbia) reversed a conviction for criminal trespass, holding that some actual "obstruction" (actual physical interference) is required for a conviction of criminal trespass. The court found that the activity of the protestors in the case did not amount to an actual obstruction because members of the public were still free to do what they wished despite protestors' presence, and that the protestors were exercising their lawful rights to convey information.

Zerbe (1981)

The defendant was found not guilty of criminal trespass, even though his actions violated statute § 18–602(F), because of the exception for lawful labor union activities provided by § 18–603. The case suggests that the labor exemption to the trespass statute for lawful union activities should be construed liberally to protect union activity, when there is no violence. *Zerbe* cited *Northwestern,* distinguishing it as a case in which the activity resulted in physical obstruction of traffic and was "accompanied by threats of violence to employees . . . ."

Note: If you wanted to cite *Northwestern* in your answer, you would do so as follows: "*Northwestern* as cited in *Zerbe.*" Why? Because the grader's "point sheet" or grading rubric will likely expect to see references to all the main cases (which, again, are those listed in the Library table of contents), so the grader will be looking to see that you cited *Zerbe* in your answer.

If Burke's activities are deemed unlawful, the union exemption will not apply. However, if his activities are deemed lawful, his engaging in union activity, even if he was trespassing, will negate the criminality of the trespass.

After reading this case, you know exactly what you are looking for when you go back to re-read the File. You want to know if Burke was actually obstructing people. If he gave them information and they turned away on their own, that may not amount to an unlawful obstruction. Armed with what you learned in the Library, you would be able to go back to the File and easily figure out what your office can prove Burke did or did not do.

You also want to know if Burke either committed acts of violence or threatened violence. We know some people said he did, but did all the witnesses' accounts match up? Can we prove this in court? Taken together, *Zerbe* and *Wallace* underscore the difficulty we may have in proving beyond a reasonable doubt that Burke had the requisite criminal intent for the trespass.

Polin (1981)

From the *Polin* case, we learn that "great bodily injury" need not be permanent or visible, but must be more than "slight, trivial, or minor." In *Polin,* the victim suffered burns, lesions, a ruptured eardrum, and an eye hemorrhage. The court cites other cases involving examples of serious injuries that all amount to great bodily injury (*Wells, James,* and *Grigsby*).

Clearly, after reading *Polin*, you want to go back to the File to see what harm Passon allegedly suffered and determine if the injuries clearly amount to "great bodily injury." If you did not see this on first read, when you go back to re-read the File, it will be very obviously troubling that Passon just plain forgot the details of some of his alleged injuries. ("How serious could they be if he forgot about them?," you must have wondered.)

Lathus (1983)

This case informs readers about two issues: what is a deadly weapon, and whether recklessness or a general intent may be sufficient for this assault crime. About the first issue, the court cites a number of other cases where objects were found to be deadly weapons, including a nail file. The court stressed that it is not just the inherent nature of the instrument but the manner in which it is used. It seems likely that a wooden stake such as that used by Burke and the other picketers would qualify, if Burke indeed used it in a deadly manner (which is still a big question).

On the second issue, the *Lathus* court found that assault with a deadly weapon is essentially a general intent crime, meaning that the intent required is only that the defendant "willfully commit" an act that has the "probable consequence" of resulting in injury to another. There is no requirement that the defendant have the specific intent to actually cause great bodily harm or death or to seriously injure this victim.

Summary of Case Work

After reading *Polin* and *Lathus*, you should have been able to zoom right in to certain facts in the File and much more readily see their significance in relation to whether or not Burke can likely be convicted on the assault charge. It was very obvious, in *State v. Burke,* that skimming the File before reading these cases just gave you general background information. In re-reading the File, after studying the Library cases, you could see much more clearly whether we now have sufficient evidence establishing that Burke actually obstructed customers and, accordingly, whether his picketing actions were lawful, and whether he possessed the requisite intent to and actually caused injuries amounting to great bodily harm. You also likely saw much more easily what additional evidence to investigate.

PULLING IT ALL TOGETHER

Once you have the law in mind, go back through the File and you will see what evidence is critical. It also becomes much clearer where evidence may be contradictory (here, different stories from different witnesses).

An organizing tip: Because both memos were organized charge-by-charge and, under each charge, element-by-element, you could actually set up one outline, copy it, and then work simultaneously to flesh out both outlines. How would that work? Well, as you are reading to insert what will have to be proven in the first memo (whether we have sufficient evidence to prove each element beyond a reasonable doubt), if a "more facts needed" question pops into your head (such as "I wonder where the property line actually ended and if Burke crossed the boundary?" or "I wonder how sharp the stick actually was?"), you could immediately scroll down and insert those questions (asking for more detail or to fill in missing information) in the appropriate place in Memo Two. This approach—writing the two memos at the same time—will not work for every PT, but the key is always to read the instructions carefully enough that you know exactly what your job is. Here, if you scrutinized the Task Memo before writing, it might well have jumped out at you that the organization was the same in both memos, prompting you to ask yourself if there was any way to take advantage of that.

Affirmative Defenses, Failing to Prove One's Case, and Credibility Problems

On PTs, I generally find that many students fall short in giving enough weight to the defense perspective. Perhaps this results from the sort of automatic IRAC training where students take fact patterns and organize them by potential causes of action or crimes. In fact, one trick that I remind students about when memorizing elements of causes of action is to put right into the laundry list "lack of defenses." I know that is not an element per se, and you know that is not an element, but if a defendant can assert a valid affirmative defense, then the plaintiff will not prevail just as surely as if the plaintiff had not proven all the elements of his or her case-in-chief to begin with.

In the *Burke* PT, most people recognize the statutory defense because the Library included a case on it. However, many downplay the credibility, bias, and other problems that are rampant throughout the *Burke* File. Think about the big picture: Why is the DA asking for a second assessment on whether to take this case to trial? He does not want surprises. He does not want to lose. You must let the DA know, as explicitly and specifically as possible, what problems he will face at trial. Of course, on the surface it looks like Burke may have committed both crimes (the trespass and the assault), but if surface analysis were all that was needed here, you would not have been given this assignment. Identifying the proof problems in this case was critical to doing well on this PT. That is what shows the grader you can think like a lawyer, not just a law student.

In addition to not always recognizing how biased witnesses were, some of the other challenges students often have with *Burke* are spending so much time on the first task that they run out of time on the second task, and wasting time writing a statement of facts (and other parts of a traditional law school memo) that was not requested in the Task Memo instructions. Study the sample answers in eProducts and compare them to the answer you wrote. Look for any places where you might improve.

SPIN-OFF EXERCISES

Spin-off exercises provide a way to gain exposure to drafting different types of documents using the same facts and law as on the PT you just completed. Spend a few minutes, now that you have completed *State v. Burke*, to think of other tasks you could have been given and how you would have handled them. Here are a few suggestions:

- Draft a letter to the defendant's (Burke's) counsel to propose a plea bargain.
- Draft a memo outlining the pros and cons of entering into a plea-bargain arrangement with Burke in this instance.

- Draft an anticipated cross-examination plan of Joe Passon, the alleged victim, showing how he may be discredited if we end up relying on his testimony.
- Draft an anticipated cross-examination plan of Deputy Coderra, the arresting officer, showing how he may be discredited if we end up relying on his testimony.
- Pretend that you represent the defendant, Mr. Burke, instead of working for the DA in this PT. Would you look at the evidence against Burke differently?

Note: In a sense, because you were asked to analyze the evidence thoroughly and look at all information that might be used to support Burke and impeach our witnesses, you really should not suddenly see the case in a new light if you were defense counsel. Nevertheless, if my simply asking you to *pretend* you are wearing the defense hat causes you to view any facts or law in a different light, great! This may be a technique (pretending you are counsel for the other side) that you want to employ more often when working on PTs, to ensure that you see the whole picture.

PRACTICE AND LAW SCHOOL AND PTs: COMPARE AND CONTRAST

This PT provides a wonderful exercise in factual analysis, and, if you get "into" it, it is very exciting. Although it may seem unrealistic that as a lawyer just out of law school you would be asked to give an assessment about whether or not to prosecute a matter that is so politically charged, it is a far more realistic assignment than a typical law school or bar exam essay question. (Precisely because a case is politically charged, new lawyers in the office or even law clerks may be asked to research and give second opinions, to have a few extra eyes look at the case before proceeding to trial.) This exam also allowed you a chance to see yourself as a prosecutor and assume a prosecutor's ethical responsibilities.

This exam forces you to look at facts in a very different manner than you look at an essay fact pattern. What do I mean? Well, in essays, as in appellate work, the facts are essentially frozen. (On appeal, you must work with the facts that were proven at trial; on a law school or bar exam essay, you must work with the fact pattern as written.) Here, though, in *Burke*, we basically only have informal statements from witnesses. Nothing has yet been proven, so no fact is set in stone. We have a victim who contradicts himself, or at least "forgets" key details. We also have witnesses who are extremely biased. This is real-world stuff!

In working through this PT with my students, I have found that many are uncomfortable with, and take time getting used to, the idea that the sources of information may be so biased. We have sheriffs who are moonlighting for the racetrack that is pressing for the defendant to be prosecuted; we have witnesses who have clearly taken sides and have a lot at stake, financially and personally; we have a victim who has a negative personal history with the defendant and thus a possible motive to fabricate testimony. However, after really understanding the assignments, students embrace this exercise and usually enjoy looking closely into credibility and bias.

Working through a practice PT exam like *Burke* helps you as a law student in many ways and even may give you an edge if you end up with some sort of criminal law-related job or internship.

KEY TAKEAWAYS

- Be skeptical on PTs. Sources of "facts" may be biased, and "facts" are not firm until they have been proven in court. (Even then, remember that a witness may be cross-examined.)
- Crimes often lend themselves to element-based analysis. Be sure to know the exact elements of each offense, and the elements of any possible defenses.
- Think about evidence you currently have and whether it is sufficient to prove each element beyond a reasonable doubt. Think also about evidence or information you may still need to discover.

2. CRIMINAL PROCEDURE

OVERVIEW OF CRIMINAL PROCEDURE[1]

In law school, criminal law and criminal procedure are very different courses. On bar exams, they are often considered one subject.

Typically, criminal law is a 1L course where you study the elements of crimes: the actus reus and mens rea requirements of homicidal offenses such as murder and manslaughter, and defenses to those crimes such as self-defense, intoxication, and insanity. You might also study structure crimes such as burglary and arson, theft crimes such as larceny and embezzlement, and preliminary (or "inchoate") crimes such as solicitation, attempt, and conspiracy.

Most often, you study these various crimes by reading appellate court cases where the defendants have argued that the prosecution did not meet its burden of proving one or more elements of a particular crime or crimes (or of a defense theory). This helps you understand the law in a certain jurisdiction. You may read a number of cases about the same crime or crimes from different jurisdictions to see how older law has evolved and/or how present law differs in different states or in the federal courts. For example, you will likely study several different tests employed in varying jurisdictions dealing with how close to the completion of the target offense a defendant's actions must be in order for that defendant to be guilty of an attempt crime. This area makes for fascinating discussion in law school, especially because we know that just thinking even the most evil of thoughts is not a crime, but action taken toward completing a crime with the intent to complete the crime may amount to a criminal act.

By contrast, criminal procedure courses in law school are often 2L courses in which you study the constitutional law that affects the rights of the accused, and the obligations and responsibilities of police and prosecutors. In most criminal procedure courses, students read cases dealing with the Fourth,

---

[1] Readers interested in this field who want an overview of the criminal justice system, from arrest to appeal, see *The Criminal Law Handbook*, Bergman and Berman, Nolo.com.

Fifth, and Sixth Amendments to the United States Constitution, looking at the defendant's rights during police stops, arrests, and searches and seizures of evidence. You also typically study the rights of an accused when the police are questioning a suspect or defendant, including due process rights, the right to receive *Miranda* warnings, and the right to counsel.

Criminal procedure courses also often look into the history and evolution of these rights, how they have been guaranteed, when and where exceptions have been carved out, and where the courts are likely to expand or curtail these rights in the future. (You study mostly Supreme Court cases in law school criminal procedure courses.)

In bar review, you will fill in gaps in both criminal law and criminal procedure. Your law school professors typically cover fewer areas than you are responsible for on the bar exam, but in much more detail. (One of my colleagues says the bar exam is 1 foot deep and 6 feet wide, whereas law school courses are 6 feet deep and 1 foot wide. Another colleague likens law school to scuba diving and the bar exam to snorkeling.)

On the bar exam, you will not typically have to have the depth of knowledge that law school courses require, but you will have to have a wide breadth of knowledge, including knowing rules that many basic law school criminal procedure courses skip. For example, you must know rules about bail, the rights to a jury trial and a speedy trial, sentencing, and double jeopardy. For a list of the topics covered in both criminal law and criminal procedure, consult the websites for your jurisdiction and/or the NCBE which will have subject matter outlines.

Note: It is a good thing that many law school courses spend so much time on arrests, searches, and seizures, as those tend to be the most heavily tested areas on bar exam criminal procedure questions.

PTs that are set in criminal law and procedure contexts may take a number of different forms. You might be asked to role-play as a government attorney (a prosecutor) or a defense lawyer. In one of those roles, you may be asked to determine whether the law and evidence support charging the defendant (or dropping charges if criminal charges have been filed) or convicting the defendant of particular crimes. You may be given statutory and/or case law that specifies what must be proven beyond a reasonable doubt, and you may have to study testimony or documentary evidence to determine what the likelihood of conviction is. You may be analyzing possible defense theories, or you may be drafting a discovery plan to determine how evidence may be obtained to defend against a conviction. You may be asked to draft an argument to a judge to suppress evidence before a trial, or to draft a closing argument to a judge or jury urging that your client should prevail at the close of a criminal trial. You may be asked to draft a trial brief or an appellate brief. You could be asked to negotiate a plea bargain, or advise a client on whether or not to plead guilty.

SIMULATED CRIMINAL PROCEDURE-BASED PT

Take three hours, go to the eProducts, and complete the *People v. Duncan* test ("*Duncan*").

TIME-CRUNCH TIPS

If you still want to write the *Duncan* exam but cannot take three hours now, here are a couple of suggestions: (1) Read the entire *Duncan* File and Library and thoroughly outline your answer, but do not write it out in full. This will likely take you about 90 minutes. (2) Read through all of *Duncan,* but in drafting your opposition to the defendant's motion to dismiss, only address the first few of the eight factors of the balancing test you will find (in your Library reading) that the courts consider when determining whether there was "custody" for purposes of *Miranda.* If you address all eight factors, you will need the full 180 minutes to complete the test, but you can shave off substantial time if you practice by addressing only some of the factors. Note that certain factors will be easier to establish than others, so in the best of circumstances, you would take the time and write out the answer in full.

INSIDE THIS TEST: TIPS AND STRATEGIES

Read the following only after you have completed the *Duncan* practice exam. You may want to print a copy of the File and Library and have it with you to reference as you read through this debrief.

Inside the File, Starting with the Instructions

I love this exam. It drills down into *Miranda*, one of the most heavily tested areas on bar exam criminal procedure questions, and it reminds us of the fundamentals: *Miranda* protects people in situations involving custodial interrogation. That means it focuses on those who are **both** *in custody* **and** being *interrogated*.

You probably did lots of studying in law school about what constitutes *interrogation*. (You might recall that it involves not just explicit questioning but also words or actions designed to elicit a response.) In this question, however, your work centered on whether this defendant, Mr. Duncan, was in *custody*. It was clear that he was being interrogated: He was questioned for nearly six hours! However, Mr. Duncan says he was also in custody, and the prosecution (us in this PT) disagrees.

Now, let's plunge in and walk through the exam. As far as Instructions, remember there are three potential documents that typically provide directions: (1) the General Instructions, (2) the Task Memo, and possibly (3) a Format Page. Here there are only two; there is no Format Page.

The General Instructions are essentially boilerplate in this exam. They tell you that you have a File and a Library—nothing unusual. They say you have three hours to complete it. The Instructions note that you are in state court, in the State of Columbia. There is only one document to draft, so you need not worry about allocating time between tasks. With nothing unusual, you only need to take a very quick glance at the General Instructions, and because there are no Format Pages, you know that all the real "directions" will come from the Task Memo.

So, on to the Task Memo! Despite being only two paragraphs long, the Task Memo is full of important detail. The first critical pieces of information you want to pull out are who you are and whom you represent. How do you find that here? First things first, look at the letterhead: "Warren County Prosecutor" in the office of "Alicia Ouelette, District Attorney" from "Averil Park, Columbia."

Next, the assignment comes from Laurie Shanks, who is the "Deputy District Attorney." Laurie Shanks jumps in, saying "*We* have indicted Raymond Duncan for the murder of Jennifer Clark" (emphasis added). You know from this first sentence that this PT is set in a criminal law context and that it involves a murder trial.

Laurie Shanks continues using the word "we" in the next few sentences, eventually saying that the defense has filed a motion to suppress and that she wants "You" (that's you, bar exam applicant) to draft the brief arguing to the court that the defense motion should be denied. Clearly, "you" are part of the "we" that is the office of the District Attorney. Thus, you work for the prosecutor's office, and Laurie Shanks is giving you your assignment, so she is likely your supervisor.

The last sentence of the first paragraph clearly requests the document you are to produce in this PT: "Please prepare a draft of a Persuasive Memorandum of Points and Authorities that argues the motion should be denied." The entire second paragraph of the Task Memo serves the same purpose as a Format Page would, telling you what your answer should contain.

Now, just because Ms. Shanks uses the word "Memorandum" does not mean you are to draft an "analytical memorandum." No. This is not a "Memorandum of Law" like the document you drafted in first-year legal research and writing. Ms. Shanks says it is a "*Persuasive* Memorandum of Points and Authorities" (emphasis added).

In some jurisdictions, and here in the fictional State of Columbia, "Memorandum of Points and Authorities" is a term of art that is essentially synonymous with the word *brief*. Even if you were unfamiliar with the term, you would know it was a persuasive document for two reasons: (1) Laurie Shanks says so, using the descriptive term "persuasive" in front of the word "Memorandum"; and (2) you know who decides what evidence should come in and what evidence should be suppressed: the judge. So, obviously a document intended ultimately for the judge (or the court) would be a persuasive document, with your job being to help the judge make the decision that favors your client, here the State of Columbia.

As we discussed earlier in this book, documents intended for someone on your "side" in litigation (for example, an attorney in your office, your investigator, or your own client) are typically analytical. In such documents, you will generally look at both sides neutrally and evaluate pros and cons. By contrast, documents that are ultimately intended for the court or the opposing side are typically persuasive in nature. In zealously representing your client, you are arguing for your client's position; you want your client's version of events, and your conclusions as to how matters should be decided, to win the day.

Notice that Ms. Shanks, your boss, asks you to prepare a "draft" of this brief that your office will be filing with the court. That is simply a way of indicating that the document will first go to Ms. Shanks, although it is ultimately intended for the court. There is nothing to suggest that it is a rough or preliminary draft. You should write the document so that it is as close as possible to being ready to file with the court.

After reading just this part of the Task Memo, even before beginning to skim the rest of the File, I might type a header and title, such as the following, in my draft answer document:

<u>Sample Memo Format in Duncan</u>

To: Ms. Shanks (or "Laurie Shanks") From: Applicant

Re: People v. Duncan

Date: [The date of your bar exam]

Please find the Memorandum of Points and Authorities that you requested below. If you have any further questions or follow-up queries, please do not hesitate to contact me.

Memorandum of Points and Authorities in Opposition to Defense Motion to Suppress Evidence

You will be able to flesh out your outline as you read, but why not get started now writing some of what you know you will eventually need?

ETHICS CONCERNS

As noted earlier in the book, bar examiners may include ethics issues in PTs. Here, Laurie Shanks specifically rules out what could have been an issue by saying, "We have, of course, turned the recording and transcript of the interview over to defense counsel." I immediately noted in the margin next to this, *"Good! No ethical issue!!"* This is just a note to remind myself that the examiners made this a nonissue. (In the practice PR PT on eProducts, an attorney took and inappropriately retained possession of physical evidence that we had to indicate must be turned over to the prosecution.) So what if Laurie Shanks had not said this? What if she had not mentioned it at all, and you thought about the question? How do you write about that (and perhaps get some credit for your thinking) when it is not directly related to your assignment? You might have simply added a caveat note to Shanks in your introduction: "We must be sure to turn over to defense counsel any and all documents or evidence we are required to turn over."

The examiners could have planted an even more explicit ethical issue by writing in the Task Memo, "I know we are obligated to turn over the recording and transcript but I am going to hold them for a while just to make it more difficult for Duncan's counsel." Then you would have had a serious ethical issue to deal with. (Note that if this were a discussable issue they expected almost all students to see, they might even have repeated that they were holding onto the evidence. If the issue was one that only some students saw, it might have counted as a bonus point.) Assuming they had included this sort of an issue, how would you have addressed this in your answer? Well, you would not mention this to the court in your draft brief. Instead, you would address it in an introductory note to Laurie Shanks, perhaps in brackets; for example:

> ["Below please find the brief you requested. Before you read that document, however, I must bring a critical matter to your attention. We have an obligation to turn over evidence such as the recording and transcript of the police interview to the defense, and I urge you to do so immediately. We must not withhold anything we are

required to provide to defense counsel, especially not for strategic purposes."]

In real life, should such a violation occur, you would want to do the same, and if necessary go over Shanks's head to Alicia Ouelette (the head prosecutor) to see that the rules are followed. It is not worth being disbarred to please or get along with any one boss or client. Better to lose your job than your license. Your license is a lifetime license: protect it as such.

One more note for now about the task: the last sentence of the Task Memo says not to write a statement of facts. So, do not write one. You will not get any extra points for drafting a statement of facts when the directions tell you not to; in fact, you may cause the grader to become biased against you from the outset for failure to follow instructions. You will also take precious time away from the argument portion of this persuasive brief, time you need to complete that critical part of your assignment. If you are uncomfortable with the idea of omitting a statement of facts because you fear the grader will think you do not know that one will be needed, you can include the following in brackets: [The statement of facts to be inserted here.] That tells the grader that you would have written a statement of facts had you not been specifically instructed to omit it. It succinctly tells the grader that you followed directions.

Skim the File

The first thing I do when approaching the File is to look at the table of contents. I want to see what my factual world is before I start skimming. Here I have four documents in addition to the Task Memo: (1) excerpts of the interview with the defendant and two detectives, which I see is 10 pages, clearly the bulk of the File; (2) the Notice of Motion to Suppress Evidence; (3) the defendant's Affidavit in Support of Motion to Suppress Evidence; and (4) a transcript of the interview of Detective Timothy James (one of the two detectives in the first interview of the defendant), conducted by my boss, Laurie Shanks. Let's take a look at each of those four documents in turn and walk through the read/skim step.

Excerpts of the Police Interview with the Defendant

Just glancing at this document, you can see it is very long. You know, based on what we said earlier in the book, that you would waste precious time if you read all of this carefully now, before you understand the law in the Library. Once you have that law, the facts that are critical will pop out, and you will easily be able to weed out those facts that are irrelevant or duplicative. If you try to read this entire transcript word-for-word now, you are likely to get mired in details you do not need to write this assignment. So, for now, at this stage, before you read the Library, just flip through this excerpted transcript to see what general background you can pick up by skimming.

Here is what I might say to myself as I skim:

> *OK, I see that these are "excerpts." (I wonder what is left out?) They are thus just parts of an interview with Raymond Duncan (the defendant) with two detectives:*
>
> *Detective James and Detective Mandel. I remember from the table of contents that there is also a transcript of an interview with this same Detective James and my boss, Laurie Shanks.*
>
> *I see that these detectives ask Duncan's permission to record, and they start developing a timeline. I remind myself not to read all of this now, because I don't know what's important yet. I just skim. I see that Detective James starts asking all the questions, and then, three pages in, the second detective, Mandel, starts questioning Duncan.*
>
> *On the fifth page of the transcript I see asterisks and again, I remember that this document was called "Excerpts of Interview" with the defendant. I wonder what was said, if anything, in those "breaks." What if anything was omitted from this transcript? Is there anything that was said that would undermine our position?*

I always tell students that if something is bothering you, make a quick note if you can say something intelligent about it, and then move on. It is not an essential part of the assignment, but might be a bonus point. Also, if it is distracting you, it might prevent you from getting on to what you are required to write.

> *Here, I decide to add a quick note to Laurie Shanks (in brackets), before the argument portion of my answer:*
>
>> ["Ms. Shanks: Before we file the Memorandum of Points and Authorities below, we should ask Detectives James and Mandel what if anything was said and what transpired where the transcript shows breaks in the record. We want to rule out any undocumented coercion, to avoid surprises. Breaks on pages 64 and 66 seem to be 20-minute breaks in the interview. But the asterisks on page 62 indicate something is missing from the transcript but for no reason. We should find out why there was a break in recording."]
>
> *Again, I'm not reading every word of this 10-page interview now, because I don't know what I'm looking for yet. I am just glancing at each page. I will come back to this after the Library. Skimming, I see a lot of polite back-and-forth, question and answer, with a number of breaks. I notice the detectives readily agree to every break and ask, as Detective James does on the bottom of page 66, "Do you still want to talk to us?" Toward the end I see Duncan confessing and the detectives placing him under arrest and reading him his* Miranda *rights. I flip back to the beginning of the transcript and see that the interview starts at 12:25 pm and ends at 6:03 pm.*

I have repeatedly suggested that you skim the documents in the File, and then go back to the File after you read the Library. That is especially true of long or complicated documents that you do not readily see the significance of.

> *The next two documents in the File are short and simple. I can read those in full, now, without wasting any time.*
>
> *The Notice of Motion to Suppress. OK, that is the defense's document that, along with the defendant's affidavit, are the documents that provide the information I will be opposing. This notice is really short. All it says is that the defendant wants the judge to*

suppress all the statements made in the January 2nd interview, and on one sole legal basis: an alleged Miranda *violation. That's it.*

The next document is the affidavit. I will skim this now, though I know I will have to return to it and read it carefully because I expect what Duncan says will be contradicted by what the detectives say. Also, this is the only document that provides Duncan's version. We are opposing his motion, so it will be critical to understand what he says happened.

I remind myself that, based on my general knowledge of the law, Miranda *requires custodial interrogation. No one could deny there was interrogation here, so I am preparing myself that the "fight" will be about whether there was custody. When I get to the Library, I expect the law will center on that issue. (And, when ultimately I see it does, I am reassured!)*

I know that whatever other details of the law are in the Library will help me see which facts support or refute the defense claims. So, I read this affidavit now, just to see what the defendant's story is. A few things pop out even now.

In the second paragraph, Duncan says he was arrested and taken into custody at 12:30 pm. I recall from just the last page of the interview that the detectives arrest him and read him his Miranda *rights at the end of the interview, closer to 6:00 pm. This is a huge discrepancy. I make a note on my scratch paper and in the margins to come back to this later. (I actually take my notes on the table of contents page in the File. Next to the Affidavit, I write "Timing of arrest?" That is enough to jog my memory later.)*

I look quickly at the other paragraphs in the affidavit. Paragraph 3 says that the detectives never tried to question him at his home. I immediately want to know (a) Did they? What do they say? And, (b) Is that important? Does it matter where the questioning took place?

The next paragraphs seem to follow the same theme: the detectives allegedly never told Duncan he could refuse to go to the station or that he could leave the police station. Again, my lawyering instincts are wondering about the significance of where the questioning took place.

Next, Duncan talks about the room unlocking only from the inside. I don't know if that's true, or if it's important. I underline and make a note to return to it when

I have read the law.

Next, Duncan says he was questioned for five hours. This appears to be true.

Next, paragraph 8 is about the cigarette breaks—I'll have to go back and look and see if they left him alone or not, or why that may be important. (I cannot really know if that is even relevant until I read the Library.)

Paragraphs 9 and 10 deal with police accusing Duncan of the crime, communicating their subjective belief that he committed it, and thus making it "objectively reasonable" for him to believe he would not be allowed to leave the station. I am now dying to have my recollection refreshed about what exactly the law requires for someone

to be considered "in custody" for purposes of Miranda. *I am itching to get to the Library, which I know will have law on this, so that I can compare Duncan's statements to the legal standard. But, even without reading the law, I am sort of shaking my head and thinking, "Well, just because the police subjectively believe I am guilty does not mean I am not free to go."*

Paragraph 11 again seems like another "so what?" to me. Who cares if the detectives say it is to the defendant's advantage to cooperate. Even without reading the Library, I don't see how that relates to whether he is in custody or not. (I remind myself that is the sole issue in the document I must draft.)

In Paragraph 12 Duncan says that the detectives claimed they had evidence against him, and it would therefore be useless to deny guilt. Again, I can't know for sure without reading the Library, but it seems that is irrelevant to the issue of custody. (Note that I am not letting myself get taken in by the "side streets," interesting facts that don't relate directly to my task; I stay focused and look for "highways": main principles and relevant facts.)

Paragraph 13 appears factual and may be important. I will know after I read the cases. It discusses how Duncan was placed in handcuffs after five hours of interrogation, left alone in the locked room, and then taken to jail.

The last paragraph notes that Duncan was advised of his Miranda *rights after the five hours of interrogation, which we knew from our quick glance at the last page of the interview document.*

I again make my mental note that I will come back to this affidavit after reading the Library, and I move on to the next and final document in the File, a five-page interview with Detective James. This one is not an "excerpt," so no worries about what may be missing. Here, James provides extra information about what happened (or at least what the detective says happened!) before, during, and after the January 2nd interview with Duncan.

I remind myself that at this stage of litigation, before trial, nothing has been proven. Every bit of information is just one side's story. The defendant has his version, presented here in the affidavit. The police have their version, presented in the two interviews. I have to draft a motion opposing the defense arguments. In doing so, I'll have to learn what the law is. I will also have to make sense of the facts, especially when it appears that facts may be contradictory. More on this later. For now I keep reading.

Laurie Shanks starts her questioning of Detective James by saying she read the interview and has questions. I can see, just by quickly flipping through, that Detective James talks about how Duncan got to the station, and that at first he was only a "subject" and not a "suspect" because he was not yet suspected of doing anything wrong. (I will make a note to figure out the difference between these terms.) I see James mentioning that Duncan was not under arrest until the end of the interview. James notes at the end of his talk with Shanks that Duncan was not restrained at any point before he was read his Miranda *rights.*

I know I will have to read this interview very carefully later, and that it will make much more sense after I read the Library.

Briefly Review Task Memo

After skimming the File and "talking to yourself" as you read, as illustrated by the preceding, you want to check back quickly with the Task Memo before going on to study the Library. This helps focus you, so that your reading of the Library becomes that precision mission we talked about early in this book, rather than the "fishing expedition" of reading cases for class. You always keep in mind what you are to produce, so that you pick up the specific information you need to draft your answer. This focus is critical to passing. You cannot write around the task: You must answer specifically and directly.

The second paragraph of the Task Memo mentions twice that the courts have identified "specific factors" that will help them decide motions to suppress evidence. Re-reading this should help you see that you want to proceed into the Library in search of "factors."

I have repeatedly noted that lists (such as of elements or factors) are often "gifts" from the examiners, providing a key for how to logically organize your answer. This exam is a great example of where the list of factors serves as a perfect organizational tool.

It may also be that where there is a lot to discuss or argue, the organization is more obvious. In exams requiring students to think much more about how to organize, the actual analysis or argument may not be as time-consuming. Bottom line: The examiners do make these PTs doable!

The Library

First thing in the Library, study the table of contents. PTs are closed-universe problems. You want to know what your universe consists of. Here our universe holds only three cases: You can quickly see that they are from the U.S. Supreme Court, the Fifteenth Circuit, and the Columbia Supreme Court, respectively (and, here, we are in the State of Columbia). Be sure to note the dates as well, as it might be significant if one or another decision is outdated.

As you read, quickly brief each of the three cases, pulling out the holdings, and determining if they are good for us (meaning they support the prosecution) or not and why.

Mathiason

Mathiason is a 1977 Supreme Court case (obviously binding because this involves federally guaranteed rights). It is good for us in that the Court ultimately found there was no custody.

Note: The very first thing I do when I read a case in a PT Library is look at the bottom line and determine if the holding is good for my client or not. Why? Typically, in a PT, you must spend more time carefully reading those cases that are *not* good for you so that you can factually distinguish them. You may simply use the ones that support your client for referencing legal rules.

Mathiason tells us that *Miranda* applies to "custodial interrogation" and defines that as "questioning initiated by law enforcement officers after a person has been taken into custody or otherwise deprived of his freedom of action in any significant way." The Supreme Court also found in this case that the defendant's freedom to leave was not restricted, despite the fact that the questioning took place in a police station. The operative facts that swayed the court were: (1) the defendant came voluntarily to the police offices in response to the police request, and (2) he was told he was not under arrest. The Court also stressed that the interview only lasted 30 minutes, and that the defendant did in fact leave after the interview.

When you go back in the File, you will want to compare these *Mathiason* facts with your case. You will have to go back to double-check both the defendant Duncan's version of events and the police officers' stories. When you do, you will see that both seem to agree that Duncan came to the station voluntarily. (Top of page 64, Duncan says "when I offered to come in for questioning"; Detective James tells Laurie Shanks, at page 71, that Duncan preferred talking at the police station to talking at his home.)

The detectives say they told Duncan at the outset that he was not under arrest; Detective James says at page 72 that he advised Duncan that "he was going to a voluntary interview and was free to leave at any time." Also, despite the fact that in his affidavit Duncan says he was arrested earlier, Duncan *asks* the detectives, well into the interview, at page 66, "if they are going to process" him. (Why would he "ask" if he believed he was under arrest?)

The Duncan interview did last much longer than the one in *Mathiason* (5 hours versus 30 minutes), and, unlike in *Mathiason* where the defendant did in fact leave after the interview, Duncan was jailed at the close of his interview.

So, although the *Mathiason* holding is good for our client, some of the key facts are distinguishable, so the case may not end up being that helpful after all. (Remember, we always want to try to find a way to use all the main cases in the Library, whether they are good for our client or not.)

WRITING TIP: USE EVERY MAIN CASE IN THE LIBRARY

You should use every case that is listed in the Library table of contents. If some of those cases cite other cases, you may—but do not have to—cite to those other cases within the main cases. Students always ask, "Will I fail if I don't cite every main case?" As I mentioned earlier, I liken PTs to the television cooking show *Chopped*, in which contestants are to use each of the ingredients in the basket provided to prepare each course of their meal. Will a contestant who omits a basket ingredient automatically be eliminated? No, but the burden weighs very heavily against that chef. Everything else must be spectacular for that chef to remain in the contest after failing to use one of the key ingredients. Think of the main cases in your Library as ingredients you must use. If you cannot use them for their holdings, cite a rule or dicta from the case, or cite the case within that case. (To get "credit" for that, be sure to cite both cases; for example, "*Jones* as cited in *Cray*.") Try as hard as possible to cite every main case in the Library.

We may want to use *Mathiason* to cite the general rules about when *Miranda* warnings are required. We also may want to refer to some of the language in the case, even if it is not the holding. *Mathiason* includes some very helpful language, ideas we may want to quote or restate in our own words in certain parts of our answer. First, *Mathiason* makes clear at page 80 that just because a person is questioned in a police station does not mean that the person is "in custody" for purposes of *Miranda*. Second, *Mathiason* adds by way of dicta (at page 80) that an officer's false statement about possessing evidence that the defendant committed the crime is not relevant to the question of "custody" for *Miranda* purposes. You might remember that Duncan was concerned that the detectives thought he had committed the crime and that they made up evidence of his being at the scene, perhaps just to determine if he would contradict himself.

If you are taking notes as I suggest on the table of contents of the Library, next to where *Mathiason* is listed, write: "* * * Helpful language at page 80." On page 80, put double asterisks next to those helpful quotes and underline them. This double asterisk method, or some other sort of note-taking system, will be very useful for you!

Cray

Cray is also good for us, in that the appellate court overturned the lower court's finding of custody and concluded that defendant Cray was not in custody for purposes of *Miranda*. A few pages into *Cray* you should notice factors. Gold! You hit the PT jackpot.

Remember that the Task Memo repeatedly mentioned factors. Such lists are often organizational gifts. *Cray* cites *Jones* on pages 82–83 and lists eight factors that courts have identified in determining whether a defendant is in custody for purposes of *Miranda*.

This is your precise issue. This is exactly what the defense Motion to Suppress, the document you are drafting an opposition to, rests on. This is what you must battle. You must show how these eight factors stack up in the People's favor. (Remember, the "People" of the "State of Columbia" are your clients.) You may logically organize your entire opposition motion around the factors. This is it. You have your "plan" on how to structure your answer. (You will soon find a sample outline.)

Once you see these factors, which you know you will use in your answer, you also need to look through and compare and contrast the facts in *Cray* to see if the court we are writing our motion to will likely find our situation parallel enough with Cray's as to also conclude that Duncan was not in custody. You should see that there are some facts that are helpful but others that hurt. For example, in *Cray*, the defendant was questioned for seven hours, and by three officers. If that was not deemed "custody," then it is arguable (and we will make the argument) that the five hours for which two detectives questioned Duncan do not necessarily amount to custody. However, the court stresses that Mr. Cray was repeatedly told ("at least eight times") that the interview was voluntary and he was free to leave. Was Duncan ever told he was free to leave?

There are a number of other differences and similarities between the facts in *Cray* and in Duncan's case. Your work, when you go back to the File, will be to pick up on these quickly, and formulate arguments to try to make Duncan's situation look as much as possible like the parts of Cray's questioning that the court found noncoercive and thus noncustodial.

Something else you want to be sure you get out of *Cray* is that the *Jones* factors are not to be followed "ritualistically." Factors are not elements. Each one need not be established. Rather, they are to be balanced. That language guides you to exactly what you will be doing in your answer. You will take each factor, one at a time, and you will try to present the evidence that establishes that factor in the light most favorable to our clients (meaning that it tends to show there was no custody). You may have to concede certain factors, but you will have wonderful ammunition to conclude your argument with: this language from *Cray* that the factors are guiding tools rather than exhaustive elements.

Adams

The last case, *Adams*, also cited the *Jones* factors, so if you missed them in *Cray* I hope you saw them in *Adams*. Any time bar examiners repeat something within a question (a PT or essay), pay special attention, as it may be a hint. I also hope that you remembered that the person giving you the assignment in the Task Memo repeatedly referred to "specific factors" in the cases. *Adams* thus reinforces what the legal standard will be, and in turn how you will organize your answer.

Adams, however, is bad for us. It is the one out of the three cases in this Library in which the court found that the defendant was in custody. So, your job will be to look carefully at the facts in *Adams* and then go back into the File and see how we can distinguish it from Duncan's case.

What stands out without even returning to the File is that the questioning of Adams was much more aggressive and threatening than that of Duncan, and that Adams was essentially told that he was not free to leave unless he confessed. (Recall how polite the two detectives in our case were with Duncan. Go back and look at that when you review the transcript.) The *Adams* court also found it important that the defendant was never told he could stop the questioning and leave.

Again, you can refer back to the Library for any details you need. Your first read of the Library is done to see what the legal framework is so that you can then go into the File and read in an efficient manner. Before you run back into the File, though, stop and spend a few minutes thinking about what you just read. Ask yourself: How does the Library fit together, and how can I begin structuring my answer?

How Does the Library Fit Together?

This step—taking time to stop and think about how the law in the Library fits together and how best to produce the task(s) you were asked to draft—is arguably the most important strategic step for success on the PT. If you are racing through the exam and never stop to think about your client and your task(s), your answer may well be off the mark. Examiners repeatedly say that the reason many fail the PT is because they fail to be fully responsive to the instructions.

In this PT, all three cases address whether particular defendants were "in custody" for purposes of *Miranda*. Reviewing your Task Memo, you know that the defendant Duncan has moved to suppress all his statements made in the January 2nd police interview; your "answer" is the argument portion of the state's Opposition Motion.

You know, based on the defense's Notice of Motion, that Duncan's sole basis for his motion is *Miranda*. All the Library cases remind you, in case you had forgotten, that *Miranda* warnings are required when the police question a defendant who is in custody.

With your first File document being a transcript detailing five hours of questioning and no Library cases about the meaning of the term *interrogation*, you know the issue is *not* whether Duncan was interrogated. All three cases deal with whether and when a defendant is "in custody" for purposes of *Miranda*, so you should begin to see your world (and how you will approach formulating your answer) crystallizing. The issue should be clear and you should now be on a very precise mission: to argue that the defendant, Mr. Duncan, was not in custody when questioned by police.

Further, based on the *Jones* factors cited in *Cray* and *Adams*, you know exactly how you will organize your answer: factor-by-factor. Now is the fun part! You get to go back into the File with purpose, with direction, and with the *Jones* factors in mind.

One quick point, though, before looking back at the File: now that you have the basic legal framework, you can begin to flesh out your "outline." Your outline may serve as a rough draft of your answer.

SAMPLE UPDATED OUTLINE

To: Ms. Shanks From: Applicant

Re: People v. Duncan

Date: [The date of your bar exam]

Please find the Memorandum of Points and Authorities that you requested below. If you have any further questions or follow-up queries, please do not hesitate to contact me.

Memorandum of Points and Authorities in Opposition to Defense Motion to Suppress Evidence

[After reading the Library, you can flesh out the introductory portion of your opposition, perhaps as follows here.]

Defendant Duncan has moved that all of the statements he made during a January 2nd interview with police detectives be suppressed based on allegations that he was questioned in violation of *Miranda v. Arizona.* The People oppose said motion, as *Miranda* warnings are only required where the police engage in custodial interrogation, and, when these statements were made, Defendant was not "in custody" for purposes of *Miranda.*

Therefore, the People urge that the Defense motion be denied.

[You might go on to add a paragraph such as the following with a bit more law and setting up the factors as your organizational scheme.]

Mathiason makes clear that "custodial interrogation" means "questioning initiated by law enforcement officers after a person has been taken into custody or otherwise deprived of his freedom of action in any significant way." *Cray* and *Adams* make clear that courts have "identified at least eight factors for consideration in making the custody determination" (*Cray* at page 82). Looking closely at those factors, as the People argue below, it is clear that the Defendant was not in "custody" for purposes of *Miranda.*

[Next, quickly list the factors, in your own words or copied from the case. In your final answer, you will want to turn these factors into persuasive headings or mini-arguments that advocate your client's position. There is more on how to draft persuasive headings earlier in this book.]

Factor 1: WHETHER SUSPECT WAS INFORMED THAT QUESTIONING WAS VOLUNTARY, THAT HE COULD ASK TO LEAVE, OR THAT HE WAS NOT UNDER ARREST, AND THAT HIS CONDUCT INDICATED AN AWARENESS OF SUCH FREEDOM

Factor 2: WHETHER SUSPECT POSSESSED UNRESTRAINED FREEDOM OF MOVEMENT DURING QUESTIONING

Factor 3: WHETHER SUSPECT VOLUNTARILY AGREED TO QUESTIONING OR INITIATED CONTACT WITH AUTHORITIES

Factor 4: WHETHER STRONG-ARM TACTICS WERE USED: DID POLICE MANIFEST A BELIEF THAT PERSON WAS GUILTY AND HAVE EVIDENCE TO PROVE IT? WERE POLICE AGGRESSIVE, CONFRONTATIONAL, OR THREATENING?

Factor 5: WHETHER THERE WAS POLICE-DOMINATED ATMOSPHERE DURING QUESTIONING

Factor 6: WHETHER SUSPECT WAS PLACED UNDER ARREST AT THE END OF THE QUESTIONING

Factor 7: WHETHER THE EXPRESS PURPOSE OF THE INTERVIEW WAS TO QUESTION PERSON AS A WITNESS OR A SUSPECT

Factor 8: HOW LONG THE INTERROGATION LASTED

Conclusion

At this point you are still in note-taking mode. By listing the factors in your draft outline, you can take notes when you re-read the File, placing support for each factor right in this draft underneath the corresponding heading. When you begin writing, you will want to turn these factors, here stated as questions, into persuasive headings. (See examples of this later in this section.) Headings in your final draft serve as a roadmap and help the court see why it should rule in your favor. (As discussed earlier in this book, in persuasive briefs to the court, headings are typically more detailed than in analytical (in-house) assignments, serving as mini-arguments in addition to being a roadmap.) Equally important, for exam purposes, headings show the grader that you followed directions, and that you read and understood the law in the Library.

> **TIP**
>
> If you are writing by hand, you will want to list all eight factors on scratch paper and then, as you go back to the File, jot down on your notes facts that support or refute each factor. If you are typing, you can just type rough notes underneath each heading as you read and edit those into final language before you submit your answer. In other words, for typists, your outline may actually serve as a rough draft of your answer. (Even some typists feel more confident hand-writing their outlines; experiment with what works best for you on practice tests before your real bar exam.)

File Re-Read

Now, with these eight factors in mind, return to the File to re-read and pick up the relevant facts. What pops out? It should be much clearer now what is and what is not significant. You are essentially on an "Easter egg" hunt, searching for evidence to show that under the *Jones* factors there was no "custody." As you find points that relate, either type the point itself under the factor in your draft, or use a shorthand system to underline the point in the transcript and type the page number where you have underlined key information under the relevant factor in your draft outline.

Here are just some of the selected points that might pop out at you in a File re-read:

- The interview starts with police politely asking if it is OK to record the interview. This potentially relates to Factor 3 (defendant voluntarily agreeing to talk) and does relate to Factor 4 (police don't usually politely request permission to record in situations where they are threatening, coercing, and using other strong-arm tactics).
- The first couple of pages of the transcript appear to be about the police getting a timeline of what happened. At the bottom of page 59, Detective

James does say he needs to assess how truthful Duncan is, but does not do so in an accusatory manner (no Factor 4).

- Next and critical, on page 60, Duncan says *he* "called [the police] back and agreed to come down to this interview." The first time you skimmed this, before you read the Library and knew about the *Jones* factors, you likely would not have seen this as significant. Now, it should just scream out at you as direct evidence from the defendant's mouth of Factor 3, that Duncan voluntarily agreed to the questioning, and, in calling them back, that he initiated contact with police.
- The fact that Duncan refers to the questioning as an "interview" seems to be further proof that he does not see this as an arrest but as more of a discussion (Factor 1). He is a suspect only because he has "a record."
- Also on page 60, when the defendant hesitates after being asked if he is sure, he begins to sound like he is contradicting himself. This is exactly what the detectives said: that he was not initially a suspect but became so only after he began contradicting himself during the interview (Factor 7).
- At page 61, Duncan asks for water and the officers say "Sure" (Factor 4). More water and a cigarette break were offered on page 63. The interrogation lasted five hours, likely to be deemed a long time under Factor 8, though not as long as in *Cray* where ultimately no custody was found. However, there were several water and cigarette breaks, so the questioning was not continuous.
- At page 63, when they take a cigarette break, they went to the roof, so they left the interrogation room. There wasn't unrestrained freedom of movement per se (Factor 2), in that the detectives accompanied Duncan, but he was allowed to move. Also, there is no indication that he was handcuffed

or restrained in any way during the questioning, at least not until the very end when they did read him the *Miranda* warnings.

- At page 66, Duncan indicates that he does not know whether he is under arrest (Factor 1) and he says that they have been polite (Factor 4) in his comments: "I appreciate the fact that you guys have been patient with me. What are you guys going to do? I mean, are you guys going to process me or what?" That is not the language of someone who is certain he is under arrest.
- Further, at the bottom of page 66, Detective James asks Duncan, "Do you still want to talk to us?" to which Duncan responds, on page 67, "Sure, I'll talk." That is clear proof of Factor 1, that the questioning was voluntary.

Now, let's look at the second transcript that we also skimmed on the first walk through the File. It should also now be clear what is and is not relevant in this document.

- At page 71, Detective James describes how it was that the interview took place at the police station, that it was at Duncan's request, and that he asked the police to drive him there (Factor 3). Also, even though the interview was at the station (a police-dominated atmosphere under Factor 5), if James is believed, the location was at the defendant's request. We know from clear language in *Mathiason* that just because questioning occurs at a police station does not make it custodial.
- At page 72, Detective James says that Duncan was driven in an unmarked police car, not handcuffed, and the police were not in uniform (again, diffusing the police-dominated atmosphere of Factor 5).
- Also on page 72, Detective James says he "did advise [Duncan] that he was going to a voluntary interview and he was free to leave at any time" (Factor 1). This would not have popped out at you as critical before reading the Library, but you likely

see now, after reading *Cray*, that this "advising the defendant that he is free to leave" is a sort of super factor, to be weighed more heavily in the balancing of factors than the other factors. The *Cray* court found this factor so powerful "that no governing precedent . . . holds that a person was in custody after being clearly advised of his freedom to leave or terminate questioning" (*Cray* at page 83).

- If Detective James is to be believed (and James again says the same thing on page 73, "I repeatedly told him that he was not under arrest and that he was free to leave"), this is very strong evidence in our favor.
- It may be somewhat of a problem that Duncan, in his affidavit, at paragraphs 4 and 5, says he was never told he did not have to go to the station or that he was free to leave. However, there are several points in the interview transcript, as we noted earlier, where Duncan indicates that he voluntarily came down for the interview, supporting the detective's version of events.
- At page 72, James indicated that Duncan was at the outset only a subject, not a suspect (Factor 7).
- At page 73, James says Duncan never asked to leave, and that Duncan's requests for breaks, including with fresh air, were readily provided (Factors 1, 2, 4).
- At page 73, James notes that Duncan was never restrained physically, something that would have been done had he been "in custody" (Factor 2). On pages 74 and 75, James compares interviews with other subjects who were questioned in the same manner as Duncan, did ask to leave, and were allowed to do so.

PUT IT ALL TOGETHER AND DRAFT YOUR ANSWER

Now, armed with details relating to each factor, you want to take stock of what you have in your notes and begin turning them into the answer you will upload. The task is a persuasive brief, so you want to try to show as much as possible that each and every factor weighs toward lack of custody. But, you are also under an obligation of candor to the tribunal. Accordingly, you may have to concede certain factors.

Note that there are full sample answers in the Online Question and Answer Bank. The following are steps to take before drafting your final answer: turning the factors into persuasive headings, and marshalling supportive facts (plugging in each fact under the relevant factor). Each of the eight factors is listed in question form and then in persuasive heading form, and there are a few thoughts on how to develop the argument relating to that heading.

QUESTION FORM: 1. WHETHER SUSPECT WAS INFORMED THAT QUESTIONING WAS VOLUNTARY, THAT HE COULD ASK TO LEAVE, OR THAT HE WAS NOT UNDER ARREST, AND THAT HIS CONDUCT INDICATED AN AWARENESS OF SUCH FREEDOM HEADING FORM:

1. **The Defendant was repeatedly informed by police detectives that questioning was voluntary and that he was not under arrest; his asking several times what detectives planned to do with him indicated clearly that he did not yet believe during the interview that he was under arrest.**

This is a strong factor to start with. To fill in what you will write under this heading, look up every place we noted that something in the File supported Factor 1. For example, you want to pick up what we wrote about Detective James indicating repeatedly having told Duncan that the interview was voluntary and that he was "free to leave at any time."

You will want to argue here, relying on *Cray*, that this factor, "advising the defendant that he is free to leave" should be weighed more heavily in the balancing than the other factors. (You may even want to quote *Cray* that this factor is so powerful "that no governing precedent . . . holds that a person was in custody after being clearly advised of his freedom to leave or terminate questioning." *Cray* at page 83.)

QUESTION FORM: 2. WHETHER THE SUSPECT POSSESSED UNRESTRAINED FREEDOM OF MOVEMENT DURING QUESTIONING HEADING FORM:

2. Defendant was never handcuffed or chained, and he was free to move about at all times during the police interview.

Here pick up the points where you mentioned Factor 2, stressing the number of times they went on breaks. (You may want to note that the fact that the detectives accompanied him on these breaks does not make the situation "custodial," comparing *Cray,* in which the defendant was not left alone at all during the seven hours of questioning and the Court still found no custody.)

QUESTION FORM: 3. WHETHER THE SUSPECT VOLUNTARILY AGREED TO QUESTIONING OR INITIATED CONTACT WITH AUTHORITIES HEADING FORM:

3. As evidenced by his calling the police back and agreeing to come to the interview, Defendant voluntarily agreed to be questioned.

Here you will pick up any facts noted earlier in support of Factor 3; there are many from Detective James detailing how they first went to Duncan's house, then left, then Duncan called them back and asked that they talk at the station rather than his house. You will also want to quote Duncan himself, as noted earlier, where Duncan admits that *he* "called [the police] back and agreed" to come down to this interview.

QUESTION FORM: 4. WHETHER STRONG-ARM TACTICS WERE USED: DID POLICE MANIFEST A BELIEF THAT PERSON WAS GUILTY AND HAVE EVIDENCE TO PROVE IT? WERE POLICE AGGRESSIVE, CONFRONTATIONAL, OR THREATENING? HEADING FORM:

4. **At no time did police engage in strong-arm tactics, and while they began to believe that the Defendant committed the crime after he repeatedly contradicted himself, they were never aggressive, confrontational, or threatening.**

Here you have a lot to write about, indicating the polite language and conduct of the police questioning, including their readily agreeing to any breaks he wanted. Duncan even thanks them for being so "patient." Just look for the places where you noted references to "Factor 4," and cut and paste those in to form your argument.

QUESTION FORM: 5. WHETHER THERE WAS POLICE-DOMINATED ATMOSPHERE DURING QUESTIONING HEADING FORM:

5. **Though the questioning took place in the police station, that, in and of itself, does not create "custody" for purposes of *Miranda,* and much of the way in which the interview was conducted diluted what might otherwise have been a "police-dominated" atmosphere.**

You must concede that the questioning took place at the police station, and that the station is a police-dominated place/ atmosphere. However, you can start by saying that the detectives tried to talk with the defendant at his home and he is the one who requested that they talk at the police station. You also have great language from *Mathiason* that you can quote to show that being at a police station alone does not equate with custody. You might also stress that the police were not in uniform, and that they did not brandish weapons, use handcuffs, or manifest any other form of police domination. Lastly, they took Duncan for several breaks, including ones on the rooftop where they got fresh air.

You might note that here there were only two officers and in *Cray*, where there were three officers questioning the suspect, no custody was found. (Then again, this may not be helpful, as Cray was questioned in his home, obviously a less police-dominated atmosphere than the police station.)

QUESTION FORM: 6. WHETHER SUSPECT WAS PLACED UNDER ARREST AT THE END OF THE QUESTIONING HEADING FORM:

6. The suspect was placed under arrest at the end of the questioning.

This is a fact you must concede. Hence, you do not have a lengthy persuasive heading. However, you can stress that the arrest came only *after* the defendant confessed, and that the detectives had no plan to arrest him when they began talking with him.

QUESTION FORM: 7. WHETHER THE EXPRESS PURPOSE OF THE INTERVIEW WAS TO QUESTION PERSON AS A WITNESS OR A SUSPECT HEADING FORM:

7. The Defendant was interviewed as a subject or person with possible information relating to the crime and only became a suspect as he began contradicting himself during the course of the questioning.

Plug in here every place you noted facts that support Factor 7. There were several, especially what Detective James said about why they questioned Duncan initially, that they questioned several other people initially, and so on.

QUESTION FORM: 8. HOW LONG THE INTERROGATION LASTED HEADING FORM:

8. The questioning, although it lasted about five hours, was peppered with breaks and was very polite, and at no time did the Defendant request that the questioning stop.

Again, you must concede this factor; the time is what it is. However, you can stress the breaks. You can stress the relaxed and polite tenor of the discussion. You can point to Cray's questioning lasting for seven hours and not amounting to custody and argue therefore that neither should the five-hour interview here.

You will then want to conclude by reminding the court that these factors need not be applied "ritualistically" (per *Cray*) and that the overwhelming majority of them weigh in the People's favor, such that Mr. Duncan should not be found to have been in custody prior to the time he was given *Miranda* warnings.

For examples of a passing opposition motion for this PT, study the sample answers located in eProducts.

SPIN-OFF EXERCISES

Spin-off exercises are a way to gain exposure to drafting different types of documents without as much of a time commitment as it would require to complete a whole new PT. I often suggest to my students that after writing any PT, they spend a few minutes thinking about other documents they might have been asked to draft based on the same law and facts. Then, take a minute to outline or write out in full (time permitting) those "spin-off" tasks. Pay particular attention to how your tone and approach might differ depending on the goal of your assignment and your audience.

Writing for the Other Side

A great thing to do is force yourself to turn around now and write the entire motion to suppress as if you were Duncan's counsel. You have his affidavit and you now know the law and are well versed in the facts from the police side. Doing this will help you see where the major holes are in your own (original) client's case. (For example, there are certain points you will simply have to concede.)

Memo to Laurie Shanks

Pretend that instead of writing the opposition motion, you were to draft a memo providing Shanks with the pros and cons of filing a suppression motion. This would probably help you focus more neutrally on where your weak spots in the original document were.

Letter to Mary Lynch, Attorney for Defendant Raymond Duncan

Assume that Laurie Shanks authorized you to propose a plea bargain to defense counsel. How would you write it at this point? Assume that Duncan has filed his notice of motion but you have not filed your opposition brief. You know where the holes in his case are, but you also know that this is not a "slam dunk" for either side. How will you urge Duncan's side to accept a deal?

Statement of Facts

You were asked not to draft a statement of facts here, but it may be a good exercise, time permitting, to at least ask yourself what you would have included in a fact statement if one had been assigned.

PRACTICE, LAW SCHOOL, AND PTs: COMPARE AND CONTRAST

Most criminal cases do not go to trial, but instead are resolved by way of plea bargain. The motion to suppress evidence is a great vehicle for creating test questions because it can be used to test either constitutional criminal procedure knowledge or knowledge of rules of evidence, both potential grounds for keeping out evidence that should not be admitted or considered at trial.

Miranda rights are very important—in law school, on bar essays, and in the real world. This *Duncan* PT is an excellent vehicle for both practical training and for reviewing a critically important area of substantive criminal procedure law (one that will also be tested on other portions of your bar exam).

For students interested in learning more about the practical aspects of the criminal justice system, from arrest to appeal, you might enjoy reading a book I co-authored with one of my former law professors: Bergman and Berman, *The Criminal Law Handbook: Know Your Rights, Survive the System* (Nolo.com).

KEY TAKEAWAYS

- When writing to a court, adopt a more formal tone than you would in writing an in-house memorandum to someone in your own law firm.
- In a persuasive brief to a court, you will often want to set up your argument portion so that each main point is written in a persuasive manner. (An example of this from *Duncan* was adapting the issue as to whether the suspect was informed that the questioning was voluntary into a carefully crafted persuasive heading that might have read something like: "The Defendant was repeatedly informed by police

detectives that questioning was voluntary and that he was not under arrest; his asking several times what detectives planned to do with him indicated clearly that he did not yet believe during the interview that he was under arrest.") Such headings are much more than labels; they are actually mini-arguments that provide the bar grader a way to see that you not only understand the law but also know what critical facts will prove or disprove the legal element or factor in question.

- A PT can "read" very differently depending on which side you represent. A great way to ensure that you are making all reasonable arguments is to first approach the exam from the perspective of the client you represent (here, the government), and then "switch hats" and see if facts pop out as significant when you consider the situation as if you were representing the other side.

3. TORTS

OVERVIEW OF TORTS

Most law schools start you off taking torts in 1L. That is good. Torts is a fairly straightforward and accessible subject. In a sense it is even easier on the bar exam, because bar essays and multiple-choice questions tend to test in less depth and certainly with fewer policy considerations than your typical law school professor.

If you are studying torts now or took it earlier in law school, you know that torts are civil wrongs. The most typical tort cases are personal injury matters. Who is bringing the lawsuit? A private party. (The government brings criminal cases.) What will the plaintiff receive if the plaintiff wins in a tort action? Typically, monetary relief called *damages*. (In criminal law cases, the defendant may be incarcerated if the government prevails.) Some plaintiffs in tort actions seek equitable relief; for example, where a plaintiff wants the defendant to stop repeatedly invading the plaintiff's land and asks the court for a court order called an *injunction*. In most tort actions that you study in 1L, though, the plaintiffs are seeking damages.

Many torts classes start with intentional torts (battery, assault, false imprisonment, trespass to land and trespass to chattel, nuisance, and intentional infliction of emotional distress), and then move on to negligence. Most courses cover negligence in great detail, often for many months. This too is good because negligence is typically the most heavily tested tort on bar exams.

Tort law also includes what is called *strict liability* or *absolute liability* (otherwise called *liability without fault*) in certain types of actions, such as those involving wild animals or ultrahazardous activities. (For example, if your pet lion mauls the plaintiff, you will be liable regardless of whether or not you took reasonable precautions to keep your lion caged.)

You may also spend time studying an area of tort law known as *products liability*, reviewing cases in which people were injured while using products. For instance, you step on a ladder (a product) to climb onto your roof and the ladder suddenly snaps; you fall off and are injured; in a more colorful example, you open a soda bottle, and drink half of the contents before you notice the floating decomposed snail in the bottle. Products liability cases may be based on five separate legal theories: intentional tort, strict liability in tort, negligence, warranty, and/or misrepresentation.

Torts courses sometimes finish with economic- and privacy-related torts such as fraud, interference with contractual relations, defamation, and causes of action relating to invasion of privacy. However, many 1L professors never get to discussing this wide a variety of tort actions, choosing instead to focus on the more heavily tested negligence and intentional torts. Some classes rush through or skip entirely torts such as malicious prosecution or malicious institution of civil proceedings, and often there is no time to cover important concepts relating to damages, such as joint tortfeasor liability, and indemnification.

Do not be too concerned with law school coverage. Every torts class covers negligence, the most heavily tested area on the bar exam. It is also likely that whatever you did cover, you studied in great depth and have a strong understanding of. That knowledge will benefit you in the long run. Just be aware of the range of topics that could be tested on your bar exam, and commit to learning, before or during bar review, whatever you either did not study or did not understand well in law school.

The following main areas in torts are typically tested on bar exams:

- Intentional torts
- Negligence
- Strict liability-based causes of action
- Products liability
- Economic and privacy-related torts
- Defenses (there are different defense theories that may be applicable to different tort causes of action; for example, in defending a negligence action, the defendant might claim that the plaintiff assumed the risk, or was contributorily or comparatively negligent)
- General principles such as those that arise when more than one party commits a tort, including joint and several liability

For a comprehensive list of torts topics covered on bar, see content scope outlines from your jurisdiction and the NCBE.

SIMULATED TORTS-BASED PT

For your practice PT, I chose a torts-based PT that centers around landowner liability in a negligence setting: a commonly tested area and one on which many law school classes spend significant time. Set aside a three-hour block of time and complete the PT, called *Carelton v. Mid-Central Shipping,* located in eProducts. Then, read the following sections to see how you did on the exam and gain further insight into what you can learn from this practice test going forward.

TIME-CRUNCH TIPS

To complete *Carelton* in two hours, if your time is simply too crunched to afford three hours, read the entire File and Library, and only answer the first part of the requested memorandum. Skip the multiple-choice questions and the second part of the memorandum. As always, if you can make the three-hour time commitment, it will be worth your while. In particular, completing the multiple-choice questions will help you assess your case briefing and analysis skills, critical components of success on the PT and in law practice.

INSIDE THIS TEST: TIPS AND STRATEGIES

Read this section only *after* you have completed the *Carelton v. Mid-Central Shipping* PT.

Overall Comments

One of the first things you may have noticed is that the *Carelton* File has 12 pages and the Library has 17 pages. That in and of itself suggests that the exam is "law heavy." When you get into the Instructions and see that your primary task is to draft a memorandum of law setting forth the theories of liability upon which your client might bring suit, you know for sure that the exam is "law heavy."

Did you see that you also had to complete a second part of the task: a fact gathering assignment? The legal memo could have taken up all your time and you had to budget carefully to leave enough time to complete that second task as well.

Note: This exam did not specify what percentage of your total points that second task was worth. If this exam were given percentage-point allocations, likely the fact-gathering assignment would have accounted for about 20% to 25% and the legal memo for about 75% of your written score.

The other very unusual part of this exam is that it includes multiple-choice questions along with the written tasks. *Carelton* is the only PT in this book that includes multiple-choice questions. The MPT and state-specific PTs today do not include multiple-choice questions. But when the PT was first introduced, the examiners used multiple-choice questions along with drafting assignments as a diagnostic to determine applicants" accuracy and thoroughness in briefing cases. (You saw, if you completed these multiple-choice questions, that they focused on the holdings and facts of the Library cases. Accordingly, these questions provide a helpful tool to test yourself on your own case briefing skills.)

Instructions

The general or so-called boilerplate Instructions, the first pages, tell you the basics: this is a PT, you have three hours to complete it, and so forth. The Instructions also state that the case is set in the fictitious state of Columbia, and that the Library includes six cases that are all from the Supreme Court of Columbia. This tells you that the cases will all serve as binding precedent, unless a later Library case overturned an earlier one. (The opposite happened here in this Library; as discussed later, the *Wiseguy* case impliedly accepted a Restatement section that had been explicitly rejected in a previous Library case. We discuss this further later in this section.)

From the Instructions, you learn that you are role-playing an associate in a private law firm, and that you represent an individual named Henry Carelton who is suing a business, Mid-Central Shipping Company. You know the case involves personal injury, so even before you get to the Library, you can put on your "torts hat" with respect to your general knowledge of the law. As noted earlier in this book, in your PT answers you will only apply the specific law from the Library; you will not cite outside case law. However, you *will* use your general familiarity with legal reasoning and general knowledge of the law. Here, because this is a tort action and thus a subject you would know well before the bar exam, you might approach the exam by asking yourself which of the main liability theories the suit will be based on: negligence, strict liability, or intentional tort theory. Furthermore, as on *every PT*, you always want to keep on your "professional responsibility hat," and be prepared to comment appropriately on matters that may raise ethical issues.

HOW WIDE IS YOUR PT UNIVERSE?

The *Carelton* Instructions say that your "universe" consists of two sets of materials: a File and a Library. Reading this, you simply nod and say to yourself, "Great, this is a regular PT. No unusual materials to work with." PTs are closed-universe assignments that almost always consist of a File (which includes Instructions) and a Library. On rare occasions, though, examiners have provided a third set of materials, such as draft trust instruments in an estate planning exam, or have omitted the Library and provided jury instructions as the law to work with. You always want to confirm your universe before you begin. Again, almost always there will be a File and a Library, but the seconds it will take to verify this by carefully reading the Instructions are well worth your while. (When a third set of materials was included, many students mistook it for extra scratch paper, because they had failed to carefully read the Instructions.)

Task Memo

The document following the Instructions is the Task Memo. First, notice the language the Senior Partner uses: he wants your help in "thinking through" the case. What does that indicate? Neutral analysis. Your job is to analyze, not to persuade. You must set forth the relevant and appropriate legal theories, but you will point out the arguments both for and against the firm's client.

Note the context in which this matter arises. Mid-Central has filed a pretrial motion to dismiss for failure to state a claim, which we must prepare to defend against. That is a fairly low threshold. In most jurisdictions, all that is needed at this stage is a showing that Henry (our client) has some legally cognizable claim. All the complaint requires is a short, plain statement of the ultimate facts that make up the plaintiff's cause(s) of action. This is not yet the trial stage where those facts must be proven by a preponderance of the evidence.

The Task Memo next provides a preview of each File document. From this overview you can get a sense of the relative importance of each document. The most critical part of the Task Memo is usually at the end, where the specific tasks that you are to complete are spelled out. This is crystal clear as the assignment is prefaced with: "In your memorandum to me, please address the following." I would star that, put a paper clip on the page, and read it several times over to be certain I understood the assignment.

After reading the Task Memo, especially these last paragraphs that Mr. Brown writes to you, you have enough information to start sketching a basic template for your answer. Before even reading the File and Library, you might have typed something like the following in your answer document:

START OF DRAFT OUTLINE FROM TASK MEMO

To: Edward Brown

From: Applicant

Re: Henry Carelton v. Mid-Central Shipping: Preparation for Response to Pretrial Motion to Dismiss

You have asked me to think through this case and discuss the theories of liability under which we can contend that Mid-Central is liable for Henry's injuries, and additionally to let you know what more evidence we should begin to gather to build our case. Please find my analysis below. I am available at your convenience if you have further questions.

PART I—Theories of Liability

Theory A ____________________

Theory B ____________________

Theory C ____________________

PART II—Additional Evidence to Be Gathered

Note: You can complete this fact-gathering section of the memo when you finish the first memo, or, to save time, you could have dropped points in here as you thought of them. In this sort of case, where you have both a legal analysis memo task and a fact-gathering assignment, you may be well served by multitasking; if you note points as they come to you, you are less likely to forget them later on.

File

Let's walk through the rest of the File now. I will highlight selected points along the way, starting with the judge's letter. Compare my thoughts to what you saw as you were reading the exam.

The Senior Partner, Mr. Brown, author of the Task Memo and the person you are writing to, told you that the judge is "an esteemed member of the retired judiciary." That is a hint that what Brown says may be particularly credible. Contrast that with the repeated warnings in the last paragraph of the first page of the Task Memo that the complaint is deficient. Brown characterizes the complaint as "slapped-together," notes that the lawyer who drafted it is no longer with the firm, and says "I am not at all sure it is good enough," indicating that we may need to amend it.

Note: Any time the bar examiners repeat something within an exam (whether a PT or an essay), *pay attention.* This is usually a suggestion that whatever is repeated is important and not to be missed.

Abner Goodfellow's letter tells you a bit more about the facts, how the injury occurred, where the plank and electrical wires ran, and what happened to Henry.

Goodfellow also stated firmly that Mid-Central put up and maintained the wires and "[t]he power company has nothing to do with this case." That is probably a hint to focus on liability of Mid-Central alone and not waste time with a discussion of possibly amending the complaint to add the power company. But: were you skeptical? Did you ask yourself, "Is Goodfellow certain? How does he know the power company has nothing to do with this? He may be a good fellow, but what if he is wrong, and our client missed out on recovery from a potentially 'deep pocket'?" If you had such thoughts, here is how to address them on a PT. In a note to your senior partner (Mr. Brown), suggest that your firm do some investigating and confirm that the utility in no way shares liability with Mid-Central. Here, the perfect place to make such a note is in the second part of your memo about factual or proof problems. You may well get credit for your thinking. Also, getting this thought out quickly (and in a place that might even help you score points) will free your mind to let the issue go and focus only on Mid-Central's potential liability, clearly the central aspect of this assignment.

NOTE-TAKING TIPS

As you read, sketch a picture of the property on your scratch paper to help visualize the scene of Henry's injuries. Draw where the plank was, where the wires were, where the river was, and where Henry was. (My Real Property professor in law school, the late great Jesse Dukeminier, taught us always to diagram property problems, and to this day I cannot read a property question without a pencil in hand.) This can be equally helpful in any subject where you have to picture a scene, such as here in *Carelton* with a torts problem. In addition to whatever other notes and sketches I make, I also write a cast of characters to keep everyone straight. For example, here in my notes I wrote:

> EBB: Edward Brown, senior partner in our firm, person we are drafting assignment for.
>
> Henry Carelton: Our client, injured in accident at M-C.
>
> M-C (Mid-Central Shipping Co.): the defendant, on/near whose property Henry was hurt.
>
> Abner Goodfellow: Retired judge. Gave facts about case.
>
> Martha Carelton: Henry's mother.

As we discussed earlier, on PT exams it is appropriate to question the credibility of certain facts. That is a key distinction between bar exam essays and PTs. On essays, you accept the facts as true and work with them. If an essay question stated, "Do not address liability of the power company," you would never waste even a second thinking, "Well, but what if the power company really were liable?" You certainly would not take time to write about it. On a PT, though, you may consider the sources of facts and assess their credibility. As in the real world, facts are not evidence until they are proven in court. Just because Goodfellow *says* the power company has nothing to do with this, I would still wonder, and I would take 20 seconds to jot down somewhere in my answer that our firm should verify this information. (Again, I would not take more than 20 seconds, because likely this is a hint, but our notation that we should follow up with this, could indicate to a grader that we are thinking like lawyers.)

There are a couple of other interesting points in Goodfellow's letter: First, he likens the Muddy River to a public street. This is incredibly important, but you do not see why until you read the cases about landowner liability where private land is adjacent to or indistinguishable from public property. *This is precisely the kind of fact that will likely not have significance to you until you read the Library, but will jump out at you after studying the cases!* This is exactly why I urge you to skim the File and then go back to read it again *after* you have briefed the Library authorities.

Second, Goodfellow states a conclusion about "causation," declaring that the wires fell as a result of the rotten pole. That too is a fact I would suggest we note should confirmed as soon as possible. (The place to note this is in the second part of the memo that focuses on fact-gathering.) As part of your general knowledge, you know that causation must be established as part of any of the applicable liability theories. Our client loses if we cannot establish causation!

Next in the File, after Goodfellow's letter, you find the Senior Partner's notes from his interviews with our client and his mother. At a quick glance, you might have seen that several questions are underlined. If you did not notice that as you were reading, look back at those interviews now. Much of what is underlined focuses on factual or proof problems—your second task! If you noticed these questions Brown posed, and if you happened to be running out of time in writing your answer, you could have turned back to these interview notes, and quickly and easily picked up enough information to write something intelligent and complete the second part of your memo in probably about five minutes.

Examiners don't always give away pieces of the puzzle, but often they give hints. Take the time to think carefully about what your assignment really asks of you, and keep that front and center as you review each of the File documents. You too might find such "hidden gold" on your bar exam, and you are much more likely to notice hints when you are clear on all aspects of your assignment.

As a professional responsibility note, you may have noticed that Brown asks Henry's mother to leave the room when he talks to Henry. Why? If you have already taken any classes in professional responsibility, you will readily see that this makes perfect sense, because Henry is the client, and even if Henry's mother is paying the bills, the attorney must respect the client's wishes. The mother might pressure or influence him if she were present. For example, he might not want to admit it if he was ditching school at the time of the injury, or was somehow at fault. Also, confidentiality may be breached if the lawyer talks with the client in the presence of a nonclient (though there may be exceptions for the parent of a minor client).

Many facts emerge from Brown's notes that are critical to your analogizing and distinguishing the cases and establishing which legal theories Henry may likely sue on. I won't list them all, but some include:

- Henry accessed the Muddy River through an open gate. On days the gate was locked, the boys did not swim there.
- The plank came from Mid-Central's warehouse and had been there "a long time."
- One of the workers admitted that the injury occurred because of the rotten pole.

These facts may have hit you as significant on the first read of the File because of your good lawyering instincts. But they definitely would have popped out as critical after reading the cases.

The next document is an internal memo from Mid-Central. (Did you wonder how our firm came into possession of this document? It could have triggered thoughts for the fact-gathering portion of your memo about subpoenaing or requesting production of other internal security documents. If you had that thought while reading, you could note it right away in your second memo.) It was important to look at the entire page of the document. Some students miss the note above the letterhead stating that the memo was posted at the warehouse *prior to* the injury. If you missed this, go back and look at it now. It is so critical! It makes clear that Mid-Central was aware of intruders on its property, before Henry was injured there. This sets up one of our arguments for Henry that even if he were a trespasser, he was a "known trespasser," which might well give rise to a higher duty on the part of Mid-Central.

As to the complaint, it alleges negligence and sets forth facts that would help show certain elements of the claim, but not all of them. Again, you know from the Task Memo that your firm plans to amend the complaint. So, at this stage, you read the draft complaint simply to pick up any helpful additional facts.

The last File document you see is the motion to dismiss. It is interesting in that it only denies intentional or willful misconduct; it does not deny liability based on negligence. Did you wonder: "Does Mid-Central think they ruled out negligence by characterizing the plaintiff as a trespasser?" After reading the Library, you see that many exceptions have been carved out to the general rule that no duty is owed to trespassers. Also, it is quite likely that your entire memo will focus on theories of negligence under which Henry can sue. Again, you would not see those theories until you read the cases. However, you likely noticed that nowhere in the File do you see evidence of intentional or willful acts on the part of Mid-Central.

Library

Before you even begin reading the Library, based just on your general knowledge of tort law, you may have a sense of what to expect in the Library. What do I mean? Well, there are no facts supporting willful action by Mid-Central, and Mid-Central was not engaged in ultrahazardous activity that might give rise to a strict liability claim. So, what is left? Negligence. Further, based on clear facts from the File (albeit facts we may seek to confirm), you know that causation and damages are not in dispute. So, what should the Library logically contain? Cases that focus on the duty and breach (of duty) elements of negligence—and that is precisely what you do find in the Library: one case asserting a general rule of no duty to trespassers and all the other cases regarding potential exceptions to that rule.

Now, I am *not* suggesting that you waste time trying to "guess" what's in the Library. After all, this is an open-book test! I am simply urging you to *think* as you read, and continuously put the PT puzzle pieces together. Keep the big picture in mind. Think about who your client is and what he wants. Think about your assignment and what the Senior Partner has told you. Think about what facts you have and what facts are missing. As you read the Library authorities, ask yourself how the cases (and/or statutes) fit together.

As discussed earlier in this book, facts are generally not relevant in a vacuum; facts are relevant as they prove or disprove elements of rules of law. Thus, it makes sense that the Library forms the organizational structure (the "tree trunk" or cause of action, and "branches" or elements, here theories proving a particular disputed element); and that the facts ("leaves") hang on or flesh out that law. The logical organization of most PT answers thus comes from some combination of the Task Memo and the law. The Task Memo tells you what to write; here it details the two parts of your memo (legal analysis and additional facts). Synthesizing the law in the Library will help you see how to organize your thoughts within the legal memo portion of your answer.

Now, let's highlight selected aspects of the Library cases. Again, they are all Columbia Supreme Court cases (which means they are all binding), so we need to pay special attention to the date on which each case was decided. As we discussed earlier in this book, in jurisdictions where this is provided, you may want to take notes on the table of contents page that lists the cases and the dates they were decided. Your goal is to cite to all the main cases in your answer, so it can be very helpful to organize all the main rules on one page. Next to each case, in addition to citing its holding (or noting the page number in the Library where you have "book-briefed" the holding), you might note whether each case supports Henry or Mid-Central. Ironically, you will likely have to spend more time carefully reading cases that seem *not* to support your client, typically because you will be searching for ways to factually distinguish them. With the cases that support your client's position, you may not have time to extensively reference analogous facts; it may be sufficient to simply pull out a helpful rule to cite.

Sample answers located in eProducts provide a sense of how thorough an answer one might produce in the allotted time. They also help you pull the law together. In addition, I have highlighted some points of interest from each of the cases in the rest of this section.

Note: You do *not* want to organize your answer case-by-case. An effective *Carelton* answer would determine the legal theories that can be distilled from the cases and analyze them theory by theory. Brown did not ask you to summarize the cases, but rather to see how they help Henry in developing legal theories upon which he may bring suit. I am running through them case-by-case here simply as a way of helping you see what you learned from reading the Library.

Scoundrel

Scoundrel was the first and oldest case in the Library. This case set forth the general rule that a landowner does not owe a duty to trespassers. This is "bad" for Henry's case because Henry most likely was a trespasser on Mid-Central's property. What to do? You cannot ignore unhelpful law: not on PTs and not in law practice. You want to strive to use every main Library case in your PT answer. When cases are bad for your client, try to distinguish them factually.

Here, the *Scoundrel* facts are distinguishable from Henry's situation in that the plaintiff in *Scoundrel* climbed a five-foot fence, whereas Henry walked through an open gate. Further, the *Scoundrel* plaintiff was in the defendant's yard at the time of the injury, whereas Henry was poised to dive into the Muddy River, a public waterway. (You may not have seen this point as essential until you read some of the later cases. Just as you want to get into the habit of skimming File facts and returning to them once you have more context, in a Library such as this, with so many cases, it can help to skim each case, then re-read them to pull out rules and distinguish facts once you have a better picture of the Library as a whole.)

Scoundrel also noted that the defendant in that case gave no license or invitation to trespassers, either express or implied. We will likely argue that Mid-Central impliedly consented, and certain employees may have even expressly consented, to the boys' use of its property to access the river. Further, the *Scoundrel* court observed that the defendant in question had no reason to suspect or anticipate the plaintiff's trespass. As a great deal of evidence in *Carelton*, including Mid-Central's own internal memo, indicates, Mid-Central had every reason to anticipate Henry's trespass.

Again, these are just some points in *Scoundrel* you might have noticed.

Wanderer

In *Wanderer* the plaintiff, who was lawfully using a public street, suddenly had to get out of the way of an oncoming cyclist, and did so by going onto the defendant's front steps. There, a loose brick from the defendant's property fell and injured the plaintiff. The court found for the plaintiff. This is a very good case for Henry, especially if the Muddy River is analogous to a street, as Mid-Central's wires fell on him while he was poised to dive.

The court articulated the rule as requiring an obstruction in the road by fault of the defendant and no negligence on the part of the plaintiff. The obstruction in our case (the plank) may be Mid-Central's fault if they left it out, or it may be Henry's fault if he put it there. (This is something we will have to determine.) The obstruction might also be the wiring which M-C controlled. Assuming we can get over the obstruction argument, and the second hurdle (that Henry is not deemed to have lacked due care himself in diving/swimming under electrical wiring), then this case may well support Henry's claim.

Poorsoul

This is another case that appears helpful to Henry. Here, the court found that the defendant had a duty to maintain a boardwalk that was essentially a "sidewalk" which, because of its placement, made ambiguous the line dividing the private property and public property. Based on this case, Mid-Central will likely be found to have had a duty to maintain the banks of the river.

Child

This case is likely not helpful to Henry because it found for the defendant against a child who was injured on a chain-link fence that formed the border between the public alley and the defendant's private property. The court used a two-part test: (1) whether the defendant should have known the post could break or fall when kids swung on it; or (2) whether the defendant had reasonable grounds to apprehend an accident from the placement of the post in the alley. The court in *Child* found that the injury was not foreseeable and therefore found that no duty was owed to the plaintiff in question.

Did you see the dicta in *Child* in the footnote that sets forth a Restatement section upon which liability might be established? The court declares, however, that the jurisdiction does not recognize this Restatement section as good law. Did you wonder why the court bothered to reproduce the section in full if it was not useful in answering the question? The answer becomes clear in the *Wiseguy* case, decided some 12 years later, which references the Restatement, suggesting that by that time the section has indeed been recognized in Columbia.

Fall

Fall is one of the best cases for Henry, as it makes clear that a duty is owed to trespassers where the owner has permitted trespassers to use the land, thus giving them an implied license to trespass. The facts appear very similar to those in Henry's case. In *Fall,* the court found that the defendant could not make a dangerous pit and leave it unprotected without bearing some responsibility to those who were accustomed to (and permitted to) use the defendant's lot as part of their way, and who, while exercising due care, were injured falling into that pit. Similarly, we would argue that Mid-Central should not be allowed to fail to maintain poles that held electrical wires directly over an area where they allowed the public to come swim.

Note: We will need to explore whether Henry himself was negligent in his diving/swimming. Other than the fact that he was likely skipping school, and that his mother said, "Everyone knows the shipping yard is dangerous," it does not appear from the facts in the File that Henry failed to use due care.

Wiseguy

Wiseguy, the last and most recent of the Library cases (decided just eight years before Henry's accident), is also not very helpful to Henry. Although it established a duty similar to that found in *Child,* the *Wiseguy* court found: (1) that no injury was foreseeable because the flagpole was not in obvious disrepair; and (2) the plaintiff (a 15-year-old, one year younger than Henry) should have been able to appreciate the danger of jumping on a flagpole.

You need to read this case carefully and distinguish it factually. For instance, you might note that while the plaintiff in *Wiseguy* admitted he knew it was foreseeable that he could be injured and simply did not know the possible seriousness of that injury, Henry seems to have had no clue at all that there was even a danger. It may well be that it takes much more sophistication to appreciate the possible danger of overhead electrical wiring randomly falling than to realize the fairly obvious danger of swinging on a pole designed to hold only the weight of a flag. Also, Henry likely had no way of knowing the poles were rotten from the inside out.

Lastly, as noted earlier, *Wiseguy* references the Restatement section, so assuming that the Restatement is now good law in Columbia, it too may provide a basis for liability against Mid-Central. You could also have written in your answer about that section as a theory Henry might assert.

YOUR OUTLINE AND ANSWERS

Once you have made quick notes on the rules from and key facts in all the cases, you should think about how they logically fit together, and update the draft outline of your answer accordingly. Again, do not summarize the cases one by one. That might be something a partner would ask a law clerk to do, but not a lawyer. As a lawyer, you need to think through the case law and figure out how the authorities in the Library as a whole fit together. Library authorities in PTs are like puzzle pieces. Once you see how they fit, you can begin to sketch out an outline of your answer.

Here, the first case (*Scoundrel*) established a general rule and the subsequent cases established a number of exceptions to that rule. Each exception may form a liability theory upon which Henry may argue that Mid-Central owed him a duty.

Notice that all the cases were about the duty element of negligence. Thus, there is only one cause of action here, but several theories upon which a duty might be established. That may have confused you at first. Students read the Task Memo and initially assume that the theories of liability that Henry will assert will be negligence, intentional tort, and strict liability. However, the only viable cause of action here was based on negligence. Unless we find more evidence, there appears to have been no intentional action on Mid-Central's part, nor are there grounds for strict liability. (Merely maintaining electrical wiring would not be deemed an ultrahazardous activity.) So, after reading the Library and File and thinking carefully, you would see that what Brown (the senior partner) had to have meant in terms of liability theories was theories under which *duty* can be established in order to bring a negligence cause of action.

Here is how you could have updated your outline after briefing the cases.

UPDATED SAMPLE OUTLINE

To: Edward Brown

From: Applicant

Re: *Henry Carelton v. Mid-Central Shipping*,
Preparation for Response to Pretrial Motion to Dismiss

Introduction

You have asked me to think through this case and discuss the theories of liability under which we can contend that Mid-Central is liable for Henry's injuries, and additionally, to let you know what more evidence we should begin to gather to build our case. Please find my analysis below. I am available at your convenience if you have further questions.

PART I—Landowner Liability Theories re: Duty Element of Negligence

A. General Rule is that there is no duty to trespassers.

[Discuss. Try to distinguish *Scoundrel* factually to show why it should not apply; for instance, in that case the trespasser scaled a five-foot wall whereas Henry walked through an open gate.]

Exceptions to General Rule

1. Public necessity (where obstruction is fault of defendant [D] and plaintiff [P] was not negligent). Cite to *Wanderer* and *Poorsoul*.

Provide your analysis here of how the case law supports Henry's claim that Mid-Central owes Henry a duty under a public necessity theory.

2. Implied consent (landowner knew that public regularly used its land and impliedly consented to that use). Cite to *Fall.* Provide your analysis here of how the case law supports Henry's claim that Mid-Central owes Henry a duty under an implied consent theory.

3. Child trespassers (landowner knew of danger and had reason to apprehend accident). Cite to *Child:* Children not likely to appreciate danger under case law. Cite to *Wiseguy:* Liability also under Restatement, rejected by earlier cases but impliedly endorsed in *Wiseguy*. Provide your analysis here of how the case law supports Henry's claim that Mid-Central owes Henry a duty under a child trespass theory.

Conclude as to legal theories available to prove duty.

PART II—Additional Evidence to Be Gathered

Write a quick introductory sentence saying something like: "Here below, per your request, is a list of some of the additional evidence we will need to prove Henry's claims."

Pick up all the questions from File documents, such as E.B.B.'s Rough Notes Interview with Henry Carelton and with Martha Carelton (Mother), and add any other questions you can think of. Because this is an internal memo and thus a less formal document than one written to the court or opposing counsel, and because of the nature of this type of assignment, it would be fine to just list in bullet points any additional evidence to be gathered. To maximize points here, however, you would want to note why you want any evidence you suggest gathering (what it would help prove or disprove and why). Conclude with one line here to show the grader that you completed the assignment, and that you followed directions. For example, "If you have any additional questions about the legal theories or factual/proof problems discussed above, or any other aspects of Henry's case, please let me know and I will address them.

It is critical to outline PT answers *before* writing. One of the main criteria you are being graded on is your ability to draft a well-organized answer that is responsive to the specific requests in the Task Memo. Again, the graders do not want to see you listing and summarizing cases, but rather pulling holdings from cases and using them to craft a thoughtful response that will be helpful given the context of the case.

You will find sample passing answers to *Carelton* in the Online Question and Answer Bank. They are provided to give you an idea of what a successful student answer might look like. As you read through them, do not judge yourself harshly, but rather look to see how you might improve on your next practice exam. Here too is a list of mistakes that students most frequently make on this exam:

1. Not finishing. Many students do not get to the second task on factual or proof problems within the allotted time.
2. Organizing case-by-case instead of theory-by-theory.
3. Including questions presented, a statement of facts, and/or other parts of a traditional law school memo that were not specifically requested in the Task Memo and would have taken precious time away from what you were directed to write about.

TIP: REVERSE ENGINEERING—WORKING FROM ANSWER TO QUESTION

A helpful exercise is to outline the sample answers. Then, look back from the answers into the question and ask yourself: What would you have needed in an outline of your own to draft these answers? Where is the most helpful information in the Library and File? How much information do you have to pull out before writing? This reverse engineering will help you become more efficient in your own organizing, outlining, and writing.

SPIN-OFF EXERCISES

Spin-off exercises are a great way to gain exposure to drafting different types of documents without as much of a time commitment as it would take to complete a whole new PT. I often suggest to my students that they spend a few minutes, after writing any PT, thinking about other documents they might have been asked to draft based on the same law and facts. Then, take a minute to outline or write out in full (time permitting) those "spin-off" tasks. Pay particular attention to how your tone and approach might differ depending on the goal of your assignment and your audience.

In *Carelton*, your task was to draft a memo to the senior partner. As spin-off exercises, using the same facts and law, try drafting a:

- Letter to Henry explaining the likelihood of success in suing Mid-Central (this would involve breaking down the law into simple and easy-to-understand language) and describing what Henry will need to go through during the process (what bringing a lawsuit really entails)
- Letter to Henry's mother about the likelihood of success in suing Mid-Central and what she, Henry, and their family will go through in this process
- Memo to a private investigator to get more facts to support Henry's case
- Questions to ask in depositions of Mid-Central employees
- Discovery plan
- Settlement proposal to Mid-Central

The following are just a few thoughts on the drafting of such assignments for a bar exam PT. Note that these are just tips; they are not sample answers and do not cover everything you might need for a top score on these tasks. Rather, they are designed to get you thinking. Also be aware that the comments do not necessarily mirror the exact concerns you would have in the "real world" litigating such a matter, but rather issues to highlight in the context of a bar exam PT.

Letter to Henry

Remember, Henry is a boy; he obviously has no legal training. Therefore, you must keep your language simple and straightforward. However, you can tell him that Mid-Central will likely try to argue that they are not responsible for his injuries because he went onto their land without permission.

You may go on to explain that based on what Henry told you, you will try to dispute Mid-Central by arguing that: (1) Henry did not realize there was a danger from wires falling, (2) Mid-Central knew kids regularly used their land to swim, and (3) Mid-Central's allowing its plank and wires to extend into the Muddy River gave Mid-Central an obligation to keep the area safe for people lawfully using the river.

You will want to explain confidentiality and attorney-client privilege and make sure Henry knows that he can and should tell you everything he knows, but that he must not talk with anyone else about the case without your knowledge, permission, or presence. You will then need to tell Henry that Mid-Central will want to talk with him, and that likely they will want to take his "deposition." You may explain simply that during a deposition, they will ask him a series of questions under oath, in their office or your office, but also reassure him that you will be there to help him. You may need to warn Henry that they are likely to ask all about his "ditching" school, and other things that he may be uncomfortable answering, but that he will have to answer the questions honestly. You can tell him you will prepare him for anything like that, but that he should know it might occur and should expect that it may well happen. You might also go on to tell him that if the case goes to trial, he may have to appear in court, and explain what that entails.

You can tell Henry that you believe you will win, but that there is always a likelihood that you will not, especially if they are able to show that he's a sophisticated 16-yearold who should have known better. You can also say that it is very likely the case will not go all the way to trial, but will settle instead (and explain what that means).

In this sort of an assignment, the graders would not be looking for everything that could possibly be said to Henry. Also, there are many ways such a letter could be organized. What they will want to see is that you have written in plain English that your client Henry can clearly understand. They will want to verify that you know that Henry, and not his mother, is the client. They will also want to see that you touched on most of the basics mentioned earlier.

Letter to Henry's Mother

Most of what was noted with respect to the letter to Henry would also be appropriate to include in a letter to Henry's mother. She is also likely to want to know about costs and timing, and she must understand the fee arrangement. You must prepare her for what happens both if he wins or if he loses, and you must warn her that litigation sometimes takes a long time. You will need to let her know that they may try to tarnish Henry's reputation, though you can suggest that they probably have more to lose by bad publicity and may want to settle (and you would explain what *settlement* means). You need her to understand that even though she is paying your bills, she is not the client, and she must not be offended when you tell her she may not be present in all your meetings with Henry, and that Henry must not discuss the case with her.

What else do you think you would include in a letter to Henry's mother? Remember, because his mother is not a professional, and definitely not a lawyer, you want to use plain, simple English. You also want to convey empathy in your tone, as she has undergone a traumatic event and likely is still dealing with many problems stemming from Henry's injuries.

Memo to a Private Investigator

On a PT, the best way to set up a memo to a private investigator is often to organize by legal theories, noting what you (the plaintiff) have to prove and what types of facts might be helpful to establish each element of each liability theory. You will likely also want to suggest that the investigator ask about information that could be damaging to your case: best that you know it now, before continuing too far into the litigation.

Successful PT answers must be well-organized. (Drafting well-organized PT answers is one of the great challenges in mastering PTs because time flies!) A first-year law student or paralegal could provide a list of the holdings of each of the cases, but thinking like a lawyer requires synthesizing the case law and presenting the legal theories in an order showing that you see how the cases relate to one another; that is, how the body of law "fits" together.

Part of what you are doing in the first half of your allotted time, while you are reading and thinking and outlining, is trying to determine what the relevant pieces of the puzzle are and how they fit together. Only after figuring out that part can you truly write an effective answer. When you work on fact-gathering documents on a PT, the key is really to make explicit why facts you want to obtain would be relevant. That is what proves you are thinking like a lawyer! A nonlawyer might just randomly list facts. (Being organized and thinking logically are the hallmarks of a skilled lawyer.)

If you are given this sort of an assignment, the examiners will likely set it up in such a way that information you disclose to the investigator working for your firm will be privileged. Remember, though, your investigator cannot just go and talk freely with Mid-Central employees, because the company is represented by counsel. However, the investigator can likely talk with any of the other school kids who were swimming, and/or ask questions of witnesses who are not Mid-Central employees (perhaps other people who run barges or boats up the Muddy River who might have seen kids swimming regularly). The investigator can pull up public records of property boundaries, and possibly school records showing how often and when Henry missed class, and many other things.

What can you think of that you would want to know to help prepare for trial? What pieces of that information could a private investigator help you find out informally, and what might have to be determined in formal discovery?

Discovery Plan

Similar to the letter or memo to a private investigator, you will likely organize a discovery plan by elements or legal theories. For each of the applicable theories, you would likely want to discuss evidence that may be obtainable using discovery tools such as depositions, interrogatories, requests for admission, and requests for production of evidence.

You may note that, strategically, it would be helpful to get the documents, admissions, and answers to interrogatories before you take depositions so that you have further information on what questions to ask. Also, obtaining these is generally less expensive than taking depositions.

Starting with the negligence theory based on implied consent allowing outsiders to freely use the property, here are a few points you might include for each discovery device:

Negligence Based on Implied Consent

Deposition

We may want to depose the foreman and a number of employees who were working at the Mid-Central shipyard when Henry was injured. We will ask them questions to find out (among other things):

- How often they locked the gate
- Whether they knew kids came onto the property to swim
- Whether each person being deposed spoke to any of the kids swimming and to relate the details of any such conversations
- Whether there were "No Trespassing" signs
- How often they serviced the poles and wiring

What else can you think of?

This sort of assignment may require you to specifically say why you want the particular information you are seeking; for example, what theories would be supported depending on which answers the people questioned provide.

Requests for production of documents

We will want to ask for any internal memoranda, email, or other correspondence relating to intruders and security. We will want the repair logs for any maintenance or repair of the electrical wiring, including the posts.

What else?

Requests for admission

We will want Mid-Central to admit that the gate was frequently left unlocked and that they knew the pole was rotted.

What else can you think of?

Settlement proposal to Mid-Central

You could well be asked to draft a letter to Mid-Central's attorney urging the defendant to settle. What are some of the points that you would make in that sort of a document?

- That Mid-Central will very likely be found liable based on one or more landowner liability theories
- That it would cause bad publicity for Mid-Central to go to trial when they were at fault for injuring a local 16-year-old boy
- That it will cost Mid-Central far more in protracted litigation than to settle now

What else would you include in a settlement letter?

PRACTICE, LAW SCHOOL, AND PTs: COMPARE AND CONTRAST

In the real world, a case like this would be all about settlement. It is possible, though doubtful, that such a case would ever make it to trial. Mid-Central undoubtedly has far more resources than Henry to mount a protracted fight, and that too might push the Careltons to want to settle. However, Henry might well make a very sympathetic plaintiff, and Mid-Central may not be able to afford bad press.

On this practice PT, none of this was your concern. You were instructed to draft documents to prepare for trial. (In other words, do not "write yourself out of the question" by suggesting that we settle and not even amend the complaint, and therefore skip drafting what was requested in your answer.) Give the bar examiners what they want and ask for!

Nevertheless, you should remember that even in the real world, the better prepared you are for trial, the stronger your negotiating position will be when working out a settlement agreement with opposing counsel. We typically do not spend a lot of time in law school talking about settlement. Traditional law exams are written in such a way that we immediately think in terms of elements of causes of action and whether the parties will or will not prevail in litigation. This PT makes a great springboard for discussion with classmates about settlement, and your role as a future lawyer in both litigating and negotiating.

KEY TAKEAWAYS

- When briefing cases in a PT Library, pull out the holding, and then try to find at least one or two key facts that distinguish the case from your client's situation (especially if the case holding does not support your client's position). Determine at least one or two facts from the cases that are analogous to the facts in your client's situation (especially if the case holding does support your client's position).
- The multiple-choice questions in *Carelton* helped you test yourself on your case-briefing skills, but your bar exam PT will likely **not** include multiple-choice testing.
- Think both about facts you know and can prove (and how they will be proven), and facts that may still have to be gathered.
- Do not just list or summarize cases case-by-case from the Library in your PT answers. Rather, strive to see how the law in the Library fits together, and organize your answer logically in a way that synthesizes the rules and shows the grader that you see how it all fits together and makes sense. In *Carelton*, you had one older case (that was decidedly bad for your client), and then a number of other cases establishing theories that were exceptions to the rule in that first case. As you studied the sample answers, you undoubtedly saw that those memoranda were organized theory by theory.

4. CONTRACTS

OVERVIEW OF CONTRACTS

When dealing with contract law, you find yourself in the world of civil litigation and/or transactional matters. Parties are making deals with one another every day in the real world. They may come to you to plan, to draft or edit contracts, or to seek relief (usually in the form of money damages) when promises made as part of a deal are broken.

A homeowner might sue a contractor for breach of contract if her home was not built as specified under their agreement. An employee might sue an employer for breach of contract if the employee is fired without good cause. A seller might sue a buyer if the buyer suddenly refuses to purchase goods that the seller delivered. These are all typical scenarios in contracts essay questions in law school and on the bar exam. They are also things that happen in everyday real life.

Breach of contract is not a crime. In fact, in many commercial aspects of society, it is considered a routine part of business to get out of agreements that are not profitable and move on to other arrangements. Damages are often thought of simply as the cost of doing business. Watch your terminology on bar exams: one may be "liable" for, but is not "guilty" of, breaching a contract.

1L contracts courses are almost always based on casebook study. In the appellate cases you read, the parties have already litigated and are now appealing lower-court decisions about contracts that typically:

- Were never properly formed
- Include conditions that were never satisfied
- Were breached, or
- Spawned disputes as to the appropriate remedies for breaches

You also may study situations where third parties are litigating about their respective rights, studying assignments, delegations, and the rights of third-party beneficiaries.

PTs, like typical law school or bar exam essays, may look at contract problems from that same perspective: hindsight, after a deal has fallen apart. However, PTs also may be forward-looking, in the context of a time when the parties are negotiating deals and want to draft contracts that will avoid or prevent future disputes. We will look at just such a drafting/revision problem in the practice PT associated with this section on eProducts.

On the bar exam, major contract issues typically arise in the following areas:

- Applicable law (common law or Uniform Commercial Code [UCC])
- Contract formation (offer, acceptance, consideration, defenses)
- Contract modification
- Conditions, discharge, breach
- Remedies (including damages, restitution, and equitable remedies)
- Third-party issues (third-party beneficiaries, assignments, and delegations)

Law school contracts courses sometimes may get to all of these areas of law, but typically do not. Many spend much of the semester on contract formation. Do not worry; contract formation is the most heavily tested area of contracts on bar exam questions. If you understand contract formation very well, you can likely learn all the other pieces of the contracts puzzle fairly easily before or during your bar review course.

In law school, you will read many cases about what it takes to make a valid offer, to accept that offer, and to then have a deal that is legally binding; in legalese, this means that along with a valid offer and acceptance, there is "consideration" or a consideration substitute such as promissory estoppel. We also study defenses to formation. Even after there is a "deal," it may be that the deal is not valid because it was oral and should have been in writing, for example; or because one of the parties did not have the capacity to enter into the deal in the first place. There are other contract formation defenses you will need to know as well, including illegality, fraud, duress, and mistake.

SO MUCH TIME ON OFFER AND ACCEPTANCE!

It shocks some first-year students just how many cases they might be required to read on the very opening piece of contract formation: what it takes just to make a valid offer. I am reminded of *Lucy v. Zehmer*, a classic contract formation case that appears in a number of contracts casebooks. I love the court's colorful language noting that Mr. Zehmer's drinking left him "high as a Georgia pine." The Zehmers had allegedly offered to sell their farm for $50,000. Lucy wanted to hold the Zehmers to the deal, but the Zehmers claimed it was all a joke.

We study the case to determine how we look at the parties' intent to enter a contract. Specifically, do we consider what these particular people were actually thinking (subjective intent)? Or do we look at whether a reasonable person would consider this an offer to contract (objective intent)? The court looks at all the facts in the case (though they all were drinking, among other key facts they wrote the deal on a napkin and rewrote it so Mrs. Zehmer could sign it), and concludes by saying that only if Lucy knew (subjectively) or should have known (objectively) that the Zehmers were joking, then no contract was formed. An offer will be judged by how a reasonable person would understand the offeror's words and conduct.

Your professor may engage in hours of hypotheticals about just this sort of situation, changing the facts to see how each shifting scenario might be analyzed. (What if they hadn't been drinking? What if they only had one drink? What if they hadn't written the deal on a napkin? What if these parties had negotiated prior deals?) If your professor plays with "what if" hypotheticals and asks probing questions that you feel certain there is no right answer to, embrace this. This is learning to think like a lawyer! Even if your head starts to hurt, enjoy the process. Listen carefully to every word that is exchanged. Engaging in this sort of intellectual sparring will serve you well: all this time spent on excruciating details about offer, acceptance, and consideration is critical to gaining a fundamental understanding of contracts and contractual relations and will help you do well on many bar exam contracts questions.

Most classes do eventually move on from contract formation to contract performance and breach. You may read cases about what constitutes a "material breach" and what might be deemed simply a "minor breach," and the effect of concluding either way. You will also learn about damages in the event of a breach, including the requirement to mitigate damages.

Your class may move quickly through contract remedies and only get to money damages. Some professors skip certain areas, assuming that you will either pick them up in bar review or in an upper-division course such as remedies, where you would learn not only more about damages but also about equitable remedies such as specific performance (where a party seeks a court order enforcing the actual terms of the contract rather than money because of a contract breach) and restitution (returning money or property so as to prevent unjust enrichment).

A WORD ON CONTRACTS REMEDIES

Legal remedies (money damages), restitution, and equitable remedies are all important for bar exams. Some professors skip these because they are covered in other classes, such as UCC or remedies courses. Other professors assume that you will get to them in bar review. It is important, especially if you do not take a remedies course in law school, that you take time, well before bar review begins, to be sure that you understand all applicable contract remedies as well as contract claims. Know how damages are calculated in typical agreements such as buyer-seller, employer-employee, homeowner-homebuilder; understand different types of damages such as expectation damages, consequential damages, and liquidated damages; and understand equitable contract remedies such as specific performance.

For a more complete list of the topics covered on bar exam contracts questions, consult the most recent content scope outlines for your jurisdiction and for the NCBE.

SIMULATED CONTRACTS-BASED PT

Take three hours and complete the PT in eProducts called *Southwest Health Center v. Computech* ("*Computech*"), an exam set, as you will see, in the contract drafting stage.

One quick historical context note will be useful before you start: *Computech* was given in July 1986 when the technology described in the problem (hardware and software) was cutting edge. You may be shocked to read about the size and costs of computer equipment then. And, as we all know, today's cell phones are enormously more sophisticated than the machines in *Computech*. That said, the lawyering work you must do to complete this task is wholly consistent with both more recent exams and real-life contract negotiating. Ignore the outdated machines and focus on determining (as the instructions direct) which contract provisions pose problems for your client such that they have to be revised, and why. You will see that concerns such as when equipment is installed, who pays shipping costs, whether warranties are sufficient, and so forth would be very similar today. (As you complete this practice test, if you happen to note something that would radically differ today, mention it. But don't be surprised if this does not appear in the sample answers on eProducts.)

TIME-CRUNCH TIPS

If you do not have three hours and must save time completing this practice PT, outline it thoroughly rather than writing it out in full. There is only one task to be completed on this PT, so it does not break naturally into parts; thus, one of the key challenges is determining how best to organize your answer and highlighting some key suggestions or additions to the agreement in question. You can read all the materials and complete a thorough outline in about 90 to 100 minutes.

INSIDE THIS TEST: TIPS AND STRATEGIES

Congratulations on finishing *Computech*! One unusual part of this case, which you likely noticed, is that the entire Library is comprised of UCC provisions. There are no cases. I chose this exam for three reasons. First, it provides an excellent example of a drafting/editing/document review task. Second, it gives you a chance to study certain UCC rules. Contracts is typically tested with both common law and UCC law, so you will know this entire area well by the time of your bar exam. Third, I wanted you to see that not all PT Libraries contain the same types of legal authorities. Most include cases, but occasionally you will have a Library such as this with different types of authorities: here, only statutes.

General Instructions

The first thing you might have noticed, in a twist on the standard PT, is that this problem is set in two different states, Columbia and Franklin. You learn later that our client, Southwest Health Center (SHC) is in Columbia (as is our law firm, which you see from the Task Memo letterhead). SHC wants to buy a computer system from Computech, a company based in Franklin. (From correspondence later in the File, you learn that Columbia is on the West Coast and Franklin is on the East Coast, an important fact with regard to several contract provisions such as shipping costs and on-site training.)

The minute you saw two states, you may have thought: Which state's law will apply? If so, great lawyering instincts! That is the exact topic in Provision 16 of the Agreement, one you may well want to suggest revising (but we are getting ahead of ourselves here!).

The Task Memo, as always, gives background information as well as detailing your specific assignment. Sometimes it also gives hints. This Task Memo stresses the date on which the computer system should be ready. (The fact that the system should be fully operational when SHC opens its doors on December 1 is noted repeatedly. Any time bar examiners repeat a fact, it is likely critical.) Thus, timing will be an important term to look out for in the contract. You might not have seen this on a first read, but you would not miss this if you re-read the Task Memo after reviewing the other File information, before writing.

You find your exact assignment on the second page of the Task Memo. Notice that before Jim Hagelund (the partner giving the assignment) details the task, he says, "I would like your help in preparing for the meeting," referring to talks he will have the next day with the administrative director of SHC, Laura Sauer. He also tells you not to go into attack mode and rip apart every provision; he acknowledges that we will not get everything our client wants, that there will be negotiation and compromise.

From this paragraph, you should already have an understanding of the appropriate writing tone for this task. You are writing to a lawyer on your team, a partner in your law firm, to help him prepare for a meeting that will discuss how SHC might negotiate with Computech about the proposed contract provisions. Helping him prepare involves thinking things through so as to inform him. This is not a persuasive assignment. You will be writing in a neutral manner, analyzing whether each provision complies or not and why, helping Hagelund see what parts of this proposed deal may have to be rewritten. (Again, his underscoring that you are not to rewrite every provision shows that your job is not to argue, but rather to inform and determine where we must protect our client.)

Your tone is also affected by the fact that you are writing to a lawyer, Jim Hagelund. Jim may need to explain certain concepts to Sauer (presumably a lay person). However, in this document you do not have to define every legal term. For example, when you mention that Computech has expressly disclaimed the warranties of fitness and merchantability, you do not have to tell Jim in plain English what these warranties are, as you would if your task were to draft a letter to SHC. As a lawyer, Jim would understand these terms. Hence, your focus will be on why Computech's attempts to get out of warranting its goods and services may hurt your client.

Hagelund details exactly what you are to draft in the next-to-last paragraph of the Task Memo: "Please read the correspondence and review the Agreement . . . ." The paragraph is full of important detail, including directing you to:

- Analyze the Agreement in light of SHC's goals
- Focus discussion on the most problematic provisions (this is also a hint on how to save time; it provides a way of avoiding perfectionist

tendencies so that you can finish within the allotted time)

- State why each problem provision is troubling, identify exactly what the problem is, and give suggestions on how to resolve it, and move on to the next provision
- Assess the importance of any revisions you suggest, noting which are merely desirable changes and which are musts for the client
- Be aware that some provisions need not be revised; even where you do urge revisions, you do not have to suggest specific language; just say what is problematic and why, and note how to resolve the problem

Again, this last part (freeing you from having to propose specific new terms) is critical to helping you finish. Examiners design PTs so that they can be finished within the allotted time. They test and retest that timing. On many PTs with drafting/editing tasks, you do have to propose specific new language. However, where the examiners realize that it will be difficult for applicants to finish in time, they either explicitly restrict the assignment or provide hints to rein it in. You must be alert to these hints, though, noticing and heeding them. (On that note, I hope you did not waste time writing a statement of facts or other things that were not requested. To finish these PTs in time, give the examiners what they want and *only* what they want.)

Read the Task Memo several times before you begin drafting your answer. Seeing exactly what to write and what not to write is essential to producing a responsive, passing-quality answer within the allotted time frame.

The last paragraph of the Task Memo is also interesting. It essentially tells you that your Library is what we called earlier in this book a "reference library": a set of authorities you are already familiar with by the time of the bar exam but that are there for your reference in case you need to look things up.

Note the last line of the Task Memo, which says, "most of [these UCC provisions] may not be relevant to your review, but where they are the basis for your recommendations, please cite to specific UCC sections." This is very helpful. First, it tells you that many of the statutes in the Library will not help you to evaluate the Computech Agreement, so (hint hint) do not pore over each provision. You could easily spend a (wasted) hour reading every word of every UCC provision—but Hagelund tells you not to. Instead, read the Library table of contents and note generally which provisions are included. Then, as you read corresponding sections of the Agreement, consult the Library selectively.

Also, though generally you do not have to cite to specific cases or code sections by number on bar exam essays, here you do: (1) because the examiners are giving you the provisions (and thus not testing your memory), and (2) because Hagelund tells you to cite to any specific sections that are the basis for your recommendations. So, for example, where you see a provision that is directly implicated, such as § 2–314 and § 2–315 (warranties that Computech expressly disclaims in Provision 12.7 of the Agreement), you will want to look those up in the Library and cite to them by code section in your answer.

Moving on to the rest of the File, the next document after the Task Memo is fascinating. These are internal notes that Laura Sauer wrote to herself after reading articles about computer systems. This is a critical list of concerns. As you read the Agreement, make sure that none of these are problematic. You may need to come back to this, though, after you have read through the Agreement. At that time, you would really see how helpful this list is for focusing in on problem areas that may require revision, such as price, warranty, getting the system operational in a timely manner, software compatibility, and training. Looking back at this list before you started writing (or even at some point during your writing) may have helped you spot some problematic provisions that you would not otherwise have thought to write about.

The next letter is from Ed Pinkney (SHC Head Nurse) to Laura Sauer. (This is in-house correspondence from two of the SHC staff.) Pinkney points out potential problems with the computer system. Like the previous document, this too helps flag certain concerns that we want to be alert to when we read the Agreement. Among Pinkney's concerns are:

1. How will SHC be protected in the event the computer malfunctions?
2. Will malpractice insurance cover errors in patient records because of computer problems?
3. How will rules requiring nurses to maintain medical records be satisfied by use of the computer system?
4. Will the system work going forward not just when it is first installed?

Like Sauer's notes to herself, this Pinkney letter also helps us focus on potential problem areas. Nevertheless, some of these are not problems with the computer system itself, but rather with the way SHC implements computer usage in its practice. So, some of these concerns are points you might address in either your introduction or conclusion to Jim Hagelund, rather than in your provision-by-provision analysis of the Agreement. (One sample answer in eProducts does just that; the other addresses Pinkney's concerns by suggesting that new provisions be added to the Agreement.) This is a great example of how much creative leeway you have in how and where to incorporate certain points in PT answers. The key here is to have seen that Pinkney raised some important concerns and to have addressed them somewhere in your answer.

WHO IS SHE AGAIN? TAKE NOTES USING A "CAST LIST"

Did you find yourself halfway into the File seeing the name "Laura Sauer" and wondering, "Who is she again?" As suggested earlier, it can be helpful to start a "cast of characters" list when you first read the Task Memo, and add to it as you read other File documents.

Sample Cast of Characters (compiled piecemeal as you come across names)

Jim Hagelund: Our senior partner, person to whom we are writing, who is helping client negotiate deal.

Southwest Health Center (SHC): Our client. New medical center set to open on 12/1.

Computech: Computer business from which SHC wants to buy computer system.

Columbia: Our state and state where SHC is located (West Coast).

Franklin: State where Computech is located (East Coast).

Laura Sauer: SHC administrative director.

Ed Pinkney: SHC head nurse.

Gene Minard: Computech Pacific sales representative.

The next File documents are letters between Laura Sauer and Gene Minard, a Computech sales representative. The first is an inquiry letter from SHC (written by Sauer). This provides important background about SHC, stressing its initial and expected needs and goals, and asks if Computech can provide the "equipment, software, and services" that SHC needs. Yet again, Sauer stresses the importance of the December 1 opening, and the corresponding need for the system to be operational at that time. Sauer also notes the importance of support services and other things SHC will need. You must re-read this letter after you read the Agreement to effectively complete the task that Hagelund asked of you: "analyze and evaluate the Agreement in light of Southwest's goals." Pay special attention to any document that highlights your client's goals and needs.

The reply from Minard is a sales pitch, and an offer for the sale of an equipment and software package. This letter is long. Skim it the first time you see it, and then re-read it later, after you have read the Agreement. It would be much easier at that time to see that Minard "sells" a number of points that seem to have changed significantly in the proposed Agreement, including the use and compatibility of independent hardware and software, warranties, maintenance, and updates (to ensure that the system works in the future). Minard references Computech's slogan, "Computech systems are designed for today and *tomorrow*" (emphasis in Minard's letter); you may suggest that your firm use this language in negotiating with Computech to get them to offer better assurances of future performance.

The last File documents are the Agreement itself and its attached Schedule of Equipment. This is the Agreement you must analyze in your answer, so you will have to read it slowly and carefully. To complete this analysis in the most efficient manner, given your assignment, use the following sequence:

- First, glance at the headings of each UCC provision in the Library.
- Then, read the Agreement through once quickly.
- Then, re-read the other File documents, starting with the Task Memo.
- Then, read the Agreement a second time, slowly and carefully. On this re-read, read with three senses simultaneously. Touch each word of the Agreement as you read aloud but softly, under your breath. Take notes as needed while you read. Reading with sight (eyes), hearing (listening to yourself mouth each word), and touch (putting your finger or pencil on each word as you read it) ensures that you are focused and attentive to detail.

Note: This technique of reading with three senses is discussed in *Bar Exam Success* (West Academic) and recommended for reading other bar exam questions. You cannot, nor should you, read every PT document in this detailed manner. You will never finish in time if you do. Nevertheless, selected documents such as one you will be working from (here the Agreement) and the Task Memo in every PT must be read precisely and thoroughly.

OUTLINING, ORGANIZING, AND WRITING YOUR ANSWER

I suggest organizing this sort of a drafting/editing assignment provision by provision. It is the easiest way to stay on track and for the grader to follow your thinking. (The Constitutional Law section of this Appendix debriefs an example of another PT with a similar type of task, analyzing a proposed speech code; you will also organize your answer to that PT provision by provision, for the same reasons.)

Start with a simple header and introduction; then evaluate each provision in order (where you suggest no revisions, say so), then conclude. (See the following draft outline and notice that both sample answers are also organized in just this way.) Most past PTs that involve drafting or editing tasks have been best organized paragraph by paragraph. This differs greatly from legal memoranda and many other tasks that are typically best organized with something akin to a theory-by-theory approach (and then subcategorized by elements or factors).

Many students find it most efficient, in this sort of an assignment especially, to start typing a draft outline as soon as they see a logical organization/structure. They then take "notes" under the relevant provisions, which notes they later turn into their final answer. You can also write notes to yourself in a draft outline; just remember to delete them in your final answer. For example, in the sample outline, see my notes "[Under each provision, note what is problematic for our client and why.]" I put them in brackets and italics to avoid forgetting to delete them in the final answer.

SAMPLE DRAFT OUTLINE

Header/Intro

To: Jim Hagelund

From: Bar Applicant

Re: Analysis of Proposed Agreement from Computech

Date: [exam date]

Mr. Hagelund,

You will find my evaluation of each provision of the Agreement from Computech below. As requested, I have addressed the most problematic concerns, especially considering how they help (or as written do not help) our client achieve its goals. Please let me know if you have any further concerns or follow-up questions.

[*Under each provision, I must note what is problematic for our client and why.*]

Provision 1: Purchase and Sale

Provision 2: Prices, Payment, and Security Terms

Provision 3: Price Protection Period

Provision 4: Taxes

Provision 5: Shipment Terms and Charges

Provision 6: Title and Risk of Loss

Provision 7: Installation

Provision 8: Acceptance of Computer Products

Provision 9: Manuals and Documentation

Provision 10: Upgrade Policy

Provision 11: Copyrighted Materials

Provision 12: Warranties

Provision 13: Limitation of Remedies and Liability

Provision 14: Delays in Performance

Provision 15: Maintenance Service and Parts

Provision 16: Governing Law and Jurisdiction

Provision 17: Miscellaneous

Other Notes [to senior partner JIM HAGELUND]

Conclusion

Because the sample answers in eProducts provide a fairly detailed analysis of each provision, here I will only briefly touch on some that should be changed. I have put some of the following comments in italics to indicate my own internal thoughts; you may have had similar reactions as you read the Agreement. Of course, you would not write this way in your final answer, (write in a tone that is appropriate to whomever is your intended audience) but often this method can help you to stay awake and alert to "interact with the document" as you think and prepare what you actually will write.

Introduction

This could have been short, simply telling the partner that he will find the analysis that he requested in this document, though you could also have noted how you organized your evaluation and that you focused only on those provisions that were the most problematic. These introductory points remind you of what you must write, and they tell the grader that you read and understood the directions. An introduction could also preview what the main problem areas will be (the main problems could also be recapitulated in a conclusion).

Provision 1: Purchase and Sale

You likely saw problems with SHC being responsible for selecting computer equipment. *[Huh? Do they really expect my client, a medical center, to do this? Isn't that what they sought out a company like Computech for?!]*

Provision 2: Prices, Payment, and Security Terms

This was not a major point because we don't have enough factual background to fully analyze price, although Sauer's notes to herself in the File suggest there may be discounts for purchases of more than $25,000. *[I would like to get my client a discount for a large purchase and perhaps for timely payment. Ah, but on the flip side, we may want more flexibility if for some reason SHC finds itself having to make a late payment. The language here unfairly favors Computech, discharging all its duties if a payment is late (with only 10 days' written notice).]*

Provision 3: Price Protection Period

You likely saw problems here, too, in the great freedom Computech would be afforded to raise its prices up to 20 days prior to shipment (with only 5 days allowed for SHC to cancel the order). You might have suggested some limit on price increases or some other way to keep our client from having to pay more than it bargained for.

Provision 4: Taxes

These concerns must be addressed by someone else in our firm. *[I will note this quickly so my senior partner makes sure to consult the appropriate person about this provision.]*

Provision 5: Shipment Terms and Charges

These are problems. As written, the delivery is F.O.B. Computech's plant, putting all transportation costs and risks of loss on our client. (F.O.B. stands for "free on board" and indicates when and where the responsibility for shipping is incurred. "F.O.B. Computech's plant" means that SHC is responsible for every cost associated with getting the goods from Computech's door to SHC's door, including loading and unloading, transportation, and insurance.) *[We may need more information from Sauer as to whether she expected these additional shipment costs and what sort of insurance SHC has. This may well be something to negotiate, ideally for F.O.B. the Southwest Health Center, but perhaps with some compromise to share costs.]*

Perhaps even more important is clause 5.2, which, as one of the sample answers puts it, allows Computech to "ship the goods just about whenever it gets around to it." *[This must be revised, because we know how important it is to SHC to be fully operational by a time certain. We should change this to specify a date certain when all hardware and software shall be shipped. We could also add a "time is of the essence" clause here.]*

Provision 6: Title and Risk of Loss

You may have thought the language stating that "Computech will assist in all reasonable ways" was too vague. You may have wanted this specified. Also, this provision reiterates what you probably discussed under Provision 5: that all risk of loss shifts to SHC the moment shipping begins. This repeats that the shipment is F.O.B. Computech's plant. Any time bar examiners repeat something within an exam, you can take it as a hint that this matter or fact is important, and you should notice it wherever and whenever it crops up.

Provision 7: Installation

First you may have read this and thought that SHC should get this pre-approval for the site and that more should be specified about the installation. Good instincts. Imagine how it would destroy SHC's opening if the goods arrived from Computech but could not be installed.

Some other problems also arise here: (1) The timing of the installation is too vague; again, we know how important timing is to SHC. (2) Does SHC have the expertise to unpack and position the equipment? *[Isn't this something Computech should do? And Computech should pay for this as well. If it were "F.O.B. Southwest Medical Center," then Computech could be made responsible for all of this. Maybe we negotiate installation issues hand-in-hand with shipment costs.]*

Provision 8: Acceptance of Computer Products

This provision is problematic both because of the limited time our client has to inspect the system, and because SHC may not have the expertise to determine whether the system is working properly. This may require either the use of a third party to ensure satisfaction or an allowance that gives SHC sufficient time to use the system to see that it is fully operational. One sample answer suggests that SHC might be given a trial period before it unequivocally accepts the equipment.

Provision 9: Manuals and Documentation

This provision would likely be obsolete today, as most manuals today are online and can be downloaded for free. As and when written, this provision may have been a problem, especially when read with Provision 11, which prohibits SHC from making copies of manuals. This should be rewritten to ensure that SHC has all the manuals and documentation it needs for everyone who will work with the computer system. *[It would also be nice to have assurances that any updated manuals will be sent free of charge and that SHC will be notified of any updates.]*

Provision 10: Upgrade Policy

This could be a problem and relates to Computech's assurances that it will provide for today and tomorrow. If tomorrow's upgrade causes compatibility problems, SHC needs assurances that changes or required "fixes" will be made and handled free of charge. If upgrades simply enhance the system, SHC may simply want more specificity regarding how SHC will be informed of them and what SHC would be charged for purchasing upgrades. *[Can we get some sort of good customer discount here?]*

Provision 11: Copyrighted Materials

See comments about Provision 9.

Provision 12: Warranties

This was one of the most problematic provisions. By drafting the provision with seven subparts and writing Provision 12.7 in all-capital letters, the examiners were likely hinting that this was important. (No way to miss the sudden shift to all caps!) Here are some standouts among the problems that you can study in the sample answers:

- SHC needs a longer warranty. *[Remember Sauer's notes to herself suggesting the need for three to six months to debug a system.]*
- SHC needs warranties for compatibility with independent hardware and software, as indicated in the correspondence between Sauer and Minard. *[Computech should warrant that the products it sells are not defective, even if those products are made by another company.]*
- SHC needs timely repairs, if service is required. *[Remember the nurse, Pinkney, having warned about what could happen to patients if the system were down too long.]*
- SHC may have to negotiate a better deal on the place where repairs will be done. It cannot be required to return hardware to Computech's plant in another state, nor should it have to pay each time a tech person comes out from Computech to help.
- Computech specifically disclaims the warranty of fitness and warranty of merchantability. SHC is entitled to the protection of those warranties under UCC §§ 2–315 and 2–314 respectively, and SHC should not allow Computech to get out of these.

Provision 13: Limitation of Remedies and Liability

[This seems far too one-sided favoring Computech, in that it allows SHC no recovery for incidental, special, or consequential damages. It is totally foreseeable that computer malfunctions might cause SHC to lose patients, or worse still harm the patients. Our client needs to have some protection for foreseeable consequential damages, along with other remedies that Computech is disclaiming. Anyway, what SHC would most want and most need in the event of a defect is specific performance—a new, working computer!—rather than money damages. Are injunctive remedies barred under this provision, too? This has to be rewritten.]

You may also have noticed the limited statute of limitations under this provision, something for SHC to be aware of.

Provision 14: Delays in Performance

Computech is already protected by the doctrine of impracticability, but this language seems to protect Computech even for some delays that it might be able to prevent or limit. At a minimum, the language should be tightened up and made less vague than "unforeseen circumstances" or "causes beyond its control."

Provision 15: Maintenance Service and Parts

You might have had no changes here, or you might have wanted Computech to commit to some time period during which it will ensure maintenance. Therefore, inserting a comment about continued maintenance was nice but not necessary.

Provision 16: Governing Law and Jurisdiction

Because this provision as it stands would force us to litigate in Franklin, you might have suggested that this be altered so that litigation could take place in Columbia or in either location.

Provision 17: Miscellaneous

The assignment prohibition is one-sided. *[Why should my client be prohibited from assigning but Computech could still assign or delegate its responsibilities? SHC chose Computech because of its expertise. Should SHC have to deal with "Chuck's*

Computer Shack" if Computech were to sell its business? I don't think so.]

Other Notes, Additional Provisions, and Conclusion

Somewhere in your answer, either in your conclusion or in an "other notes" or additional-provisions-type section, you want to be sure to include Pinkney's concerns about responsibility for overseeing the computer data, hacking and security concerns, and so on.

Note: If this problem were set in today's environment, computer security and information safety might have been given much greater emphasis than they were in 1986.

After reviewing the entire agreement and studying the sample answers located in the Online Question and Answer Bank, you can see that there were certain points that almost everyone spotted and others that only some students noted. As you review the sample answers, focus on how to improve your reading, note taking, analysis, and writing. Do not get frustrated if you did not see everything in the sample answers. Also, notice that both answers got passing grades, even though they were very different. In this assignment, there was a lot of room for differences in approach, level of detail, and creativity of analysis.

SPIN-OFF EXERCISES

Spin-off exercises provide exposure to different document types without taking time to learn new facts and law. Having completed *Computech*, spend a few minutes thinking of other tasks you could have been given (using the same facts and law), and how you would have handled them. Here are some suggestions:

1. Negotiation with Computech

Pick a few provisions that are particularly problematic, such as the delivery, training, warranties, and remedies provisions. Pretend that you will be negotiating with counsel for Computech tomorrow. Write a dialogue of what you would say, what you expect your Computech counterpart will say, and how you would respond as to each problem area.

2. Parade of horribles

Pretend that SHC signed the contract as is. Picture it being the New Year's holiday, a month after the target opening for SHC. Write a list of everything you can imagine that might have gone wrong between now (negotiating the deal) and January 1. Some examples might be that Computech is late in delivering the computer equipment, they deliver the wrong equipment, the equipment breaks down, some of the SHC staff were not trained well enough and are having problems using the computers, and so on. For everything that you can imagine might have gone wrong or could go wrong in the future, write whether SHC is protected under the proposed contract or not and why.

PRACTICE AND LAW SCHOOL: COMPARE AND CONTRAST

This is an extremely practical exam, and totally hands-on. You studied a proposed contract and advised your boss on what our client should accept and what the client must renegotiate in order to meet its needs. The perspective you had to adopt in this problem was forward thinking: acting as a "preventive" lawyer rather than a litigator. The client was smart to get counsel involved early on to see that it entered into the best deal possible, especially given how integral this computer system was to the new business the client was starting.

Many lawyers never see clients until problems are so far advanced that lawsuits seem inevitable. Many other lawyers spend most of their time handling problems just like this one, often on a much larger scale.

To finish this exam in the allotted time, you had to be selective about what you commented on and how much you said about provisions that you thought needed revision. There was certainly enough fodder for discussion that you could have written for six hours or more, saying something intelligent about each and every provision—but three hours was the limit. So, this test was very "real world" in its content but limited in its scope to satisfy exam conditions.

TIME CRUNCHES IN THE REAL WORLD

Sometimes the time constraints on exams appear ridiculous and far-fetched. In fact, especially in today's fast-paced world, lawyers often get emails or texts from clients expecting immediate answers. It would not be unusual for a client to email an agreement to a lawyer with a note saying, "I'm going in to meet about the deal in about an hour. Let me know if this contract seems OK for me to sign as is or if I should suggest changing anything."

I hope you saw how different this test was from the typical contracts essay question, which usually looks at a situation after the parties' agreement has been breached (or, sometimes, where a contract was never properly formed in the first place). In such essay exams, you can approach them as a law student and think about issue spotting and IRAC. You can try to see yourself as a litigator on essays, looking at the fact patterns as the attorney for each side respectively and determining what rights can effectively be asserted (and why), who will likely prevail (and why), and what remedies the prevailing party will be entitled to (and why).

With this PT, your role was very different. No problems have occurred yet. The parties have not even consummated their deal. They are just talking so far. This exam required you to put on your various hats as counselor, problem solver, planner, and predictor. I hope you enjoyed this forward-thinking role. If you liked it a lot, consider doing some work in the transactional or preventive law arena. If you are still in law school, take some electives in contract drafting, estate planning, and other transactional areas.

I also hope you had fun with this practice exam and now feel confident that you could effectively handle any sort of drafting or editing task you might see on your bar exam. I also hope it helps you continue your important transition from law student to lawyer.

KEY TAKEAWAYS

- This practice exam helped you see the difference between PTs set in the litigation context (more common) and those set in a transactional context, such as the *Computech* problem.

- This PT also helped test your problem-solving skills, particularly the need to analyze the agreement in light of your client's goals and needs. You had to know what those goals and needs were, and think about how each provision satisfied or failed to satisfy the client's concerns.
- In this sort of editing/document-analysis type of task, often the most logical organization is simply to proceed clause by clause (or paragraph by paragraph). You could have to draft a contract or contract provision for a PT, but more likely you will have to edit one, or analyze the provisions of a document such as this to see if it meets your client's needs and/or is lawful. You may also face similar types of tasks set in a wills or trust context, a business associations context, or some other planning/transactional area of law.

5. CIVIL PROCEDURE

OVERVIEW OF CIVIL PROCEDURE

Civil procedure issues tested on bar exams range from pretrial concerns, such as jurisdiction, joinder of parties, joinder of claims, and discovery; to posttrial matters such as issue preclusion (collateral estoppel) and claim preclusion (res judicata).

Law school civil procedure course coverage varies greatly. Many classes spend most of their time on jurisdiction: which courts may hear which cases. Students read dozens of cases on subject matter jurisdiction and personal jurisdiction, covering traditional jurisdictional bases and long-arm statutes. Venue concerns, critical in practice and tested occasionally on bar exams, may or may not be discussed in class.

Some classes start with and quickly cover pleading requirements, then highlight the professor's favorite topics (perhaps Rule 11 or class action rules). All of these are fair game on the bar exam. So too is discovery, the lifeblood of litigation, something that is often absent or rushed through in traditional law school civil procedure courses.

Bottom line: You will typically have to study and learn numerous procedural rules in bar review to be ready for the bar exam, especially because many jurisdictions test your knowledge of both federal and state-specific civil procedure.

Note: A bar exam essay may be brought in one court but include *Erie* or removal issues such that you have to discuss both federal and state court matters within the same question.

For a list of the topics covered on bar exam civil procedure questions, consult the most recent content scope outlines for your jurisdiction and the NCBE.

SIMULATED CIVIL PROCEDURE-BASED PT

Piccolo v. Dobbs, our civil procedure based PT, located in eProducts, is a multistate PT (MPT) designed to be completed in 90 minutes. I recommend you make every effort to complete the exam within that time, in one sitting with no interruptions. If you do not finish, draw a red line after the 90 minutes have passed and then finish up, noting how much additional time it took to complete the assignment. If possible, set aside about two hours before you begin so that immediately after you complete the 90-minute exam, you can read the rest of this section to see how you did and to gain further insight into improving your work on future exams.

TIME-CRUNCH TIP

If you have a habit, something you do while studying—such as drinking coffee or checking your phone every time you get a text—wean yourself off that habit so you can focus solely on your exam for the entire testing period. Bar exams often test in several-hour blocks. You may go to the bathroom if you need to during a session, but you may not go out to eat, drink, or smoke. Students who have gotten used to sipping tea, or stopping for a cigarette, or checking a social media site on their phones, may be in for a rude shock when they are unable to indulge these habits during the bar exam. Break such habits well before the actual exam and develop your ability to concentrate for a minimum of three hours at a stretch.

It is recommended that you spend 45 minutes reading and outlining *Piccolo* and 45 minutes writing your answer. Refer back to earlier in the book for strategies on how to approach PTs generally, if you want a refresher. Important reminder: On the actual MPT, you may *not* rip or tear any pages of the exam. Check to see if your bar exam allows you to use paper clips. If permitted, you can clip important pages such as the Task Memo or table of contents to easily refer back to them and help you stay organized.

TIME-CRUNCH TIPS

This exam is designed to be completed in 90 minutes, so it is already shorter than the previous PTs you have completed. If you are still crunched for time with this assignment, read all the materials and complete the argument portion of this task, but skip the statement of facts. If you have very little time but still want to dig in and do some quality work, read everything, write the statement of facts, and simply outline the argument section. (Be sure that your outline includes the persuasive headings you will use in the body of your argument.)

INSIDE THIS TEST: TIPS AND STRATEGIES

You will notice a Table of Contents that lists both the File contents and the Library contents or legal authorities. Here there are five items in the File and three in the Library. We will walk through both the File and Library in this section, highlighting points you may have picked up on. If you did not notice everything, do not be concerned. That is exactly why you are practicing these PT exams! Also, you may have noticed some points while re-reading that you did not notice when you first skimmed through the File. Again, this is perfectly normal; it's the reason you train extensively before actually taking the bar exam.

Debriefing the File

The first document in the File is the Task Memo, and from a close read of that document, you can develop your "cast of characters." As soon as you begin reading, you see that Alice

Nagle is the first named partner. She is also the person giving you your assignment.

We represent Pat Piccolo. The defendant is Julia Dobbs. Note that the examiners have given you a plaintiff whose name begins with "P" and a defendant whose name begins with "D." Bar examiners often use this sort of naming on essays, and you really want to thank them when they do, as it will help you keep the parties straight. In any law exam, you also want to remain aware of the roles each person plays, as that drastically shapes the analysis and often the conclusions you reach.

TIP: REFER TO PARTIES BY THEIR ROLE RATHER THAN THEIR NAME

When writing bar essays and sometimes PTs, it can be helpful to rename the parties using their roles rather than their names to keep each party straight; for example, refer to a landlord and tenant as such, rather than as they might be named on the exam. (For example, the first time you mention the name, write: "Tanya, the Plaintiff and Tenant bringing this action ('Tenant') and Larry, the Defendant Landlord ('Landlord') who is being sued.") Many students use "P" and "D," which is fine and can also help; however, because it is so easy to confuse Ps and Ds after hours of typing or writing, it may be more helpful to refer to people by their roles.

The suit here is filed in federal court. The passenger in our client's car was killed in the accident in question. There are problems now with discovery. Specifically, we have had difficulties in obtaining certain statements. We will need to make a request that the court order the other side to produce the recordings and transcripts of the interviews with the defendant and the key witness.

The task is to draft an argument in support of a motion to compel. The person giving us this assignment could not be more explicit. She says: "Your brief should argue that, under the facts of our case, we are entitled to get the transcripts and tapes." What do you get from this? Within the first few minutes of starting this PT, you understand that your job will be to persuade the court to order the other side to give us the transcripts and tapes.

What about the format of that argument? How do we know how to set up our argument? In the document after the Task Memo, the examiners give you a format page for persuasive briefs and memoranda. This is a gift, letting you know exactly how to set up your answer: simply follow the format provided in that memorandum.

Here, you are told to provide a statement of facts and an argument. You are further instructed that the argument section should be broken down by the main reasons supporting your position and that each of these should start with a proper and carefully crafted persuasive heading. The examiners describe such persuasive headings as a "specific application of a rule of law to the facts of the case and not a bare legal or factual conclusion or a statement of an abstract principle." They then provide an example of improper and proper headings.

In this type of persuasive assignment, your carefully crafted headings may be the most important part of your assignment: They essentially provide a roadmap of your entire argument. Once you study the Library and understand the main reasons that support your argument—in other words, the reasons why the plaintiff should be entitled to the tapes and transcripts—draft your headings using this format. Mirror the tone and structure of the proper heading examples.

PERSUASIVE HEADINGS ARE ESSENTIAL IN BRIEFS TO A COURT

Here are additional examples of proper and improper headings, reproduced from past California PTs. (All credit for this language to the California Committee of Bar Examiners.) Study these examples and review the information from earlier in the book on how to draft persuasive arguments to the court.

> *Improper*: Defendant had sufficient minimum contacts to establish personal jurisdiction.
>
> *Proper:* A radio station located in the State of Franklin that broadcasts into the State of Columbia, receives revenue from advertisers located in the State

of Columbia, and holds its annual meeting in the State of Columbia, has sufficient minimum contacts to allow Columbia courts to assert personal jurisdiction.

Improper: The evidence is sufficient to convict the defendant.

Proper: Evidence of entry through an open window is sufficient to satisfy the "breaking" element of burglary.

Note: In this PT, you are not instructed specifically to write an introduction or conclusion, but, as long as you write them quickly so they do not take time away from what was actually requested, adding these can help let the grader know you understood and completed the assigned task(s).

Based on directions in the Task Memo and your general knowledge of how to put together complete answers, minutes into reading this exam you could already have begun a rough outline of the basic format for your answer.

SAMPLE OUTLINE FROM THE TASK MEMO

TITLE—[Optional but helpful. Here, this could simply be:]

Argument in Support of Plaintiff's Motion to Compel Discovery

INTRODUCTION—[Optional but again useful. For example:]

To: Alice Nagle

From: Applicant (your name on the bar exam)

Re: *Piccolo v. Dobbs*, motion to compel discovery:

[Here you might add one sentence telling Alice Nagle that below she will find the persuasive argument requested.]

STATEMENT OF FACTS

This was specifically requested in the Task Memo, so in this PT, you must draft a statement of facts. As discussed earlier in the book, it is typically best to omit a statement of facts on PT assignments unless you are instructed to write one. When instructed to do so, as here, failure to include a statement of facts may well result in your failing the exam.

ARGUMENT

Persuasive Heading 1 Body of argument 1 Persuasive Heading 2 Body of argument 2 Persuasive Heading 3 Body of argument

CONCLUSION

[Optional, but helpful.] A quick conclusion signals to the grader that you completed the assignment. In a brief to the court such as this, your conclusion could be one sentence recapping the relief you are seeking, such as: "For all the foregoing reasons, Plaintiff prays that this Court will compel production by the Defendant of the requested tapes and transcripts."

Look how much information can be gleaned from a close read of the Task Memo and Format Memo! You are only two pages into your File, and you already have a sense of how to tackle this PT, and a draft outline! Armed with this organization and structure, as you read the rest of the File and Library, you can plug relevant information directly into this template and flesh out your answer.

Let's now walk through the rest of the File. The next document is "Excerpts from Deposition of Julia Dobbs." Remember, she is the defendant, the person our client is suing. Our boss, the senior partner, Alice Nagle, took this deposition. As you skim these excerpts, contradictions in the defendant's testimony may pop out at you, but you may not yet realize what is and what is not critical. Basically, this first read/skim of the File simply allows you to get the lay of the land. When you return to these documents after studying the Library, what is important from the File will be obvious.

The next File document is "Excerpts from Deposition of Ted Wallace." Again, our boss took the deposition. Who is Ted Wallace? He is a witness. (Did you notice that in this exam, the witness's name starts with a W, the plaintiff's name starts with a P, and the defendant's name starts with a D? Thank you, bar examiners!)

Wallace was at the scene of the accident and subsequently befriended the defendant Dobbs. He also hired Dobbs's father as his lawyer in an unrelated matter. (Your antennae may have been raised here, wondering about Wallace's bias in favor of Dobbs.) These excerpts also note that this witness talked with our boss two day after the accident. There appear to be some contradictions in Wallace's statements, but again you may not have noticed these until you re-read the File, or you may have noticed but not considered them relevant or important until you had a good grasp on the law in the Library.

The last document in the File is "Excerpts from Deposition of Alan Isaacs." Note that his name starts with an "I" and he works for the insurance company that insured the defendant Dobbs. What Isaacs says will be critical to the arguments in your motion, but you cannot know that until you familiarize yourself with the law in the Library.

One thing Isaacs notes is that the only eyewitnesses were the defendant Dobbs and Ted Wallace. This tells you that Wallace and Dobbs are the only people able to give us information about the accident and why the statements they made right after the accident are so important in preparing our case. After reading the Library, you will learn that this is a major component of one of your arguments.

We also learned from the deposition excerpts that neither Dobbs nor Wallace testified at Dobbs's criminal trial. Again, you may not have seen the relevance of that point on your first skim, but why that is important becomes clear once you know the law. Let's jump in now and take a look at the law in the *Piccolo* Library.

Library

There is an excerpt from one statute, Federal Rule of Civil Procedure (FRCP) Rule 26. This is a rule you would know by the time of your bar exam, because civil procedure is tested on other parts of the bar exam as well. There are also two cases. That is the whole Library. (Didn't I tell you that 90-minute PTs would be easier after having completed 3-hour practice PTs?!)

Two subsections of FRCP Rule 26 are excerpted: FRCP Rule 26(1) and FRCP Rule 26(3). They basically state that everything that is not privileged is generally discoverable; however, documents and items prepared in anticipation of litigation may only be discoverable upon a showing "that the party seeking discovery has substantial need . . . and that the party is unable without undue hardship to obtain the substantial equivalent . . . by other means." The provision continues to note extra safeguards even when a substantial need is shown, to protect against disclosures of lawyers' or other representatives' "mental impressions, conclusions, opinions, or legal theories."

Pacamor, the first case, provides mostly law; it has sparse facts. The action was one alleging false advertising. Certain customer surveys were sought to be protected against compelled discovery. The lower court ordered them produced and the decision was affirmed in the case in our Library. A great deal of what is written in this case will be helpful to your understanding of the applicable law and to the drafting of the argument in support of the motion.

There are a couple of particular points you should have seen in *Pacamor*: the work-product doctrine must be "narrowly construed," and the "burden of proving the material was prepared in anticipation of litigation" is on the person asserting the privilege. In our case, that would be Dobbs.

Perhaps the language in *Pacamor* that will be most useful to us in this part of our argument is this: "Materials assembled in the ordinary course of business . . . are not protected, even if the party is aware that the documents may also be useful in the event of litigation." Why? Isaacs thought this matter might go to trial because it involved a death, but it was arguably still not prepared "in anticipation of litigation," as Isaacs was not certain there would be a lawsuit. No case had been filed at the time these recordings were made.

The next case, *Basinger*, is more closely aligned with our case in terms of facts. There is an insurance company seeking to protect accident-related documents from discovery. The first point the court made is that the documents were not prepared in anticipation of litigation—exactly what we will try to argue (though we may not prevail on this argument). However, the court's second point is that even if the subject documents were so prepared, that protection can be (and in *Basinger* was) overcome by a showing that the information could be obtained elsewhere.

We will need to distinguish the facts in our case from those in *Basinger* with a clear showing that the information from Dobbs and Wallace *cannot* be obtained elsewhere, that the reports made to Isaacs by these witnesses are the only information available, that we tried to depose Dobbs and Wallace and could not get the equivalent information by other means. Also, because Dobbs and Wallace spoke to the investigator quite soon (close in time) after the accident, their statements would be considered "unique," per *Basinger*. All of this will help us prove we have a clear need for the statements we seek.

OUTLINING YOUR ANSWER

After reading the Library, sit and think about an appropriate organization to pull all of this together. How do the puzzle pieces fit? Try to see if the law forms a "tree" with "branches" and what facts ("leaves") you need to hang on each branch in order to prove your arguments. (If you do not remember the tree metaphor for organizing PTs, this is a good time to review earlier sections in the book on PT organization.)

Here, looking at a combination of FRCP Rule 26, *Pacamor,* and *Basinger*, what strikes you? Do you see the prongs you will have to set forth to make the argument that we need the tape recordings and transcriptions that Isaacs took of Dobbs and Wallace on the day after the accident? (These argument prongs are your tree "branches.") Look in the statute, and then (hint!), look at the headings and subheadings in *Pacamor*. Something like the following should emerge in your mind as you seek a logical organizing principle:

1. The tapes and transcriptions are discoverable under FRCP 26(b)(1).

2. The tapes and transcriptions are not privileged as attorney work product because they were not prepared in anticipation of litigation.
3. Even if the tapes and transcriptions are deemed attorney work product, they are discoverable because the plaintiff has a substantial need for them and is unable without undue hardship to obtain the substantial equivalent elsewhere.

If you look closely at the headings in *Pacamor*, you see that they mirror this logical organization. It is not unusual for examiners to give you such organizational hints in PTs.

As you read PTs, always be on the lookout for lists: lists of steps, headings, factors, or elements. Here, these logical analytical steps, the headings in *Pacamor*, track the rule sections FRCP 26(b)(1) and 26(b)(3), and the court's thinking in *Pacamor*. The examiners gave you this organization. You should have seen it if you looked carefully. If you did not notice this organizational hint when you were taking this practice exam, go back in now and see if what I am saying makes sense. If it does, great! The whole purpose of completing practice tests is to learn from the process. The more practice PTs you complete, the more you will become attuned to seeing one or more logical ways to organize and outline your answer. Sometimes there is more than one sensible organizational method. If that's the case, just pick whichever makes the most sense to you. Just remember that the examiners always make PTs solvable puzzles that do fit together in some logical way.

Plugging the Legal Argument into the Format of Your Answer

You can also go back now and flesh out the outline you started drafting when you first read the Task Memo.

[Title]

Argument in Support of Plaintiff's Motion to Compel Discovery

[Introduction]

To: Alice Nagle

From: Applicant

Re: *Piccolo v. Dobbs,* motion to compel discovery

Please find the argument you requested below.

Statement of Facts

Here fill in facts that you carefully select as pertinent to your argument. It may be helpful and quicker to draft this portion after you draft your argument section so you know which facts you relied on. Just be sure to save enough time for this!

Argument

You may want to start with a sentence that sets the stage: for example, "For the reasons stated below, Plaintiff seeks to compel the production of tapes and transcripts of interviews Alan Isaacs took of Julia Dobbs and Ted Wallace."

Persuasive Headings

Next come your three persuasive headings and the arguments supporting each. Here are examples:

I. Because they relate directly to the subject matter of the case at bar, the tapes and transcriptions are discoverable under FRCP 26(b)(1).

[Here insert your full argument, interweaving law and fact to persuasively prove the point in this heading.]

II. Because the tapes and transcriptions were prepared by an investigator before a case was filed and not in anticipation of litigation, they are not privileged as attorney work product.

[Here insert your full argument, interweaving law and fact to persuasively prove the point in this heading.]

III. Even if the tapes and transcriptions were considered attorney work product, they should be deemed discoverable here because the plaintiff has a substantial need for them, in that they are the only fairly contemporaneous statements made, and the plaintiff is unable without undue hardship to obtain the substantial equivalent elsewhere.

[Here insert your full argument, interweaving law and fact to persuasively prove the point in this heading.]

Conclusion

"For all the foregoing reasons, plaintiff prays that this court will compel production by the defendant of the requested tapes and transcripts."

Writing the Answer

Your next step would be to re-read the File, take notes, and write your answer. Armed with a logical organization, your job is to flesh out the facts to support each prong of your argument. Going back into the File at this point, the information you need about the circumstances surrounded the taking of information from Dobbs and Wallace should pop out because you know exactly what you are looking for.

On this re-read of the File, notice things you may not have seen initially. For example, you quickly and easily see why it matters that neither Wallace nor Dobbs testified at trial or talked to anyone else at the scene of the accident, and that they refused at the time to talk with our law firm. This bolsters the point that there is no other way for us to get the critical information provided in their statements. It also shows that what they said in those statements is unique because it was provided to Isaacs "fairly contemporaneously" with the accident.

You also readily see why it is critical to nail down what Isaacs thought about the case (because it involved a death, he "felt" that it was "virtually certain that a lawsuit would be filed"). But go back and review the facts, and you see that at that time Isaacs had not yet consulted with counsel and was not acting at the direction of counsel.

These and other facts may not have seemed important on the first read, but now, after studying the Library, they should jump out at you as critical. Do you now see why the SS-BROW system works so well? SS-BROW stands for:

- **S**tudy the Instructions
- **S**kim the File
- **B**rief the Library Authorities
- **R**e-Read Instructions, File, and Library as needed
- **O**utline
- **W**rite

You will find the Drafter's Point Sheet, which summarizes what needs to be included to pass this PT, in the Online Question and Answer Bank.

SPIN-OFF EXERCISES

As we have seen in previous sections, spin-off exercises are your opportunity to leverage the time investment you made in reading this Library and File, and picture how you would write your answer if you had been asked to draft a different type of assignment using the same facts and law.

Representing the Opposing Party

First, before you even change the assignment, try thinking about the exact same assignment as if you were representing Dobbs rather than Piccolo. How would your argument change? Other than the result (your asking to keep the documents privileged and not compel turning them over to the plaintiff), what else would differ? How about the way you argue whether the statements were initially taken in anticipation of litigation? (Hint: This may be a much stronger argument for Dobbs than for Piccolo. Bar examiners often make you work on the PT by giving you the "weaker" side in a particular conflict.)

Offer of Settlement

Now imagine you are still representing Piccolo, but this time counsel for Dobbs sends our client a letter offering to settle. What might that letter look like? What would be a reason they might try to persuade Piccolo to settle, and what might we advise Piccolo on how to think through the offer?

Prepare for the Other Side's Deposition of Our Client, Piccolo

This assignment asks you to anticipate the questions the other side would ask our client. To think this through, you first want to look at the types of questions that our boss, the senior partner Alice Nagle, asked Dobbs, Wallace, and Isaacs in the initial depositions. Looking at documents in one PT File can help you prepare if you end up having to draft that sort of document in a later PT.

What do you think counsel for Dobbs may be looking for in deposing our client? Is there any information out there about what happened that day that might possibly place some sort of blame or some part of the fault for the accident on our client? If so, we must know that, and we must advise Piccolo on how to answer questions.

Letter to Piccolo

How would you draft a letter to Piccolo explaining what we are doing in the case: that we are going to court to compel the other side to grant our discovery request? Piccolo is a lay person. Will she even understand the word *discovery*? How will you explain it? Practice explaining this in easy-to-understand terms; the process will help you ensure that you understand the discovery process and tools, and will help you prepare for a PT where your task is to write to a lay person.

Cross-Examination of Wallace, Dobbs, and/or Isaacs

Assume that our motion was denied and we are now in trial trying to discredit these witnesses based only on the information we now have. Can you think of what you might want to ask on cross-examination to help prove our case and/or cast doubt on the credibility of these key witnesses? To draft your cross-examination plan, for each main topic of questioning, write the following:

- Your proposed question
- The witness's anticipated answer
- Opposing counsel's likely objection
- Your response to the objection

- The court's likely ruling

Note: You will find much more on cross-examination in the "Evidence" section of this Appendix.

PRACTICE, LAW SCHOOL, AND PTs: COMPARE AND CONTRAST

This PT provides a very realistic accident fact pattern and a plausible discovery dispute. The legal issues in the assigned task were narrow, specific to this motion to compel. Arguments about discovery are commonplace. When litigating smaller cases, it may not be cost-effective to engage in protracted discovery battles, and people may give in or settle such matters. Here, because it involved an insured motorist who killed someone, this may well be the type of case an insurance company would fight hard over.

This exam helps you to think about discovery rules—what is and what is not discoverable—from both parties' perspectives. It therefore provides great experiential training in a realistic setting.

KEY TAKEAWAYS

- This practice exam helped you master actual bar exam timing, as this PT was designed to be completed, start to finish, in 90 minutes. This is very representative of what you will see on your exam.
- This PT provided excellent exposure to a commonly tested PT task, a brief in support of a motion. You had to draft a persuasive though accurate statement of facts and a persuasive argument section (the main body of your brief) with "carefully crafted" persuasive headings. Practice writing such headings; they are the key to this sort of persuasive task.
- Like many PTs, this PT included organizational hints that, if you recognized them, were time-savers and helpful guidelines. Here, the hints were that the headings in the *Pacamor* case mirrored the same logical organization that you might well have used in setting up your answer.
- The Library here, with the hints noted earlier, reminds us not to just read and brief the cases and rush to begin writing.

To succeed on PTs, sit back for a bit before taking fingers to keyboard and think carefully about how each case helps or hurts your client's position and how all the cases and statutes fit together. The examiners will want to pass you if you produce a well-organized, thoughtful answer that is responsive to the instructions.

6. EVIDENCE

OVERVIEW OF EVIDENCE

In law school evidence classes, we generally study rules and principles that govern how facts are proven in court. People may *think* that what someone tells them or what they read online is what really happened. In a lawsuit, though, unless someone's words or documents or other physical items are admitted in court as evidence (or were admitted into the record as part of pretrial discovery), these cannot really be considered "the facts." They are perhaps the alleged facts, or facts anticipated to emerge, but they are not the definitive story.

Even when "facts" are first accepted in court at the trial level, they are still only the evidence that one side presented. The other side will present its story with other evidence and/or by casting the first side's facts in a different light. Each side will poke holes in the other's evidence, by impeaching witnesses and pointing out contradictions or other reasons that evidence is unreliable.

What emerges from this litigation process is eventually "frozen" as the factual record. That record is generally the "story" an appellate court considers when making its ruling to uphold or overturn a lower court.

In law school, we study most subjects by reading appellate cases, so when an opinion discusses "the facts," those are what was proven at trial (in the lower court). Similarly, essay questions in law school and on bar exams typically include paragraphs (sometimes pages) of facts that are meant to be taken as true for purposes of the exam. You do not want to be in cross-examination mode when reading essay-question fact patterns. On bar exam essays, you never think "what if" a fact were not as it is stated. It *is* so stated, in the particular manner written, and you must use it as given. You may use the fact to support or refute the existence of an element of a cause of action or crime or defense theory, but you must not waste time wondering whether something in an essay fact pattern "really happened." Law essay exams are almost always based on hypotheticals and written to see how you *use* the facts as they are presented.

In sharp contrast, in PTs, just as in investigating cases as a lawyer and establishing facts in court, doubt and credibility are major concerns. As you will see in the PT to be completed in this section, your job might well be to destroy the believability of someone's "story."

PTs such as this evidence-based PT may feel more like the "real world." It may be fun to see yourself more as an attorney than a law student. At the same time, practicing with this sort of PT is also helping you to review important rules of evidence that you will likely be tested on in your evidence class and on the bar exam.

In most law school evidence courses:

- You will study how evidence is presented (rules about which witnesses can testify about what and how) and how it is rebutted (how witnesses may be impeached).
- You learn about what is relevant and why sometimes even evidence that is logically relevant (directly on point!) can be excluded. (You all know one reason: where the prejudice outweighs the probative value.)
- You learn how some evidence can be kept out of court (for example, communications that are privileged).
- You typically spend a lot of time on the hearsay rule and exceptions to it.

For a list of the topics covered on bar exam evidence questions, consult the most recent content scope outlines for your jurisdiction and the NCBE.

Several of the key points on the list of what you will likely cover in evidence class are integral parts of the PT you are about to complete, including, but not limited to, relevance issues, impeachment concerns, policy objectives achieved by restricting evidence of subsequent remedial measures, and more. *Dodson v. Canadian Equipment Company* is a great test. I hope you have fun with it!

SIMULATED EVIDENCE-BASED PT

Complete the three-hour *Dodson v. Canadian Equipment Company* located in eProducts.

TIME-CRUNCH TIPS

I suggest that you write this whole exam as one three-hour exam. However, if you prefer to complete this exam in two 90-minute sittings, that is fine too. This exam was designed to be broken into two 90-minute exams, each with one task. Here's what to read for the respective tasks: All of the File except the "Excerpt from Interrogatories to Canadian Equipment Company" is relevant to the first task. The law that relates to the first task includes most of the Federal Rules of Evidence (FRE) excerpts and the *Christmas v. Sanders* case. When you are ready to complete the second task, review the File (skipping the Format page on witness cross-examination, the report from the investigator John Ripka, the arrest record, and the "Excerpt of the Deposition of Denise"). For the second task, also be sure to read the "Excerpt from Interrogatories to Canadian Equipment Company." The law that relates to the second task is FRE Rule 407, the Columbia Products Liability Act (CPLA), and the *Moe*, *Walker*, and *Stewart* cases.

INSIDE THIS TEST: TIPS AND STRATEGIES

Welcome to evidence in action!

The General Instructions are fairly boilerplate in this exam. They tell you the basics about how much time you have, that cases are not real, that you may use short cites, and so on. The only information in the General Instructions that is unique to this problem is in the second paragraph, which tells you that you are set in the fictitious 15th Federal Circuit.

Note: When you get to the Task Memo, you see that this exam involves a negligence and product liability case, and thus is not a "federal question"; but from the complaint you see that you are in federal district court under diversity jurisdiction.

Also, at the end of the Instructions, you see that each of the two tasks is weighted equally.

The Task Memo is never boilerplate, and that is where we start getting all the information that will really help us on this PT. Let's look at how the Task Memo starts: "I need your help preparing for trial." From this we know that the role-play takes place before the trial. We learn that we represent the plaintiff.

Did you notice who is giving you the assignment? Elizabeth Duke. Who is that? Well, the Task Memo is written on firm letterhead, and the firm is called "Freeman, Duke, and Woolridge," so in all likelihood the person giving us the assignment is the second named partner in your law firm, Ms. Duke.

Next in the Task Memo, we learn a little about the case. Our client is suing a company, Canadian Equipment Company (CEC), the manufacturer of her car. We are claiming that our client was seriously injured (she's a paraplegic as a result of the accident) when the car's glass sunroof shattered.

We also learn that we are in a contributory negligence jurisdiction. The Task Memo tells us, but we should also understand from our general knowledge of tort law, that means that if our client should be found to have been in any way negligent herself, her negligence claim against CEC will be barred. She is bringing two claims, though. The senior partner tells us that this contributory negligence issue makes the second claim, the strict liability claim under products liability, "all the more important." This makes sense because, as you know, claims based on strict liability would not be barred even if the plaintiff were at fault.

Now comes another interesting part, the real-world stuff. Our client's sister, Denise Johnston, was a passenger in the car at the time of the accident. The sister is a key witness whose testimony is essential to our negligence action—but our client and her sister are not talking. Ironically, they were meeting to try to reconcile on the day of the accident. Unfortunately, in part because of the accident, they are now more distant than ever. In fact, we are told that Denise is likely to sue Esther (our client).

Are you feeling a little sorry for Esther right now? She was terribly hurt, she is embroiled in litigation with the car manufacturer, and her sister Denise is likely going to sue her! It gets worse. Not only might the sister (Denise) sue our client, but your job, your first task, is to draft a cross-examination plan that will "destroy" Denise's credibility. (Even if they are estranged, it may still be very hard for Esther to be responsible for causing any further pain to her sister.)

The second assignment is a legal memo discussing whether federal or state law will apply on the question of introducing evidence of subsequent remedial measures. This is a more straightforward assignment, likely similar to memos you completed in your legal research and writing course. Most students find the law a bit complicated in the second assignment, but they find the task very clear. By contrast, many students find the law easier in the cross-examination plan, but find the format and organization of that task to be challenging.

The next page is a classic Format page. This document tells you exactly how the examiners want you to set up this cross-examination plan.

Note: If you have prepared for cross-examination in a trial advocacy course or working in a law firm, and you set up your plan differently, forget what you did before. Set up this assignment exactly the way this Format Memo tells you to. As in every PT, the Format Memo (if they give you one) and the Task Memo are the most important documents. You are being tested in large part on following directions.

After you understand the assignments, then skim the File. Read quickly just to get the main points. If you do not clearly see the significance of a document, come back to it after reading the relevant Library authorities and it will make more sense.

The next page is the accident report. There is a diagram and narrative. The narrative is simple, just a paragraph, but you likely saw that it contains a significant internal contradiction. It says at first, "Passenger, Denise Johnston, stated that she wasn't sure what had happened." She also said that her sister was driving under the speed limit. Then, in the last line, it says that an officer "spoke to Ms. Johnston after she was admitted to the hospital" and this time she said that "her sister hit the sunroof because she wasn't wearing a seatbelt."

You should ask yourself (and later on cross-examination ask Denise!), why at first she said it could have been a deer that shattered the sunroof *or* her sister's head, but then a short while later she said definitively it was her sister because she wore no seatbelt.

Now, I know I said to "skim" the File the first time you go through it, but what I am referring to in the accident report was just one paragraph. It was easy to read, and if the contradictory stories popped out at you on the first skim, great. Take note. If at first you did not see this conflicting information, you would have seen it the next time you went back through to re-read the File.

The next document is the complaint. You should glance at documents like this for two reasons:

1. It is part of this PT, of course, and it tells you what claims we (the plaintiff) are asserting. Notice, as to Claim 1, that we say the car impacting the guard rail caused the sunroof to shatter. We also say the plaintiff was wearing a seatbelt.
2. Review the complaint with an eye toward how to draft such a document if you were asked to do so on another PT. Just look at the components: (a) jurisdiction, (b) a short, plain, factual statement that shows which facts give rise to each of the claims (here there are two claims: negligence and products liability), and lastly, (c) a prayer for relief and signature. That's it. You could draft something like that if your assignment were to draft a complaint!

The next document is the answer. This is the defense reply to our complaint. No surprise: they deny everything, and assert that our client was not wearing a seatbelt. (You now know what some of the "fight" on which this lawsuit is centered is going to be about.)

The next document is an investigation report. This is a list of all of Denise Johnston's arrests. Note that there is also an arrest report. Denise, remember, is the sister of the plaintiff, Esther Dodson. Denise was a passenger in the car at the time of the accident, and now, allegedly, wants to sue her sister (our client). This document relates to the first task, the cross-examination plan. The minute you saw this report, you likely suspected that we would be attempting to impeach Denise's credibility with some of these past crimes. If you did not think about that yet, you would have immediately thought of it when you read the *Christmas* case in the Library.

Lists on PTs, whether they are fact-based or law-based lists, can often provide helpful organizational and writing hints. Here, this list of Denise's arrest record is a gift. Students completing this exam sometimes make the mistake of combining the items listed (for example, putting all the fraud charges together). By doing that, though, students may be losing points. Denise was prosecuted separately for each charge, at different times and under different circumstances, and each may form the basis of impeachment. (Recall from your study of evidence different ways to impeach someone, including felony convictions, convictions for felonies or misdemeanors that involve dishonesty, prior inconsistent statements, and more.)

The next document is an excerpt of a transcript of a deposition taken of Denise Johnston. We will want to look at this carefully to see if she contradicts herself at all, and any other information that might be valuable to us in preparing our cross-examination of her. Just reading deposition transcripts in the File will help you get in "the zone" and ready to think in a question-and-answer format, which is how you will have to draft your cross-examination plan.

The last document is excerpts from interrogatories (questions and answers) that we sent to the defendant. This relates to the second assignment, the memo. *It is absolutely critical*—but you would not necessarily see or understand why this is so important on the first skim, before you have read the

Library. After you read the cases, this piece should have fallen right into place.

In these responses, the defendant is saying that the company changed the type of glass it used in sunroofs from the tempered glass that shattered in the accident to laminated glass; however, it is also saying that it is not feasible to use laminated glass for sunroofs. As you probably know already, and as you will read in the Library, evidence of subsequent remedial measures (such as changing the type of glass used in the sunroofs) is generally not admissible as evidence of negligence, but it may be used for other reasons, such as to impeach a party who denies the feasibility of the subsequent measure. The answer for Interrogatory No. 10 is about as close to a "smoking gun" as you will find in a PT-type assignment, and it provides very useful information to incorporate into your answer to the second task.

Library

As noted, this PT divides neatly into two separate 90-minute exams. In the Library, the documents separate out as follows: Most of the FRE provisions and the *Christmas* case relate to Task A. FRE Rule 407, the Columbia Products Liability Act (CPLA), and *Moe*, *Walker*, and *Stewart* all apply to Task B. You can likely tell, just from glancing at that allocation of authorities, that Task A is a bit more fact-heavy and Task B a bit more law-heavy.

Note: You are likely (or will be by the time of the bar exam) familiar with most or all of the FRE sections. (These will be tested on other portions of the bar exam as well.) For that reason, I would treat the FRE excerpts here as a "reference library," if I need it. I would start by skimming the titles of each section, and later go in and read the provisions in detail as needed. (As usual, the cases had to be studied and briefed as if new to you.)

If you take a step back and consider what you will be using these provisions for in Task A, discrediting Denise, you might have noticed that the titles of each section provide a sort of roadmap of the topics you will likely question her on: past crimes, character evidence, prior statements. (Not all PTs contain such hints, but where they do you must be alert and notice them. If you did not, go back and scan the rule headings in the FRE excerpts.) Some of the FRE sections may also provide reasons why the defense will object; for example, where our questions lead to evidence that is more prejudicial than probative. The *Christmas* case also provides further guidance on what can and cannot be used to impeach.

In Task B we will compare and contrast state law and federal law (here the CPLA with FRE 407), and then use the cases to determine which law our court will likely apply in this sort of diversity action. You may already be thinking state substantive law and federal procedural rules, but not so fast: Is the rule about subsequent remedial measures substantive or procedural? Reading through the Library, you see that there is not necessarily a clear answer. Should that bother you here? No, because your task is to write a memo to your senior partner about the issues. This is an in-house, analytical document, and you might well end up concluding that the law is not 100% in our client's favor. That is fine. Recall what the senior partner wrote in the Task Memo: "Write an objective memorandum for me discussing which of the statutes will be applied, the theories supporting admission of this information, and the likelihood that each theory would be successful." This necessarily means that you will objectively set forth the situation, explaining that which tends to favor our client and that which does not. Your conclusion may well be one that begins with the word "Likely."

The issue again is the policy exclusion regarding evidence of subsequent remedial measures. You all learned about this in evidence. It is the law's way of saying that we don't want the fact that people fix problems after accidents to be held against them and lead to conclusions about their liability. Let's say I am a store owner. You fall on my carpet. Assume I am certain that you fell because of your own dizziness (you were drunk at the time). However, I decide to go ahead and replace the carpet after your accident, thinking that it does have some small rips in it that someone might get hurt on eventually, even though I know those rips are not what caused your injury. If I replace the carpet and a jury hears about it, jurors might jump to the conclusion that my making the repairs means I must have been at fault. Knowing that my good deed could be used against me would discourage me from taking precautions to keep my premises safe for others. Because we don't want people to be "chilled" in taking positive actions to make the world a safer place, we limit use of such action in evidence.

You will see by studying the sample answers in eProducts what you should have pulled out of each of the cases, what would be a thorough cross-examination plan on the first task, and what would constitute enough analysis to be a passing answer on the second task.

PUTTING IT ALL TOGETHER

For the first memo, the cross-examination plan, the key is really to follow the sample in the Format Memo. It is easy to get hung up and feel the need to write long Q&A scenes as if in a movie, but that is not what the example indicated. The witness's answers need not be lengthy; in fact, that is not really very important. (In the sample, the answers are just "Yes.") It's the questions that are important: they contain the precise information we are trying to elicit, and they suggest what we want jurors to conclude. In cross-examination, we ask leading questions that contain the desired answers. All we are doing is looking for confirmation, which essentially then turns our questions into facts (unless the judge sustains an objection to our question, or strikes the witness's response).

Additionally, the key here was to separate issues. Do not ask a question that combines queries about multiple inconsistent statements and/or multiple arrests. Just the way the sample illustrates, let each Q&A set focus on one circumstance to impeach Denise, then move on to the next, and the next.

For the second memo, the law may have seemed confusing and could have thrown you. Remember, the purpose of the memo was to help your boss understand the law in the context of our case. So, what was the difference between the two laws? Which law benefits our client, and why? How do we convince the court to use the "better" law? And, if the court decides not to use that better law, how might we prevail anyway?

The Task Memo asked which statute will be applied, the theories supporting admission of the information, and the likelihood of success of each theory. Our problem is that the laws conflict. Your memo should explain the differences, noting that under state law we cannot use this evidence unless feasibility is brought up first by the other side and we are impeaching. However, the federal statute says we may assert this evidence affirmatively, in our own case, to show feasibility. Study the sample answers in eProducts for a sense of how each task should have been handled.

SPIN-OFF EXERCISES

Spin-off exercises provide a way to gain exposure to drafting different types of documents using the same facts and law as on the PT you just completed. Spend a few minutes, now that you have completed *Dodson,* to think of other tasks you might have been given and how you would have handled them. Here are a few suggestions.

Mediation Between Esther and Denise

Right now, the litigation is between Esther and CEC, and Denise will likely be testifying for CEC. It appears likely that Denise may also end up bringing her own lawsuit against Esther. If so, Esther may want to propose mediation. Try drafting a dialogue of the various stages of a mediation between Esther and Denise. What might the mediator say to both sisters together? What might the mediator say in private caucus with each? What sorts of win-win agreements might be possible to help the two resolve their difficulties without litigation?

Typical stages of a mediation:[2]

> *Introductory*—During this part of the process, the mediator helps the parties create a safe environment in which to discuss difficult topics. Depending on the parties' experience with mediation, the mediator may provide a process overview: the role of the mediator, what will happen in various mediation sessions, and confidentiality. During this phase, parties may agree to ground rules for the conduct of the mediation (e.g., ensuring that only one person speaks at a time) and a general timetable for the

---

[2] Slightly adapted from U.S. Department of Health and Human Services, "Mediation," available at http://www.hhs.gov/dab/divisions/adr/mediation/process.html.

process. This phase includes a joint session among parties, during which opposing sides have an opportunity to state their views and desired outcomes.

Problem-Solving Stage—During this stage, parties principally focus on issues, interests, options for resolution, and criteria for evaluating those options. Parties may meet separately with the mediator to share confidences and fully consider options in private.

Closure—During this phase, parties decide whether and on what terms to resolve the dispute. The mediator may help them draft a document that reflects any commitments they wish to make. As needed, the agreement then may have to be passed to others for approval. If parties do not reach agreement, the mediator makes sure they understand why and what next steps are available to them.

Letter to Esther

Let's say that in addition to the cross-examination plan of Denise, the senior partner asked you to draft a letter to Esther explaining to her what we need to accomplish in this cross-examination and why. You might start by explaining the parts of a trial and what cross-examination is, but you will want to go on to prepare Esther that this may be hard. Her own sister is going to be discredited (and, if we do our job well, her sister will look very bad when we are finished). What can you say to Esther to prepare her?

Settlement Offer to the Defendant, CEC

Why might CEC be inclined to settle? Are some of their witnesses less than credible? Might they benefit from some sort of confidential or sealed agreement? What sorts of things did their expert, Dr. Leyhe, say that might make for terrible publicity if they were to emerge at trial? Also, what if CEC loses? How much money might they have to pay to someone as severely injured as Esther? Might they cut their losses and give her sufficient damages right now to make her as whole as possible, and not drag her through an extensive and difficult trial? Try drafting an offer of settlement to present to counsel for CEC.

PRACTICE, LAW SCHOOL, AND PTs: COMPARE AND CONTRAST

This PT was evidence-based, but the underlying claim was grounded in tort. (One cause of action was based on alleged negligence, the other on strict liability in tort.) This is a reminder that while we tend to study evidence as a discrete subject, it is all about the information that comes in to prove or disprove elements of claims in other substantive areas: here torts. In other words, in this PT, as in practice, you were simultaneously "in" both the world of evidence and the world of torts. Further crossing subjects, the second task was more a civil procedure question as to which law governs, state or federal. Accordingly, some see this PT as an evidence/civil procedure cross-over.

Whereas certain bar exam essays test multiple subjects, law school courses "silo" learning into discrete buckets: You will not sit down to your evidence final in law school and see a constitutional law question. In real life, though, clients often come to you for help in one area and it quickly becomes apparent that their problems cross into numerous other areas. (Someone may come to you for a divorce and child custody matter. One or the other spouse may then have to file for bankruptcy. There may be tax consequences. Real property may be sold. Depending on how complicated things get, you may have to consult with another attorney or refer parts of the case to someone else to handle. That is reality.)

This PT also differed from a typical evidence essay in that here you were actually framing the question-and-answer courtroom dialogue. You might have felt more like a screenwriter than a law student. This is litigation prep in action. Nevertheless, even within this "realistic" drafting, the exam was still about the testing more than reality in this respect. In real life, you never want to ask a question on cross-examination that you don't know the answer to. Here, for exam purposes, it was fine to draft some questions to which you were not certain how the witness would respond. It was also fine to draft questions that you knew would be objected to (even when those objections would likely be sustained), because your purpose was to show the grader that you understood all the law and facts in the Library and File. It would have been a much more difficult assignment had you been asked only to think of questions that you believed would not be objected to.

So, in some ways, the *Dodson* PT was realistic and gave you a snapshot of the kind of lawyering you might do in practice. In other ways, it was still an exam, testing you on what you read and how to apply the law to the facts. I hope you enjoyed this work, zealously advocating on behalf of your client, and that at least for a moment you saw evidence law come to life!

KEY TAKEAWAYS

- This practice exam exposed you to a task that required a very precise format: the cross-examination plan. Not only did you have to write detailed information, but the examiners also wanted it set out in the exact way they instructed. (As is often the case on PTs, *Dodson* tested your ability and willingness to follow instructions, as well as your lawyering skills.)
- This PT was in the evidence section, and a great many of the issues (especially with regard to the cross-examination) were evidentiary concerns, but the underlying case was a torts cause of action; some of what was tested in the second memo (about which law applies) you may well have studied in a civil procedure course. This illustrates how PTs "cross over" from one subject to the next, rather than putting subjects in airtight boxes or silos as law school tends to do.
- This PT provided a good example of a "reference Library," in terms of the provisions that the examiners noted were from the Federal Rules of Evidence. The sections were there for your reference if you needed to review them, but you probably did not need to study each FRE section. Because evidence rules are typically something you need to know for the bar exam, these provisions would have seemed familiar by the time of the actual bar exam. The Columbia rule (the Columbia Product Liability Act), and the cases, were of course new to you (as are all cases in PT Libraries, no matter how familiar they may look!).

- This exam was divided into two 90-minute PTs, so it provided great practice in both skills and timing.

7. CONSTITUTIONAL LAW

OVERVIEW OF CONSTITUTIONAL LAW

Many law school constitutional law classes focus on due process, equal protection, and the First Amendment: freedom of speech, religion, the press, and association. (There is so much to study with the First Amendment alone that it is often broken out as a separate semester course.) On bar exam questions, you typically must be fluent in these rules and principles and also many others, including (but not limited to) standing, ripeness, and mootness; legislative powers (interstate commerce, taxing and spending, war powers and other powers relating to foreign affairs); federal preemption; eminent domain; and more.

For a list of the topics covered on bar exam constitutional law questions, consult the most recent content scope outlines for your jurisdiction and the NCBE.

SIMULATED CONSTITUTIONAL LAW-BASED PT

This multistate PT (MPT) was designed to be completed in 90 minutes. Go to eProducts, take 90 minutes, download *In re: Gardenton*, and draft your answer. Then return and read the rest of this section to see how you did and to learn from the practice test experience.

TIME-CRUNCH TIPS

This is a 90-minute exam. I would strongly urge you to find a full hour and a half and complete this exam under timed conditions. If you do not have the time at this sitting, take 45 minutes and read all the facts and law, and just outline the memorandum. Come back another time when you have an additional 45 minutes and complete the writing assignment.

INSIDE THIS TEST: TIPS AND STRATEGIES

Congratulations on finishing *Gardenton*! (Again, if you have not completed this exam, please download it from the eProducts and do so now.) This is a great question. It is different from assignments you have seen before if you have been working through the PTs in order.

This practice PT was shorter than some of the other PTs in this appendix. (*Gardenton* was designed to be completed in 90 minutes, so naturally your legal and factual universes were smaller than in the three-hour PTs.) The *Gardenton* Instructions and File consisted of only three documents: the Task Memo, the transcript of the meeting with Kantor, and the proposed code in question. Your Library had small sections of the U.S. Constitution, the Franklin State Constitution, and the Franklin Education Act (FEA), along with three short cases.

NOTE-TAKING TIPS

Unlike the three-hour PTs that we have seen in earlier, which include a separate table of contents for the File and Library, this MPT has one table of contents (TOC) for both. Where you have a TOC that you can write on, you can use it as your central note-taking page. Or, you can take notes all on one page of scratch paper or at the beginning or end of your answer document file (that you will delete before uploading). Especially if you are rushing to finish, it is convenient to have all your notes in one place. This is much more efficient than searching through notes you wrote on every page of the File and Library to find points you want to make. You can still "book brief" within the cases, but also note the page numbers where you wrote key points on your table of contents page.

Let's say there is language from the *Hazelwood* case that you want to quote. Underline it and put a double asterisk next to that language in the case itself. Then also place a double asterisk on the table of contents page next to the *Hazelwood* entry and jot down something like "1st A Rts of students not same as Con'l Rts @ p. 6." This note reminds you to return to page 6 to reference the exact language you underlined. And, this "book-briefing" saves you the time that it would otherwise take to write more about the case in your notes.

Try this approach. See if it helps you to make your table of contents your one-page "go-to" resource guide, to organize what you will need to write your full answer.

The key to success on this PT (as on all PTs!) is to carefully read the Task Memo and clearly understand your assignment. Here the Task Memo was from Frank Eisner. I always suggest looking at the letterhead on File documents. Here, you notice that "Eisner" is the second named partner on the firm letterhead. From this you know that the person giving you this assignment appears to be one of the senior partners in a private law firm; you are an associate at this firm. Remember, as on every PT, your name as you write it in your answer is "Applicant." (Do not ever write your real name or any identifying information other than your exam number or whatever else the examiners direct you to write.)

This Task Memo is typical. The first paragraph provides a summary of who the client is, what that client's immediate problem is, and what the client's goals are. You want to read this Task Memo slowly and carefully.

I urge you to get in the habit of reading the Task Memo aloud but under your breath. Touch each word as you read. This reading with your eyes, ears, and voice will keep you focused and attentive to detail. (This reading strategy, detailed in *Bar Exam Success* (West Academic) is especially important on bar exams where you must complete a PT in the afternoon and are tired from the morning portion of the exam.)

Re-read the Task Memo after you skim the File. Read the Task Memo again after you study the Library, before you draft your answer. Re-reading the Task Memo a few times gives further insight into the assignment. You process the information differently as you get more "into" the problem. You notice important points that may not have seemed critical at first read. Re-reading also ensures that you follow directions—the most important key to passing the PT.

IT IS EASY TO FORGET THE DIRECTIONS!

PTs contain a lot of information, and much is asked of you in a short amount of time. It is easier than you would think to forget all or part of your instructions by the time you start writing, especially if you only read the Task Memo once. A stark reminder comes every time I teach PTs where the task is to draft a closing argument. Inevitably, at least one student will write the argument for the other side. Why? The examiners often place applicants on what appears to be the unenviable side. The more you read, the more you think of arguments for the other side, and the easier it becomes for those who did not review the instructions to forget whom they represent. On one PT, applicants were to represent the party that seems to have done exactly what it is being accused of: exerting undue influence over an old lady to change her will in their favor before she died. Time after time, students get so persuaded by the law and facts that there was undue influence that they end up arguing for the wrong side, all because they failed to go back and carefully re-read the instructions. Another mistake in that same problem is that students forget that the judge already concluded, early in the case, that the testator had capacity and the argument now centers on only one issue: undue influence. They end up needlessly arguing capacity issues, a colossal waste of time. Moral of the story: Re-read the Task Memo several times as you complete each PT.

What exactly do we learn from the *Gardenton* Task Memo? Frank Eisner, your boss, consulted with Dr. Edwina Kantor, who is the president of the Gardenton Board of Education. You know, again from looking at the letterhead, that your firm is situated in the city of Gardenton in the State of Franklin. Kantor was clearly consulting Eisner and your firm not as an individual but in her capacity as Board president. The Board wants to adopt a communications code for the local public high school. (You likely underlined the word *public*, because you know that rules may differ for public and private schools.)

You also learn the Board's main goal: to get a code adopted that is as restrictive as possible so that it helps the school prevent the publication of offensive material. Always pay attention to any information (in the Task Memo or other File document) that details or hints at the client's goals and needs. Such language helps you to effectively perform the problem-solving skill that is one of the main skills tested on the PT. (The skills tested on PT exams are discussed extensively in earlier parts of this book.) Picking up on language in the Task Memo and/or File about your client's needs also shows the graders that you are detail oriented, a critical skill for successful lawyering.

It appears that the Board must present a proposed communications code for public comment, and Kantor wants advice for herself and the other Board members for preparing to face public questioning. The Memo describes the heated emotions on both sides of this issue: the free speech advocates, irate about censorship, on the one side; and the parents and civic groups on the other side, who are equally outraged about what they see as profanity and sexually charged material coming from the school.

The last paragraph of the Task Memo gives you specifics on what you are to draft. Note that you are writing to your senior partner. We have talked in the past about using simplified plain English when writing to non lawyers and more sophisticated legal terminology when writing to lawyers. In this *Gardenton* task, you are role-playing a lawyer writing to another lawyer. Thus, you may freely cite cases and use legal terms that in a client document you would want to define, simplify, or avoid.

Note also that this is an in-house document, for this senior partner (your supervisor) to use in advising the Board of Education. The Task Memo uses the term "evaluate," so you know that this is an analytical memorandum wherein you are looking at this situation as a neutral. You are anticipating what language will help achieve the Board's goals, where those goals are achievable. You will also note where what they seek to accomplish may not be permissible. In other words, you do not want to treat this as if it were a brief and you were arguing persuasively to urge that every provision of the proposed code be adopted as written. Rather, you are studying each provision to see whether it passes constitutional muster or not, and why, and to propose edits where they would be necessary or helpful.

The Task Memo specifies that you are to evaluate the preamble and each provision of the proposed code. The word *each* is repeated several times. Any time bar examiners repeat something, pay attention. Here this repetition suggests a provision-by-provision organization for your analysis. Caution: In rushing to write, students sometimes start with Provision 1, forgetting to analyze the preamble, and thereby lose precious points. The Memo goes on to explicitly spell out your tasks. You can highlight or underline this part of the Memo or write a note to yourself on scratch paper or as a rough outline in the document that will ultimately become your answer. (Be sure to delete any notes to yourself before uploading your answer.)

For example, after reading this Task Memo, I might write something like the following to myself:

In my answer, I must:

- Identify *the* legal issues *that can give rise to* constitutional challenges *of each of the provisions* and *analyze whether each such provision is likely to be found legally permissible.*
- Make suggestions *to delete, modify, or add language as needed to help our client (the Board) achieve its goal (of presenting the most restrictive code permissible).*
- Conclude as to whether each provision is or is not permissible.
- *Also, for each conclusion about permissibility and for each editing suggestion,* explain and support my reasoning with specific references to the facts and law. *In other words, write WHY I came to particular conclusions or made specific editing suggestions.*

What I wrote for myself is not the exact verbatim words of the directions, but rather a way of breaking those directions down and putting them into words that help you tell yourself exactly what to do. (See examples following for how I use this framework to outline my answer.)

You will get points *both* for saying which provisions are permissible even without revisions, and for saying which must be rewritten, so long as in each instance you say why. Your job here is not just to jump to those provisions that may be impermissible, but to critically review each and every provision.

It helps to read the Instructions a few times over and really think carefully about who you represent and why and what your job is. Here, once you do that, you may well begin to develop an organizing structure for your answer, even before you read the rest of the File and Library. You may have even noted something like the following and put it immediately into a blank document on your computer.

FIRST ROUGH DRAFT OUTLINE

Header

To: Frank Eisner

From: Applicant

Re: Proposed Communications Code:

Date: ___ [If you write a date, use the date you are taking the exam.]

Introduction: [Even though the Task Memo did not explicitly direct you to draft an introduction, short introductions are important. Introductions tell the grader to expect to find what was requested; in other words, introductions declare that you followed the directions. They do not have to be long, and in fact long introductions waste time and sometimes make it look like you did not understand the actual assignment. Here, one sentence would be sufficient]:

"Here below is the analysis of the proposed code that you requested. Please contact me if you have any follow-up questions."

[Legal Issues Giving Rise to Constitutional Challenges]—optional

Most students completing this test identify the legal issues for each provision while analyzing the permissibility of the provision. Others interpret the directions as first requesting a short few paragraphs noting some of the major legal concerns; for example, that the FEA grants more significant rights to students than does the Constitution, and that the level of scrutiny of particular restrictions on communication will be determined in part by whether the publication in question is seen as a public forum or a limited public forum.

If you included this sort of preliminary legal analysis before your provision-by-provision analysis of the code, write your introduction as follows:

"Here below is a brief exploration of the legal issues that may give rise to constitutional challenges in this matter, followed by the provision-by-provision analysis of the proposed Code that you requested. Please contact me if you have any follow-up questions."

[Again, this tells the graders that you followed directions.]

Analysis of Proposed Code

Preamble:

a) Legal issues raised? Permissible? Why/why not?

b) Suggested edits and reasons for edits?

Provision 1:

a) Legal issues raised? Permissible? Why/why not?

b) Suggested edits and reasons for edits?

Provision 2:

a) Legal issues raised? Permissible? Why/why not?

b) Suggested edits and reasons for edits? [And so on with each remaining provision.]

Conclusion [again, at most one or two sentences.]

Without even reading the Code or the rest of the law and facts, just from reading the directions, you could have come up with this sort of a logical (albeit rough-draft) structure for your answer. You could type it right into your answer document, as a sort of skeleton outline of what you will edit into your final answer.

After you read the Code (on page 4 of the File), you will be able to build on that skeletal structure, fleshing out descriptive headings with the title (subject) of each provision. Rather than referring to the first provision simply as "Provision 1," it will be clearer for graders if your heading reads: "Provision 1: Professional Standards of English and Journalism." (See the updated outline later in this section.)

Also, to help the grader easily follow your analysis, keep your numbering consistent with the Code's provisions. Some students mark the Preamble as heading 1, which requires that the analysis of provision 1 be labeled as heading 2. That can confuse graders. Instead, give your discussion of the Preamble a heading that uses the word "Preamble" so that the discussion under your first heading addresses the first code provision, the discussion under your second heading addresses the second code provision, and so on.

ORGANIZING EARLY WITH YOUR OUTLINE AS A DRAFT ANSWER

For many people, it helps to get an organizational structure started and typed into your exam-answer file document as soon as possible into your reading of each PT. That way your "notes" or outline form the first draft of your final answer. It's not always as easy as on this exam to see a logical structure. Sometimes you really have to sit and think about how the Library authorities fit together and how that structure merges with the task you have been given to settle on a logical format for answering the assignment. Nearly always, though, your organizational structure (how to set up your answer) comes from some combination of the Task Memo, Format Pages if there are any, and the Library authorities.

File Review

After the Task Memo, all the File contains is a transcript and the draft Code. Skim the transcript of the discussion with Dr. Kantor. You won't understand the legal significance of all the facts until you have read the Library, so do not waste time with a detailed reading at this stage. Here are a few things you may have seen in the Transcript, even during a skim: points that certainly would have popped out as significant when you re-read after studying the Library:

- Kantor first discusses what she calls "degenerating quality" of the subject matter and language in student publications. Then there's mention of problems with student theater.
- The next question and answer, about how wide the audience is for the paper and plays, is a perfect example of something that won't make a lot of sense until after you have read the Library. *Lopez*, the second case in the Library, explains the forum analysis, wherein public property may be divided into public, nonpublic, and limited public forums. The *Lopez* case equates a public forum with a "traditional soapbox" where "prior restraints are rarely permissible." A nonpublic forum such as an administrative informational bulletin is one where the school would have "full power to regulate access and content." Somewhere in the middle, is a limited forum, where "school officials must demonstrate that the particular regulation of student expression advances a compelling state interest."

After reading *Lopez*, when re-reading the File, Kantor's answers to the questions about the circulation of the student newspaper, and who attends the school theater productions, pop out. You will re-read them, after reading *Lopez*, and you will readily assess as to what sort of forums these are and how that affects what sort of expression must be allowed.

You will likely have concluded that the school newspaper is a limited public forum, as are the small school plays, but you may have seen the regular annual live theatrical productions as public forums and as such subject to greater scrutiny. This is open to interpretation. You will get points not so much for concluding one way or the other as for your analysis, so long as you explain your reasoning, support it, and follow it through to its logical conclusion.

- At the bottom of page 2, Kantor mentions several alleged problems: reporting without adequate fact checking, use of profanity, potentially defamatory statements, and stories that are not "in good taste." Kantor also talks about the "sexually charged" and "morally questionable" subject matter of theater being objectionable. Without even getting to the Library, your lawyer instincts may rise up inside you to a point where you think to yourself: "*Well, I can see how defamation might be prohibited, but it sure sounds wishy-washy to try to stop something that is 'not in good taste.'*"

If you do not have that sort of gut reaction, that is fine; the cases spell out what may and may not be prohibited. You will study them, then come back to this transcript (and of course to the proposed Code itself, which is what you need to analyze), and the relevant facts will then become clear. The point is that, for many students, it can be very reassuring to realize that you are already "thinking like a lawyer," when your eyebrows raise at certain suspect facts.

THINK LIKE A LAWYER AND KEEP A COOL HEAD

Have you ever found yourself in a social conversation listening to someone say something abstract and think, "Void for vagueness." That's when you know law school has sunk in! It's a good thing to think like a lawyer; it's also good on PTs and in law practice, to remain calm. As you read through this PT, you may have realized that you do not want to get swept up in the community debate aspect of this situation. That is not your job. Your tasks are very clearly spelled out: analyze the constitutionality of the preamble and each provision of the proposed code. Keep your focus. (Imagining yourself thrust into the middle of a community debate may help you get "into" the role-play aspects of the PT, which is fine. It is great if you can enjoy these exams! Just do not allow your emotions or biases to sidetrack you from your task.)

PTs always include interesting detours. I like to say that on PTs you must "take the highways, not the side streets." You have to finish in 90 minutes; you cannot afford to lose sight of the narrow focus of your assignment. The time flies. If you pursue "side streets" or interesting tangents, you will not complete the main parts of what is specifically asked of you.

Page 3 of the File talks more about the politics of the situation: that the proposed Code was supposed to have been secret but that it got out and everyone is preparing for battle. This is interesting, and tells you why Kantor needs you to analyze the Code, but it doesn't really relate to producing your exam answer. Remember, there are always tangents on PTs. They are testing you on your ability to sort relevant from irrelevant information, so there will always be some facts that do not help answer the specific questions you are asked to write about.

Nevertheless, these background facts again do help you immerse yourself in the role-play. They help you see why this matter is so important to Kantor, and so urgent. You might expect that everyone on both sides of this issue will be scrutinizing the Code, so in your analysis, you must help Kantor and the Board see exactly what is and is not permissible and why.

- One of the last points Kantor makes is to reiterate the Board's goals: "The main thing is that we be able to censor unacceptable language and morally questionable subject matter that runs counter to our educational goals, especially things that open us up to suits for libel and slander and invasion of privacy."

The word "censor" might well have hit you as a flag reminding you that, in the big picture, this is a case about prior restraints of free speech, something that even in the case of high-school-age children is not to be done lightly or without adequate justification. Nonetheless, you know that your mission, as you proceed, is to consider just how much of this "unacceptable language and morally questionable subject matter" can be curtailed. Off to the Library to find out!

MOTIVATIONAL NOTE

Try to have fun with these PTs as you work through them. You control the exam; the exam does not control you. It's open book; it's all there for you. You can read and re-read as many times as you need to. The examiners take pains in drafting these PTs to ensure that they are doable, meaning finishable, within the time limits. Assume that you will eventually "get it," and you are more likely to relax and complete your PTs skillfully. Panic, and you are more likely to be blocked and not see what is clear and relevant. Above all, remember that all you have to do is produce a passing answer. You are not writing an amicus brief for the Supreme Court!

One last document in the File, though, before you get to the Library, is the Code itself. This is the document you will work from when you get to writing, as your job is to analyze and suggest edits for the preamble and each provision of this proposed Code. You will not know whether each provision is permissible until you have read the Library, so scan them quickly now, study the Library authorities, and then return to this Code. However, after even a quick skim through the Code, you can update your outline as follows:

UPDATED DRAFT OUTLINE

To: Frank Eisner

From: Applicant

Re: Proposed Communications Code

Date: [date of exam]

Introduction

Here below is the analysis of the Code that you requested. Please contact me if you have any follow-up questions.

[Legal Issues Giving Rise to Constitutional Challenges]—optional

A few short paragraphs noting some of the major legal concerns (for example, that the FEA grants more significant rights to students than does the Constitution and that the level of scrutiny of particular restrictions on communication will be determined in part by whether the publication in question is seen as a public forum or limited public forum).

[Again, if you included this sort of preliminary legal analysis before analyzing the Code, provision by provision, I would suggest writing your introduction as follows:]

> "Here below is a brief exploration of the legal issues that may give rise to constitutional challenges in this matter, followed by the provision-by-provision analysis of the proposed Code that you requested. Please contact me if you have any follow-up questions."

Analysis of Proposed Code

Preamble:

a) Legal issues raised? Permissible? Why/why not?

b) Suggested edits and reasons for edits?

Provision 1: Professional standards of English and journalistic style

a) Legal issues raised? Permissible? Why/why not?

b) Suggested edits and reasons for edits?

Provision 2: [This provision refers to both language and depictions; I have addressed each separately here.]

—Language not in "good taste" and considering age, experience, and maturity

a) Legal issues raised? Permissible? Why/why not?

b) Suggested edits and reasons for edits?

—Depictions not in "good taste" and considering age, experience, and maturity

a) Legal issues raised? Permissible? Why/why not?

b) Suggested edits and reasons for edits?

Provision 3: Verification of fact and quote accuracy to "satisfaction of teacher supervising"

a) Legal issues raised? Permissible? Why/why not?

b) Suggested edits and reasons for edits?

Provision 4: Permission for quotes or photos from adult or parents if minor, with exception for group photos

a) Legal issues raised? Permissible? Why/why not?

b) Suggested edits and reasons for edits?

Provision 5: Prohibition against publications that:

a) Are libel, slander, or violate privacy rights;

b) Contain profanity (judged by local newspapers as standard);

c) Criticize or demean any public official, including school administrators and teachers;

d) Are deemed by principal not to be in school's best interests. For each of these, assess:

- Legal issues raised? Permissible? Why/why not?
- Suggested edits and reasons for edits?

Provision 6: Prior approval by principal before publication/distribution.

a) Legal issues raised? Permissible? Why/why not?

b) Suggested edits and reasons for edits?

Conclusion

I hope the preceding analysis helps you prepare for your meeting with Kantor and the Board. If you have any additional questions, please let me know.

Library

The first document you find in the Library is the First Amendment, which, by the time of the bar exam, you would be very familiar with if you weren't even before that. Everything else in the Library is new.

You recall, of course, that you are located in the fictitious State of Franklin. The Franklin Constitution's provision on free speech is interesting but not terribly helpful to you in terms of guidance on what is or is not permitted speech. (What exactly does it mean to "be responsible for the abuse of" the free-speech right?)

The Franklin Education Act (FEA) section, however, is very interesting, useful, and clearly broader than the U.S. Constitution in terms of respecting student rights. Under this section, students appear to have wide-ranging free-speech rights, though expression that is "obscene, libelous, or slanderous" is prohibited. Also prohibited is speech inciting unlawful action on campus, violations of school regulations, or "substantial disruption of the orderly operation of the school."

From what Kantor said to Mr. Eisner, it does not look like these are the main concerns that the Board has, although Kantor did suggest that there were some publications bordering on defamatory. Also, the FEA clearly allows prohibition of defamatory speech. This FEA section may not prevent some of the other concerns Kantor brought to our attention, however. Thus, you should expect to find further clarification in the cases.

The last paragraphs of the FEA section deal with student editorial control. This grants students responsibility for "official school publications" (a term defined on this same page), with the limitation that "it shall be the responsibility of journalism advisers or advisers of student publications within each school to supervise the production of student staff, to maintain professional standards of English and Journalism, and to maintain the provision of this section."

The "standards of English and Journalism" language might have popped out at you, and if you flip back, you will see that this language is mirrored almost precisely in Provision 1. So, right away, you could have gone into your draft outline document and explained why, per FEA § 48, Provision 1 is likely fine as drafted.

Remember, as you read each case, that your goal is to figure out which provisions are acceptable, which are not, and why, and to make suggested edits to help the Board redraft the Code to achieve its goals. You will not simply brief the cases, but use them to help explain why certain provisions are or are not permissible. Students too often jump into PTs and start writing by just briefing (or worse still, summarizing) each case and not writing the tasks as directed in the Instructions. Throwing case-by-case summaries of law into your answer is a sure way to fail this sort of exam.

In eProducts, you will see the grader's point sheet, which give specifics on exactly what was expected in a passing answer to this assignment, so I will not detail every point. Rather, I will simply highlight some key points from each case. Be sure to study the point sheet carefully after reading this section.

Hazelwood is a Supreme Court case from 1988. *Lopez* and *Leeb* are both more recent and from Franklin Courts (*Lopez* was in the Franklin Supreme Court, and *Leeb* was a Franklin Court of Appeal case). Remember, states may not provide less protection than the federal government, but they may provide greater protection. (I like the often-referenced image that the federal Constitution is a floor, not a ceiling.) It may well be that *Lopez* and *Leeb* discuss greater protections afforded under the Franklin Constitution, Franklin statutes, and Franklin courts than in *Hazelwood*. Still, *Hazelwood* is factually very similar to our subject and helpful for our client, as the Supreme Court in *Hazelwood* reversed the circuit court and affirmed the district court's ruling that favored the school district.

Hazelwood gives a great deal of deference to the principal and to the school board. For example, note the language in *Hazelwood* that "A school need not tolerate student speech that is inconsistent with its basic educational mission, even though the government could not censor similar speech outside the school." The court recognized the school's right to remain neutral in areas of public controversy and says that only when censorship "has no valid educational purpose" will the First Amendment be implicated and "require judicial intervention to protect students' " constitutional rights.

Lopez again favors our client, allowing the school the right to restrict expression that includes profanity on the grounds that it violates "the professional standards of English and journalism" under the Franklin Education Act. *Lopez* does note that the restriction is to be of the objectionable language (in that case, certain "four-letter words") and not the content of the student speech; in other words, not the ideas or opinions expressed. *Lopez* confirms that its holding that § 48 of the FEA allows "prior restraint of profane student language" is consistent with both the United States and Franklin Constitutions. The *Lopez* court also provides very useful analysis of the public, nonpublic, and limited public forum standards. The court says that school publications (and here the court defines these broadly to include school newspapers, yearbooks, and theatrical productions) are a limited public forum, and as such the school, in order to regulate student expression, must show that the "regulations are narrowly drawn" to achieve "compelling state interests" and must be "sufficiently precise" so they are not vague. This should have given you a great deal of food for thought in reviewing provisions of the proposed Code, as many of them were far too vague to let stand.

Lastly, a few highlights from the *Leeb* case underscore that the State of Franklin provides greater protection to students than the Supreme Court did in *Hazelwood*. Even with greater deference to students, though, the *Leeb* court nonetheless ruled in the school's favor, finding that the principal had justifiable concerns supporting his prohibition on distribution of a student newspaper edition that included photos the principal considered "damaging" to certain students' reputations. *Leeb* did remind us that under the leading Supreme Court case, *New York Times v. Sullivan*, even a school "may not censor defamatory material that is not actionable because it is privileged or deals with a public figure without malice." Reading this should have led you directly to advise editing or deleting Provision 5c, that part of the proposed Code prohibiting criticism of public officials. *Leeb* concluded with some useful dicta about revising school communications codes to comport with legal requirements—our exact task in this PT.

Again, those are just some highlights. You should have seen a great deal more in each of those cases. With that backdrop, though, take a few minutes to study the grader's point sheet in the Online Question and Answer Bank, and compare this to your own answer to see how you did on this exam. Investigate how these comments analyzing the legality of each provision compare to what you wrote in your answer.

SPIN-OFF EXERCISES

Spin-off exercises provide exposure to different document types without taking time to learn new facts and law. Spend a few minutes, now that you have completed *Gardenton*, thinking of other tasks you might have been given and how you would have handled them. Here are a few suggestions.

1. Draft a persuasive document instead of a neutral one. Imagine that the Board had adopted the proposed Code as is, without ever consulting you, and is now being sued by a free-speech organization on behalf of students who were censored. Draft a persuasive memo to help Frank Eisner argue in court that the Code is constitutional.

2. Draft a persuasive statement opposing the Code that might be made orally by a student group or a civil rights group at the Board meeting that is open to public comment. Then, draft an equally persuasive statement that would be read aloud by a parent committee supporting the Code.

3. Represent a student instead of the Board of Education. Pretend that a Gardenton High School student ("Student") wrote and wants to star in a one-person play dealing with high school angst. The script includes themes relating to the lack of funding for the arts in public schools, teenage stress and anxiety, drug usage, sex, and gender identity issues. The drama teacher showed the principal the script, and the principal said that Student would not be allowed to perform the show. Student and his parents want to sue High School and Principal and come to you for legal consultation:

a. Draft a two-part memo that (i) advises Student of his rights, and suggests alternative courses of action Student might pursue, and the pros and cons of each, and (ii) asks Student any follow-up questions you need answered to know how best to advise Student going forward. For example, would you want to know if the language used in the play is profane (i.e., is it filled with "four-letter words"), or is it simply about a mature subject matter that is worded in socially appropriate terminology?

b. Draft a persuasive letter on Student's behalf to the school principal urging that the student be allowed to perform the play. For the purposes of this exercise only, assume that (i) you are a junior associate in the Franklin law firm of Allen, Eisner & Thomas, (ii) that neither you nor your law firm has any conflict of interest with your firm's having advised the Board and that you may freely represent Student, (iii) that the proposed Communications Code has not yet been adopted, but that (iv) all the constitutional and case law in the Gardenton Library controls.

PRACTICE, LAW SCHOOL, AND PTs: COMPARE AND CONTRAST

Gardenton provides a scenario that differs greatly from many typical law exams. In many ways, it reflects much of what certain lawyers actually do in practice. Clients often bring documents to their lawyers to edit to make sure they comply with legal requirements. The exercise you were asked to complete in *Gardenton* is not much different in principle from reviewing a contract, provision by provision, to determine if each is lawful and in the best interests of your client. (You saw just that sort of an exercise in the practice contracts PT debriefed in this appendix.) Here, of course, you were analyzing the document in terms of constitutional restrictions, but the same type of thinking was required. Also, it is easy to picture clients coming to you to ask about how to draft and/or edit contracts. If your client is a school board, you can see that they might come to you for advice on all sorts of policies and documents, from employment and building contracts to communications codes.

Unless you took a drafting course (an elective in most law schools), or unless you work for a law office that does transactional work, you are probably much more familiar with essay and analytical legal memo formats than you are with deleting, adding, or modifying language to achieve a client's goals. Nevertheless, drafting and editing work is the lifeblood of many law practices.

CLIENT COUNSELING

> If you enjoy these sorts of tasks and are interested in client counseling, you may want to look into the ABA Law Student Division's Client Counseling Competition https://www.americanbar.org/groups/law_students/events/competitions/client-counseling/. This competition was inspired by the career of one of my mentors, the late Louis M. Brown, an attorney and professor fondly referred to as "the father of preventive law."

This PT provides a great tool to help you transition to thinking as a transactional lawyer would at this early stage of representation: ensuring that documents are drafted so as to prevent later litigation rather than looking at what has already occurred and determining the legal rights and remedies of the parties at that stage.

PT Pep Talk

PTs are open book and, at least to a certain extent, "real world." Take a moment to appreciate this exam. Hopefully, you had fun with it! I would love to see you get to a place of confidence in how to approach and tackle these PTs where you are certain you can handle anything they throw at you. Wrestle with and master the time and data management challenges now, ahead of time, so that you can actually have fun with the PT on your bar exam.

PTs are not contrived hypotheticals designed to see how many rules you memorized, as some essays seem to be. Nor do

PTs require the extreme speed with which you must analyze and pick the best answers on multiple-choice questions.

You must complete questions in other testing formats on your exam. They too can be fun. For many, the issue spotting and the strategy of taking MCQs, eliminating wrong answers by ferreting out inconsistencies and errors, make these questions like a game, challenging in a way that is similar to other tricky word games. Many also view the legal analysis portion of written exam questions as an intriguing puzzle—issue spotting and seeing how facts prove or disprove particular elements of rules of law.

Try to enjoy all the practice tests you complete, and learning process generally. As with most work and study, to the extent you can have fun with the process, the more engaged you will be and the more likely you will be to succeed.

A Word on Memory and Enjoying the Process

Some parts of the bar exam test critical reading and analytical skills and can help immensely in training you to be a successful lawyer, also depend heavily on memory, despite the fact that much of today's lawyering does not. Lawyers use tablets, computers, and smartphones to help them remember a lot of what they need on a day-to-day basis. PTs by contrast, like much of law practice, are open book. You can look up rules, and you can take some time to actually think about them. (PTs do not allow time for deep reflection but they can feel more leisurely a pace than the more rapidly paced multiple choice sections.) Again, though, I am not knocking MCQs. For many, taking these types of questions is an exhilarating experience, albeit exhausting; it is empowering to know that you can read rapidly through so many different legal scenarios and be able to critically reason through each one.

Again, if you let yourself, you can really enjoy all of bar preparation, especially PTs. Your memory gets to relax a little because they are open book, and you get to dive right into real-world struggles and help your clients. *Gardenton* is a perfect example. This happens all over the country: students want to express themselves, and parents and other community members are often offended by what students say. Schools and school boards are frequently stuck in the middle, as in *Gardenton*: they must follow education laws and guidelines, but they do not want to alienate the community or become ensnared in scandals that can disrupt their basic task of educating students. You get the opportunity to jump into the thick of the situation, learn what both the state and federal governments require and permit, and provide useful advice in a very realistic scenario.

Tell me honestly: If you could complete this exam as part of a pass/fail class, not worrying about your "grade," wouldn't you have fun? Even though the bar exam is a high-pressure, high-stakes exam, I urge you to get into that mindset. *Have fun*. Get into the role-play. You will do just as well, if not better, than if you are totally stressed out. Also, if you are enjoying yourself you will stay awake, focused, and not get as easily distracted as people often do with this long an exam.

Remember, too, that even on the bar exam, you are still in the "safe" world of simulation as compared with law practice. What do I mean? You have stimulating cases to work on, with fascinating and sometimes complicated facts and/or law, but you will be awarded points for identifying the issues and theorizing logically about the likely outcomes, without actually being responsible for the results. So long as you explain your reasoning, you likely will do well on the exam, if you do just that: answer thoroughly and logically, often no matter what your exact conclusion is. Students often return and tell me after graduation that the best part of law school was getting "credit" for seeing both sides of issues and not having to worry about who would actually "win," as they do in practice.

I hope you enjoyed the *Gardenton* practice test and saw it as part real-world and part simulation role-play, but entirely useful, as you continue your training to succeed on both the PTs and in law practice.

KEY TAKEAWAYS

- This PT was set in a different context than many of the typical litigation-oriented PTs. In this exam, you were proactively counseling your client (the School Board) about what would likely be permissible in their proposed communications code and what would not be. Your tone and presentation had to take this into account.

- When writing to a judge or opposing counsel, your job may be to persuade. Here, you were writing to your senior partner to help advise the client, so your job was to analyze as more of a neutral observer and counselor. For that reason, it was just as important to note which provisions were likely permissible as it was to note which had to be revised and why.
- This PT task was also a problem-solving and a drafting/editing exercise, in that you were asked to make suggestions about deleting or adding particular language that would help your client achieve its goals.

8. PROFESSIONAL RESPONSIBILITY

OVERVIEW OF PROFESSIONAL RESPONSIBILITY

Professional responsibility (PR) or legal ethics are not only required courses in law school, but also required for licensure in nearly every state. Specifically, almost every state requires you to pass the Multistate Professional Responsibility Examination (MPRE) in addition to passing your state's bar exam. Because you have so much exposure to ethics rules during law school, it is possible that most of what you will learn in bar review will actually be a review in this subject. That said, there may be areas that are new to you, or that you did not fully understand or see the implications of in law school.

The MPRE tests rules regulating attorneys and judges, whereas most bar exam PR essays test ethics issues relating mostly to lawyers. (In fact, the easiest way to spot a PR issue on a bar exam essay is the presence of a lawyer in the fact pattern!) The most heavily tested PR areas on bar exams include:

- How you gain and how you can lose the right to practice law
- Working with and/or supervising other lawyers and nonlawyers
- Advertising for and soliciting clients
- Managing client money (fees and funds)

- Becoming and staying competent to represent clients
- Zealously representing clients
- Conflicts of interest
- Confidentiality

For a comprehensive list of the subjects covered on the MPRE, consult the most recent MPRE Subject Matter Outline published by the National Conference of Bar Examiners on their website, ncbex.org/exams/mpre/preparing/. Many of these rules are fair game for other parts of the bar exam as well.

SIMULATED PROFESSIONAL RESPONSIBILITY-BASED PT

Take three hours and complete *In re: Deale* on eProducts.

> **TIME-CRUNCH TIPS**
>
> This PT requires you to complete one single task chock full of ethical issues. Professional responsibility is tested on almost all bar exams in some form or other, so I urge you if at all possible to find three hours and complete this test in full. If you cannot find that time now, please read the entire File and Library (using the SS-BROW system) and outline the memo. In your outline, be sure to identify all the ethical problems that have occurred and the potential ethical problems, and note what points you would have discussed if you had had the full three hours to analyze them. You can do this in about 90 to 100 minutes. Plan to come back and write out your answer in full when you have more time.

INSIDE THIS TEST: TIPS AND STRATEGIES

Now that you have tackled *Deale*, let's look together at its File and Library, and see how you did. As you know, you find instructions in the first pages in General Instructions, a Task Memo, and/or Format Pages.

Deale included a standard (nearly boilerplate) set of General Instructions. These Instructions noted that there were statutory authorities as well as cases, but there was nothing unusual (no third set of material beyond the File and Library, for example) and no percentage split, as there was only one assignment to produce.

The Task Memo

The Task Memo gives background about Ms. Amanda Deale, our client, and the City Council she serves on; it further states that she also serves on a property development subcommittee that has been under investigation. The language used by Jim Klein, the partner giving you the assignment, is interesting: "After reading over the transcript of the interview [between Deale and Mark Craven, another lawyer in our firm], I think there may be some ethical problems." The first time you read this, you may have just thought, "Oh, OK, perhaps I'll see some ethical issues." Going back to this, after reading the File and the Library, you were likely screaming to yourself, "*Really*, Mr. Klein? You think there were problems?! Duh! Mark Craven will be lucky if he's not disbarred!" Note I said "screaming to yourself." Whatever you think when you read, make certain that your answer is written in a professional and respectful manner.

Mark Craven's words and actions were deeply troubling, and in a number of instances appear to clearly have violated ethical rules and principles. If you did not see the problems on your initial skim of the File, you would have seen them on your re-read of the File after you investigated the Library contents.

Jim Klein next indicates that while still zealously protecting Deale's rights and adequately preparing her for the grand jury, "it is imperative that our representation of her be totally consistent with the demands of professional responsibility." That comment sets the stage for your careful review of the last paragraph, which explicitly gives you your task:

> Based upon your review of the file, write a memo to me that identifies and analyzes ethical problems that have already occurred and potential ethical issues affecting either our client or our firm. To the extent that these issues present problems to our client or to us, describe how I should solve them.

Right in this assignment language, you have a structure for your answer and a rough draft outline. Here is the skeletal framework:

To: Jim Klein

From: Bar Applicant

Re: *In re: Deale*: Past and Potential Ethical Problems Affecting Client and Law Firm.

Date: [date of the exam] Memo

I. Ethical problems that have occurred

II. Potential ethical issues affecting client/firm Conclusion

To make your memo easy to follow, you will include descriptive subheadings that identify past problems and potential issues and list them under each appropriate main heading. Based on your knowledge of the PT generally, you should expect to see ethical rules in the Library, and facts in the File, that trigger ethical issues. (If you keep this outline as an open document on your computer, you can note issues right in the outline as you see them.)

Once you understood the directions, following the SS-BROW steps, you should have skimmed the File, studied the Library, then returned to the File to flesh out your outline and pick up enough factual information to write a thorough answer.

Skim the File

Why again do we skim the File? You should see right away, here in *Deale*, why that step is so important. There is so much in the File! If you don't know more precisely what you're looking for, you will get bogged down in irrelevancies. That is precious time you cannot spare. Also, although your instincts and general knowledge of PR law may help you see some of the ethical issues, you will not see them all or be able to fully analyze them until after you read the Library. That is why you skim the File first, then study the Library, and then re-read the File.

Before checking out each of the File documents, I suggest a quick look at the File table of contents, to see what your world is. There are six documents, including the Task Memo. The first

File document (after the Task Memo) is the interview that Craven conducted with Deale, our client. You know from the Task Memo that there are problems in Craven's interview; Jim Klein said so specifically. For now, though, just flip through it and get a flavor. If anything pops out at you, fine, but don't spend time trying to make all the facts make sense yet. (When you return to the File after reading the Library, you will study Craven's interview word for word, because Klein told you that is where the problems are. At that time, what is significant will be obvious.)

You see there is a lot of discussion about property called the "Wharf Building." You might have noticed Craven asking to keep a document and might have made a mental note to review attorney duties with respect to retaining physical evidence.

You see Craven speculating on what is and is not covered under the subpoena. (You might recall from your look at the File table of contents that the subpoena itself is in the File.)

Other things will become obvious in the transcript, if you didn't see them on the first skim, including: (1) Craven's revealing to Deale confidential information, a "hush-hush deal," about another client; and (2) Craven seemingly counseling Deale that she can hide documents and/or evade responding to questions at the grand jury. These are both very significant problems that you need to look at carefully when you re-read the File. (The examiners were undoubtedly giving you a hint that confidentiality duties were violated by having Craven refer to the other client matter as a "hush-hush" deal.)

The next document is the partnership agreement, which, among other things, lists who owns what percentage interest in the Wharf Building.

Next is the subpoena. You might have noted the language in Paragraphs 1 and 2, which appears to request a fairly broad sweep of documents.

The next document is an internal memo from Mark Craven to Jim Klein (the person to whom we are writing), in which Craven lets us know that Deale wants us to represent her secretary, Stuart Levy. Craven says Deale wants Stuart "to have a lawyer who is sensitive to [Deale's] interests." This should scream out at you as problematic. Even without looking in the Library, you know that an attorney must zealously represent the client. If we represent Levy, then Levy is the client—and if his interests are potentially adverse to Deale's, then there may be a conflict of interest issue with our current client, Ms. Deale. You might have written something just like this paragraph as draft notes the minute you saw this, and then edited the point into a more thorough paragraph in your answer after reviewing the Library authorities.

The last File document is a newspaper article that gives you a bit more background on the city council's alleged favoritism with respect to the city development.

The Library

The table of contents shows that the Library contains five authorities: two statutes and three cases. The statutes are from the U.S. Code and the Columbia Rules of Professional Conduct, which Rules the table of contents states are identical to California Rules of Professional Responsibility. Because this was a California bar exam, this signaled to applicants that they were already familiar with these rules (as this was law they would have had to apply on a PR essay). An MPT could easily note that Library statutes are substantially similar to statutes you are familiar with, such as the Model Rules of Professional Responsibility.

Caveat: Do not study PTs to master specific rules of law. It is true that many of the PR rules in this Library are similar to those in other jurisdictions, and it is hoped that completing this PT helped bolster your general knowledge of PR at the same time it helped train key lawyering skills. Nevertheless, as we have said throughout this book, you must not expect to use practice PTs to master particular rules for your bar exam. Examiners may use fictitious law for PT exam purposes. Even if a PT is from your own jurisdiction, case holdings may have been changed for exam purposes, or the Library law may be outdated. So remember, practice PTs provide excellent skills training in the context of subjects you need to master, and they help you gain fluency in general areas of law that will help in turn when you go to master the rules in your jurisdiction.

In this Library, as always, read the cases in full as if they were new to you, and brief them using the surgical briefing method described earlier in the book. Still, because of your presumed general familiarity with professional responsibility statutes, it makes sense here to first read the titles or headings of the statutes before spending time studying each provision.

Scanning these headings, you see from the criminal code sections that the following are crimes: Tampering with a witness, victim, or an informant; Perjury; Subornation of perjury; and Destruction of evidence. If Mark Craven (the lawyer in our firm whose actions we are writing about in our PT answer) counseled any of those things, then he acted in a way that advised a violation of the law. Again, you know from your general knowledge of PR rules that advising someone to violate the law is itself a violation of an ethical rule, and you see that specifically set forth in the Library in Rule 3–210.

Looking next at the Columbia Rules of Professional Conduct, among other things you see:

- A duty to maintain client confidences (3–100)
- Prohibitions against acting incompetently (3–110) and against bringing actions that are not in good faith (3–200)
- Obligations not to advise someone to violate the law (3–210), to avoid representing parties with adverse interests without informed consent, and certain other requirements (3–310)
- Duties to the tribunal (5–200) and a prohibition, with some exceptions, not to act as a witness in a case in which you are representing a party (5–210)
- A prohibition against suppressing evidence (5–220)
- Rules about prohibited contact with witnesses (5–310)

Again, all of the titles of these code sections raise possible ethical violations, most of which occurred or will potentially occur given the facts in this File. You might note as subheadings in your outline, right when you see them, any violations you think Craven committed.

Note: All of these provisions deal with ethical obligations of lawyers. The task you must wrestle with is what the lawyer in our own firm, Craven, did or said that raises or potentially raises issues for our firm or our client. Nothing in this Library is about the city council's obligations or about what Deale's obligations as a government official may be. (Students frequently make the mistake of focusing not on what Craven did wrong but on what Deale did wrong. If you were confused about this, let the Library be your guide. It's nearly all about the duties of lawyers.)

The cases are interesting, and each raises different areas of ethical concern. I will walk through them here, in this debriefing, case by case, but in your answer, you want to reference the cases as they relate to possibly unethical behavior in the past and potential future ethical violations committed by Craven and/or our law firm. As I have warned throughout this book, you do not want to write a summary of each case, case by case, in your answer. (Here your answer should have been organized violation-by-violation.)

Bronston, a Supreme Court case, holds that it is the responsibility of the questioner, the lawyer, to ask precise questions and ferret out the truth when a witness answers a question in a literally honest manner but in a manner that nonetheless misleads by what it leaves out. The burden is on the lawyer to ask follow-up questions and get the full picture. So long as the witness is honest, she or he is not committing perjury. When you go back to the File, what will pop out is that Craven starts to advise Deale accurately about her obligation to answer truthfully but without obligation to volunteer information. Then, however, Craven goes on and tells Deale she "can always say she doesn't remember." What? (Did you stop yourself wondering if you read this wrong? I remember reading it five times the first time I saw this PT, thinking, "Did Craven really just say what it looks like he said?") I hope this jumped out at you as very wrong. If you remember something and under oath say you do not remember, you are committing perjury. By advising Deale that she "can always say she doesn't remember," Craven seems essentially to be telling her to perjure herself. Big problem! The next case, *Edwards*, reminds us that physical evidence does not become privileged simply because it is given to or taken into custody by an attorney. The attorney may keep evidence in a criminal case only long enough to prepare a defense, but then must turn over the evidence to the prosecution. You may remember, and the rules tell you, that this may be done anonymously. There is no need to say how the evidence came into the lawyer's possession. However, an attorney cannot keep the evidence for too long. Reading *Edwards* should have made you think, when you went back into the File, about the partnership agreement that Craven took from Deale.

The last case, *Elliott Saul*, reiterates (in the context of a grand jury situation) that so long as the client knowingly and intelligently consents, an attorney may represent more than one person subpoenaed before the grand jury. Here, this basically points us in the direction of making certain we have informed consent from Stuart Levy, whom Deale wants us to represent. Although there may be ethical issues with that representation (the one we looked at earlier of Deale wanting us to be "sensitive" to Deale's issues in representing Levy, rather than Levy's, and the possible conflict of interest), it still may be possible to represent both Deale and Levy if the proper consents are obtained. This is another issue you would study carefully, perhaps moving back and forth between re-reading the relevant pages in the File and reviewing the relevant law as you write.

Study the sample answers in eProducts and compare and contrast them to your answer.

SPIN-OFF EXERCISES

Using the same facts and law as in *Deale*, try drafting the following assignments:

1. A letter to Amanda Deale advising her specifically about her obligations with respect to the grand jury subpoena and her obligation to answer questions truthfully. Also inform her explicitly in your letter that if Stuart Levy wants us to represent him, we will owe a duty to him and not to her during that representation. Discuss, as well, the potential conflict of interest in representing both her and Levy. Note that even though Deale is a politician,

to our knowledge she is not a lawyer, so write in a tone appropriate for Deale.

2. A letter to Mark Craven notifying him of ethical violations you believe he committed and what must now be done about those violations.

Note that in this case, the senior partner, Jim Klein, would likely deal directly with his partner, Mark Craven. But what if this were a small firm, or if Mark Craven were a solo practitioner you worked for? How do you think you would handle this situation? What would you do if Mark Craven were your boss and had directed you to file frivolous motions for the purposes of delay?

Related Substance Abuse Concerns

What if you have reason to believe that part of why Craven engaged in such egregiously unethical conduct (including revealing client confidences and counseling our client to hide documents and evade responding to questions) is that Craven has an alcohol or drug problem? What do you do with that information? Do you talk with Craven? Do you talk with another, more senior, attorney for advice? Do you report Craven to an ethics hotline?

Let's say further that you are a new junior associate, just out of law school. Craven and your boss Jim Klein are much older than you, and they are close friends. You think that Klein does not see or does not want to see or admit that Craven has a substance abuse problem. But Craven has taken you to lunch and ordered far too many drinks on a number of occasions, you have seen Craven stumbling in the elevator when he leaves at the end of the day, and you are certain that Craven needs help. Draft a paragraph of the dialogue you might have with Jim Klein about Craven.

Another scenario: What if Craven is much older than Klein? Craven, now in his eighties, was Klein's mentor, and Klein does not at all want to see that Craven is slowing down. How do you handle expressing your concerns about Craven's behavior? (Note that the American Academy of Neurology estimated that up to 50% of people over the age of 85 experience some dementia.[3])

Lastly, what if working for Klein and Craven is so stressful that you find yourself drinking to calm yourself down each afternoon, or that you drink before meeting with them, or before going to court on matters they send you on that you are not comfortable with? What if they both drink often during the work day and pressure you to join them?

Would you be able to recognize if you have a substance abuse problem? What steps might you take to help yourself?

Note: If you think I am making up unrealistic scenarios here, think again. Substance abuse is an enormous problem in our profession and one you must be aware of. You must actively work to stay healthy yourself and to understand and comply with ethical obligations when you encounter others who are using and possibly abusing drugs or alcohol. (I don't say "if" but "when.")

In addition to spinning off assignments based on the *Deale* File and Library, while you are thinking practically about professional responsibility, try to answer these few short PR-related hypotheticals.

1. You are Plaintiff's counsel. You just received a request from Defense counsel to continue the hearing you had set for tomorrow morning. You went to some length rearranging your own calendar to make the hearing date and time work, and you believe that opposing counsel attorney is asking for the continuance to stall. How do you handle the situation?

2. You are in court on your first case ever. You are speaking to the court clerk, who is rude. The clerk says that you and your client are wasting the court's time, and suggests that you do not know how

[3] From Richard Carlton, *A Closer Look at Depression and Cognitive Decline in Senior Attorneys*, Cal. B.J., Apr. 2016, https://apps.calbar.ca.gov/mcleselfstudy/mcle_home.aspx?testID=108.

to handle yourself as a lawyer. What do you say or do?

3. You are in court litigating a particularly thorny issue, and, on a quick break from the proceedings, your client tells you that he intends to just "skip certain details" if the court asks him about them. How do you handle the situation? Is this a *Bronston* type situation where it would be up to the court to ask the right questions? Should you advise your client to answer truthfully but not volunteer additional information? Write a short paragraph on how you would respond to your client.

4. You have met with your client once. At the close of the initial meeting, after telling you a bit about her case, and after your explaining how you could potentially help her, she gave you a large retainer. Before your next meeting, she tells you that she and her adversary have tried going to a mediator and hope to resolve things without a lawyer and no longer need your services. How do you handle the situation?

5. You are acting as the mediator for two parties. With your help, they have reached a preliminary agreement, and you have encouraged them each to have outside counsel read it before they sign it, if they wish. One of the attorneys phones to yell at you, insinuating that you are biased or being "paid off" because the agreement is so one-sided. How do you handle the situation?

6. The court is set to hear your argument, and the judge says, "Counselors, I have a docket full of important matters this morning, and you both are wasting my time. Go out in the hallway and figure this out. Come back in 30 minutes with a solution." You are taken aback by the judge's tone. Opposing counsel (who is a much more experienced lawyer than you are) tries to push you into a compromise, but you really believe, based on the facts and law,

that your client should prevail. How do you handle the situation?

PTs and PT spin-off exercises are among the best places and times to think about ethical issues and prepare yourself to face trying situations.

PRACTICE, LAW SCHOOL, AND PTs: COMPARE AND CONTRAST

Ethical issues in real life do not typically come wrapped in neat packages the way they do on law exams. (Even in this fairly realistic PT, the bulk of the many professional violations nearly all appeared in one short transcript.) In actual practice, PR issues may sneak up on you. You may not know for certain if something is permissible or not; it may be a gray area and you may need advice. If so, seek advice from another trusted lawyer. Lawyers are typically very generous with their time in terms of mentoring less experienced colleagues. There are also ethics hotlines at many state bar offices, where you can call and get advice anonymously. If you sense that something isn't right, make some inquiries, do some research, and find out for certain what you must do, what you may do, and what you may not do. Trust yourself.

Ethics issues in practice may be laden with peer pressure, or heavy-handed top down intimidation—some with veiled (or not-so-veiled) threats that you may lose your job unless you engage in the prohibited conduct. The hypothetical I suggested earlier (where you pretended Mark Craven was your boss and was pushing you to file frivolous lawsuits) is all too realistic. I have heard many lawyers discuss how they were asked to engage in unethical behavior when they were new to practice, including being directed by more senior lawyers to mishandle client trust funds, disregard contrary legal authorities, and/or delay proceedings to gain a competitive advantage. Things you might think would only come up on an exam unfortunately do arise in practice. Protect your license and your reputation, at the same time as you fight for your clients.

Bottom line: The price of failing to understand ethical rules (and follow them) in practice is far higher than on exams. The worst you can typically do on an exam when you don't see or understand what is at issue is fail and have to retake the exam or course. This is not something I want for any of you, but it is not tragic. In practice, however, you may lose your license, your reputation, and all that you have worked for your whole life—not to mention what your client may lose as a result of your behavior. As you well know, some attorneys end up in prison. So, do everything in your power to protect this law license that you are working so hard now to earn. Guard it as one of the most precious things you will ever have the privilege of calling yours.

Further protect your ability to become licensed by following all Honor Code and other rules in law school, and keeping your moral character record such that you will be deemed fit to practice law by the jurisdiction of your choosing.

KEEP YOUR OWN PRIVATE LISTS

A very senior and extremely experienced attorney I knew advised young lawyers to keep two private lists, and to update those lists every time they worked with another attorney (in or outside of their own practice):

1. A list of attorneys you want to work with in the future, people to whom you would give the benefit of the doubt if they ever need it. (Jot notes to remind yourself of particularly reputable actions the attorney took while you were interacting with him or her.)
2. A list of attorneys you do not want to work with, or, if forced to work with, whom you will not trust or give the benefit of the doubt. (On this list, note anything the attorney did that was underhanded, unprofessional, or unethical, so that you remember why you do not trust this person in the future.)

Whether we keep them as written lists or mental lists, we all keep such lists. People will remember what you do that is right and honorable, and what you do that is not, starting in law school (and even earlier). It takes a lifetime to cultivate a good reputation, but only a moment to destroy one.

Bottom line: PR issues on PTs and essays are often derived from real life. Many of the scenarios you will have to identify and analyze, and sometimes make recommendations about, are problems and violations you see regularly reported against practicing lawyers. The difference between both types of exams and real life is that the consequences in the latter can be devastating, even irreparable. Learn your rules of ethics and learn them well!

KEY TAKEAWAYS

- This practice exam helped raise your awareness of the types of ethical issues that may well arise on a PT. In this PT, the underlying legal backdrop was professional responsibility, but any one of the concerns in this PT may be planted in a PT based on any other legal subject as just a single issue for you to identify and discuss. For example, you could have a wills and trusts problem where you were drafting an estate plan and a lawyer in your firm revealed the confidences of another client.
- Having completed this PT, you should have your antennae up for potential ethical issues and a good sense of how to address ethical issues in future PTs.
- This PT showed a very realistic (unfortunate but realistic) scenario of a client pushing the attorney to "bend" or outright break the rules for that client. In real life, it can be tremendously difficult to call out (or report) the unethical behavior of a colleague. Nonetheless, you must know what your own duties are, and follow the rules of professional conduct. You work too hard for your law license to lose it.

9. REAL PROPERTY

OVERVIEW OF REAL PROPERTY

The term *real property* connotes land, as opposed to "personal property" or moveable items also known as *chattel.* Law school property classes and the bar exam both focus on the former: land. (On bar exams, issues relating to personal property most often arise in torts contexts, where someone may be interfering with or destroying personal property or in criminal law contexts, where someone may be trying to steal it.)

Chattel that is attached to real property will likely be deemed a fixture and part of the real property, not separate personal property. Likewise, growing crops are considered part of the land until they are cut (such as for harvest), after which time they become personal property.

In law school, often in 1L, you learn about how real property is acquired (often by sale), and you need to know a fair amount about land sale contracts.

Note: In contracts class, you learn that contracts for the sale of land must typically be in writing. You will likely also pick this up in your property course with further study of the Statute of Frauds and its exceptions, as it applies to interests in land.

Land can also be acquired by adverse possession, and the government can acquire land by eminent domain; the former you will probably study in law school, but, depending on your professor, the latter you might not get to until bar review.

You will learn about deeds or land ownership documents; what constitutes a valid deed; and rules with respect to delivering deeds, transferring deeds, and recording deeds. You will also learn about different types of recording statutes.

In law school property classes, you study restrictions on the use of land such as easements, profits, covenants, and equitable servitudes. You learn about present possessory estates and future interests in land. (These terms should seem familiar: fee simple, fee tail, life estate, possibility of reverter, and remainders.) Most law school classes and bar exams also test concurrent estates, including joint ownership such as joint tenancy, tenancy by the entirety, and tenancy in common. You may have studied and should know rules about present landowners protecting the interests of future owners (waste), and rules that would prevent unreasonable restraints on transferability (alienation) of property, such as the rule against perpetuities.

You may or may not cover landlord-tenant rules in law school, but they are often tested on other parts of the bar exam. For a list of the topics covered on your bar exam, consult the most recent content scope outlines for your jurisdiction and the NCBE.

SIMULATED REAL PROPERTY-BASED PT

I chose the *Westside Community Corporation* (*Westside*) PT for confidence-building reasons. In it, you will tackle the dreaded "rule against perpetuities" (RAP). It is not that difficult to understand, but it has gotten a bad "rap" (pun intended!). It seems odd to say that I picked what some view as an impossibly tricky topic to build confidence, but what I want is for you to get to a place where you believe that you can handle anything the examiners throw at you, even the RAP.

Go ahead and take three hours and complete the *Westside* PT found on eProducts. We'll debrief it together after you finish and you will see that it isn't that bad at all!

> **TIME-CRUNCH TIPS**
>
> If you do not have time now for a full three-hour PT, but still want to do some work with this practice exam, read all the materials and complete just the first memo, comparing the prior Columbia law and new Columbia statutes. Skip the second memo advising the board about the proposed alternatives. This should trim off at least 30 minutes of the time needed to complete this exam.

INSIDE THIS TEST: TIPS AND STRATEGIES

Walking through the *Westside* File, as always the first and most important document is the Task Memo. In the Task Memo, we learn that the partner (Meherrin, the person to whom we are to deliver our assignment) has met with the executive director of our client, the Westside Community Development Corporation (Westside). Immediately, knowing our client is a corporation, we can expect to hear about the board of directors. Sure enough, in the next sentence we learn that the board is negotiating with the Lewiston Historic Preservation Society (LHPS) about "the transfer" of the old Lewiston High School property (High School).

I suggest starting a "cast of characters" on your scratch paper. You may end up having lots of people and parties to keep track of in a PT. It can be helpful to start notes on who is whom, like a program for a play. Here, you can begin that already, reading the Task Memo.

- Meherrin = our boss (partner in our firm)
- Westside = our client
- Paulette Wade = Westside's executive director
- LHPS = party negotiating potential lease/sale of high school with our client

Did you wonder why Meherrin used the word "transfer" rather than "sale"? The next sentence provides a hint. Our boss refers immediately to the lease that is in the File, but says that the board is considering two alternatives. The lease must be one. We will find out more as we read.

Some students freak out when next they see mention of the rule against perpetuities (RAP). It is imperative to stay calm and not panic. Just keep reading, and think as you read; talk yourself through the instructions:

> *What is my exact task? Draft a memo that analyzes the prior and new Columbia law on the RAP. (I do not have to know this by heart. The Library will have everything I need.) Then, I need to draft a second memo analyzing the two alternatives, and determining which is better and why, to help my boss to best advise the Westside board.*

At this point, at what would be only about two minutes or less into reading this PT, you can start a draft outline. You can either write this outline on scratch paper or type it into a blank document file on your computer that will eventually become your final answer.

Header and Introduction to Meherrin

Memo I

Analysis of prior law and new law of RAP and how it affects Westside's alternatives. Does new law eliminate old problems?

Memo II

Analysis of alternatives. Which is better for Westside and why?

Conclude Memo II with advice to give to board.

Most often, Instructions tell you how much each task is worth. When they do not, make an educated guess based on how much material relates to each task and how complex each is: *Here, the first memo is the law-heavy document; it incorporates analysis of both prior and new law, so likely there is more to say here than in the second memo, which is more of a problem-solving and factual analysis document. In that second memo, I must evaluate the pros and cons of each of the two alternatives. Sounds like something that can be written more quickly than the first memo.* This is how your reasoning might lead you to allocate a bit more time to the first task, if the percentages are not specified. Here, it is likely that the first memo would have been worth about 60% (with about 40% of that 60% focused on prior law and 20% on the new law) and the second memo worth about 40% of the total.

> The next File document is a short letter to our boss from Westside's executive director, Paulette Wade. It tells us that her main goal is to obtain access to the Fine Arts Building to get started constructing a new cultural and arts center. Wade says that the board is interested in getting control of the entire school property. She also spells out very precisely the two alternatives that our boss noted in the Task Memo:
>
> 1. Lease the High School's Fine Arts Building, with an option to purchase the entire property (lease-option), or
> 2. Purchase the entire school, with LHPS retaining an option to buy it back (sale/buy back). You can update your draft outline with this new information.

Header and Intro

Memo I

Analysis of prior law and new law of RAP and how it affects Westside's lease-option and sale-buy back. Does new law eliminate old problems?

Memo II

Analysis of alternatives: which is better for Westside and why?

1) Pros and cons of leasing the High School's Fine Arts Building, with an option to purchase the entire property (lease-option), or

2) Pros and cons of purchasing the entire school with LHPS retaining an option to buy it back (sale-buy back).

Conclude Memo II with advice to give to board.

Note that the letter tells our boss not to "worry about the specific dollars and cents." We might learn more about the money in later File documents, but this also may be a hint that the money is not the biggest factor in this decision.

The next document is a draft lease. Before knowing all the law in the Library and having more familiarity with the rest of the facts, you may want to just make a mental note that the lease is here in the File for you to return and read it when you have more context for fully understanding it.

The next document is a letter from the LHPS to the board. Among other key facts, you learn in this correspondence that the Historical Society has already rejected two offers from prospective buyers offering $3 million because those buyers were not willing to commit to preserving the historical character of the school. That is LHPS's primary concern. We also learn that LHPS acquired the property from the school district precisely because of concern that a new buyer would destroy the character of the property, but that when LHPS does sell the property it will have to pay 75% of the proceeds to the school district. LHPS explains that it cannot sell only a part of the school, as our client seemingly wants, but would consider leasing us just the Fine Arts Building. (Notice how I am jumping into the role-play and thinking of the client as "us." The more "into" these PTs you get, the easier they will be to understand.)

LHPS further suggests that a sale of the entire property may be possible even at a "modest" below-market price, if there were a buy-back option (on an equally modest basis). That way

LHPS could later find a buyer that was willing to both keep the history preserved and pay market value.

You should already be beginning to see some of the pros and cons of each alternative. If not, do not be concerned. Keep reading and re-reading. The minutes of the Westside Board clearly set out the positions of different board members. Remember, too, that the whole File will make more sense after you read the Library.

The next document is another letter, this one from Westside to a foundation seeking money for a grant. This provides a lot of background on both Westside and on the high school site. It will come in handy when exploring the pros and cons of the various alternatives, in your second task. For example, you learn from this letter that the Fine Arts Building needs extensive renovations, and you learn that although Westside immediately wants just that one building, it may eventually need the whole property. The next document is minutes from a July 1 Westside Board meeting. Skim it now and come back to it after you have read the Library. Some points will make sense on this first skim. Others will not be clear until after you know the law. As you read, add to the cast of characters you started when you began the Task Memo, to keep everyone straight. Next to each name, you can jot down the person's position vis-à-vis the two alternatives:

- Meherrin = our boss (partner in our firm)
- Westside = our client
- LHPS = party negotiating potential lease/sale of high school with our client
- Paulette Wade = Westside's executive director
- Ashleigh McKenzie = Chair of Westside Board
- Wade Herndon = Secretary of Westside Board
- Jane Kovnat = President of LHPS
- Reverend S.C. James Dawes = Board member
- Jenny Alley = former dancer and presumably board member
- Ellis Hart = lawyer

- Nicole Figures = CPA

In the minutes, in addition to learning different board members' positions, we also learn that although the million-dollar grant request was not approved, Westside was awarded $250,000 for renovations to the Fine Arts Building if Westside leases or buys it.

The minutes go on to detail several people's positions on a lease versus a sale. You could have started writing some of these positions right into your outline under the pros and cons of each alternative.

The minutes end by authorizing Wade to negotiate either the lease or a sale, so long as the board approves.

The last File document is language from LHPS about each option. You can look at this now, but you will need to come back to the specific language after studying the RAP law in the Library in order to determine how these provisions do or do not comply with the rules.

Note: If your lawyering instincts saw a red flag by the language "at any time" in both the lease and sale language, you are on the right track! Perhaps you were thinking: *Does that really mean <u>any</u> time? Any time at all in the far distant future? In other words, they could have this right in perpetuity? That would mean they could essentially keep their interest in the property locked up forever. . .* Ah, now that you see it, this rule against perpetuities won't be that hard to understand! (If you did not see this yet, do not be concerned; the first case, *Symphony*, and later cases, especially *Citgo*, should have started to make the RAP clear.)

Off to the Library to tackle the RAP in more detail.

Library

This Library contains sections of the Probate Code and four cases. I will highlight some points in each, specifically places you might have gotten detoured and points you should have seen.

Probate Code

The first section listed, § 21201, tells you that this chapter supersedes prior common law. Thinking back to your directions, you already might sense that the statutes will primarily give you the information you need on the second part of Memo 1 (the analysis of the new law). Logically, you might deduce that the cases will then provide what you need for the first part of Memo 1 (the analysis of prior law). What this means is that you really must read the cases and then come back to the statutes to see how the statutes fix problems that occurred under the old law. (Note how, as you read, you want to continually think about what your exact assignment is, and ask yourself how pieces of the Library and File fit into that assignment.)

I will review the rest of the statutes now, but you might well just have skimmed the statutes at first and then come back to them after reading the rest of the Library. They make much more sense when you have the context.

The second section listed, § 21205, gives the modern rule against perpetuities.

The next section, § 21220, provides for a remedy; in the case of a violation, the court "shall reform a disposition in the manner that most closely approximates the transferor's manifested plan distribution." Under this section, the court will also limit the nonalienation period to 90 years. You may not see the significance of this at first read, but after reading all the cases, and going back to the Task Memo, File, and thinking about how they all connect, you will see that this allows for the possibility of the court coming in and fixing a RAP problem should the transfer to Westside pose such a problem.

Perhaps the most interesting section, § 21225 lists exceptions or interests that are specifically excluded from the rule. This is gold. Your assignment (in the second part of Memo 1) is to describe how the new law eliminates problems with prior law. Reading carefully, you will see a few exceptions that potentially apply here, namely:

- § 21225(a) on non-vested . . . arising out of nondonative [or "commercial"] transfer, and
- § 21225(e) on charity-to-charity giving.

Also note that § 21225(g) excludes interests that would have been exempt under prior law; as you learn from reading the case law, in the lease alternative, if the option is considered part of the lease and not independent (or "in gross"), it will be excluded under prior law and under current law via § 21225(g). You will note in the sample answers in eProducts how some of these points were mentioned only briefly.

Again, if the statutes were not clear on first read, it would help to read the cases and then come back to the statutes. Note too that only some, but not all, of the subsections in § 21225 were applicable to our case. So, if you did not see how a section applied, it was important not to spend too much time trying to make it fit. (Always remember that on PTs, you will be sorting relevant from irrelevant material.)

All of the cases were applicable and I hope you saw how at least some of the statutes applied. Let's look at the cases now.

Note: Remember, the directions tell you that you can abbreviate cases. You get no "extra credit" for providing full cites. Do not waste time writing complete case citations.

Symphony

This case provided the old RAP rule: that prior to the adoption of the Uniform Statutory Rule Against Perpetuities (USRP), a future property interest was invalid "unless it must vest, if at all, not later than 21 years after one or more of the lives in being at the creation of the estate and any period of gestation involved."

In addition to literally stating the rule, *Symphony* also helped explain the purpose of the RAP in plain English. Did you begin to see it? The basic idea of the RAP is to invalidate interests in property that vest too remotely (generations into the future); the rule thereby stops landowners from excessively restraining the free transfer of property in the far-off future. Very descriptively, *Symphony* explains how 17th-century judges used the RAP to try to limit the "dead hand of landowners [from] reaching into future generations."

Think about it in the terms of the facts of our case. Do we as a society want this (albeit historic) high school property site locked up forever in the hands of LHPS? Do we want them controlling the property for generations to come? Or do we want new owners, such as our client Westside, to be able to come in and reinvigorate the property and help it grow to meet the present community's needs? I realize I am oversimplifying, but no matter what law you find in the Library on PTs, you need to step back, see the big picture, and try to make the rules make sense to you in the context of this role-play.

You cannot allow yourself to be intimidated by any rules you see in a PT Library or any facts you see in a PT File. This is why I included *Westside* in this book!

Again, though, you may have had to read this and the language of each alternative (on the last File page) several times to see their significance. Eventually, you would see that the lease option is potentially problematic as worded because it allows for indefinite renewals and so could continue beyond lives in being plus 21 years. The sale-buy back may also pose problems because, under the current wording, LHPS could exercise its option "at any time after sale."

Symphony also cites *MTA*, a case that distinguishes options from preemptive rights, and explains why the latter (also called *rights of first refusal*) do not violate the RAP. A right of first refusal would likely provide another way to possibly get around the RAP problems under prior law, something we will write about in Memo 1.

Temple Hoyne Buell (Temple)

The *Temple* case provides "fixes" for the RAP problems, namely adding a savings clause (or time limitation language) or deleting language that makes an option binding on heirs, successors, and assigns. This is also a very important problem-solving tool that we may want to write about in Memo 1.

Citgo

In the *Citgo* case, you learn that purchase options (such as the one contemplated by Westside) may be exempt from the (old) RAP if they are adjunct to a valid long-term commercial and nondonative lease. (Is this a commercial lease? It might be considered one, or it might be analogous to one, though it could also be considered a charitable venture.) You will see how the sample answers in eProducts analyzed this.

However, *Citgo* may not apply because, in *Citgo*, the option could be exercised any time *during* the lease; whereas, in our case, the language allows LHPS to exercise the option *at any time* starting two years *after* the lease.

Even if *Citgo* is distinguishable, we might still argue that some of the policy applies and should help save the lease because it furthers the goals behind the RAP, namely stimulating improvement and development of the property. This property has been unused for nearly 20 years, and our client is offering to come in and bring the location to life with arts and culture.

Shaver

This is the only case that discusses the new law. *Shaver* discusses USRP § 21225, giving insight into its nonapplicability to commercial nondonative transactions. Hence, you might reference *Shaver* in your discussion in Part 2 of Memo 1 regarding how the new law eliminates RAP problems.

THE BIGGEST CHALLENGES IN THIS PT

What many found challenging here included:

1. Finishing, as there was a lot to discuss. A success strategy here (and with other PTs that seem overwhelming) is to write briefly on each part, finish, and then return to add more detail if time permits.
2. Getting "thrown" by the RAP. Just read it and analyze it like any other rule of law. Do not assume that you cannot understand it. It is no more complicated than much of the rest of what you study in real property. Of course, depending on your professor and the casebook you use, you may study some RAP cases that are extremely complex, but if tested on the bar exam, RAP issues will likely be fairly straightforward. Also, as the USRP is adopted in more states, casebooks seem to be dropping many of the particularly complex RAP cases.

PUTTING IT ALL TOGETHER

After initially briefing the cases, go back and look at the Task Memo and remember your assignment. In the first memo, you are to analyze the old law and recommend how to avoid the RAP even under the old law, and then analyze how the new law eliminates RAP problems. After reading these cases, re-reading the File, and maybe re-reading the law (especially if it was confusing on first read), you should have seen several ways to fix the problems under the old law. Then, after putting together Part 1 of Memo 1 (on the old law), go back and review the USRP provisions and *Shaver*. You will immediately see how the new law helps eliminate RAP problems: namely (as noted earlier), with provisions excepting the commercial nondonative transfer and the transfer from charity to charity. After that, move on to the second memo on the pros and cons of each alternative.

How would this all fit into the outline we started earlier?

To: A. Hilliard Meherrin

From: Applicant

Re: Westside Community Development Corp. and Effects of Rule Against Perpetuities on Plans to Lease or Buy Property on the High School Site.

Memo I: Analysis of prior law and new law of RAP and how it affects Westside's lease-option and sale-buy back. Does new law eliminate old problems?

The traditional rule against perpetuities poses potential problems with both the lease option and the sale-buy back. As to the former, because the lease may be renewed indefinitely, it may extend too far into the future. Also, under the second option, because LHPS could exercise its buy-back option at any time in the future, that too would violate the rule as strictly construed.

Analysis of prior law

[Ways to possibly solve lease-option problems under old law]:

- Make option adjunct to the lease and not independent of the lease.
- Discuss and cite cases, including *Citgo*.

- Include a termination date for the lease option.
- Discuss and cite cases, including *Temple.*
- Make sure the option right does not transfer to successors in perpetuity.
- Discuss and cite cases, including *Temple.*

[Ways to possibly solve sale-buy back problems under old law]:

- Show why it is part of a commercial nondonative transaction.
- Discuss and cite cases, including *Symphony.*
- Include a termination date for the buy back.
- Discuss and cite cases, including *Temple.*
- Insert a preemptive right (or right of first refusal) clause. Discuss and cite cases, including *Symphony.*

Analysis of new law

Several changes in the new law will help, particularly the following exclusions:

Show why it is part of commercial nondonative transaction. Discuss, cite *Shaver* and § 21225(a).

Show why it is a charity-to-charity transfer. Discuss, cite *Shaver* and § 21225(e).

Memo II: Analysis of alternatives: which is better for Westside and why?

Many of the Westside staff and board members expressed strong opinions about Westside's acquiring space on the old high school site. The following is a summary of the pros and cons of each alternative, and a recommendation based on a review of all views as a whole as to which path would best serve our client.

1) Pros and Cons of Leasing the High School's Fine Arts Building, with an option to purchase the entire property ("lease option"), or

Alternative 1 gets Westside the Fine Arts Building right away, and Westside has the money to complete the necessary renovations on that one building from the

Rappaport Foundation grant. This alternative also gives Westside a purchase option, which, depending on how the language is read and interpreted, may give Westside the right to buy the property for quite a long time. The purchase option protects Westside in this way, and also allows Westside time to raise more money to fix the rest of the buildings (and perhaps eventually build additional buildings) on the site.

2) Pros and Cons of Purchasing the entire school with LHPS retaining an option to buy it back ("sale-buy back").

Alternative 2 gives Westside the entire property and accordingly the potential to grow and expand further in the future, so at first it may look like the better option (and several board members seem to favor it), but (a) can Westside afford to buy the whole property? And (b) will LHPS come snatch it back (with the buy-back provision as written) and take it all away from Westside? (And will knowledge of the mere existence of LHPS's preemptive right to repurchase cause hesitancy on the part of prospective tenants to rent space on the property? Will this cause similar problems for Westside too in terms of future grant applications?)

Conclude Memo II with advice to give to board.

On balance, after evaluating both the positions of the Westside Board and staff and the soundness of each option, quite likely the lease option is the better of the two alternatives for Westside.

Note: More important than your actual conclusion was that you explained your reasoning and clearly set out the pros and cons, and the importance of avoiding a focus on merely technical compliance with the RAP. Also, although *Holland* discussed legal malpractice, it brings up an important strategy available to a lawyer who has the luxury of drafting documents instead of defending documents after the fact (in litigation). The board members will want to avoid the expensive and distracting litigation that may arise if the RAP issue is questionable. We're looking to stay out of court here, not for a winnable case. Thus, the solution should be clear and obvious compliance with the letter and spirit of the perpetuities rules.

Memo 2 should have been much easier after writing Memo 1, because Memo 1 really already forced you to think about both alternatives. Memo 2 just makes more explicit the task of evaluating the pros and cons of each alternative, and, if you have time, summarizing the specific positions of various Westside staff and board members. Review the sample answers in eProducts for more details.

SPIN-OFF EXERCISES

Spin-off exercises are a great way to gain exposure to different types of documents without as much of a time commitment as it would take to complete a whole new PT. Now that you have completed the *Westside* memos, think about other documents you might have been asked to draft based on the same law and facts. Pay particular attention to how your tone and approach might differ depending on the goal of your assignment and your audience. Consider how you would draft an answer if your task were to:

- Make a presentation to the board advocating the lease option as the better of the two alternatives (and why). Write out your words exactly as you would speak to board members. Anticipate questions that particular board members may ask and indicate how you would respond. How does this assignment differ from writing a memo to your boss about how to advise the board?
- Draft an investigation plan. What, if any, additional information would you like to help choose the best alternative for Westside?
- Edit the draft lease in the File and/or draft a proposed sale agreement.

PRACTICE, LAW SCHOOL, AND PTs: COMPARE AND CONTRAST

This again is a fabulous and realistic transactional problem. You are not set in a litigation context at all; thus, this is a very different type of assignment from a typical law school property essay question where it is likely that facts have already taken place which give rise to a potential lawsuit. Here in *Westside*, you are thinking forward to help your client make a legally sound decision that accomplishes the organization's goals. The perspective you had to adopt in this problem was that of a "preventive lawyer" (planning well to avoid ever having legal issues in the first place), rather than that of a litigator. Though some clients do not seek the advice of a lawyer until litigation is inevitable, the client here was smart to get counsel involved early on to help determine which alternative was better. We see similar assignments that ask you to roleplay as attorneys with a similar perspective in the constitutional law and contracts PTs debriefed in this appendix. If you enjoy these sorts of tasks, you might take additional transactional courses in law school and intern for or get a job in a firm that does transactional work.

Congratulations, too, on grappling with a tough area of the law on this practice exam. There is a tendency, both on exams and in real life, especially for beginning lawyers, to get nervous when they don't have all the answers—but this is normal. Do not pretend. Competency of counsel does not mean you know everything off the top of your head. You may have to study to become competent, or associate with more knowledgeable and experienced counsel.

In law school and in studying for the bar exam, it is very important not to get frustrated. Do not even think that there are areas of law that you cannot understand. If you were smart enough to be accepted by a reputable law school, there is an overwhelming likelihood that you are smart enough to understand every rule or concept you encounter in law school and studying for the bar exam. That does not mean it will be easy! You may have to read things many times over. You may have to seek help and ask for explanations, possibly from multiple sources (professors, classmates, and academic support faculty). You may also need to read trustworthy explanatory resources such as hornbooks or treatises. Still, with enough dedicated, focused hard work, you *will* get it.

KEY TAKEAWAYS

- This practice exam helped steel you for the worst, and hopefully empowered you to see that you must not "freeze" on the PT portion of the bar exam if a PT is set in the context of a subject of law that you either do not know or do not like. (There may even be subjects you dread or fear, though I urge you not to fear anything on the bar exam; just prepare well and face the beasts!) Note this applies on essays and multiple choice questions as well. There may be subjects you like more or feel more comfortable with, but you cannot panic or turn off when faced with questions in your least favorite subjects. In fact, I would recommend that as part of your practice, you complete extra questions in any subjects you secretly hope will not be on the bar exam, so that you are well prepared (and not psyched out) if they are.

- This PT gave you some further exposure to statutory as well as case analysis in that part of the exam that required you to analyze the new and old laws.
- Although the first memo task was heavy on legal analysis skills, the second memo task also worked your problem-solving skills. You needed to consider how each alternative would help your clients or not, and why, and conclude by giving them advice.

10. FAMILY LAW

OVERVIEW OF FAMILY LAW

Family law comprises both divorce and marital property division laws, as well as laws about child support, child custody and visitation, and related family issues. Family law matters are handled in state court, and family laws differ from state to state. There are some threads that are common with child custody and visitation concerns generally, namely that family courts typically look at what is in the best interests of the child. However, the law discussed in a particular PT may or may not be the same as your state's laws, and should be used *only* to provide a legal context for this hypothetical case and *not* for purposes of learning what law might govern in any other case.

SIMULATED FAMILY LAW-BASED PT

Take three hours, and complete the memo requested in the *Stolier v. Wallach* PT located in eProducts. Though set in a family law context (the main question you are concerned with is visitation rights), your assignment is essentially an investigation/discovery plan (implicating civil procedure rules). Thus, this PT is good practice in both family law and civil procedure.

This is yet another reason why PTs are realistic: They often cross over different subjects. Law school divides study into distinct subjects, but all kinds of matters may arise in the context of family law practice, including bankruptcy, criminal concerns, education law, tax law, and more.

Enjoy the *Stolier* exam, and after you have drafted your answer, read the rest of this section.

TIME-CRUNCH TIPS

This PT requires you to complete one memo (essentially a discovery plan). If you cannot take a full three hours to do this, please read the entire File and Library and outline your answer. Try to at least quickly identify the legal elements at issue, evidence that proves or disproves facts related to each element, and sources of obtaining such evidence. You can do this in about 90 to 100 minutes.

INSIDE THIS TEST: TIPS AND STRATEGIES

Now that you have tackled the *Stolier* PT, let's look together at the File, starting with the Task Memo and the Library, and see how you did.

The Task Memo

The Task Memo is written to you, Applicant (who you are on the PT) from Marsha Pushkin. A quick glance at the letterhead shows Pushkin as the third named partner. Assuming Marsha is that partner, we understand we are in a private law firm and working for one of the named partners.

The very first sentence is the most critical of the entire PT. "We represent Celia Stolier and are trying to help her establish the right to regular visitation with her granddaughter, Joanna Wallach." It would have helped to have returned to that sentence, and everything in this Task Memo, several times as you read, outlined, and wrote, to keep your eyes on the bottom line.

In PTs, as in practice, what your client wants is the baseline. The bar examiners use the PT in part to see if you can help the client achieve the client's desired objectives.

Your boss, Pushkin, then goes on to provide some background about the parties and how the parties got to the point they are now. Joanna's mother died, and her father and stepmother refuse to let Celia (our client and the grandmother) see Joanna (the granddaughter who is now living with her father). Pushkin outlines a history of "bad blood" between the father and grandmother, but suggests that Celia and Joanna had an "excellent" relationship.

When you first read this, were you wondering how Pushkin knows this? If so, your lawyering instincts are excellent. So often, our concerns in PTs and in law practice are with how facts are proven.

Note: Pushkin goes on to indicate that litigation is now the only choice. Remember, the Task Memo is helping define your task by situating you in context, telling you what your assignment is and also what it is not. This language lets you know not to write about settlement or alternative dispute resolution (both viable possibilities in real life, even given the fact that reconciliation has thus far failed). The PT is an exam, though, and the examiners write the questions to be answerable within the time limits, so you want to be sure to pick up on clues regarding what to write about and what not to write about.

Your boss (Pushkin) then says she has gathered some cases and statutes (what you will find in the Library) and that she has communicated with some of the players (opposing counsel and our client's brother-in law), giving a preview of what we will find in the File, with a very important hint.

Pushkin tells you, "There is no doubt that the facts here are seriously in dispute." What a wonderful sentence! First, this underscores another great difference between PTs on the one hand, and essays and multiple-choice questions on the other. PTs often set up that very real-life situation where different people see things differently, where there are two or more sides to every story, and where a huge part of the job of a lawyer is determining what happened and how that can be proven. You do not want to "fight the facts" on MCQs and essays; they are fixed, set in stone. Your job on essays is to determine how you will use the facts as given to prove or disprove the applicable legal rules raised by the relevant legal issues. Second, and more specifically relating to this PT, this sentence hints that you should expect to see contradictions in the File, and perhaps provides a hint that your task may involve some determination about what facts can credibly be established. You of course hold that last thought until you read exactly what your boss wants you to draft. Still, this sort of thinking gets you primed to understand your assignment, something underscored in the next paragraph.

"Before we draft the Petition . . . I need your thoughts on how we should go about gathering the facts." This is followed by a paragraph that starts: "What I need from you is . . . ." Underline or highlight that part of the Task Memo; it is your guide, your bible. Here is where those who read slowly and carefully will do so much better than those who are hurrying to get to the File and Library. Slow down now, and read every word. Why? You will be graded in large part on whether you give the examiners what they want (whether you follow directions!). Here, Pushkin is (or, really, the bar examiners are) telling you precisely what your assignment is: "a well-organized, thorough but not unduly repetitive statement as to how we can obtain the evidence needed to show the court that our client should be granted the right to visit her grandchild." That is your precise assignment.

Equally important is the next sentence telling you what the assignment is *not*: "Please do not burden this memorandum with a general discussion of the legal right to visitation, as I am aware of those requirements." This is critical for PT purposes because you will typically be able to finish the PT only if you give the graders what they want and only what they want. If you give them extras, you will not be rewarded, unless you have first thoroughly covered everything that was requested. This really is important. You may well appear before a judge who asks you to speak on one thing and not another; you will likely annoy the judge, and perhaps lose, if you do not comply.

The next part of the Task Memo is really a Format Memo in disguise. It sets forth exactly how to set up your answer, with examples. (Examples on PTs are gifts!)

Note: If you were confused about how to organize your response on this exam, I would ask how carefully you read the last two paragraphs of the Task Memo.

This is how I would have translated that information immediately into my rough draft outline, before I even began skimming the File or reading the Library:

I. Elements that must be established to grant visitation rights

II. Element #1

—Items of evidence to prove or disprove facts relating to element #1, and

—Source(s) of such evidence

Element #2

—Items of evidence to prove or disprove facts relating to element #2, and

—Source(s) of such evidence

Element #3

—Items of evidence to prove or disprove facts relating to element #3, and

—Source(s) of such evidence

And so on for however many elements we have.

This, of course, is a most basic skeletal outline, but it starts helping me visualize what I will need to draft to be responsive to the directions. I urge you to get into the habit of outlining as soon as you see an organizational structure or a directive to respond to.

Next, I would actually have mapped out the examples given in the Task Memo so I have a format to follow that makes sense in context, not just a skeletal outline. Pushkin gives one required element, facts that might establish that element, and how we might prove those facts. I translated those examples into outline form as follows:

I. Elements that must be established to grant visitation rights

II. Element #1

—Items of evidence to prove or disprove facts relating to element #1, and

—Source(s) of such evidence

Element #___: Joanna has a desire to visit her grandmother.

—Fact that proves this element: Joanna wrote a letter expressing this desire to her grandma.

—Discovery/investigation needed to establish this fact: Have Joanna's letter authenticated, possibly by Celia or by admission of father.

—Fact that proves this element: If Joanna had told one of her teachers that she wanted to see her grandma.

—Discovery/investigation needed to establish this fact: Interviewing and perhaps taking depositions of Joanna's teachers.

Element #___

—Items of evidence to prove or disprove facts relating to this element, and

—Source(s) of such evidence Element #___

—Items of evidence to prove or disprove facts relating to this element, and

—Source(s) of such evidence

III. Conclusion

I would have kept this outline, with examples, as sort of a "cheat sheet" in front of me as an open document, so that I could type in ideas as I thought of what facts to investigate, and place them into the logically related part of my memo.

Note: I added space for a conclusion at the end of my memo. It will not be long because it was not specifically requested, but it will wrap up and serve to notify the grader that I completed the assignment.

Because it was not requested, you would not want to waste precious time writing a statement of facts in this Memo. That was easy to see (we hope!) and something we have stressed throughout this book: *follow the directions*. They will tell you what they want. Write the assignments as the bar examiners direct you, and not as you learned in school or at work. (That said, I do realize that just previously I said to add a very short conclusion even if that wasn't requested; but doing so will not take time away from your work and it adds substantial value in showing the grader that you finished.) What may have been a bit trickier was determining how much to put into the first part of the memo that your boss requested: the setting forth of the required legal elements. We will look at that in more detail after exploring the File and Library.

For now, with a big-picture sense of what our client wants and what she is fighting, and a fairly detailed sense of the type of document we are to produce, you want to get the lay of the land: first factually, by quickly skimming the File; second, by briefing the authorities in the Library and understanding what those critical elements are that will frame your whole task; and third, by going back and carefully reading the File to pick up what you need to write your answer.

Skim the File

If you flip back to the table of contents of the File, you see that the File consists of all notes and letters. You see from your careful read of the Task Memo that the facts are in dispute and that your job will be to organize facts as they establish elements. Here, a very quick look at the File is all you want to do until you get to the Library and identify those elements.

You might want to get into the habit of thinking of the File as just general background, much of which may be irrelevant, until you know what the legal framework is. Only then can you pull out what is truly significant from your File. So, at this first skim, just familiarize yourself with what is in the File, eyeballing for a sense of each document.

Notes of Interview with Our Client

Again, you do not yet know what is critical in this document; until you understand the law, you won't. Still, this document does give you background on a number of different people. As you read, you may want to write a "cast of characters" on scratch paper (or in part of your answer file that you will delete before uploading), so you remember everyone. Just as a program names the actors who play certain roles in a play, you can add quick notes about each person as you see him or her described in the File documents. For example:

- Marsha Pushkin: senior partner and my boss, person I am writing task to
- Celia Stolier: client
- Joanna Wallach: client's granddaughter, person client wants to be able to visit
- David Wallach: Joanna's father, opposes Celia's visitation requests
- Fred Andrews: Wallach's attorney
- Elizabeth Lawton: deceased mother of Joanna (divorced from David Wallach before she died)
- Harry Breckenridge: Celia's brother-in-law, very ill
- Wanda Breckenridge: Celia's sister, now deceased. Joanna lived with her great-aunt Wanda and great-uncle Harry when Joanna's mother divorced and then after she died, before Joanna moved to live with David Wallach and his new wife. Wanda and Harry wanted and were awarded visitation.

If it helps you can take your cast-of-characters list and make it into a "family tree" to visualize how the people in this PT are related.

Notes to File

This document is a chronology of sorts. There are some red flags, but nothing you can yet make sense of. There are references to "surprising allegations" about our client in a letter from the Wallachs' lawyer. We don't know what they are, but we know we have a letter from the attorney, so we can look for those when we get to that document. There is also a reference to a new person to add to our cast of characters, Karen Hegel, but we don't know who she is yet. This too will likely become clear as we keep reading, but we can add her name to the list with a question mark for now.

Letter to Fred Andrews, the Wallachs' Attorney

When you first skim the File, you may not see why this letter was important, but after you read the Library, you note that it is critical for thoughts on why Joanna will benefit from visitation with Celia: She benefits from (1) continued contact with maternal blood relatives, and (2) financial and material support that Celia can provide.

LETTER TO ANDREWS AS SAMPLE SETTLEMENT LETTER

There's another important thing about the letter from Pushkin to Andrews: it provides a great sample of a settlement letter. It says what our client wants from Andrews' client, and how his client can benefit from granting our client's request. It concludes by making clear that our client intends to pursue relief in court if an informal agreement cannot be reached. If you end up having a settlement letter assignment on a PT, this is a very useful example of what you might write in this sort of task.

Reply Letter from Fred Andrews, the Wallachs' Attorney

This reply letter is easy to read, and again, as with the letter from Pushkin to Andrews, should be read both with an eye toward the facts that we need to look into in this case, and with a sense of how we might draft a reply refusing a settlement request on behalf of our client if that were the task in a future PT. The "surprising allegations" about our client that were alluded to earlier in the File are now clear: the claim is that Celia "abandoned" her own daughter when she was young. We do not know exactly how this fits in to the assignment, because we still have not read the Library and do not yet know the legal framework. We also do not know if this is true or, if it is, whether Celia has a reasonable explanation. Remember, David Wallach is allegedly biased against our client and may have reasons to fabricate statements that hurt her. However, as we are in an investigatory stage, preparing to go to court to make requests for relief on behalf of our client, we must learn about all potentially damaging as well as all helpful evidence.

Notes of Interview with Harry Breckenridge

From these notes we learn a bit more about Harry's physical condition, particularly that it is "precarious," and about the significant contact the Breckenridges had with Joanna (her living with them for a time, etc.), and how Celia often came to visit during that time. Harry spoke very positively about the grandmother-granddaughter relationship. Pushkin asked him about family photos and he said he and Wanda had taken many and thought they were in a box. He also provided some details about Celia's and Elizabeth's backgrounds: how Celia's multiple marriages contributed to why Elizabeth stayed so often with the Breckenridges and how Celia came to be wealthy.

Notes from Second Client Interview

In the second interview, Celia gave our boss more details on her own background, including depression, recent counseling with a psychiatrist named Jane Peters (another person to add to the cast of characters), and time spent 32 years ago in a psychiatric center. Celia also mentioned that Harry had given boxes of Wanda's things to a friend, Karen Hegel (the person we added to our cast of characters earlier but could not identify). Celia notes that she and Hegel are not on speaking terms, but does not say why.

Letter from Joanna to Celia

Lastly, we have a handwritten letter, purportedly from Joanna to Celia, saying she misses Celia. If you remembered, or if you had taken notes on the Task Memo examples, Marsha Pushkin mentioned the letter in connection with proving the element of the child's desire to see her grandmother.

We have now skimmed the File and come full circle. We know a bit about the situation and we know one element of the legal framework (what the senior partner gave us from the Task Memo). We need to see what the Library reveals in terms of what all the other elements are.

The Library

First notice that this Library is a nice mix of statutes and cases. As we have said with statutes, before you study each word of them, figure out whether they are statutes you are familiar with (for example, excerpts from a code you are already charged with knowing for the bar exam, such as the Federal Rules of Evidence; if so, you can treat them more like a reference Library) or whether they are statutes governing a particular area relevant to your PT case (if so, you must read them carefully as if they were brand new to you).

The first rules you have are from the Columbia Rules of Civil Procedure (CRCP). You do not have language specifically telling you that they are substantially similar to the Federal Rules of Civil Procedure, but a quick look reveals that they cover basic discovery tools. You know this! (Or you would by the time of the bar exam.) Each numbered section covers a different discovery device. In case you forget, or blank on the exam about these, you can glance through these to remind yourself what each device is and how and when you can use it. For example, you can see that as a party, you can take depositions of any person (party or nonparty), whereas you as a party can only send interrogatories to other parties.

At this point, I would simply scan the headings of each of the CRPC sections, listing the five formal discovery tools they have provided sections for on scratch paper, or highlighting each heading: depositions, interrogatories, requests for admission, requests for identification/production of documents, and physical/mental examinations.

You may already be matching up these devices in your mind with our cast of characters to determine what sort of further information you might want from whom. Or, you might just hold this list so that when you get to figuring out what facts you want to prove, you can look back to this list to see if any of these rules and devices will help you prove what you want to establish.

Along this line, note that buried in the first paragraph under the code section on depositions is the following: "Upon leave of court, the deposition of a potential witness may be taken, notwithstanding the absence of a pending action, where good cause exists to believe the witness may be unavailable at the time suit is filed." Anything pop out at you? Harry Breckenridge is very ill. He has positive things to say about the relationship between Celia and Joanna, something he witnessed at first hand over many years. We may want to immediately request permission from the court to depose him now, in case he gets sicker and is unable to talk with us on the record, and determine what exactly we will want to ask him.

Next, we have four sections from the Columbia Civil Code. This is not something we are familiar with; it clearly relates directly to the particulars of the *Stolier* visitation issues. We will have to read these sections as if they were brand new. They are not terribly long or complex, though, so we may want to glance at them now and then go back and re-read them carefully after we read the three cases.

Two of the cases, *Whitaker* and *Hawkins*, are Columbia Supreme Court cases, and thus binding in our case, which will be filed in state court in Columbia. The third case, *Douglas*, is from the Court of Appeals of Indiana, so it is merely persuasive authority in Columbia. However, *Douglas* is cited by the *Hawkins* court, so its reasoning appears to be compelling to our Columbia Supreme Court.

Remember, per the Task Memo, we are not supposed to be writing a treatise on grandparental visitation, simply a quick summary of the elements we must establish. (Other PTs have asked for lengthier legal memos; this is more of a discovery plan organized by the components of the applicable legal standard.)

Looking strictly at § 3108, we see it applies in certain proceedings (not how Celia's matter arises) and only to parents. However, the court may order, "in its discretion," certain "reasonable companionship or visitation rights" to "any other person having an interest in the welfare of the child." Also, *Hawkins* allows the court-ordered grandparental visitation in special circumstances in situations such as *Stolier's* where there is no pending divorce proceeding.

Whitaker holds that "grandparents may be granted visitation rights under Section 3108 if the trial court finds that such visitation is in the child's best interest." *Whitaker* further holds that the § 3108 factors for determining the "best interest of the child" for custody apply for visitation purposes as well.

So, Marsha Pushkin in the Task Memo asks for "elements." Those essentially appear to be two: whether Celia is a person "having an interest in the welfare of Joanna," and whether ordering visitation with Joanna is in Joanna's "best interests" as determined by a set of five factors that the court will look to as guidelines.

Note: Factors are not the same as elements. Elements must each be proven in order to establish a cause of action, defense, or other legal theory. Factors are not applied rigidly, but typically assessed on a sliding scale: if most of the factors are clearly established, the standard may be found to be satisfied even if proof of a certain factor or factors is weak. Taking the cases and statutes as a whole, it appears clear that the standard the court will be looking to in making its determination will be whether or not the visitation would be in the best interest of Joanna.

Armed with the legal framework, I would revise my outline before I go back into the File and look for facts that prove each factor.

Updated Outline

<u>Legal standard that must be established to grant visitation rights</u>

First that Celia qualifies, as Joanna's maternal grandmother, as "any other person having an interest in the welfare of the child" under § 3108. And, next, considering the following five factors in § 3108, that ordering visitation with her grandmother is in Joanna's best interest:

(a) <u>Joanna's wishes</u> [and note that she is only eight years old, so this is not mandatory but within the court's discretion to consider]

—Brainstorm here, listing items of evidence to prove or disprove facts relating to Joanna's wishes, and sources of proof for each such item of evidence.

(b) The wishes of Joanna's parents. [Get creative here and consider not only her one living blood parent, but perhaps her stepparent and perhaps Breckenridge who stood for some time in a parental role.]

—Items of evidence to prove or disprove facts relating to Joanna's wishes, and sources of proof for each such item of evidence.

(c) The child's interaction and interrelationship with her parents and any other person (such as grandparent) who may significantly affect the child's best interests.

—Items of evidence to prove or disprove facts relating to Joanna's wishes, and sources of proof for each such item of evidence.

(d) The child's adjustment to home, school, and community.

—Items of evidence to prove or disprove facts relating to this factor, and source(s) of such evidence.

(e) The mental and physical health of all persons involved in the situation.

—Items of evidence to prove or disprove facts relating to this factor, and source(s) of such evidence.

Conclusion

TIP: PAY ATTENTION TO INFORMATION THAT IS REPEATED

The § 3108 factors are set forth both under the Civil Code Sections and again in *Whitaker*. This is a hint that the factors are important and should be used in your answer. As I've said throughout this book, lists, especially lists of elements or factors, are often organizational gifts in PTs! Also, anything the bar examiners repeat within a question is worth paying special attention to.

PUTTING IT ALL TOGETHER

With that sort of an outline, I go back into the File and essentially begin plucking out facts (and ideas on how to prove them) to plug into the appropriate section of my outline. Because we are in the first stages of planning what to investigate rather than at the stage where we are arguing before the court, we can brainstorm here and be fairly creative. As long as the graders see that you are suggesting facts that are relevant to proving each factor and are proposing ethical and lawful ways of gathering and establishing those facts, you should get points for all your ideas.

For example, for the fourth factor, Child's Adjustment to Home/School/Community, my first thought was to show that Joanna is not as well-adjusted where she is now and that she would be better off if she were allowed to visit with her grandmother.

- Review court records if they can be unsealed, reports and accounts of teachers, counselors, and clergy people to find out how well-adjusted Joanna is. (Are there "Grandparent and Me" classes at the local community center that Joanna could be a part of if Celia were in her life?) Much of this information could be collected informally through simply talking with people, though some we might need to depose; for sealed records we would seek leave of court under Columbia Civil Code § 3121.
- Request a physical inspection of the father's home to determine if Joanna is comfortable there and also if there is anything lacking that perhaps Celia's material resources might help provide.
- Mental evaluation of Joanna, perhaps. Have a counselor talk with her and see if she is well adjusted, if she misses her grandmother, and so on.

You can see from this list that it is brainstorming, but in a way that shows what information we are seeking, why, and from what sources: responding exactly to the directions and what was asked of us in the Task Memo.

Go ahead now and study the sample answers in the Online Question and Answer Bank. Compare and contrast them to your own answer, looking for ideas on how to improve what you wrote. Pay special attention to the organization of your answer.

SPIN-OFF EXERCISES

Taking the same facts and law as you had in the *Stolier* PT, try drafting the following:

- A dialogue of a mediation between Celia Stolier and David Wallach. Be sure to note what the mediator would say, and what each party would say, both when they are together and when each meets privately with the neutral mediator.
- A second settlement letter from Marsha Pushkin to Fred Andrews, in addition to the letter on June 15, 1989, to Fred Andrews, again requesting and pushing harder on visitation rights for Celia Stolier.
- Next, assume for the sake of this assignment only that David Wallach fired Fred Andrews; write a letter from Marsha Pushkin directly to David Wallach.

How would the content and tone of your letter to Mr. Wallach differ if you were writing to his attorney or if he was unrepresented? Both of these suggested exercises are designed to help you think about the differences between writing in plain English, so that a lay person can easily understand your points, and writing to fellow lawyers. (Remember, you are a lawyer on this exam!)

The PT often requires an awareness and appreciation of the differences in communication with lay people versus lawyers. Are there any bits of jargon or terms you have come across that you might need to define? Lastly, how does the goal of mediation differ from what the goal in your settlement letter would be?

Next, assume that a hearing on visitation has been set and the court requests both briefing before the hearing and oral argument at the hearing. Draft the following:

- A brief to the family court urging that Celia Stolier be granted visitation rights
- An oral argument to the family court judge arguing that Celia Stolier should be granted visitation rights

How would the last two assignments differ? What might you include in a written brief in advance of a hearing that you would not say orally, or vice versa? In both instances your audience is the judge, but in the former the judge will presumably sit and read what you wrote, whereas in the latter the judge is listening to what will likely be a fairly quick statement in open court.

PRACTICE, LAW SCHOOL, AND PTs: COMPARE AND CONTRAST

This exam posed a problem that is not uncommon, especially in today's world of frequent divorces, blended families, grandparents living longer, and so on. However, unless a grandmother like Celia Stolier were very wealthy (and here note that built into the File was the fact that Celia had inherited substantial wealth), it is not likely that she would have the money to engage in discovery and have an extended court battle to visit her granddaughter. More likely, in the real world, this would be a matter handled either informally, with or without the brief intervention of a lawyer, or through some sort of mediation. Nevertheless, the *Stolier* problem is a great exercise for a law student, because it combines a basic governing principle of family law (best interests of the child) with fact-gathering work using informal and formal discovery tools.

Family lawyers often work with both issues relating to divorce and property division and issues relating to children. All kinds of other matters may arise in the context of family law consultations, including bankruptcy, criminal concerns, education law, and more. Family lawyers may specialize, but they often are called on to refer parts of their cases to others who know more about particular slices of their clients' problems. Law school courses may be more siloed: some might focus more extensively on marital property division, which may be tested more heavily on bar exams; others might focus on issues relating to children and families. Some law schools include children's rights courses and clinics, where the issues that students grapple with may extend to children facing violence, educational or health care challenges, neglect, and other problems (civil and/or criminal), both within their families and outside the family setting such as in foster care or schools settings.

As you work your way through law school, if this is an area that interests you, look both at what family law-related courses and/or clinics your school offers. Look also at externships or clerkships that may be available in local legal organizations, clinics, or law offices. Consider both paid and volunteer positions, so you can gain as much experience as possible. You might also consider getting trained as a mediator and helping with some family law mediations; this is something you can do without a law license.

Family law is an important area on many state bar exams and in real life. Whether you end up practicing in the area or not, some exposure to the area can be helpful, as you will inevitably encounter questions at some point from family, friends, or colleagues who need advice in family law matters.

KEY TAKEAWAYS

- This practice exam helped train your factual analysis skills. It was less "law heavy" and much more focused on seeing which facts (and finding new facts) that help prove the elements your client has to establish to secure her visitation rights. This is an excellent skills-training PT even if you have no interest at all in family law. Just having to pull the key rules out of the Library, and then think of facts to prove each element, was superb PT success training.
- Breaking down the facts that prove or disprove each element and the sources of such evidence (how and where you find and establish such facts) provided an excellent exercise and training for any PT that involves discovery or fact investigation. Studying the answers, you see that this question asked you to consider both formal and informal discovery—a very realistic exercise.

- This PT also provided very explicit directions, with a specific format, and thus tested your ability and willingness to follow instructions as well as your other lawyering skills.

INDEX

References are to Pages